1976–77 EDITION

DOLLARWISE GUIDE TO PORTUGAL

By STANLEY HAGGART
and DARWIN PORTER

Prepared for
TAP
THE INTERCONTINENTAL
AIRLINE OF PORTUGAL

Copyright © 1970, 1972, 1974, 1976

by
THE FROMMER/PASMANTIER PUBLISHING CORPORATION
All rights reserved

Published by
THE FROMMER/PASMANTIER PUBLISHING CORPORATION
70 Fifth Avenue
New York, New York 10011

Distributed by
SIMON AND SCHUSTER
A GULF+WESTERN COMPANY
630 Fifth Avenue
New York, New York 10020
671-10956-1

Distributed outside the USA and Canada by
FLEETBOOKS
c/o Feffer and Simons, Inc.
100 Park Avenue
New York, New York 10017

Manufactured in the United States of America

CONTENTS

INTRODUCTION	A DOLLAR-WISE GUIDE TO PORTUGAL	1
	The Reason Why	1
CHAPTER I	GETTING THERE	12
	1. Air Transportation	12
	2. Traveling within Portugal	16
CHAPTER II	THE SCENE IN PORTUGAL	19
	1. A Capsule History	21
	2. Dining and Wining	24
	3. The Hotel Outlook	28
CHAPTER III	SETTLING INTO LISBON	30
	1. Navigating Your Way	33
	2. Public Transportation	35
	3. The ABC's of Life	36
CHAPTER IV	THE HOTELS OF LISBON	40
	1. The Deluxe Choices	41
	2. Leading First-Class Hotels	42
	3. Middle-Bracket Hotels	44
	4. Full-Board Bargains	46
	5. The Budget Range	47
CHAPTER V	THE RESTAURANTS OF LISBON	49
	1. The Deluxe Trio	49
	2. The Medium-Priced Range	50
	3. Less Expensive Restaurants	52
	4. The Budget Range	54
	5. Seafood on the Left Bank	55
	6. The Foreign Colony	55
	7. The Special Spots	56
	8. Hard-Core Budget	57
CHAPTER VI	ESTORIL, CASCAIS & SINTRA	60
	1. Estoril	62

	2. Cascais	66
	3. Oitavos	72
	4. Guincho	73
	5. Queluz	74
	6. Sintra	76
	7. Mafra Palace	80
	8. Ericeira	82
	9. Vale do Lobos	82
CHAPTER VII	**THE SIGHTS OF LISBON**	84
	1. The Alfama	85
	2. Belém	88
	3. Museums and Galleries	92
	4. The Churches of Lisbon	96
	5. A Bullfight Spectacle	97
	6. Other Sights	98
CHAPTER VIII	**NIGHTLIFE IN AND AROUND LISBON**	101
	1. The Fado Clubs	102
	2. The Capital After Dark	104
	3. Estoril by Night	106
	4. The Clubs of Cascais	108
CHAPTER IX	**SOUTH OF THE TAGUS**	110
	1. Azeitao	111
	2. Sesimbra	112
	3. Portinho da Arrábida	113
	4. Setúbal	113
	5. Palmela	115
CHAPTER X	**ESTREMADURA**	117
	1. Obidos	118
	2. Caldas da Rainha	119
	3. Berlenga Islands	120
	4. Alcobaça	120
	5. Aljubarrota	121
	6. Sao Martinho do Porto	122
	7. Nazaré	122
	8. Batalha	124
	9. Fátima	125
CHAPTER XI	**THE ALGARVE**	128
	1. Sagres	131
	2. Lagos	132

	3. Portimao	136
	4. Praia da Rocha	138
	5. Silves	141
	6. Armaçao de Pera	142
	7. Albufeira	142
	8. Praia de Quarteira	146
	9. Vilamoura	147
	10. Vale do Lobo	148
	11. Faro	148
	12. Sao Brás de Alportel	151
	13. Olhao	152
	14. Monte Gordo	153
CHAPTER XII	**ALENTEJO AND RIBATEJO**	**155**
	1. Évora	156
	2. Beja	159
	3. Vila Viçosa	160
	4. Elvas	162
	5. Marvao	163
	6. Castelo de Vive	163
	7. Estremoz	163
	8. Vila Franca de Xira	165
	9. Santarém	166
	10. Tomar	167
CHAPTER XIII	**COIMBRA AND THE BEIRAS**	**169**
	1. Leiria	170
	2. Figueira da Foz	171
	3. Coimbra	173
	4. Conimbriga	177
	5. Bussaco	178
	6. Curía and Luso	179
	7. Aveiro	180
	8. Caramulo	182
	9. Viseu	183
	10. Serra da Estrêla	185
	11. Castelo Branco	186
	12. Abrantes	186
CHAPTER XIV	**PORTO AND ITS ENVIRONS**	**187**
	1. The Hotels	188
	2. Where to Dine	189
	3. What to See and Do	191

	4. Exploring the Coast	195
	5. Deep in the Environs	197
CHAPTER XV	**THE MINHO DISTRICT**	200
	1. Guimaraes	201
	2. Braga	202
	3. Barcelos	203
	4. Esposende	204
	5. Viana do Castelo	205
	6. Valença	206
	7. Pousada-Hopping in Minho	207
CHAPTER XVI	**MADEIRA AND THE AZORES**	208
	1. Settling into Funchal	210
	2. Excursions in Madeira	218
	3. Discovering the Azores	221
	4. Ponta Delgada	223
	5. Exploring Sao Miguel	225
	6. Terceira	226
	7. Faial	228
CHAPTER XVII	**A GRAB BAG OF CHARTS**	229
	1. Menu Translations	229
	2. A Capsule Vocabulary	232
	3. Currency Exchange	233

MAPS

PORTUGAL	4
LISBON: THE MAJOR BOULEVARDS	32

When a $ is not a $

Portugal is one of the most inexpensive countries in which to travel in Europe. But first-time American visitors often panic at price quotations, because Portugal uses the same $ sign to designate its currency. The escudo is written as 1$00. The dollar sign is written between the escudo and the centavo, of which there are 100 to the escudo.

There is no fixed rate of exchange between the escudo and the dollar. At press time, one escudo was worth approximately 4¢ in U.S. coinage, meaning you could buy 26 escudos with one dollar. There is no way to predict what the escudo will be worth when you arrive—so check with a banker, at home or in Portugal, for the latest information.

Introduction

A DOLLAR-WISE GUIDE TO PORTUGAL

The Reason Why

AT THE DAWN of the Renaissance "Age of Exploration," mariners believed that two-headed fork-tongued monsters—big as houses—lurked across the "Sea of Darkness," waiting to gulp a caravel down their fire-lined throats. It was even feared that white men turned black if they ventured near the equator.

In spite of these formidable problems, Portugal—in what has been called its "épopée of yesteryears"—launched legendary caravels on missions that became historic: Vasco da Gama to India, Ferdinand Magellan to circumnavigate the globe, Dias to round the Cape of Good Hope. In time, Portuguese navigators explored two-thirds of the earth!

Although the Iberian country was in the vanguard of worldwide exploration, it has never been as successful in attracting visitors to its own shores. Outside of Greater Lisbon, the Algarve, and Madeira, it remains unknown and undiscovered by the main-line tourist. That fact is particularly lamentable because Portugal offers so much in the way of sandy beaches, art treasures, a delicious cuisine, unique Manueline architecture, cut-rate handicraft shopping buys, a mild climate, low hotel tariffs, and friendly people.

But Portugal's anonymity has changed, partly due to the recent political unrest. The news is out: the country is what one newspaper columnist dubbed, "the bargain basement vacationland of Europe." That appellation will suffice if it's not mistakenly interpreted to suggest lack of quality. Portugal is a first-rate attraction.

The country may be small—roughly about the size of Maine—but, like Mighty Mouse, it packs a powerful punch. Connecting you with its life forces is one of the aims of this book.

We have set for ourselves the formidable task of seeking out the finest in Portugal—its best way of life—and condensing that between the covers of this book. The finest includes not only descriptions of important cities, towns, villages, and sightseeing attractions, but recommendations of hotels, restaurants, bars, coffee houses, and nightspots as well.

Part of the philosophy of this book is based on the premise that the best need not be the most expensive! Hence, our ultimate aim—beyond that of familiarizing you with the offerings of Portugal—is to stretch your dollar power . . . to reveal to you that you need not always pay scalper's prices for charm, top-grade comfort, and gourmet food.

In this guide, we'll devote a great deal of attention to those old tourist meccas, Lisbon, Estoril, Cascais, Sintra, focusing on both their obvious and hidden treasures. But they are not the full reason why of this book. Important as they are, they simply do not reflect fully the widely diverse and complicated country that Portugal is. To discover that, you must venture deep into the provinces.

Unlike many nations in Europe, Portugal defies a clear, logical, coherent plan of sightseeing. It is a patchwork of treasures, with many of the choicest items tucked away in remote corners. To sample the best of Portugal, especially some of its most intriguing living conditions, you'll have to seek out a faraway country estate deep in the heartland, or perhaps a 14th-century monastery now converted into a pousada (tourist inn) in the old Roman city of Evora in Alentejo, even an 18th-century palace in Seteais, where Lord Byron worked on "Childe Harold" in the front garden. Living outside of Lisbon whenever possible will, of course, give you a chance to get acquainted with the Portuguese, which is a more difficult task in most capital city hotels.

THE PEOPLE OF PORTUGAL: Meeting the Portuguese, after all, is perhaps the most important reason for making the jaunt. They have developed a decidedly different character from that of Spain, their sister nation on the Iberian peninsula. Those who travel among and mingle with the Portuguese usually return home filled with a special warm response for the people. They are easily approachable, extraordinarily helpful, and you may find after you've left that you have cultivated several lifetime friends and correspondents.

Physically (generally speaking, of course) the Portuguese are rather short in stature with swarthy complexions. The women are quite attractive, though their bodies are often hidden behind a regional garb. The men play their roles well, with bravura flair at times, especially when they fancy themselves as conquistadores.

In Lisbon, the people generally dress well—at least in the business district. However, in the country, you'll meet the people of the heartland with their all-purpose, all-weather clothing. Women with black shawls draped around their shoulders carry baskets of produce balanced on their heads. These same women work in the fields with their men, sowing seed, guiding oxen, carrying milk jugs, harvesting. Forming a colorful sight, they wear folded clothing, their hands bandaged, wide caps covering their heads from the powerful summer sun. Children are often attired in sweaters and labor in the fields alongside their parents.

The north of Portugal is more industrial, especially in and around Porto; while in the south, the Algarve, the approach to life seems more casual, the attitude more relaxed and friendly.

In Portugal, the family as an institution remains firmly entrenched. Many of its people have no close friends outside the family unit. The Catholic Church still enjoys strong power and prestige over many segments of society. It is rare to meet a Portuguese Protestant or members of other faiths.

Although ladies of the sociedade have become increasingly sophisticated in the past few years, their counterparts down the economic and social scale are still of a more traditional character. Unlike Finland, where women have achieved equal status with men in all professional fields, the Portuguese woman remains in her time-honored position. But she's usually more than a housewife. If her husband's a fisherman, she may help repair the nets, then sell the catch in the streets. If she's married to a farmer, she'll spend part of her day in the fields with her husband, returning to their cottage in the evening to do all the housework, cooking, and the mending. A hard life!

In all, a proud people worthy of knowing.

It may be presumptuous to give you reasons why to go to Portugal. Dozens may have already occurred to you, ranging from trying to find where you hid that microfilm when you were spying for the Allies in World War II, to putting a tracer on your ancestors to determine if you are descended from royalty or hangmen. We'll merely add a few that you may not have thought about . . .

(1) To learn the meaning of saudade

The word is hard to translate, evoking a mood of melancholy—a sense of sadness expressed most dramatically in Portuguese music. One scholar called it ". . . the nostalgic memory of past greatness, the myth of a golden century, the deep sense of loss which has been called Atlantic melancholy." You'll most certainly want to listen to saudade's most heartthrobbing and poignant expression, the fado—Portugal's most authentic and absorbing art form. Classically beautiful singers, such as Celeste Rodrigues, sister of the world-famed Amália, will entertain you in Lisbon. Clutching a traditional black shawl around herself, she raises her sensitive voice in the dimly lit tavern near the Alfama and the docks—singing the plaintive and poetic songs of her people. It doesn't matter whether you understand the words. The power and dynamic quality of the lament transcends language, forming its own vocabulary, finding its own reality.

(2) To do something really majestic

Atop the highest turret of the seemingly impregnable fortress of St. George in Lisbon, the sounds of the quays and streets merely hum far below. A great eagle encaged within the fortress bewails its captivity. And whenever all sounds seem to have faded, the unnerving screams of one of the castle's white peacocks knifes the tranquility. Then you understand why the ancients trembled at the harsh, discordant shrieks of this bird—supposedly ill omens, harbingers of war, blood, and death.

Below, great ocean-going vessels trudge out of the custard-brown harbor toward the blue Atlantic. Cast before you are ancient facades and chipped slate backsides; teeming narrow city streets and rolling hills; awesome religious monuments; and steel and glass testimonies to technology. You can sit straddled upon a giant cannon which once protected the wealthiest of maritime empires and which trembled through many an earth tremor. In a glance you can view Roman occupation, Visigothic walls, Moorish remains, conflict with Spain, the cradle of the Portuguese empire, the modern world—a continuum of time unbroken.

(3) To jump off a train or park and forget your car as you wander back into the Middle Ages

Involve yourself in the rural life, the very soul of Portugal. To sample a way of life fast disappearing, go to, say, **Entrocamento,** in the bull-breeding province of Ribatejo. This village, like so many others in Portugal, exudes the simple rusticity and warmth of a people still connected spiritually to the grapes and the land on which they grow.

From any street you can see the outskirts of the vineyards, in which cork trees are abundantly interspersed. Streams flow swiftly through the vineyards

DOLLAR-WISE GUIDE TO PORTUGAL

on their way to the nearby Tagus. You can follow one up into the foothills; and if you possess or can borrow a string and hook, chances are that you'll be having fish for supper.

The men come in from the fields at dusk, heading directly for the taverns for many carafes of deep purple wine topped with an inch of froth. An entire family—including the mother, the father, the children, even the friends—works behind the serving tables, drawing glasses from the damp cool casks. Once inside one of these bustling taverns, an olive-skinned habitué will motion you toward a serving table, give a quick jerk on his earlobe, a wink of the eye from under a dark beret, and a repeated flip of his thumb toward his lips—the lever on the cask creaks!

(4) To build bridges to other people

As crusty as cork bark, but as hard as an olive pit, yet as warm as life really ought to be, the people of Portugal are the greatest experience in this still provincial country. Their bridges of giving are strong and sturdy. Those accustomed to a smile or friendly gesture used to cover an ulterior motive may find themselves clumsy in dealing with the Portuguese. But once you let yourself go, venturing into the countryside and exposing yourself to the Portuguese way of life, you'll feel the organic kindness of a remarkable people.

For example, you might stop a white-bearded farmer in Alentejo, innocently inquiring about directions. Don't be surprised if he invites you inside his family compound, where all the activity really takes place. It is here where he grows the produce that feeds his large family, barters with his neighbors, and generally carries on the business of living. He'll ask you to warm yourself at a corner hearthside fire, while he takes out a large loaf of bread, slicing it and spreading it with home-churned butter, then coating it with farm-grown honey kept in a large crock. Wine made from his own grapes will be offered in ceramic mugs.

When you leave, don't be surprised again if he tells you with conviction that the next time you pass through, you're to bed down as a guest of his family!

(5) To feel the impact of the sea

While the Portuguese fishermen are the challengers of the sea, the women are the guardians and sentinels. At **Nazaré,** Portugal's most colorful fishing village (north of Lisbon), the ritual of launching and bringing in those brightly painted Phoenician-inspired boats is as regular as the tidal rhythm of the sea. The bearded fishermen, in their long tasseled stocking caps and plaid shirts, push out to the sea, paddling furiously, riding through the fury of the first breaker. When at sea, they search for the best fish-producing waters, letting down their nets and depositing their catch at the bottom of the boat. Hopefully, they will return to shore early with smiles of victory; but too often their return is delayed. Tragically, an occasional storm may rise suddenly to strike them down.

As the sun sinks, the women of Nazaré—frozen like classical women in stone—wait on the beach for the return of their men. They have spent the first portion of the day gossiping and repairing nets; but when it's time for the homecoming of the fleet, they gather quietly at the water's edge. Standing there in lonely vigil, they say not a word, as there is a silent understanding among them. While the custom of the young girls is to wear seven bright petticoats, the older women are nearly always draped in black. There is no one who has not lost a father, a brother, or a son. Tightening their woolen black shawls around themselves, they gaze out to the now-darkening sea, squinting their eyes, searching for the first signs of the high-bowed seeing eye boats.

When the fleet appears, the women cross themselves many times in gratefulness to their protector saint, then rush out to do their part in unloading the boat. Teams of oxen are hitched up ready to bring the boats in safely on the beach, so as not to lose the precious cargo.

The sea gives life and it takes it away.

We'll turn now to a closer examination of our pleasant task.

DOLLAR-WISE—WHAT IT MEANS: In brief, this is a guidebook giving specific details (including prices) about Portuguese hotels, restaurants, bars, sightseeing attractions, nightlife, and tours. Establishments in *all* price ranges have been documented and described.

About ten percent of the recommendations include the luxury hotels such as the Palácio at Estoril, while another 35 percent suggests inexpensive accommodations: budget hotels, guest houses, or country inns such as the Estalagem da Santa Iria in the heart of the scenic Templars town of Tomar, offering provincial-styled bedrooms with private baths overlooking a gently flowing river—and costing only about $10 a night for two persons.

On the other hand, the greater number—55 percent—fall in that great in-between price category of the middle bracket. For example, in Lisbon you can ensconce yourself at the ultra-contemporary Tivoli Jardim in the center of the city—where your colorful bedroom with its tiled bath goes for around $18 nightly for a double.

In all cases, establishments have been judged by a strict yardstick of value. If they measured up, they were included, regardless of price classification. The uniqueness of the book, we think, lies in the fact that it could be used either by a society matron with lorgnette ("We always stay at the Albatroz in Cascais") or by an escudo-lean collegian ("There's this little restaurant in Lisbon that serves you a big spread for less than a buck").

But the major focus of the book is centered neither on the impecunious nor on the affluent whose gold rests in numbered accounts in Zurich. Rather, our chief concern is the average, middle-income-bracket voyager who'd like to patronize the almost wholly undocumented establishments in Portugal—that is, the first-class hotels (around $10 to $12 per person for a room with private bath and a continental breakfast), or some of the better, though less heralded, restaurants where you can often get a superb dinner for around $4.

In Portugal, of course, a first-time visitor is often bewildered as to what to see. The country suffers from lack of publicity. People know of Lisbon—and that's about it.

However, we've penetrated deep into remote villages, such as baroque Lamego in that province over the mountains, Tras-os-Montes. Naturally, all the big-time attractions are explored as well—ranging from Byron's glorious Eden at Sintra, to the sunny beaches of the Algarve, to the coastal villages of the north.

To show you what we have in mind in the way of where you'll be sleeping and dining, here is . . .

A CALDEIRADA OF BARGAINS: Borrowing the title of this heading from the classic fish stew of Portugal, we'll preview some of the delectable establishments awaiting you. In our journeys through every province of the country, we have discovered charm and comfort offered for little cost, or else establishments where the homemade or creative touch of their proprietors lifts them far above the ordinary. For a truer understanding of what dollar-wise means, we'll recall only a few as examples, though you'll meet dozens more in the pages ahead—perhaps discover some all on your own when you actually go to Portugal.

—A converted hillside monastery providing living in Lisbon, overlooking the Tagus River. The 16th-century convent offers today's comforts blended with the mellowed atmosphere of yesterday: antique-filled bedrooms, corridors, and living rooms; ecclesiastical sculpture; bronze torchiers; time-aged paintings. Oddly shaped bedrooms open onto a cloistered garden. For all of this, including three top quality meals provided by a spirited Gallic lady owner, you'll pay only $30 (U.S.) daily for two persons.

—Or perhaps a crow's nest, stone-built modern inn, perched near the crest of a mountain at Caramulo. This estalagem retreat is favored by artists who appreciate a genuine Dufy on the wall, a blazing fire before an open hearth for after-dinner coffee, a panoramic view from the dining room, and immaculately kept and cozy bedrooms with private balconies and tiled baths. All this, plus three country-style meals (lots of second helpings!), costs only $25 (U.S.) for two persons per day.

—Or perhaps you'll be drawn to the splendid life in the historic Roman city of Evora, staying at a luxury pousada (a government-run tourist inn). In this converted 14th-century monastery, you'll pay only about $15 per person per day—based on double occupancy—for three regional meals, a bedroom filled with handsome antique reproductions, and a tiled private bath. You can wander through a Manueline-styled cloister, pause beside a gurgling marble fountain, and drink the local wine in the former monks' dining hall.

—Finally, you may want to become a guest in an ancient stately home (quinta) on the faraway island of Madeira, at a converted private estate, with its own sun-pocket swimming pool. Two persons can stay here in individualized bedrooms with tasteful antiques for $15.99 (U.S.) daily. That low figure includes a delicious homemade breakfast served on a silver tray on the flagstone terrace overlooking the harbor.

What about restaurants?

—In the kitchen of the former royal palace at Queluz, outside of Lisbon on the road to Sintra, you can enjoy a gourmet meal in a regal setting. You dine on high ladder-backed chairs under a towering vaulted ceiling, with stone arches, a fireplace, and a 15-foot marble-topped chef's table laden with appetizing food. For $5.90 (U.S.), you can order a top-level dinner—such as a regional soup, seafood bubbly with cheese, acorn-sweetened pork that is tender and juicy, and a homemade almond cake, plus assorted cheese from the neighboring countryside as well as fresh fruit.

—Back on the island of Madeira, you can savor a hearty-style meal in a provincial hillside tavern—a setting of sun terraces overlooking the bay at Funchal. For only $2.34 (U.S.), an order of skewers of garlic-studded charcoal-broiled hunks of tender beef will be hung on a hook over your table. The rich juices are mopped up with crusty homemade bread fresh from the oven.

SOME DISCLAIMERS: No restaurant, inn, hotel, pensao, or nightclub paid to be mentioned in this book. What you read are entirely personal recommendations—in many cases, the proprietors never knew their establishments were being visited or investigated for inclusion in a travel guide.

A word of warning: unfortunately, costs change—and they rarely go downward. The government virtually imposes rent control on its hotels, and many establishments have gone on four or five years before changing their tariffs. Owing to sudden improvements or upgrading, other places have sky-rocketed their tabs.

Always, when checking into a hotel, inquire about the tariff. This policy can save much embarrassment and disappointment when the time comes to settle your bill. Unfortunately, you cannot ever insist on being charged the precise prices quoted in this book, though every effort has been made to secure the accurate tariffs as much as they were foreseeable.

THE ORGANIZATION OF THIS BOOK: Here's how *Dollar-Wise Guide to Portugal* sets forth the information it provides:

Chapter I, directly ahead, deals with ways of flying to Portugal, and then with various modes of transportation within the country. Naturally, the focus is on the least expensive means of transport—on such items as excursion fares and off-season discounts.

Chapter II turns the spotlight on "The Scene in Portugal"; it's meant to fortify you for your plunge into the country by outlining its history, providing tips on the best food specialties and wine, and previewing the hotel outlook.

Chapters III through VIII take on a huge task—that of exploring the hotels, restaurants, sightseeing attractions, and nightlife not only of **Lisbon**, but of the leading resorts along the Costa do Sol (**Estoril** and **Cascais**), and of **Sintra**. Documented first are the deluxe and first-class hotels, followed by those in the middle bracket and budget range. Beginning with the most expensive and elegant restaurants, such as Tavares and Aviz, the list continues downward to the lowly beer tavern serving an icy cold stein and a juicy steak at prices you didn't know existed any more. Nightlife, especially fado, can be found in a wide variety of places, ranging from a rowdy sailors' bar in Lisbon to a posh discotheque in Cascais.

Chapters IX and X move outside of Lisbon for a trip south of the Tagus to the fishing port of **Setúbal** and the three-castle district, to the resort village of **Sesimbra**, and to the cove of **Portinho da Arrábida** at the foot of the Arrábida hills. Heading north—though still based in Lisbon—you can explore the fortress town of **Obidos**; the 12th-century Cistercian monastery of **Alcobaça**; the 14th-century battle abbey at **Batalha**; the fishing village of **Nazaré**; the world-famed pilgrimage shrine at **Fátima**, and the historic Templars city of **Tomar**.

Chapter XI heads to the **Algarve**, the African-looking southernmost province of Portugal. Stretching along the coast from Sagres to Vila Real de Santo Antonio, it spans a distance of about 94 miles. For those who like beaches and sunshine, it sends out a call—and the tariffs are low.

Chapter XII also bites off a big hunk—**Alentejo** and **Ribatejo**. Ribatejo is a land of pastures famed for its bull breeding. Chief target: Tomar. The Alentejo is a district of olive trees and cork, its major tourist goal the old Roman city of **Evora**.

Chapter XIII explores **Coimbra**, famous for its university dating from 1290, and the environs, especially the former royal palace and forest of **Buçaco** and the remains of a Roman settlement at **Conimbriga**.

Chapters XIV and XV do the same for Portugal's second city, **Porto** (where Port wine is shipped out to the world), and for the **Minho** district in the northwestern corner of the country. Hotels, pousadas, sights, whatever, are detailed.

Chapter XVI heads out into the Atlantic for the mountainous, vegetation-rich island of **Madeira**, centering at **Funchal**. Finally, our trip concludes in the remote **Azores,** referred to as the "daughters of the ocean" and "recently" discovered in the 15th century.

Chapter XVII caps the book with vital minutiae: menu translations, capsule vocabularies, and a currency conversion.

AN INVITATION TO READERS: Like all the Dollar-Wise books, *Dollar-Wise Guide to Portugal* hopes to maintain a continuing dialogue between its writers and its readers. All of us share a common aim—to travel as widely and as well as possible, at the best value for our money—and in achieving that aim, your comments and suggestions can be of aid to others. Therefore, if you come across an appealing hotel, restaurant, nightclub, even sightseeing attraction, please don't keep it to yourself. We'll send free copies of the next edition of this book to readers whose suggestions are printed in it. And the letters need not only apply to new establishments, but to hotels and restaurants already recommended in this guide. The fact that a listing appears in this edition doesn't give it squatter's rights in future publications. If its services have deteriorated, its chef grown stale, its prices risen unfairly, whatever, these failings need to be known. Even if you enjoyed every place and found every description accurate, a letter letting us know that, too, can cheer a gray day. Send your comments to Stanley Haggart and Darwin Porter, c/o **The Frommer/Pasmantier Publishing Corporation,** 70 Fifth Avenue, New York, N. Y. 10011.

THE $10-A-DAY TRAVEL CLUB: In just a few paragraphs, you'll begin your exploration of Portugal. But before you do, you may want to learn about a device for saving money on all your trips and travels; we refer to the now widely known $10-a-Day Travel Club, which has gone into its 12th successful year of operation.

The Club was formed at the urging of readers of the $10-a-Day Books and the Dollar-Wise Guides, many of whom felt that the organization of a Travel Club could bring financial benefits, continuing travel information, and a sense of community to economy-minded travelers in all parts of the world. We thought—and have since learned—that the idea had merit. For by combining the purchasing power of thousands of our readers, it has proved possible to obtain a wide range of exciting travel benefits—including substantial discounts to members from auto rental agencies, restaurants, sightseeing operators, hotels, and other purveyors of tourist services throughout the United States and abroad.

In order to make membership in the Club as attractive as possible—and thus build a Club large enough to achieve the above goals—we have agreed to offer members immediate benefits whose value exceeds the cost of the membership fee, which is $8 a year.

And thus, upon receipt of that sum, we shall send all new members, by return mail, the following items:

(1) The latest edition of any *two* of the following books (please designate in your letter which two books you wish to receive):

Europe on $10 a Day
England on $10 & $15 a Day
Greece on $10 a Day
Hawaii on $15 a Day
India on $5 & $10 a Day

Ireland on $10 a Day
Israel on $10 & $15 a Day
Mexico and Guatemala on $5 & $10 a Day
New Zealand on $10 a Day
Scandinavia on $15 a Day
South America on $10 a Day
Spain and Morocco on $10 a Day
Turkey on $5 & $10 a Day
Washington, D.C. on $10 & $15 a Day

Dollar-Wise Guide to England
Dollar-Wise Guide to France
Dollar-Wise Guide to Germany
Dollar-Wise Guide to Italy
Dollar-Wise Guide to Japan and Hong Kong
Dollar-Wise Guide to Portugal

(Dollar-Wise Guides discuss accommodations and facilities in all price categories, with special emphasis on the medium-priced.)

Whole World Handbook
(Prepared by the prestigious Council on International Educational Exchange, the Whole World Handbook—updated for 1976-7—deals with more than 1,000 programs of student travel, study and employment in Europe, the Near East, Africa, Asia, Australia and Latin America.)

Where to Stay U.S.A.
(By the Council on International Educational Exchange, published in cooperation with the American Revolution Bicentennial Administration, this extraordinary guide is the first ever to list accommodations in all 50 states that cost anywhere from 50¢ to $10 per night.)

(2) A copy of **A Getaway Guide to New York**—a newly revised 208-page pocket-size guide, including discount coupons worth up to $100 at hotels, restaurants, night spots and sightseeing attractions throughout the New York area.

(3) A copy of **Surprising Amsterdam**—a 192-page, pocket-size guide to Amsterdam by Arthur Frommer.

(4) A one-year subscription to the quarterly Club newsletter—**The Wonderful World of Budget Travel**—which keeps members up-to-date on fast-breaking developments in low-cost travel to all areas of the world.

(5) A voucher entitling you to a $5 discount on any Arthur Frommer International, Inc. tour booked by you through travel agents in the United States and Canada.

(6) Your personal membership card, which, once received, entitles you to purchase through the Club all Arthur Frommer Publications for a third to a half off their regular retail prices during the term of your membership.

These are the immediate and definite benefits which we can assure members of the Club at this time. Even more exciting, however, are the further and more substantial benefits (including, in particular, a comprehensive grant of reductions and discounts on travel accommodations and facilities in numerous areas), which it has been our continuing aim to achieve for members. These are announced to members throughout the year, and can be obtained by them through presentation of their membership cards. Equally interesting has been the development of the Club's newsletter, which has now become an eight-page newspaper, and carries such continuing features as "The Travelers' Directory" —a list of members all over the world who are willing to provide hospitality to other members as they pass through their home cities; "Share-a-Trip"— offers and requests from members for travel companions who can share costs; advance news of individual and group tour programs operated by Arthur Frommer International, Inc.; discussions of freighter travel; tips and articles on other travel clubs (air travel clubs, home and apartment exchanges, pen pals, etc.) and on specific plans and methods for travel savings and travel opportunities.

If you would like to join thousands of other travelers from all parts of the world who are now members of this exciting organization, and participate in its exchange of travel information and hospitality, then send your name and address, together with your membership fee of $8, to: $10-a-Day Travel Club, Inc., 70 Fifth Avenue, New York, N.Y. 10011—and remember to specify which *two* of the books in section (1) above you wish to receive in your initial package of members' benefits.

And now we start. The first step toward a vacation in Portugal is getting there. For suggestions, see Chapter I, coming up.

Chapter I

GETTING THERE

1. By Air
2. Traveling within Portugal

ALTHOUGH LISBON is a major gateway city to Europe, to old-time travelers it seemed isolated. In bygone days, one went to France or England first, then began the Grand Tour, perhaps (but most likely not) stopping over in Portugal.

Air transportation has changed this habit, and more and more sun-seeking travelers are beginning their European adventure in Lisbon. In terms of its distance from North America, Portugal is one of the closest of all European countries. It costs less to fly from New York to Lisbon than from New York to Paris, Amsterdam, Frankfurt, Geneva, Munich, or Copenhagen.

Moreover, in planning your trip to Portugal, there are several available methods of cutting your air transportation costs. We'll first discuss the basic structure of airfares to Western Europe, and finally deal with methods of traveling within Portugal, once you arrive.

1. By Air

PLANE ECONOMICS: The basic premise from which you begin is that all the major international airlines other than tiny Icelandic charge exactly the same fares. All of these lines—both American and foreign—belong to the International Air Transport Association (IATA), which prescribes fares, and periodically revises them, on a uniform basis for all its members.

The following sets of fares went into effect on April 1, 1975, and will remain valid until March 31, 1976. As we go to press, IATA is in session to determine what, if any, fare revisions there will be after that date. It would be safe to assume that there will be an increase of 5-10%. Since that's only a guess, we suggest that you check with any international air carrier or travel agent if you are planning to travel after April 1, 1976.

In each case, the figures set forth below represent *round-trip* rates from New York, economy class, on a jet aircraft. To determine the approximate fare

GETTING THERE 13

from your own town, merely add the cost of transportation from where you live to New York.

Round trip between New York and	Winter Season*	Shoulder Season*	Peak Season*
Amsterdam	$612	$ 692	$ 866
Athens	914	1016	1174
Barcelona	632	700	892
Berlin	680	748	936
Brussels	612	692	866
Copenhagen	668	734	922
Frankfurt	668	734	922
Hamburg	668	734	922
Helsinki	760	822	1012
Istanbul	948	1008	1166
Lisbon	584	666	806
London	584	666	806
Madrid	612	692	866
Nice	724	802	960
Oslo	668	734	922
Paris	612	692	866
Rome	794	868	1010
Stockholm	726	790	976
Vienna	740	802	988
Zurich	668	734	922

*"Winter season" is November through March: "shoulder season" April, May, September and October eastbound, April, May, June and October westbound; "peak season" is June through August eastbound, July through September westbound.

The round-trip fare to these cities from Montreal is, generally, about $17 less than the above; the round-trip fare from Houston is some $180 more. You'll receive a 50% reduction for children between the ages of two and 12, and a 90% reduction for infants under the age of two. If you're not a child or infant, and still want to lower the fare, read on:

14- TO 21-DAY EXCURSIONS: A first way to cut the cost of your air transportation to Europe is by taking a 14- to 21-day "excursion"—which simply means that you plan a trip of from 14 to 21 days' duration. If, under this plan, you go for a minimum of 14 days, but return no later than midnight of the 21st day following your day of departure, you'll realize a saving that can range as high as nearly $180 off normal round-trip fares. Here are the 14- to 21-day excursion rates in both the "basic" excursion season (September through May eastbound, October through June westbound) and the "peak" season (June through August eastbound, July through September westbound), again round trip by jet, between New York and the following European cities:

14- to 21-day round-trip excursion, between New York and	Basic Season	Peak Season	14- to 21-day round-trip excursion, between New York and	Basic Season	Peak Season
Amsterdam	$588	$681	Hamburg	$634	$726
Athens	769	875	Helsinki	748	839
Barcelona	618	712	Istanbul	782	893
Berlin	644	736	Lisbon	541	631
Brussels	588	681	London	541	631
Copenhagen	634	726	Madrid	588	681
Frankfurt	634	726	Munich	644	736

14 □ DOLLAR-WISE GUIDE TO PORTUGAL

Oslo	634	726	Stockholm	704	798
Paris	588	681	Vienna	679	770
Rome	714	804	Zurich	634	726

These fares are available for Monday-through-Thursday departures only; if you fly transatlantic on a weekend, you'll pay a $15 supplement for eastbound ocean crossings on Fridays and Saturdays, westbound crossings on Saturdays and Sundays.

22- TO 45-DAY EXCURSIONS: And you can even go cheaper. Since 1975, the airlines have offered a 22- to 45-day (minimum 22 days, maximum 45 days) excursion fare that descends to a truly remarkable level—as little as $508 round trip between New York and Athens in winter, $546 in "shoulder" months, $664 in peak season (see the list of regular economy fares above for an explanation of the seasons). And what's more, they'll give you a further reduction off these 22- to 45-day excursion rates if you'll buy your tickets at least 60 days in advance. Here, first, are the round-trip 22- to 45-day fares for persons purchasing their tickets *within* 60 days of departure:

22- to 45-day excursion, round trip between New York and	Winter Season	Shoulder Season	Peak Season
Amsterdam	$374	$451	$541
Berlin	415	483	582
Brussels	374	451	541
Copenhagen	399	468	565
Frankfurt	399	468	565
Hamburg	399	468	565
Istanbul	524	585	713
Lisbon	363	432	527
London	363	432	527
Madrid	374	451	541
Munich	415	483	582
Oslo	399	468	565
Paris	374	451	541
Rome	450	522	628
Stockholm	435	505	603
Vienna	440	511	623
Zurich	399	468	565

And here are the rates you'll pay if you purchase your 22- to 45-day tickets *more* than 60 days in advance of departure:

Advance purchase 22- to 45-day excursion, round trip between New York and	Winter Season	Shoulder Season	Peak Season
Amsterdam	$320	$350	$446
Athens	461	492	598
Berlin	355	384	494
Brussels	320	350	446
Copenhagen	340	369	474
Frankfurt	340	369	474
Hamburg	340	369	474
Istanbul	472	507	621
Lisbon	295	325	410
London	295	325	410
Madrid	320	350	446

Munich	355	384	494
Oslo	340	369	474
Paris	374	350	446
Rome	388	433	544
Stockholm	345	385	490
Vienna	371	404	525
Zurich	340	369	474

As with the 14- to 21-day fares, there's a surcharge for the weekend use of 22- to 45-day excursion fares: $15 for eastbound trips on Fridays and Saturdays, $15 for westbound crossings on Saturdays and Sundays. *And there is a cancellation "penalty" charge on advance purchase fares: 10% of the fare or $50, whichever is higher.*

One drawback to the 22- to 45-day excursion fares: they permit no air stopovers on the way to your destination. What's the impact of that "stopover" rule? Well, that can best be understood in the context of our next discussion, which deals with the "extra-city" bonus available on non-excursion air fares or (to a more limited extent) on 14- to 21-day excursion fares:

ADDITIONAL CITIES FOR NO EXTRA FARE: Look again at our chart of basic air fares to Europe. Those prices will appear somewhat lower to you when you realize that they can be made to cover not only the expense of traveling to Europe, but also of traveling *within* Europe.

The key to this feat is the so-called "extra-city" system, which, on a non-excursion ticket, permits you to stop free at any of the European cities on the way to, and on the way back from, your ultimate destination. Conceivably, you could incur no extra transportation costs whatever!

The same extra-city privileges are provided on a 14- to 21-day excursion flight, but only for five cities (two on the inbound flight, two on the outbound flight, plus the point of turnaround).

Does this save money? Emphatically, yes. Your round-trip fare, you see, is calculated according to the mileage, along the straight-line route from New York to your destination. But the cities in which you can stop along the way are not always on the straight-line route; many involve considerable detours. This added mileage comes to you free under the extra-city plan. In fact, your transportation costs within Europe are thus reduced to not much more than they would be by train. And, since most major European cities are separated by only an hour or two of flying time, the extra-city system conserves large portions of your vacation time that would otherwise be spent in weary train trips.

GO NOW, PAY LATER: Thus far, you've made a single round-trip ticket serve for much of your transportation, both to and through Europe—but the cost of that ticket is still a substantial one. To ease the burden of the initial outlay, all the airlines permit the purchasing of tickets on an installment-payment basis. This plan permits you to avoid the necessity of paying your entire fare all at once, and instead to pay simply $50-or-so down, and the remainder in installments over three to 24 months.

You should apply for a pay-later plan at least ten days before you expect to pick up your plane tickets. No collateral is required. You merely fill out a form, furnish a couple of references, and sign your name. If you have any sort of earning power, your application will be approved. I know a woman who was able to obtain a ticket, installment-style, at a time when she was working as a researcher for $110 a week.

16 DOLLAR-WISE GUIDE TO PORTUGAL

Naturally, any installment purchase device adds a slight amount in interest charges to the ultimate cost of your ticket; it's a money-delayer, not a cash-saver. Still, it's a useful arrangement that avoids an immediate, substantial depletion of your travel funds.

2. Traveling within Portugal

TRAINS IN PORTUGAL: Underdeveloped when stacked against the more industrialized nations of Western Europe. Still, the connections between the capital and more than 20 major towns are mainly electric and diesel. Express trains run between Lisbon and Coimbra (the university city), as well as Porto. Leaving from Lisbon's waterfront, electric trains travel along the Costa do Sol (Estorial and Cascais) and on to Queluz and Sintra.

At any rate, nobody complains about the prices charged: 0$54 per kilometer in first class, a little more than 0$36 per kilometer in second class. Discounts up to 20 percent are granted on Weekend Tickets, valid only from 5 p.m. on Fridays till noon on Sundays. Parties of ten or more can apply at any Portuguese railway station for substantial reductions if the total combined rail miles exceeds 31.

In Lisbon at the **Statium Apolónia,** connections can be made for international services and the Northern and Eastern Lines. **Rossio** serves Sintra and the Western Lines; and at the **Cais do Sodré** connections are made for the Costa do Sol resorts of Estoril and Cascais. Finally, trains leave from the **Sul e Sueste** for the Alentejo and the Algarve. In addition, express trains connect Lisbon to all the major capitals of Western Europe, and there is a direct link with Seville.

Railway information and tickets on the **Portuguese National Railroad** may be obtained in North America from its representative, the **French National Railways,** 610 Fifth Avenue, New York, N.Y.; 323 Geary Street, San Francisco, Calif.; 11 East Adams Street, Chicago, Ill.; 1500 Stanley Street, Montreal, Quebec.

Eurailpass

This pass is obtainable for periods of 15 days, 21 days, and one, two, or three months at the price of $130, $160, $200, $270, and $330, respectively. The holder is entitled to unlimited first-class rail transportation and many bonuses —either free or with substantial reductions. Travel on this pass must begin within six months of the day of issue, and the first day of validity has to be stamped in at the railroad station where travel is commenced. For children, the already-mentioned rate reductions apply.

Travel agents in all towns, and railway agents in major cities in the United States, sell Eurailpasses. Readers who live elsewhere can write to: Eurailpass, Box Q, Staten Island, N. Y. 10305.

The pass is sold only in North America, and is good throughout Western Europe, except in the British Isles and Finland.

Student Railpass

This is available in North America to bonafide students under 25 years of age. It is valid for two months of unlimited *second-class* travel in the same 13 countries as the Eurailpass. However, supplements and seat reservation fees aren't included in the $195 price. The bonuses are the same as for Eurailpass.

TRAVELING WITHIN PORTUGAL 17

Before leaving for Portugal, you can get complete details from travel agents in all towns and railway agents in such major cities as New York, Montreal, Los Angeles, or Chicago. You can also write to Eurailpass, Box Q, Staten Island, N.Y. 10305.

CAR RENTAL: For most travelers, it's best to have a rented car at your command. That way, you're your own free agent, capable of savoring the hidden charms of Portugal that are often inaccessible by public transportation. While there are no superhighways, the roads are quite good, providing access to hard-to-reach gems, undiscovered villages, mountain passes with panoramic views and waterfalls, rustic country inns, and off-the-beaten-track sandy beaches and coves.

You'll have to decide if it's more economical for you to rent a car with a straight daily or weekly charge, plus either a per kilometer rate, or an unlimited mileage arrangement. Many agencies do not offer you a choice. But a firm that does is **Carop/Europcar**, a branch of Contauto, a European firm with 600 depot stations on the continent. The office in Lisbon is at the airport and at 24-C Avenida António Augusto de Aguiar (tel. 53-51-15), and there are branches at Faro (the center of the Algarve), Faro Airport, Albufeira, Praia da Rocha, Portimao, Lagos, Porto (the capital of the north), Porto Airport, and Funchal (the capital of Madeira Island).

In high season (April through October), seven price groups of cars are offered, the rates including maintenance, touring documents, oil, insurance, but not gasoline. The daily rate with unlimited mileage for a Fiat 126 (a tiny four-seater) is 420$ ($16.38); for a Morris 1000 or Fiat 127, 475$ ($18.53); for a VW 1300, Simca 1100 GLS, Renault 5, or Fiat 128, 585$ ($22.82); for a Cortina or Marina, 715$ ($27.89); for an Opel 1900, Ford 17M, Chrysler 180, or Opel 1900 automatic shift, 860$ ($33.54); for a VW Minibus (8-9 passengers), 1,100$ ($42.92); and for a luxurious five-passenger Mercedes 220, the fee is 1,230$ ($47.97). The daily rate for the same vehicles, with a per kilometer fee, is 175$ plus 1$80 ($6.90) per kilometer for the Fiat 126; 200$ plus 2$ ($7.88) for the Morris 1000; 220$ plus 2$80 ($8.65) for the VW 1300; 250$ plus 3$30 ($9.89) for the Cortina; 275$ plus 4$ ($10.53) for the Opel 1900; 375$ plus 4$60 ($14.82) for the VW Minibus; and 470$ plus 5$50 ($18.55) for the Mercedes 220.

For seven days or more, subsequent reductions are granted. In low season, November to March, lower prices are quoted. If you are going on to Spain, or elsewhere, ask about the "rent it in Portugal, leave it in another country" plan.

Write to or speak with the friendly and most helpful manager Victor Manique. He'll send you a detailed brochure and will reserve a car for your arrival. If you want to tour in the grand manner, in a Cadillac or other luxurious car, Mr. Manique will arrange it at a lower cost than any competitive car rental firm in Portugal.

Of course, **Hertz** and **Avis** are well represented in Lisbon, with offices at Lisbon airport. The downtown office of Avis is at 11 Avenida da Liberdade; that of Hertz at 113 Avenida da Liberdade.

Also highly recommended is **Brunauto**, at Rua Joaquim Bonifácio 10A (tel. 539168). Their cars are new, and the genial owner—Mr. Bruno—is most eager to help Americans enjoy Portugal. Their staff is, of course, English-speaking, and gives personal service. And the price is right!

Brunauto also has branches in the Algarve at Faro, Lagos, Praia da Rocha, and Monte Gordo. There are offices also at the airport in Lisbon and at the airport in Faro.

By now you've bought your plane tickets and are on your way. Coming up next—some handy reading matter during your flight about the food, history, and hotels of Portugal.

Chapter II

THE SCENE IN PORTUGAL

**1. A Capsule History
2. Dining and Wining
3. The Hotel Outlook**

IN AN INCREASINGLY mechanized age, there is still Portugal!
It is a land of gardens and natural produce, of abundant flowers, a place that still values the artful or artless homemade touch. The wine you drink may be from your host's own casks, the tablecloth before you made by his wife, the bread fresh from the oven and baked by a daughter-in-law.

A long line of expatriates—including exiled royalty—has discovered what has long been called "the last foreign country of Europe." The society has been termed feudal, and that forms part of its medieval charm for many. But revolution and change are in the air. Even so, visitors are still rare in the more remote parts of Portugal. One Canadian couple were themselves the subject of sightseeing interest as they made their way through a village en route to a church built in the 14th century.

A small country at the southwestern edge of Europe, Portugal measures only 136 miles at its widest point, 350 miles at its longest span.

You can divide your Portuguese holiday into four parts, spending the first leg of your trip in **Lisbon** and at the Costa do Sol resorts of **Estoril** and **Cascais.** Perhaps you'll allow time for a series of day trips from the capital, going to **Sintra, Nazaré, Tomar, Fátima, Obidos,** as well as the scenic spots south of the **Tagus.**

Maybe you'll devote the second phase to one of the hotels on the **Algarve** in the south, studded with sandy beaches (en route to the Algarve, you can detour through the Alentejo district, stopping at the old Roman city of **Evora,** for example).

Before leaving continental Portugal, you should experience the relatively unknown north. Go there to see towns and monuments—**Coimbra, Porto** (home of port wine), **Viana do Castelo**—and some of the country's finest scenery. Before beginning your homeward trek, you can wind down in the islands, either **Madeira** or in the more remote **Azores.**

Hopefully, on your Portuguese holiday you'll allow for recuperative days in the sun and at the sea—all of which will fortify you to drink from Lisbon's chalice: hearing fado songs, seeing its museums, attending a bullfight, an opera, dining in a palace, browsing through numerous handicraft shops.

When traveling through the countryside, it's best to plot your trips so that you'll stop over at the government-owned pousadas (tourist inns), ranging from restored castles on the Atlantic coast to mountain chalets.

Essentially, Portugal is a land of . . .

SOUNDS, SMELLS, AND SIGHTS: Windmills clacking in the Atlantic wind . . . farmers burning dried eucalyptus leaves . . . the plaintive sound of fado echoing through the narrow streets of Lisbon's Alfama . . . lonely varinas —draped in black—waiting at the surf, their melancholy faces wrinkled by the harsh sea wind . . . purple wisteria cascading over the walls of mosaic courtyards . . . starfish-scattered sands . . . plodding oxen pulling carts along ribbon roads . . . sun-baked, grape-yielding slopes . . . the stark ruggedness of the seascape . . . sun-scorched, bull-breeding plains . . . houses bathed in birthday cake colors with contrasting azulejos in ivory white, mustard gold, indigo blue, and emerald green . . .

Wicker baskets of eels steeped in the scent of the sea . . . terraced rice fields evoking the Orient . . . the pine groves of Leiria . . . bullock carts trundling across arched bridges . . . a ringing of a church bell in a mountain village . . . fields of cork . . . coasts of cliffs . . . the singsong litany of a fish auction . . . lemons, snowy almonds, and cactus . . . richly embroidered regional costumes . . . black-shawled women mending nets . . . horseback-riding campinos . . . the violent grandeur of the "Mouth of Hell" . . . pagan festivals . . . medieval monasteries . . . and women filling their jugs at fountains, as in Biblical times.

THE SEASONS: "We didn't know we had an April," one Lisbon resident said, "until *that* song came out." "April in Portugal" is famous—both the song and the season. Then there are those who prefer May, or a day in late September, and especially October. Summer may be the most popular season, vacations being timed as they are; but for the traveler who can chart his own course, spring and autumn are the delectable seasons.

For Americans, the climate of Portugal most closely parallels that of California. The Portuguese, of course, consider their climate one of the most ideal in Europe—and it is. As in California, there are only slight fluctuations in temperature between summer and winter—the overall mean ranging from 77 degrees Fahrenheit in summer to about 58 degrees Fahrenheit in winter. However, the rainy season begins in November, usually lasting through January.

The proximity of the Gulf Stream allows Portugal's northernmost province, the **Minho**, to enjoy mild, though very rainy, winters, even though it's at approximately the same latitude as New York.

Snow brings many skiing enthusiasts to the **Serra de Estrêla** mountains in north-central Portugal; but, for the most part, winter entails only some rain and lower temperatures in the other provinces.

The **Algarve** and especially **Madeira** are the exceptions to the rule: they enjoy warm and temperate winters. Madeira, in fact, basks in its high season in winter. The Algarve, too, is somewhat of a winter riviera, attracting sunworshippers from both North America and Europe. Summers in both the Algarve and Madeira tend to be long and hot, crystal clear and dry.

Lisbon and **Estoril** enjoy 46 to 65 degree Fahrenheit temperatures in winter, those figures rising to between 60 and 82 degrees Fahrenheit in summer.

Travelers have dubbed the country—whose terrain ranges from wooded fertile valleys, to mountains, to sun-baked slopes, to flat coastal expanses, to rolling pasturelands, to windswept plains, to sandy beaches—a "country for all seasons."

1. A Capsule History

Early in their history—the 12th century to be exact—the ancestors of today's Portuguese decided they didn't want to be associated with their Spanish neighbors in León and Castile. The split that was to occur followed a typical medieval pattern of indiscretion, ambition, jealousy, open conflict, and the emergence of a popular hero around whom the people could rally in a cause of independence.

First, the indiscretion. The 11th-century ruler of the Spanish kingdoms of León and Castile, Ferdinand the Great (otherwise the First), handed over the county of Portugal to his illegitimate daughter Teresa. The land south of the Tagus was at that time held by the Moors. Unknowingly, the king had launched a course of events that was to lead eventually to the birth of another nation.

Ambition. Teresa, though born out of wedlock herself, was firmly and securely bound in marriage to Henry, a Count of Burgundy. Count Henry seemed to accept his father-in-law's gift of Portugal as his wife's dowry. Upon the king's death, Henry perhaps coveted the territories in Spain as well, but his own demise cut short further aggrandizement of territory.

Jealousy. Teresa now ruled in Portugal, casting a disdainful eye and an interfering nose into her legitimate sister's kingdom in Spain. Teresa lost no time mourning poor Henry, but took as a lover a Galician count, Fernao Peres. Teresa's constant refusal to guard her own affair with Peres and stay out of everyone else's affairs led to open strife with León.

Her son, Afonso Henriques, was terribly displeased with his mother's actions. Life being so short in those days, he probably wanted to hurry the day when he could rule in her place. Their armies met at Sao Mamade in 1128. Teresa lost and was banished along with her lover.

Ungrateful son or not, Afonso Henriques was to become the George Washington of Portugal. In 1143 he was proclaimed king, and official recognition eventually came from the Vatican in 1178. His enemies in Spain temporarily quieted, Afonso turned his roving eye toward the Moorish conquerors in the south of Portugal. Beefed up by the armed might of the Crusaders from the north, the Portuguese conquered Santarém and Lisbon in 1147. Upon his death in 1185, Afonso was succeeded by his son Sancho I, who continued his father's work of consolidation of the newly emerged nation, which was threatened with recurring attacks by the Moors. His heir Afonso II ruled for 12 years, beginning in 1211. Like his father and grandfather, he carried on the war against the Moors.

Sancho II was an adolescent when he ascended the throne. Extremely devout, he returned much to the clergy that had been confiscated during his father's reign. He scored numerous victories over the Moors. However, he couldn't pacify the clergy and was eventually excommunicated. His brother Afonso III was named king, ruling from 1248 to 1279. During the latter's reign, the Algarve, the southern district of Portugal, was finally taken from the Moors, and the capital was moved from Coimbra to Lisbon.

The new king Dinis, the son of a bigamous marriage, ruled Portugal from 1279 to 1325. He is sometimes known as the poet king or the farmer king. He founded the country's first university, in Lisbon, in 1290. Dinis married an Aragonese princess, Isabella, who was later canonized—although evidence indicates that the vigorous young king would have preferred a less saintly wife! Isabella was especially interested in poor people, and they spread a legend about her. It seems that she was sneaking bread out of the palace to feed them when her husband spotted her and inquired as to what she was concealing. When she revealed the contents to Dinis, the bread miraculously turned into roses, so the story goes.

The son of these two famous monarchs, Afonso IV, could hardly wait until his father stepped down from the throne. He, too, was involved in wars with Castile and the Moors, chiefly the 1340 battle of Salado, but is remembered today for having had assassins murder his son's mistress, the legendary Inês de Castro.

Early in life his son, who would later rule as Pedro I, was betrothed to marry a Spanish princess. However, he fell in love with her beautiful lady-in-waiting. Inês was deeply attracted to him, and their affair blossomed. Eventually, Inês was banished from the country, although she returned upon the death of the Spanish princess to live openly with Pedro. Jealous sycophants in court persuaded Afonso IV to sanction her murder, which was especially blood curdling. Though he was to know other women, Pedro seemingly never recovered from the shock of seeing his dead mistress. Patiently he waited until his father died. Upon his becoming king, he set out to seek revenge. Tracking the assassins to Spain, he had them returned by force to Portugal, where he had their hearts torn out. (One of the assassins managed to escape to France.) But the king did not stop there. He ordered that the body of Inês be exhumed. The members of the court were summoned, and forced to pay homage by kissing the hand of Inês, who had been interred for at least four or five years. She was then royally attired and regally placed on the throne beside her husband. Inês, and later Pedro, were buried at Alcobaça, where their tombs are visited frequently today.

During Pedro's reign (1357-67), the influential representative body, the Cortes (an assembly of clergy, nobility, and commoners), began to gain ascendancy, while the majority of the clergy, pretentious and greedy for power, fought the sovereign's reform measures, thus allying the people more strongly with the crown. Pedro's son, Ferdinand I (1367-73), saw Portugal invaded by Castilian forces, Lisbon besieged, and the final demise of his dynasty.

In 1383, rather than submit to Spanish rule, the Portuguese people chose the illegitimate son of Pedro as regent. The house of Avís was thereby established. Joao de Avís (1383-1433) secured Portuguese independence by defeating Castilian forces at Aljubarrota in 1385. His union with Philippa, the granddaughter of Edward III of England, produced the seed which was to mark the emergence of Portugal as an empire—Prince Henry the Navigator.

Henry's demand for geographical accuracy and exploration, his desire to attain the legendary wealth in gold and ivory, slaves and spices of the East and "Terra Incognita," and his patriotic and spiritual desires to promote Christianity by joining with the fabled Christian kingdom of Prester John and driving the Moslems out of North Africa—all drove Henry to explore. Facing him was a Sea of Darkness where ships supposedly melted in the equatorial regions, sea serpents flourished, and strange beasts sought to destroy any interloper.

Henry established a community of scholars at Sagres on the south coast of Portugal to develop navigational and cartographical techniques. He infused the court with his zeal and brought his nation to face a destiny imminent from the time of their earliest contacts with Phoenician and Greek mariners. Henry was responsible for the discovery of Madeira, the Azores, Cape Verde, Senegal, and Sierra Leone—and he established the blueprint for continued exploration during the reigns of Durate I (1433-38), Afonso V (1438-81), and Joao II (1481-95).

In 1482 Portuguese ships explored the mouth of the Congo; in 1488 Dias rounded the Cape of Good Hope; and in 1497 Vasco da Gama reached Calicut (Kozhikode) on India's west coast, clearing the way for trade in spices, porcelain, silks, ivory, and slaves. The original appellation of the Cape of Good Hope—the Cape of Storms—might have been a more prophetic one.

The Treaty of Tordesillas, negotiated by Joao II in 1494 for as yet undiscovered lands in the Western Hemisphere, ensured Portugal's possession of Brazil, not discovered until 1500. Utilizing the inflowing wealth of the whole empire, Manuel I (the Fortunate, 1495-1521) imprinted his imagination and name upon great movements of art and architecture. His reign inspired Portugal's Golden Age. By 1521 the country had begun to tap the natural resources of Brazil and had broken the spice-trade monopoly formerly held by the Venetians. She was mistress of nearly all accesses to the Indian Ocean. At her noontide, she stood as the first of the great maritime world empires.

Joao III (1527-57) ushered the Inquisition and the Jesuits into his unwieldy empire. With his son Sebastian's disappearance in action in Morocco in 1578, leaving Portugal without an heir, the way was opened for Spanish control. Philip II of Spain claimed the throne and began 60 years of Spanish domination. In the East, Portugal's strength had been undermined by Dutch and English traders.

A nationalist revolution in 1640 brought a descendant of an illegitimate son of Joao I to the throne, Joao IV. This began the house of Braganza, which was to rule until the 20th century, as well as a long series of revolutions and intrigues in Portugal's history. Joao IV arranged an English alliance, wedding his daughter to Charles II. For her dowry he "threw in" Bombay and Tangier.

The Treaty of Lisbon with Spain in 1668 gave Portugal recognized independence. In that same year the Cortes ousted King Afonso VI, replacing him with Pedro II.

All Saints Day, 1755. The great earthquake destroyed virtually all of Lisbon. In six minutes 15,000 people were killed, many thousands while attending morning masses. The Marquis de Pombal, adviser to King José (1750-77), became a dictator, completing the process he had begun years before, transforming the inert absolutism into an active despotism. Much that he did—such as limiting the power of the Inquisition, rebuilding Lisbon after the earthquake—was good. He beefed up such industries as silk, fishing, even diamonds. But his expulsion of the Jesuits in 1759 earned him powerful enemies throughout Europe.

In 1793, under the threat of Napoleon, Portugal joined a coalition with England and Spain. An insane queen, Maria I (1777-1816), plus an exiled royal family, made military overthrow an easy job. The Cortes was summoned by the military junta, a constitution was drawn up, and Maria's son, Joao VI, accepted the position of constitutional monarch in 1821. Joao's son Pedro declared independence for Brazil in 1822; and in 1853, after a series of intrigues and battles within the royal family, he returned to Portugal and restored the constitution.

The year 1853-1908 felt the rumble of republican movements that assaulted the very existence of the monarchists, as exemplified by the dictatorial government of Carlos I, "the painter king." In 1908 Carlos and the crown prince were assassinated at Black Horse Square in Lisbon. Manuel II ruled for two years before being overthrown in an outright revolution on October 5, 1910. (He died in England in 1932, the last of the Portuguese monarchs.)

Portugal was a republic!

Instability was the watchword of the newly proclaimed Republic, with revolutions occurring two or three times a year. Portugal failed in her attempts to remain neutral in World War I. Influenced by her old ally, England, she commandeered German ships in the Lisbon harbor, which promptly brought a declaration of war from Germany.

The precarious foundations of the Republic collapsed in 1926 when a military revolt established a dictatorship, with Fragoso da Carmona at its head. He remained president until 1951, though only as a figurehead. António Salazar became his finance minister in 1928, rescuing the country from a morass of financial difficulties. He went on to become the head of state. In World War II, he asserted his country's neutrality, although he allowed British and American troops to occupy the Azores in 1943.

In 1955, Portugal joined the United Nations. Salazar suffered a stroke in 1968 (he died in 1970), and Premier Marcelo Caetano succeeded him.

The old dictatorship was overthrown by the revolution of April 25, 1974, after which a Communist-Socialist government was set up, which is radically changing not only the political, but the social and economic structure of the country.

As we go to press the situation continues to be unstable, though Portugal's Socialist leader, Mario Soares, who won free elections in 1974, has been promised aid from Common Market countries which hopefully will help to stabilize the situation.

2. Dining and Wining

Portuguese food was summed up well by Mary Jean Kempner in her *Invitation to Portugal:* "The best Portuguese food is provincial, indigenous, eccentric, and proud—a reflection of the chauvinism of this complex people. It takes no sides, assumes no airs, makes no concessions or bows to Brillat-Savarin—and usually tastes wonderful."

WHAT TO EXPECT: The first main dish you're likely to encounter on any menu is bacalhau (salted codfish), the o fiel amigo (faithful friend) to the Portuguese. As you drive through fishing villages in the north, you'll see racks and racks on which the fish is drying in the sun. It has literally saved the lives of thousands from starvation, and the Portuguese not only are grateful to it—they like it as well.

Foreigners may not wax as rhapsodical about it, though it's prepared in imaginative ways, reportedly one for every day of the year. Common ways of serving it include bacalhau cozido (boiled with vegetables such as carrots, cabbage, and spinach, then baked in a mixture); bacalhau à Bras (fried in olive oil with onions and potatoes and flavored with garlic); bacalhau à Gomes de Sá (codfish that has been stewed with black olives, potatoes, onions, then baked and topped with a sliced boiled egg); and, finally, bacalhau no churrasco (barbecued).

A Kettle of Fruits of the Sea

Aside from codfish, the classic national dish is caldeirada, once described as the Portuguese version of a savory Mediterranean bouillabaisse. Prepared by the lady of the house, it is a simple kettle of fish, with bits and pieces of the latest catch. From the kitchen of a competent chef, it's a pungent stew with choice bits and pieces of fruits of the sea.

Next on the platter is the Portuguese sardine, which many gastronomes have called elegant. This unassuming fish goes by the pompous name of Clupea Pilchardus, and is found off the Atlantic coasts of Iberia as well as France. Many of the sardines come from Setúbal, a city south of the Tagus which is most often visited on a day trip from Lisbon. As you stroll through the alleys of the Alfama, or pass along the main streets of small villages throughout Portugal, you'll see women kneeling in front of braziers on their front doorsteps, grilling these large sardines left behind for domestic consumption. To have them grilled, order sardinhas assadas.

Shellfish is one of the great delicacies of the Portuguese table. Its scarcity and the demand of foreign markets have led to astronomical price tags.

However, tourists devour them—many lamenting later when the bill is presented to settle damages. The price of lobster or crabs literally changes every day, depending on market quotations. Therefore, the tariff doesn't appear on the menu. Rather, you'll see the abbreviation, Preço V., meaning variable price. When the waiter brings one of these crustaceans to your table, inquire as to the price. That way you'll avoid shock when your sin is tallied up.

If you do decide to splurge, make sure you get fresh shellfish. Many of these creatures from the deep, such as king-sized crabs, are cooked, then displayed in restaurant windows. If they don't sell that day, we suspect the chef places them there tomorrow.

When fresh, santola (crab) is a delicacy. It's often served stuffed (santola recheada), though this specialty may be too pungent for unaccustomed western palates. Amêijoas, the baby clams, are a reliable item of the Portuguese kitchen. Lagosta is translated as lobster; in fact, it's really a crayfish, best when served without adornment. If you see the words piri piri on the menu following lobster, rush for the nearest exit. This is a sauce made of hot pepper from Angola. Jennings Parrott once wrote: "After tasting it you will understand why Angola wants to get it out of the country."

In Pursuit of an Incomparable Morsel

Many Portuguese begin their meals with percêbes, roughly translated as goose barnacles. These little devils are the subject of much controversy. One local newspaper in Lisbon suggested to tourists that if they "can bear their repulsive appearance," they'll find "an incomparable morsel of delicious seafood" within. Others claim that all they taste from barnacles is brackish sea water.

There will be no controversy among those who are partial to camaraoes (shrimps). Most restaurants serve a heaping, delectable platter full—but be forewarned—after devouring the meal, you will most assuredly need a bath!

A wide variety of good-tasting and inexpensive fish dishes are also available: salmonete (red mullet) from Setúbal; robalo (bass); lenguado (sole); and the sweet-tasting pescada (hake). Perhaps less appealing to the average diner, though preferred by many discriminating palates, are eiros (eels), polvo (octopus) and lampreías (lampreys), the latter a seasonal feature in the northern Minho district.

Of course, another way of beginning your repast is to select from the offerings of trays of acepipes variados, Portuguese hors d'oeuvres, which might include everything from a sea creature known as "knife" to the inevitable olives and tuna fish.

Meat, especially beef and veal, is less satisfying. Porto residents are known as "tripe eaters." The specialty is dobrada, tripe with beans, a favorite of the workers. The cozido à Portuguesa is another dish much in demand: a stew often employing both beef and pork, along with fresh vegetables and sausages. The chief offering of the beer tavern is bife na frigideira, beef in a mustard sauce, usually served with a fried egg on top, all piping hot in a brown ceramic dish. Thinly sliced iscas (calf's livers) are usually well prepared and sautéed with onions.

The best meat in Portugal is porco (pork), which is usually tender and juicy. In particular, order porco Alentejano, fried pork in a succulent sauce with baby clams, often cooked with herb-flavored onions and tomatoes. In the same province, cabrito (roast kid) is another treat, flavored with herbs and garlic. Chicken tends to be hit and miss, and is perhaps best when spit roasted a golden brown (frango no espeto).

In season, game is good, especially perdiz (partridge) and codorniz estufada (pan-roasted quail).

The Question of Olive Oil and Garlic

From the soup kitchen, the most popular broth is caldo verde, literally green broth. Made from cabbage, sausage, potatoes, and olive oil, it is commonly encountered in the north. Another ubiquitous soup is sopa Alentejana, simmered with garlic and bread among other ingredients. The Portuguese housewife is canny, knowing how to gain every last morsel of nutrition from her fish, meat, and vegetables. The fishwives make a sopa de mariscos by boiling the shells from fish, then richly flavoring the stock and lacing it with white wine.

The basis of much Portuguese cooking is olive oil. However, the oil seems blander than that used extensively in Spain. Furthermore, chefs in most Portuguese hotels—certainly first-class ones—offer more of a routine international fare than they do the regional cuisine. If you don't like olive oil, ask that your fish or meat be prepared sem azeite (without olive oil) but com manteiga (with butter). Garlic is also used extensively and forms the basis of many dishes. However, if you select anything prepared to order you can request that it be sem alho (without garlic).

Time and time again in Portuguese restaurants you'll be asked if "you want a second helping, sir?" It's customary in most establishments to order soup (invariably a big bowl filled to the brim), then a fish and a meat course. Potatoes and/or rice are likely to accompany both the meat and fish platters. This banquet is simply too much for many, particularly those second helpings.

Menus are not usually posted in the windows of Portuguese restaurants, making shopping around impossible. In many restaurants, the chef features a prato do dia—that is, a plate of the day, actually several listings. These dishes are prepared fresh that day, and often are cheaper than the regular offerings. In regional dining rooms (not in first-class restaurants and hotels), you'll sometimes see two price listings after an entree. The first price is the tariff if one person orders the dish, the second tab is if two persons select the same main course. This system is known as the famous "double portions" of Portugal. Having two persons order the same entree amounts to only a small saving, but the custom is highly favored in escudo-wise Portugal.

The Sugaring of the Egg

Locked away in isolated and remote convents and monasteries, nuns and monks created such original sweet tooth concoctions that they surely had to confess their sins! Many of these same delectable dessert specialties have been handed down over the years and are nowadays sold in little pastry shops throughout Portugal. In Lisbon or Porto, and a few other Portuguese cities, you can visit a salao de chá (tea salon) at four o'clock in the afternoon where you can sample these delicacies. Regrettably, too few restaurants feature regional desserts, many relying on caramel custard or fresh fruit.

Portugal doesn't offer many egg dishes, except for the omelette which all countries enjoy. However, the egg is used extensively in many of the sweets. Although egg yolks cooked in sugar may not appeal to you, you may want to try some of the more original offerings. Perhaps the best known are ovos moles (soft eggs sold in colorful barrels) that originate in Aveiro. From the same district capital comes ovos de fio (string eggs).

The most typical dessert is arroz doce, rice pudding flavored with cinnamon. As mentioned, flan or caramel custard, appears on all menus. If you're in Portugal in summer, ask for a peach from Alcobaça. One of these juicy, succulent yellow fruits will spoil all other peaches for you forever! In first-class restaurants, the waiters go through an elaborate ritual of skinning it in front of you. Sintra is known for its strawberries, Setúbal for its orange groves, the Algarve for its almonds and figs, Elvas for its plums, the Azores for their pineapple, and Madeira for its passion fruit. Some people believe that if you eat too much of the latter, you'll be driven insane!

Cheese (queijo) is usually eaten separately and not with the fruit, as in France. The most common varieties of Portuguese cheese are made from sheep or goat's milk. Popular entrees include quejo da serra (literally, cheese from the hills). Another much-in-demand cheese is queijo do Alentejo, plus queijo de Azeitao. Many prefer queijo Flamengo (similar to the Dutch Gouda cheese).

Dining hours in Portugal are much earlier than they are in Spain. The best time for lunch is between 1 and 2:30 p.m., from 7:30 to 9 p.m. for dinner.

The Pleasures of Port

One of the joys of dining in Portugal is to discover its regional wines. With the exception of Port and Madeira, they remain little known in Europe.

Port wine is produced in a specially designated region on the arid slopes of the **Douro.** Only vineyards within this area are recognized as yielding genuine Port wine. The wine is shipped from Portugal's second largest city, Porto, which the English have dubbed Oporto.

Port—drunk in tulip-shaped glasses—comes in many different colors and flavors. The pale dry Port makes an ideal apéritif, and you can request it at the same time you might normally order dry sherry. The ruby or tawny Port is sweet or medium dry, usually drunk as a liqueur after dessert. The most valuable Port is either vintage or crusted wine. Crusted Port does not mean vintage—rather, it takes its name from the decanting of its crust. Vintage Port is the very best wine. In a period of a decade, only three years may be declared vintage.

Port is blended to assure a consistency of taste. Cyril Ray called it "one of the heartiest and handsomest of wines." Matured in wooden casks, the "wood ports" are either white, tawny, or ruby red. At first, the wine is a deep ruby color, turning more the color of straw as it ages.

Port wine has "perpetuated and glorified the fame of Porto," as one citizen put it. The first foreigners to be won over by it were the English—a drinking tradition dating back to the 17th century. In more recent times, however, the French import more of the wine than the British. The grapes are still crushed by barefoot men; but this shouldn't alarm you as the wine is purified before it's bottled.

Falstaff's Soul for a Glass of Madeira

Although its greatest chic was in times gone by, Madeira wine remains popular. It was highly favored by the early American colonies. Made with grapes grown in volcanic soil, it is fortified with brandy before it's shipped out.

The major types of the Madeira are Sercial (a dry wine, drunk as an apéritif, once a favorite with characters in Galsworthy novels); Malmsey (the dessert wine that the Duke of Clarence allegedly asked to drown in to escape torture at the hands of his brother); and Boal (a heady wine used on many different occasions, every place from a banquet following a hunt to an off-the-record tête-à-tête).

Perhaps one of the finest statements ever made for Madeira wines is the following: "It gives vivacity to a social gathering, profundity to a solitary meditation, helps a man to think well of his friends and to forgive his enemies . . ."

Feminine, But Virile

Among the table wines, our personal favorites are from the mountainous wine district known as **Dao**. Its red wines are ruby-colored, their taste often described as velvety, whereas the white wines are light and delicate enough to make a fit accompaniment to Portuguese shellfish. From the sandy dunes of the **Colares** wine district, near Sintra, emerges a full-bodied wine made from Ramisco grapes (this wine is served at the famous Palácio de Seteais deluxe hotel). Of Colares wine, a Portuguese writer once noted that it has "a feminine complexion, but a virile energy."

The vinhos verdes (green wines) have many adherents. These light wines—low in alcoholic content—come from the northwestern corner of Portugal, the Minho district. The wine is gaseous, as it's made from grapes not fully matured. Near Estoril, the **Carcavelos** district produces an esoteric wine—commonly served as an apéritif or else with dessert. As it mellows, its bouquet is more powerful. Finally, the **Bucelas** district, near Lisbon, makes a wine from the Arinto grape, among others. Its best known wine is white, with a bit of an acid taste.

Drinking water is safe in Lisbon, along the Costa do Sol (Estoril and Cascais), and in Porto. In less visited towns and villages, you may want to be extra cautious and order bottled water. You can ask for it to be with or without "gas."

Beer (cerveja) is gaining new followers yearly. One of the best of the home brews is sold under the name of Sagres, honoring the town in the Algarve which enjoyed famous associations with Henry the Navigator.

3. The Hotel Outlook

The government-sponsored pousadas—similar to Spain's paradores—were originally created for Portuguese holiday seekers in remote sections of the country. Now they are crowded during the peak months. The pousadas, usually in a setting of physical beauty—perhaps on the ledge of a mountain—are strategically located. Often they are in accommodation-lean sections: everywhere from a cliffside inn at Henry the Navigator's Sagres to a feudal castle in the walled town of Óbidos. The tariffs are low, and a guest can't stay more than five days, as there is usually a waiting line of other pilgrims. Special terms are granted to honeymoon couples!

Not only the capital, but the Costa do Sol resorts, are riddled with attractive, serviceable, small, contemporary, and inexpensive accommodations, with a tiled private bath going with every room. Accommodations are available to fit all pocketbooks, ranging from the Lisbon Ritz to the Palácio at Estoril down to the lowliest pensao (boarding house).

In the 1960s, many enterprising and cost-concerned Germans and Scandinavians discovered the **Algarve** coast, that southernmost strip of Portugal, with its endless miles of some of the finest beaches in Europe. The sun-seekers from the Teutonic lands poured in like the invading Visigoths of old. They were subsequently followed by Americans and Canadians—all wanting in on the suntanning and surf-riding bonanza. The Algarve at present boasts some deluxe hotels, as well as dozens of first- and second-class establishments, plus lots of low-cost boarding houses.

In the north, **Porto** has also wakened from its hotel slumber—its newest hotels finding immediate acceptance. Many provincial towns, such as **Viseu, Tomar, Leiria,** have well-run, first-class hotels. However, other out-of-the-way towns and villages have not yet aroused themselves to meet the needs of projected tourism. Although some of the most interesting centers don't offer enough varied quality accommodations as of yet, there are ways to work around this handicap. For example, one can often bed down in the vicinity of a tourist zone, visiting important shrines or sights on day trips from a more pleasing base elsewhere.

Funchal, the capital of **Madeira,** is well stocked with top-grade hotels, notably the world-famed Reid's. For budgeteers, many cost-saving accommodations are available, especially the quintas (old stately homes converted into inns—usually surrounded by gardens and furnished with family antiques). Even the **Azores** offer pleasant lodgings, but they're very limited.

For a more detailed breakdown of the hotel classifications and price guidelines, refer to the introduction to "The Hotels of Lisbon," Chapter IV.

There's just so much to learn about a country before plunging into it. Now it's time for the actual experience. Our TAP plane is about to land in Lisbon, where our voyage of discovery will begin.

Chapter III

SETTLING INTO LISBON

1. Navigating Your Way
2. Public Transportation
3. The ABC's of Life

IN ITS GOLDEN AGE, it was called the "eighth wonder of the world." Travelers returning from a trip to Lisbon reported that its riches rivaled those of Venice.

As one of the greatest maritime centers in history, the Portuguese capital has enjoyed exotic riches from the far-flung corners of its empire. Aside from the wealth of cultural influences, Lisbon stockpiled goods, beginning with its earliest contacts with the Calicut and Malabar coasts.

Treasures from the Orient brought in on Chinese junks to Indian seaports eventually found their way back to Lisbon: porcelain, elaborate and luxurious silks, rubies, pearls, and other rare gems. The abundance and variety of spices from the East—tea, indigo, turmeric, ginger, pepper, coconut, cumin, betel— were to rival even Keats' vision of "silken Samarkand."

From the wilds of the Americas came valuable red dye-wood (Brazilwood), coffee, gold (discovered in 1698), diamonds (unearthed in 1729), and gem stones. All this extensive contact signaled a new era in world trade, with Lisbon sitting as the grande dame of maritime empires, the hub of commerce between Europe, Africa, and Asia. And then came . . .

THE GREAT EARTHQUAKE: "From Scotland to Asia Minor, people ran out of doors and looked at the sky, and fearfully waited. It was, of course, an earthquake," as once chronicled a *Holiday* article. Tidal waves, 50 feet high, swept over Algeciras, Spain. The capitals of Europe shook.

It was 9:40 on the morning of All Saints' Day, November 1, 1755. The churches were packed to overflowing; smoky tapers and incense burned upon the altars. After the initial shock, 22 spasms followed. Roofs caved in; hospitals (with more than 1,000 patients), prisons, public buildings, royal palaces, aristocratic town houses, fishermen's cottages, churches, and houses of prostitution —all were toppled. Overturned candles helped ignite a fire that would consume the once-proud capital in six days, leaving her a gutted, charred shambles.

Voltaire captured much of the spiritual and fatalistic tenor of the feelings of the people in *Candide*. In one part, he wrote: "The sea boiled up in the harbor and smashed the vessels lying at anchor. Whirlwinds of flame and ashes covered the streets and squares, houses collapsed, roofs were thrown onto foundations and the foundations crumbled;" all told, 30,000 inhabitants were crushed beneath the tumbling debris.

When the survivors of the initial shocks ran from their burning homes toward the mighty Tagus, they were met with walls of water 40 feet high. Estimates vary, but the final tally of all who died in drownings and the six-day holocaust that followed is put at around 60,000.

Voltaire was cynical in commenting on the aftermath of the disaster, particularly the auto-da-fé that followed: "It was decided by the University of Coimbra that the sight of several people being slowly burned with great ceremony was an infallible means of preventing the earth from quaking."

PLAYING THE COQUETTE GAME: Today, the "new" Lisbon is distinctly feminine. In fact, she was once called a coquette. Under a stark blue sky, her medley of pastel-washed houses dazzles, like a city in North Africa. The Tagus has been called her eternal lover.

Sea gulls take flight from her harbor, where trawlers from Africa unload their freight. Pigeons sweep down on Black Horse Square. From the Bairro Alto (upper city), cablecars carry its denizens down to the waterfront. On narrow lanes and dark cobbled alleyways, barefoot varinas rush by with wicker baskets of fresh fish on their heads. The sidewalks are more characteristic, the black and white mosaics forming arabesques.

At times, a country town atmosphere prevails. From many Lisbon hotel rooms, you are wakened in the morning by the crowing of roosters. Streets bear colorful names or designations, such as the Rua do Açúcar (Street of Sugar). Fountains abound: one, the Samaritan, dating from the 16th century. Wide, symmetrical boulevards split through the city to new high-rise apartment houses, while in other quarters laundry hanging from 18th-century houses laps the wind.

It is a city that gives nicknames to everything from its districts (the Chiado, named after a poet) to its kings. Fernando, who built one of the most characteristic walls around Lisbon, was honored with the appellation, "The Beautiful."

THE LEGEND OF ULYSSES: Lisboans have always known they were special. Regardless of how fanciful the legend, it has its adherents. In the Alfama, many of the residents claim unabashedly that Ulysses founded their city. Others more scholarly maintain that the Phoenicians or the Carthaginians were the original settlers. The body of the country's patron saint, Vincent, is said to have arrived in Portugal on an abandoned boat, with only two ravens to guide it. It is further alleged that the birds lived in the Cathedral tower until as late as the 19th century.

The Romans settled in Lisbon in the first century B.C., building a fortification on what is now St. George's Castle. The city was captured by the Visigoths in the 5th century A.D., this conquest later followed by long centuries of Moorish domination beginning in 714 A.D. The first king of Portugal, Afonso Henriques, captured Lisbon in 1147. But it wasn't until 1256 that King Afonso III moved the capital there, deserting Coimbra, the major university city of Portugal.

Now in its seventh century as the headquarters of the Portuguese nation, Lisbon is the westernmost capital of continental Europe. Part of its legend is that it spreads across seven hills, like Rome. If that statement were ever true, it has long since become historical, as Lisbon now sprawls across more hills than that. Most of it lies on the right bank of the Tagus.

32 DOLLAR-WISE GUIDE TO PORTUGAL

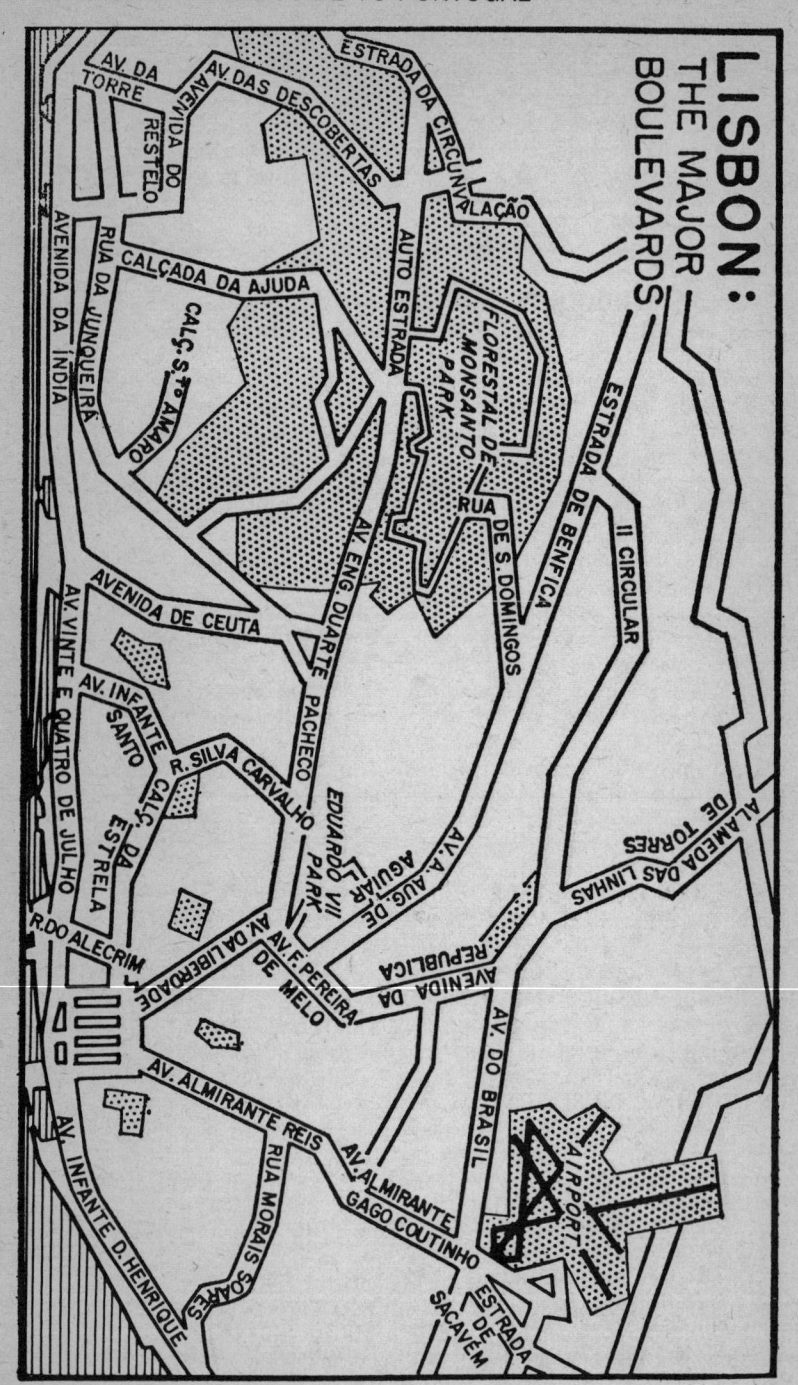

1. Navigating Your Way

No one ever claimed that getting around Lisbon was easy. Streets rise and fall across the legendary seven hills, at times dwindling into mere alleyways. But exploring it and ultimate discovery make the effort worthwhile.

Lisbon is best approached by way of its famous gateway, the **Praça do Comércio**, bordering the Tagus. Like a formal parlor, it is one of the most perfectly planned squares in Europe, only rivaled perhaps by the Piazza dell'-Unità d'Italia in Trieste, Italy.

Before the earthquake of 1755, Commerce Square was known as **Terreiro do Paço**, the palace grounds, as the king and his court lived in now-destroyed buildings on that site. To further confuse matters, English-speaking residents refer to it as **Black Horse Square**, so named because of a statue (actually a bronze green) of José I, a Portuguese king. The monument from the 18th century was created by Machado de Castro, who dominated Portuguese sculpture in his era.

Today, the square houses the Stock Exchange and various ministries of government. Its center is used as a parking lot, which destroys some of the harmonious effect of the praça. In 1908, its most monumental event occurred, the reverberations of which were heard around the world. King Carlos I and his older son, Luís Filipe, were fatally shot by an assassin. Although it would hold on for another two years under the rule of a younger prince, the House of Braganza collapsed that day on Black Horse Square.

Directly to the west of the square stands the City Hall fronting the **Praça do Município**. The building itself was erected in the latter 19th century by the architect Domingos Parente.

Heading north from Black Horse or Commerce Square, you enter the hustle-bustle of the Praça Dom Pedro IV, popularly known as **The Rossio**. The "drunken" undulation of the sidewalks, with their arabesques of black and white, have led to the appellation—used mainly by tourists—of "the dizzy praça." Here you can sit, sipping strong unblended coffee from the Portuguese provinces in Africa, while a boy gives you one of the cheapest and slickest shoeshines in Europe. The statue on the square is that of the Emperor of Brazil, Pedro IV, himself a Portuguese.

Opening onto The Rossio is the **Teatro Nacional Dona Maria II**, a freestanding building whose facade has been preserved. In 1967-70, workmen gutted the interior to rebuild it completely. If you arrive by train, you'll enter the **Estaçao do Rossio**, whose Manueline exuberance offends those sensitive to architecture. The Tourist Bureau on this square is in the Palácio Foz.

Separating The Rossio from the Avenida da Liberdade is the **Praça dos Restauradores**, named in honor of the restoration—that is, when the Portuguese chose their own king and freed themselves from 60 years of rule by Spain. That event is marked by an obelisk.

The main avenue of Lisbon is the **Avenida da Liberdade**, a handsomely laid out street dating from 1880, and once called the antechamber of Lisbon. The Avenue of Liberty is like a mile-long park, with shade trees, gardens, and center walks for the promenading crowds. Flanking it are some of the finest shops, headquarters for many major airlines, travel agents, coffee houses with sidewalk tables, and such important hotels as the Tivoli. The comparable street in Paris would be the Champs Elysées; in Rome, the Via Veneto.

At the top of the avenue is the **Praça Marquês de Pombal**, a statue erected in honor of Pombal, the 18th-century prime minister credited with the reconstruction of Lisbon in the aftermath of the earthquake. He is depicted with a lion.

Proceeding north, you'll enter the splendid **Parque Eduardo VII**, named to honor the son of Queen Victoria who paid a state visit to Lisbon. In the park is the **Estufa Fria**, a greenhouse that is well worth a visit.

The business district of Lisbon is called **Baixa**, its architecture characterized as Pombaline, referring to the 18th-century prime minister again. Many of the major Portuguese banks have their headquarters here. Running south, the main street of Baixa separates Black Horse Square from the Rossio. In fact, a triumphal arch leads from Black Horse Square to the **Rua Augusta**, itself sheltering many clothing stores. The two most important streets of Baixa are the Street of Silver (Rua da Prata) and the Street of Gold (Rua da Ouro). Of course, they were never paved with gold or silver, but take their names from the silver and goldsmiths whose shops were (and still are) found there. The most famous one: **Sarmento.**

If you head west from Baixa, you'll enter an even smarter shopping district known as the **Chiado**. From its perch on a hill, it is traversed by the **Rua Garrett**, honoring the Portuguese poet and dandy of the 19th century. Many of the finest shops in the city, such as the Vista Alegre, a china and porcelain house, are here. One coffee house, in particular, **A Brasileira**, has been a traditional gathering spot for the Portuguese literati.

Continuing our ascent, we arrive at the **Bairro Alto** (the upper city). This sector, reached by trolley car, occupies one of the legendary seven hills of Lisbon. Many of its buildings were left fairly intact from the 1755 earthquake. Containing much of the charm and color of the Alfama, it is of interest mainly because it is the center of some of the finest fado cafes in Lisbon, such as **A Severa, Lisboa à Noite,** and **Adega Machado.** In addition, some of the best restaurants in the city are found here, as well as unpretentious taverns featuring hearty Portuguese cuisine.

To the east of Black Horse Square lies the oldest district of Lisbon, the **Alfama.** For a more detailed description of this section, refer to Chapter VII, "The Sights of Lisbon." Saved only in part from the devastation of the earthquake, the Alfama was the old Moorish sector of the capital. Centuries later, before the earthquake struck, it was the residential district of aristocrats. Nowadays, it is occupied mainly by stevedores, plus fishermen and their barefoot varinas.

Overlooking the Alfama is **St. George's Castle**, once a Visigothic fortification, although it was used by the Romans before that. Destroyed and rebuilt so many times that its history is a jumble, the present castle dates from the 12th century.

On the way to the Alfama, on the Rua dos Bacalheiros, stands the **Casa dos Bicos** (the House of the Pointed Stones). Although this early 16th-century town house is not open to the public, the mansion is graced with a facade studded with diamond-shaped stones. And though it was partially demolished by the earthquake, it remains an impressive sight.

In the west, on the coastal road to Estoril, is the suburb of **Belém** (Bethlehem). It contains some of the finest monuments in Portugal, a few of which were built during the Age of Discovery, near the point where the caravels set out to conquer new worlds (at Belém, the Tagus reaches the sea). At one time, before the earthquake, Belém was an aristocratic sector filled with elegant town houses.

Two of the principal sightseeing attractions in all of Portugal stand here: the **Jéonimos Monastery**, erected in the 16th century in the Manueline style, and the **National Coach Museum**, the finest of its kind in the world. Actually, Belém is Lisbon's museumland, containing as it does the **Museum of Popular Art**, the **Ethnological Museum**, and the galley-stuffed **Naval Museum**.

On the south side of the Tagus, where a puce-colored smoke billows out from the factories, is the left bank settlement of **Cacilhas**. It is inhabited mainly by the working class, although visited by right bank denizens for its seafood restaurants, such as the Floresta (see our dining recommendations). You can reach the settlement by way of a bridge or by taking a ferry boat across, leaving from Black Horse Square.

Of course, the most dramatic way to cross the Tagus is on the **Ponte 25 de Abril** the longest and most expensive suspension bridge ever erected in Europe, the total outlay exceeding $75 million. The bridge opened up that sector of Portugal lying south of the Tagus. Its towers peaking at 625 feet, the bridge is 7,473 feet long. Standing guard on the left bank is a monumental statue of Christ, depicted with his arms outstretched.

If you don't have a private car, you'll need to know something about:

2. Public Transportation

Inexpensive, though inadequate at times. Yet considering the hilly terrain of the city and the fact that many of the streets were designed for donkey carts, the Portuguese manage very well. However, even the most skilled chauffeurs have been known to scrape the fenders of their clients' rented limousines while maneuvering through the narrow alleyways.

A lot of the city can be walked around, especially by those adept at hill climbing. However, to get from one point to the other—say from the Alfama to the suburb of Belém—you'll need public transport or your own car.

THE TAXIS: Taxis in Lisbon tend to be cheap and are a most popular means of transport for all but the most economy minded of tourists. The taxis usually are diesel-engined Mercedes, charging a basic fare of 5$ for the first 500 yards. After that, you'll be assessed another pittance for each additional 250 yards. The driver is allowed by law to tack on another 50 percent to your bill if your total luggage weighs in at more than 66 pounds.

Many visitors anchor in at one of the Costa do Sol resort hotels, such as the Palácio in Estoril and the Cidadela in Cascais. If that is your situation, then you'll probably find taxi connections from Lisbon prohibitively expensive. The fare must be negotiated. The driver has a choice of turning the meter down and letting it tick up a fat tab, or else of setting a straight fare for the journey. Whichever he elects, it's not cheap. Far preferable for Costa do Sol visitors is the electric train system (see below).

TRAMS AND BUSES: Among the cheapest in Europe. You'll pay only 1$ (4¢) to 5$ (20¢) for a ride. The trolley cars, such as those that make the steep run up to the Bairro Alto, are usually painted a rich Roman gold. The green doubledecker buses, on the other hand, come from London—and look as if they need Big Ben in the background to complete the picture. If you're trying to stand on the platform at the back of a jammed bus, by the way, you'll need both hands free to hold on.

At the foot of the Santa Justa elevator, that Eiffel-designed structure lying on the **Rua do Ouro** or Street of Gold, a stand will give you a schedule pinpointing the zigzagging route of these trams and buses. Your hotel concierge should also be of help to you.

SUBWAYS: The underground decor of Lisbon's Metro stations is usually more impressive than the network itself. Designated by large "M" signs on the street, the stations are elegantly adorned with colored glazed tiles. A single fare is only 2$5 (10¢). One of the most popular runs—and likely to be jampacked on corrida days—is from the Avenida da Liberdade to the Campo Pequeno, that brick-built bullring away from the center of the city.

FERRY BOATS: Long before the advent of the Ponte 25 de Abril, the reliable ferry boats chugged across the Tagus, connecting the left bank with the right. They still do, and are as popular as ever, as many Portuguese find the bridge too expensive to traverse with their automobiles. Therefore, they leave their cars at home and take the ferry boat to work.

Most of the boats leave from Black Horse Square, heading for Barreiro and Cacilhas. The one-way fare on the ferry boat is about 2$ (8¢) per passenger. You can take your car over on the ferry as well for around 25$ (98¢). Or else you can drive on the:

PONTE 25 DE ABRIL: As mentioned, this suspension bridge—the largest ever built in Europe—connects Lisbon with its left bank and south of the Tagus district. For a small car, the toll charge is 10$ (39¢), increasing to 20$ (78¢) for a larger automobile. Not only can you take the bridge to reach Cacilhas, but you can use it for such cities as Setúbal in the south, and Évora, the old Roman city in the east.

Finally, there is that most important means of transport, the:

ELECTRIC TRAINS: Lisbon is connected with all the towns and villages along the Portuguese "Riviera" by a smooth-running electric train system. You can board the train at the waterfront **Cais do Sodré** station in Lisbon, heading up the coast all the way to Cascais, the end of the run where you'll be delivered practically to the doorstep of the famous Fim do Mundo (End of the World) restaurant.

Both first- and second-class seats are offered, and the rides are cheap. For example, if you go all the way—that is, Lisbon to Cascais—in a first-class seat, the one-way fare is 15$ (59¢). From Lisbon to Estoril, the one-way fare in a first-class seat is 12$50 (49¢).

Sintra, that third major destination in the environs, is not reached by the electric train. You must go to the Estaçao do Rossio station, opening onto the Praça Dom Pedro IV or The Rossio, where frequent connections can be made.

3. The ABC's of Life

It's maddening to have your trip marred by an incident which could have been avoided, providing you'd been tipped off previously. Hocking your watch, renting a fur, seeking medical care, getting your hair cut, or ferreting out the nearest toilet, can at times become paramount problems. Although we don't promise to answer all these needs, there are a variety of services in Lisbon that can ease your adjustment into the capital.

The concierge in your hotel is a usually reliable dispenser of information, bullfight tickets, "man-to-man" advice about whether you can "bring somebody back to the room," or assistance in pleading with your wife to speak to you again after your too-friendly attention to a fadista. However, should your hotel not be staffed with an English-speaking person, or should you desire more

LISBON: USEFUL INFORMATION 37

immediate or more detailed answers to your questions, the following brief summary of some of Lisbon's facets of life may prove helpful.

AIRLINES: For ticket sales, flight reservations, information about the city and the country itself, you can get in touch with the polite and very efficient personnel of **Transportes Aéreos Portugueses (TAP)** at 3 Praça Marquês de Pombal (tel. 53-88-51).

AMERICAN EXPRESS: Will hold or forward mail for you. There, too, you can buy traveler's checks, tickets for tours, or exchange currency. **STAR** in Lisbon is the representative of American Express and accommodates your banking and mailing needs from its offices at 4-A Avenida Sidónio Pais (tel. 53-98-71). It is open daily from 9 a.m. until 12:30 p.m. and from 2-6 p.m. weekdays; closed on Saturdays and Sundays. The offices are a good hike from downtown Lisbon.

BABYSITTING: Check with the staff at your hotel for arrangements. Most first-class hotels can provide competent women or young girls for babysitting from lists which the concierge keeps. At smaller establishments, the girl is likely to be the daughter of the proprietor. Rates are low. Remember to request a babysitter in the morning if you're going out that evening.

BANKS: Check with your home bank before your departure, as many banks in Canada and the United States may not have affiliates in Lisbon. The majority of banks open at 9 a.m., close at noon. Afternoon hours are from 2 to 3:30. A trio of major Portuguese banks: the **Banco Português do Atlântico**, 112 Rua Áurea; the **Banco Espírito Santo e Comercial de Lisboa**, 95 Rua do Comércio; at the airport, a branch of **Banco Lisboa & Açores** is open at all hours day and night including holidays.

CURRENCY: The exchange rate is approximately 26 escudos (26$) to the U.S. dollar.

CUSTOMS: You'll be asked how much tobacco you're bringing in: the limit is 200 cigarettes or 50 cigars. One still camera with five unexposed reels of film is allowed duty free; also a small movie camera with two reels; a portable tape recorder; a portable record player with ten "used" records; a portable typewriter; a portable radio; a portable musical instrument; and a bicycle (not motor bikes).

Campers and sportsmen are allowed to bring in one tent and camping accessories (including a kayak not exceeding 18 feet), a pair of skis, two tennis rackets, a tackle set, and a small firearm (for hunting only) with 50 bullets.

Pets brought into the country must have the okay of a local veterinarian and a health certificate from their home country. A normal-size bottle of wine and half a pint of hard alcohol are permitted, as is a "small quantity" of perfume and a half pint of toilet water.

ELECTRIC CURRENT: Many North Americans find that their plugs will not fit into sockets in Portugal, where the voltage is 220 AC, 50 cycles. Adapters and transformers may be purchased once you're in Lisbon.

HOLIDAYS: Watch those holidays and adjust your banking needs, or whatever, accordingly. Aside from the regular holidays, Portugal has a few of its own: Universal Brotherhood Day on January 1; the anniversary of the Republic, October 5; a Memorial Day to the country's greatest poet, Camoes, June 10; Assumption Day, August 15; All Saints Day on November 1 (ironically, this was the date Lisbon was destroyed in the earthquake of 1755); Independence Day on December 1; and "Our Feast of the Immaculate Conception" on December 8. Good Friday and the Feast of Corpus Christi are also holidays, but their dates are different every year.

LANGUAGE: One writer suggested that Portuguese "has the hiss and rush of surf crashing against the bleak rocks at Sagres." French and English are commonly spoken in Lisbon, along the Costa do Sol, and in Porto. In most small villages and towns, hotel staffs and guides usually speak French, though English is making greater inroads. The native tongue is difficult, but the people are helpful and patient. Gestures often suffice.

LAUNDRY: Most hotels in this guide provide laundry services, but if you want your garment returned on the same day, you'll often be charged anywhere from 20 percent to 40 percent more. Simply present your maid or valet with your laundry or dry cleaning (usually lists are provided). Note: materials needing special treatment (such as orlon or other synthetics) should be called to

38 DOLLAR-WISE GUIDE TO PORTUGAL

the attention of the person handling your laundry. Some establishments we've dealt with treated every fabric as if it were cotton.

MEDICAL CARE: The concierge at your hotel can usually put you in touch with the house doctor, or summon him in case of emergencies. You can also call the American Embassy, 39 Avenida Duque Loulé (tel. 55-51-41), and ask the staff there to recommend a physician who speaks English; or the British Hospital (tel. 67-10-07), where the telephone operator, staff, and doctors all speak English.

NEWSPAPERS AND MAGAZINES: The international edition of *The Herald Tribune* is sold at most newsstands in Lisbon, either in major hotels or along the street. The *Trib* is also sold in leading newsstands throughout the country, in Porto, and in the Algarve.

PASSPORTS: If you lose your passport, and if you're an American or Canadian citizen, you can apply for a new one at the **American Embassy,** 39 Duque Loulé (tel. 55-51-41), or the **Canadian Embassy,** 2 Rua Rosa Araújo (tel. 56-25-47).

PHARMACIES: The Portuguese government requires selected pharmacies (farmacias) to stay open at all times of the day and night. This is effected by means of a rotation system. So check with your concierge for locations and hours of opening of the nearby drugstores. The local newspapers list the ones open 24 hours each day.

POST OFFICE: While in Portugal you may have your mail directed to your hotel or hotels, to the American Express representative, or to General Delivery, Lisbon. Your passport must later be presented for mail pickups. Open 24 hours a day, the General Post Office is at Praça dos Restauradores.

TIPPING: The following tips on tipping are merely guidelines:
Hotels: The hotels add a service charge (known as a serviço), which is divided among the entire staff. But individual tipping is also the rule of the day: 5$ to the bellhop for errands run, 5$ to the doorman who calls you a cab, 2$50 in simple inns or hotels; 5$ to the porter for each piece of luggage carried; 25$ to the wine steward if you've dined often at the hotel (more if your stay has been extended beyond a week); 40$ to the chambermaid on short stays.
    In the first-class or deluxe hotels, the concierge will present you with a separate bill, outlining your little or big extras, such as charges for bullfight tickets, etc. A gratuity is expected in addition to the charge, the amount depending entirely upon the number of requests you've put to him.
    Hairdressers: For a normal haircut, men should leave 5$ behind as a tip to their barbers. But if your hair is cut at the Ritz don't dare leave less than 10$. Beauticians get 20$; a manicurist, around 10$.
    Taxis: Figure on about 20 percent of the regular fare for short runs. For longer treks—as, for example, from the airport to Cascais—15 percent is adequate.
    Porters: The porters at the airport or train stations generally charge you 5$ per piece of luggage. In addition to that, you should add two or three escudos.
    Restaurants: Most restaurants and nightclubs add 13.1 percent for service and government taxes. As in hotels, this serviço is distributed among the entire staff, including the waiter's mistress and the proprietor's grandfather—so extra tipping is required. Add about 5 percent to the bill in moderately priced restaurants, up to 10 percent in deluxe or first-class establishments.
    Services: Hatcheck girls in fado houses, restaurants, and nightclubs expect at least 2$50, as do the women who stand on sentinel duty in the washrooms. The shoeshine boys of Portugal are the most undertipped creatures in Portuguese society, getting only one escudo for a 2$50 shine. Here we recommend greater generosity if you feel like it.
    Helpful Hints: Learn the value of Portugal's currency and its relation to the people as you dispense your gratuities. Tips in the country are generally low, higher in Lisbon and Estoril. However, service personnel are expecting more every year. It is well to remember that exorbitant tipping in another country—given its economic structure—can be as unwise as undertipping is cruel.

TOURIST OFFICE: The Information section of the State Tourist Department is housed in the Palácio Foz, at the Praça dos Restauradores (tel. 36-70-31) in Lisbon. If you desire travel information or facts about Portugal before heading there, you can make contact with the **Casa de Portugal** (Portuguese Tourist and Information Office), 570 Fifth Avenue, New York, N.Y. 10036. Tel. 581-2450.

LISBON: USEFUL INFORMATION 39

TOURS: Lisbon travel agents will book you on organized tours. One of the most popular such agencies is **STAR,** the Lisbon representative for American Express, at 4-A Avenida Sidónio Pais (main office), tel. 53-98-71, close to Eduardo VII Park-South (Marquês de Pombal Square), starting point of its tours. It also has a downtown branch office at 14 Restauradores Square (tel. 36-25-01).

At the height of the season, from March 1 to October 31, most of the major tours are operated on a daily basis, excluding Mondays and holidays. St. George's Castle, Belém's Jerónimos Monastery, the National Art Gallery—all are highlighted by different city tours which stress particularly fascinating cultural, historical, or scenic attractions.

"Touristic Lisbon" and **"Old Lisbon"** are popular morning tours, departing at 9:30. **"Touristic Lisbon"** and **"Artistic Lisbon"** are afternoon trips leaving at 2:30. The cost of each of these tours is 130$ ($5.07).

The **Lisbon-Mafra-Sintra-Escoril** special departs daily, except Tuesdays, at 9:30 a.m., costs 380$ ($14.82), and includes lunch. It's a beautiful excursion out into the environs.

For 400$ ($15.60), you can journey north on a 12-hour trip to the walled city of **Óbidos** and the fishing village of **Nazaré.** The jaunt departs on Tuesdays, Thursdays, and Saturdays, from April 1 to October 31, at 8:30 a.m. Another popular year-round 12-hour tour, the **Nazaré-Fátima** special, can be had for the same price.

In the next chapter, we'll tackle the more specific problem of settling into Lisbon—that is, finding a suitable hotel in the price range you desire.

Chapter IV

THE HOTELS OF LISBON

1. The Deluxe Choices
2. Leading First-Class Hotels
3. Middle-Bracket Hotels
4. Full-Board Bargains
5. The Budget Range

WHEN YOU CHECK into a hotel, you'll see the official tariffs posted in the main lobby as well as somewhere in your room, perhaps at the bottom of the closet. These rates are dictated by the Directorate of Tourism and are strictly regulated. It's really a form of rent control. They include the 13.1 percent service charge and tourist tax which in previous years were added on separately.

Most hotels will allow you to keep your room or deposit your luggage there until noon. From that point on, the manager can add the cost of an additional full day's rent to your bill.

When checking into a hotel, clear up the all-important question of how many meals, if any, you plan to take in the dining room. Full pension means a room and three meals a day; half pension a room, breakfast, and at least one other meal. It is proper for the hotel clerk to ask which of those main meals—either lunch or dinner—you'll be taking. Those on the half- or full-pension plans must pay for a meal even if they miss it. It saves you money to take full or half board, as you are granted a reduction in the overall rate, as opposed to staying at a hotel and taking your meals there on an à la carte basis. But the manager is not obliged to grant you a discount on a pension plan unless you are staying at his establishment two full days and nights.

Should an infraction occur—such as overcharging, etc.—you may demand to be given the Official Complaints Book. In this tome you can write your allegations. The hotel manager is then obligated to turn your comments over to the Directorate of Tourism, where they are reviewed by a staff to see if any punitive action should be taken against the establishment.

Hotels in Portugal are rated from five stars to one star. The difference between a five-star hotel and a four-star hotel will not always be apparent to the casual visitor. Often the distinction is based on square footage of bathrooms and other technical differences.

When you go below this level, you enter the realm of the second-class hotel and the third class, the latter comprising the most raw-boned and least-recommended hotels in Portugal, although some can be quite good.

Tourist inns, not government run, are known as estalagems. Often these offer some of the finest accommodations in Portugal, many decorated in the native or típico style—representing topnotch bargains.

The residências are a form of boarding house, except without board. Only a room and breakfast are offered at these establishments. The pensao is a Portuguese boarding house that charges the lowest tariffs in the country. The deluxe pensao is a misnomer. The term simply means that the pensao enjoys the highest rating in its category, although the accommodation is decidedly not luxurious. A luxury pensao is generally the equivalent of a second-class hotel. The boarding houses are great finds for the budget hunter. Often many of them prepare a good local cuisine with generous helpings. For bottom-of-the-barrel type living, there are both first-class and second-class boarding houses.

Coastal hotels, especially those in the Algarve, are required to grant off-season (November to February) visitors a 15 percent reduction on the regular tariff. To attract more off-season business, a number of establishments extend this, starting the reduced rates in mid-October and granting them until April 1.

1. The Deluxe Choices

THE TOP CHOICE: American ladies in boots, black velvet pants, and chinchilla swagger jackets walk their pet poodles on the grassy center strip fronting the entrance. Where does this scene take place? At **The Ritz**, 88 Rua Rodrigo da Fonseca (tel. 68-41-31). Now a landmark, the hotel was built in the late 1950s.

The Ritz was once given worldwide exposure in a many-page spread in Life. There in dazzling color you saw the richness of its lavish suites, furnished with museum-quality antiques or reproductions (many of which were made at the famous Fundação Ricardo do Espírito Santo Silva). Of course, in this popular magazine you were shown the romantically contrived suites. If you book into a typically modern room, you'll more likely get unfrilly blond furnishings. The duality in the decor has its amusing moments, especially when teddy bear wooly armchairs are set in vast bank-style lobbies.

The suites have the finest style and decorative taste of all first-class Portuguese hotels. Slender mahogany canopied beds, with fringed swags, marquetry desks, satinwood dressing tables with tip-mirrors, plush carpeting—no wonder the Ritz was preferred by such famous guests as President Eisenhower, Germany's Kurt Georg Kiesinger, Lord Snowdon, Faisal of Saudi Arabia, even Jerry Lewis, John Wayne, Audrey Hepburn, and Sammy Davis Jr. The modern rooms facing the avenue are cheaper, the more expensive ones with terraces opening onto Edward VII Park. All are air conditioned and sound proof, with modern tiled baths with double basins.

For a double room, including a continental breakfast, the tariff ranges from 890$ ($34.71) to 1,490$ ($58.11). In a single, the rate goes from 595$ ($23.21) to 1,015$ ($39.59). The more luxurious rooms, with antiques or reproductions, rent for 1,120$ ($43.70) for one person, 1,600$ ($62.40) for two. If you require a sitting room, the price is 940$ ($36.66) extra, 470$ ($18.33) extra for a boudoir. All rates include service and taxes.

The main dining room is dignified and pleasant, and the Grill Room is traditionally decorated (see our restaurant recommendations in the next chapter). Breakfast is usually brought to your room on a tray, but alternatively there is a breakfast room overlooking the avenue—with wooden marquetry panels on its gleaming marble walls. In addition to the bridge and reading rooms, the Ritz Bar is a magnet. Lodged in a corner of the hotel, overlooking the terrace and park, it offers everything from a Pimm's No. 1 Cup to a Mint Julep.

OTHER DELUXE HOTELS: Hotel Diplomático, 74 Rua Castilho (tel. 56-20-41), is a semi-luxurious structure in the gilt-edged section of the city, near the Ritz and the Park of Edward VII. The two-story-high lobby and lounge is dominated by an overscaled mural in reds and oranges, the creation of George Bramdeiro, who exhibits in modern galleries. Guests receive visitors in the hidden away mezzanine lounge, with its brightly colored contemporary furnishings. Adjoining the bar is an open sundeck terrace, where you can relax and enjoy a panoramic view of most of the hills of Lisbon. On the ground floor is a modernistic dining room—enlivened by wall murals, a cubist-styled ceiling, and a highly polished silver meat trolley. A complete table d'hôte meal costs 140$ ($5.46).

Spread among the 11 floors are the tasteful bedrooms, which have small balconies and excellent city views, plus central heating and air conditioning if required. The majority of the rooms are clean-cut, with no extra frills, each dominated by a long built-in headboard, with "airplane pilot" buttons to summon room service or the maid. Pristine walls with simple flowing draperies create a restful background for well-selected furnishings, such as built-in chests, armchairs, and desks. The baths, one to each room, are tiled. The manager Belmiro Santos has set three price levels, based on the size and location of the room. Singles range from 300$ ($11.70) in low season to 350$ ($13.65) in high season; doubles are in the 445$ ($17.36) to 520$ ($20.28) range. Note: low season is November 1 through March 31; high season is April 1 through October 30. Breakfast and taxes are included in the prices.

Sheraton, 1 Rua Latino Coelho (tel. 57-57-57), a huge 30-story colossus, was opened in 1972 and contains 400 rooms. It can be seen from miles away, and, in turn, the views from its windows are panoramic, sweeping over the whole of Lisbon. Like most other Sheratons around the world, its emphasis is on slick American-type comfort.

This blockbuster of a hotel, in the modern part of Lisbon, not far from Pombal Square, features a penthouse restaurant called "The Panorama," where à la carte dishes go for about 200$ ($7.80) to 250$ ($9.75). Downstairs is the Alfama Grill, serving Portuguese specialties and providing fado music. There's also a Caravella coffee shop, with a table d'hôte menu for 110$ ($4.29). Hamburgers here cost 60$ ($2.34), a ham steak goes for 70$ ($2.73), and a sirloin and salad is 90$ ($3.51). The hotel has many amenities, including a garage, pool, and a complete health club. The rooms are comfortably furnished, with individually controlled heating and air conditioning, wall-to-wall carpeting, marble sinks in the bathrooms, and direct-dial telephones. The rather steep price of a single ranges from 665$ ($25.94) to 825$ ($32.18). Doubles cost from 940$ ($36.67) to 1,150$ ($44.87).

Avenida Palace, 123 Rua 1 de Dezembro (tel. 36-01-51), is Lisbon's leading hotel link with the past, a world reflected by glittering crystal and antiques. The second-floor drawing room attracts those partial to the age of silk-brocaded wall paneling, fringed velvet draperies, crystal chandeliers, marquetry tables, consoles, and handwoven Portuguese carpets. Five tall windows in the dining room, itself studded with velvet chairs, overlook the avenue. The location is bull's eye—right at The Rossio, minutes from fado clubs, restaurants, and shops.

The restored bedrooms are furnished in the old manner, with 18th-century antiques or reproductions, and are air conditioned and centrally heated. The walls are paneled, often with gilt trim. Crystal prisms hang from the wall sconces and chandeliers, and beds are styled in an old-world way, but with soft mattresses. All the spacious bathrooms have that luxury aura—the walls and floors in Portuguese marble. In high season, with breakfast included, a single rents for 382$ ($14.90) and up; a double for 564$ ($22).

2. Leading First-Class Hotels

Hotel Tivoli, 185 Avenida da Liberdade (tel. 53-01-81), has many enticing features that make it the first choice of many seasoned travelers. First, its location is choice—right on the fashionable main boulevard of Lisbon. Second, it's large enough to accommodate more than 600 guests—hence, its public facilities are bountiful. Third, its prices are low, considering its amenities and the quality of service. The two-story-high reception lobby with an encircling mezzanine lounge is almost arena-sized, with comfortable islands of furniture arranged on Oriental rugs.

The wood-paneled O Zodiaco restaurant is decorated with Easter-egg-colored chairs and a wall plaque depicting astrological signs. Meals are all à la carte. Adjoining the restaurant is a homelike salon with a wood-burning fireplace, Oriental rugs, and restrained accoutrements. On the top floor, the O Terraço offers a view of Lisbon. Here, à la carte meals are provided, with the emphasis on steaks and chops, which you select yourself and have cooked on a tiled charcoal grill.

The regular room prices are scaled according to position—the larger and more expensive ones facing the boulevard. Singles are 465$ ($18.14); doubles are 665$ ($25.94). The air-conditioned rooms contain a mixture of modern and traditional pieces, with solid fabrics and walls making for a restful background. All have private baths. Taxes and service are included in the tariffs.

Tivoli Jardim, 7-9 Rua Júlio C. Machado (tel. 53-99-71), is the sister to the above-mentioned hotel. Here you'll find more contemporary design in the lounges and bedrooms than at the Tivoli. Set in back of its namesake, avoiding the traffic noises from the Avenida da Liberdade, it features a free parking area for guests. The air-conditioned structure is graced with cliff-hanging balconies, two shafts of elevators, and well-styled bedrooms.

The rooms themselves are consistent, with a restrained decor. The walls are rough white plaster, the carpets scarlet, the furnishings basic built in, with reading lights, maid-summoning bells, channel music, as well as comfortable armchairs with coffee tables, and a wall of glass (curtained off at night) leading to the balcony with its rattan furniture. The baths have overall patterned tile, with a bidet, shower, and tub. Singles are 330$ ($12.87) and 355$ ($13.85), and

LISBON: FIRST-CLASS HOTELS

doubles are 460$ ($17.94) and 510$ ($19.89), including breakfast. The rooms overlooking the garden in the rear are a little cheaper.

There are adequate public lounges. Portuguese business people have found the Jardim ideal for meeting clients in the cathedral-high lobby, with its wall of glass through which the Iberian sun pours. Dominating everything is a ceiling-high tapestry, in sunburst colors. The tiled and marbled floors are peacock blue and emerald green, the staircase leading to the mezzanine a blood red. The dining room is tasteful, with its white brick walls and green tables—its wall niches filled with Portuguese ceramics. Within view of most of the tables is a convoluted bronze sculpture, framed by a picture window. For quick meals, the Jardim's zippy, regional-styled snack bar gets the business.

Príncipe Real, 53 Rua de Alegria (tel. 36-01-16). "I do everything myself here—make beds, carry luggage, everything," claims the remarkable owner of this remarkable little hotel, Senhor José Lousada de Rezende. Actually, he's exaggerating: he not only has one of the most skillful and efficient staffs of any hotel in Lisbon, but a surprisingly large one considering the size of his establishment. For example, one maid is assigned only six rooms. That way, Senhor Rezende feels, he can keep things more personal and homelike.

The modern hotel, a convenient five-minute walk from the Avenida da Liberdade, is quite disarming. Behind its rather impersonal facade lies a petite world of fine living. No wonder the Ritz uses it for overflow guests! The living room, quite private seeming, is eclectic, revealing the tastes of the owner, who scouts the north for unusual antiques. Carved wooden pieces, ecclesiastical figures, Oriental rugs, a wide stone fireplace, an ornate pirate's chest, copper water jugs with flowers—whatever, it's warm and inviting. Guests get acquainted in the adjoining small bar, dramatically styled with fire engine red tiled tables, ebony banquettes, and wood-paneled walls.

The same selectivity and care extends to the highly individualized bedrooms—compact, tasteful little worlds. The beds are reproductions of fine antiques, with excellent mattresses. Each room is color coordinated, a happy blending of plain fabrics with florals. In the bathroom, you're likely to find purple towels, lavender toilet paper, and a lilac-stemmed glass for your toothbrush. You'll be charged 370$ ($14.43) in a single room; 570$ ($22.23) in a double; and 782$ ($30.50) in a triple—these tariffs including a continental breakfast, taxes, and service. Breakfast is served in a glassed-in rooftop room. Here early risers are treated to Lisbon's most sensational sunrise. The sun first backlights St. George's Castle, topping the mountain on the far side of the city, as if some master electrician had wired the setting for a Son et Lumière show. When the sun pops over the mountain, red rays catch the tops of taller buildings, gradually illuminating their sides with gold. A fantastic shadow-play. The breakfast room has a beamed ceiling and 18th-century-styled red velvet chairs. What a way to meet the new day in Lisbon! And the waitress—who has one of the prettiest smiles in a city where smiles are prettier than most—usually remembers whether or not you prefer tea or coffee.

A *Los Angeles Times* columnist called the Príncipe Real ". . . one of the finest small hotels in Europe." We concur. We had to go to the cellar one day to get a packing box—there the floors sparkled, too, as well-scrubbed as those in the lobby. A beautifully kept hotel, indeed.

Dom Carlos, 121 Avenida Duque de Loulé (tel. 53-90-71), just off the Praça Marquês de Pombal, faces its own triangular park, dedicated to the partially blind Camilo Castelo Branco, a 19th-century "eternity poet." The curvy facade of the hotel is all glass, giving guests an indoor-outdoor feeling, reinforced by green trees and beds of orange and red canna. In summer, there is air conditioning; in winter, central heating.

The hotel offers 73 bedrooms, including 17 suites. Many of the bedrooms—containing private baths and television—are paneled in reddish Portuguese wood. The Nordic-inspired furnishings are softened by the occasional use of accessories, such as a hand-carved cherub or collage. The single rate is 335$ ($13.05) daily, increasing to 514$ ($20.05) for a double. In a suite, suitable for three, the tariff is 675$ ($26.33), including breakfast.

The lobby-lounge is satisfactory, but even more inviting is the mezzanine salon, where sofas and chairs face the park. Intriguing is the dining room, with its curving glass, polished Danish chairs, slat-board ceiling—and especially its 110$ ($4.29) table d'hôte dinners. In addition, there's a miniature drinking bar, with modern leather chairs, ideal for a tête-à-tête. The hotel also has a sauna.

Flórida Hotel, 32 Rua Duque de Palmela (tel. 541-71), is one of the most highly recommended modern hotels clustered around the circular Praça Marquês de Pombal, with its statue of the prime minister who rebuilt Lisbon after the earthquake. Against a contemporary background, the public rooms utilize a vibrant palette of colors. Facing a glass wall, the main lounge is decorated with pillars of Portuguese marble. Against one wall is a painting by António Alfredo. The grill room provides meals in a setting of Nordic-styled armchairs and plaid draperies. A snack bar opens onto a view of the plaza. There's yet another "view" dining room, more conservatively decorated in shades of midnight blue. In the Bar de Inverno guests congregate for healthy-sized drinks.

The bedrooms are ingeniously designed, fitting the shape of the curving building and making use of stark, primitive colors. Often you'll get a U-shaped desk and sofa as a room divider, with two armchairs forming a living room area. The rooms contain wall-to-wall windows, blond furniture, minuscule closets, and bathrooms with wide-grained marble. Singles range in price from 210$ ($8.19) to 290$ ($11.31), and doubles are in the 335$ ($13.07) to 410$ ($15.99) category. All taxes are included.

Hotel Lutécia, 52 Avenida Frei Miguel Contreiras (tel. 71-70-21), is away from the center, toward the airport, offering 143 air-conditioned rooms, plus eight suites, that have distilled beauty and space and yet are utter simplicity. The ambience is caused by the slimline leather and wood armchairs, the wall-hung desk and dressing table, a roomwide headboard and walnut and leather paneling complete with push-buttons, reading lights, and telephones. The baths are tiled, with a tub and shower combination, and large wrap-around towels on heated rods. Breakfast is available either on your private balcony or in the second-floor morning room. The tariff for one person is 302$ ($11.78) per day, increasing to 405$ ($15.80) for a double. Two persons in one suite pay 860$ ($33.54). Taxes and service are included.

Its 12 stories are set back from a busy thoroughfare, with a formal driveway entrance. The public lounges consume most of the first two floors, though you must take an elevator to the top for the open-view dining room. Also up in the sky is a bar with red leather love seats and stools, potted palms, prints of schooners, and a picture-window view of Lisbon. The snack bar is open till 2 a.m., where a hearty meal will run around 110$ ($4.29), including taxes.

Mundial Hotel, 4 Rua Dom Duarte (tel. 86-31-01), right in the heart of everything, rises eight floors on the curve of a street. The top-floor restaurant offers a view of St. George's Castle and the Alfama. A short walk to The Rossio, theaters, and shops, the Mundial is skillfully managed by Ivan Blovsky, who has brought an efficient, friendly atmosphere with him. Everything is properly manicured and polished, and the hotel is high on the preference list of European businessmen.

The rooms—150 in all with private bath—are comfortable, spacious, and restrained in decor. The baths are tiled, each with a bidet, shower and tub combination, and plenty of mirrors and shelf space for toilet articles. In a single, the rate is 350$ ($13.65). Doubles rent for 500$ ($19.50), breakfast included.

The lobby is sedate, with a glass wall of ivy and gift displays. The sky-view dining room provides both indoor and outdoor meals, according to the weather. For 140$ ($5.46), you can get a better-than-average four-course table d'hôte meal. Tucked away is the tiny Oriental-style bar on the roof—ideal for that special tête-à-tête. The birds in the cages sing love songs.

3. Middle-Bracket Hotels

Hotel Albergaria da Senhora do Monte, 39 Calçada do Monte (tel. 86-28-46), is a special little hilltop hotel with a unique character. It's perched near a belvedere, the Miradouro Senhorado Monte, in the Graça district, a spot where a knowing Lisboan takes his favorite person for a memorable nighttime view of the city, the Castle of St. George, and the Tagus.

Built originally as an apartment house, the hotel has been converted into a clublike establishment, with lots of semi-lavish touches for those seeking an unusual atmosphere. The living room is intimate, with large tufted sofas and over-scaled tables and lamps. The drinking lounge is yet another favored gathering spot.

Many leveled corridors lead to the excellent bedrooms, all 27 of which contain private baths and verandas. The rooms reveal the touch of the decorator, especially the gilt-edged door panels, the grass-cloth walls, and the tiled baths with bronze fixtures. No room is a rubberstamp duplicate. A single with bath rents for 210$ ($8.19) to 276$ ($10.77); a double with bath for 300$ ($11.70) to 395$ ($15.41), the tariffs including a continental breakfast; 13.1 percent is added for service and taxes. In a suite for two, the rate is 395$ ($15.41).

Hotel Fenix, 8 Praça Marquês de Pombal (tel. 53-51-21), enjoys a front-row position on the circular plaza dedicated to the 18th-century prime minister of Portugal. From most of its bedrooms, you can view the trees on the avenue and in Edward VII Park. A semi-modern hotel, the Fenix is run by the Torralta chain.

The hotel is favored by many clients who have timetested their stays here, enjoying its cleanliness and comfort, the modern tiled baths, the Nordic-type furnishings. Each of the compact 125 bedrooms is uncluttered, containing upholstered armchairs and many amenities. In a double or twin-bedded room, the daily rate is 490$ ($19.11); 310$ ($12.09) in a single, including breakfast.

The brightly furnished and air-conditioned two-floor reception lounge, with a cozy bar-lounge on the mezzanine, is much favored. Another plus is the grill room in the hotel, the Bodegón, worthy of a separate recommendation as a restaurant.

LISBON: MEDIUM-PRICED HOTELS

Infante Santo, 14 Rua Tenente Valadim (tel. 60-01-44), is on a secluded tree-shaded street near the docks where the great liners tie in, lying 1.4 miles from the Cais de Sodré, the electric train departure point for the Costa do Sol resorts. Built on the side of a high-rising hill, it has two tiny elevators to take you to the top of its eight floors. Almost all of its 27 bedrooms contain good-sized balconies where you can order your morning breakfast, while enjoying the Tagus.

The emphasis is on modern bedrooms with space for sitting, adequate closets, and amenities such as radios, televisions, and reading lamps. The bedspreads and draperies are in simple, yet vibrant, tones, contrasting with warm grained wood and pastel walls. Tiled baths with a shower-tub combination come with each room. For a double, tariffs range from 285$ ($11.12) to 370$ ($14.43) daily; in a single, from 200$ ($7.80) to 250$ ($9.75). Service and taxes are included.

On the lower floor is a separately owned restaurant, reached by an outside staircase, serving luncheon or dinner for 130$ ($5.07). Breakfast is 30$ ($1.17). Mostly, guests like to utilize the drinking lounge, decorated with oak walls, leather armchairs, and tiled abstract fish scenes on the walls. The corridors have pleasant touches, using decorative framed tiles of regional scenes.

Jorge V Hotel, 3 Rua Mouzinho da Silveira (tel. 56-25-25), is a neat little hotel of today's design, with good amenities, low prices, and a choice location a block off the Avenida da Liberdade. Its butternut yellow and white facade contains rows of cellular balconies, roomy enough for guests to have breakfast or afternoon "coolers." A wee-sized elevator takes you to a variety of rooms at different price levels. The rooms aren't generous in size, but adequate—not glamorous, but comfortable in a compact way. All have small tiled bathrooms, telephones, and radios.

Tariffs vary according to position, with the cheaper rooms facing the rear. Singles cost 280$ ($10.92), including breakfast, with doubles renting for 395$ ($15.41).

The reception lounge shares space with a bar in bright, stark colors played against white. For 125$ ($4.88) you can order a table d'hôte meal in the dining room, itself pleasantly decorated and dominated by a central table with baskets of fresh fruit and cheese. But the room most favored by guests is a regional-style combination drinking bar and breakfast room of nicely melded aggregate stone and wood paneling. Napery is a crisp white, and a center table tempts with fruits piled high in baskets and a big condiment tray.

Flamingo Hotel, 41 Rua Castilho (tel. 53-21-91), has an informal, friendly atmosphere. It goes beyond the cliché, "a home away from home," as many a home never had the care and attention showered upon it that the Flamingo gets from its manager Diamantino Andrade. He got off to a running start by learning American ways in Rhode Island, where he lived for a while with relatives. For a time, he was the manager of the deluxe Palácio at Estoril.

His hotel lies in the "Park Avenue" section of Lisbon, near the Ritz, close to the best shops and restaurants. On its seven floors, the hotel offers 35 compact bedrooms, decorated and maintained in a homey fashion, with a liberal use of modestly contemporary furnishings. Including breakfast, service, and taxes, the rate for a double or twin-bedded room ranges from 345$ ($13.46) to 410$ ($15.99). In a single, the tariff is 225$ ($8.78) to 280$ ($10.92) nightly. Every room has a private bath with a tub-shower combination, plus a bidet.

In winter, everything is kept snug by central heating; in summer, a few rooms are air conditioned. The dining room is decorated in white and puce, with overhead indirect lighting. Smoked duck is one of the chef's specialties. Off the lounge is a little bar, where the bartender learns quickly to mix your favorite drink. The most important community area is the rear garden terrace, where summer furniture is set up and surrounded by vines and semi-tropical greenery.

Presidente Hotel, 13 Rua Alexandre Herculano (tel. 53-95-01), is a small-scaled establishment—near the Avenida da Liberdade on a busy street corner. It's recommended to families, as children under nine are granted a 50 percent reduction; babysitting can be arranged; there's a laundry on the premises, and a permanent medical service.

The general atmosphere, including the furnishings, is of good taste. Though the 58 bedrooms are small, they are nicely laid out, with chestnut built-in headboards, including radios, bed lights, and telephones. There are double-view windows, a small entry with two closets, bathrooms tiled in happy colors, snow-white walls and bedspreads, and even a valet stand. The high-season rate, with breakfast, for a double, is 395$ ($15.41); in a single, 280$ ($10.92). In the wood-paneled mezzanine lounge, only breakfast is served.

The public rooms, all the suites, and 15 of the bedrooms are air conditioned. The modestly sized reception lounges are on three levels, connected by wide marble steps.

Rex Hotel, 169 Rua Castilho (tel. 68-21-61), is another family favorite, a modern hotel only minutes from the Ritz, the Avenida da Liberdade, and the Park of Edward VII. Every one of the 77 bedrooms at the Rex is complete with a tiled private bath and is furnished in a homelike manner, with matching fabrics, sitting areas, TV, refrigerator bars, air conditioning, and (in some rooms) breakfast balconies. Incidentally, North Americans who like a belt-stretching breakfast can order one for 35$ ($1.37).

The bedrooms are priced according to placement and size. The tariff for a double is 370$ ($14.43); a single, 270$ ($10.53).

Guests seek out the cozy bar, Club 37, or the solarium terrace and breakfast room on the top floor where the view of Lisbon is memorable. There's a restaurant on the top floor with a panoramic view, where a meal will cost you from 120$ ($4.68) to 150$ ($5.85).

The **Hotel do Reno**, 195-197 Avenida Duque d'Avila (tel. 481-81), and the **Hotel Príncipe**, 201 Avenida Duque d'Avila (tel. 53-61-51), lie only about a 10-minute taxi ride from the heart of Lisbon. Although run as competitors by different owners, they are two almost identical small modern hotels, heretofore enjoying heavy patronage by Germans and Scandinavians. But they attract English and American visitors as well. Both of them provide good, substantial, and clean rooms with private baths (and, in most cases, private balconies). Each puts an emphasis on the bedrooms rather than the public lounges, though providing a small lobby and bar, along with separate dining rooms.

The first of the economy twins, the Do Reno, has been upgraded to three stars. It has a nice bar at the main entrance, and its sitting room has been enlarged. The bedrooms are tailored and contemporary, each provided with a small sitting area that includes a desk and an armchair. Singles cost 285$ ($11.12), with breakfast; doubles, 440$ ($17.16), including a continental breakfast. A true bargain is the full-board rate of 270$ ($10.53) per person daily. Typical Portuguese food is served in the dining room—decorated with vibrant carpet and chairs, resting under a blue ceiling.

The Príncipe (not to be confused with the first-class Príncipe Real recommended previously) is the second of these compact, quite commercial, but comfortable little hotels. A successful choice, it enjoys lounges and a very good dining room. For a room with breakfast, the rate for a single is 270$ ($10.53), that tariff increasing to 407$ ($15.87) for a double or twin-bedded room with breakfast. Spread among the hotel's eight floors are enough beds to accommodate 100 travelers, who use two elevators for their ascent. At both establishments, children up to eight years are granted a 50 percent reduction.

4. Full-Board Bargains

York House, 32 Rua das Janelas Verdes (tel. 66-25-44), provides the drama of the past with the conveniences of the 20th century. York House was once a 16th-century convent, and is outside the center of traffic-filled Lisbon, attracting those who want peace and tranquility. Long known to the English and embassy personnel, it is almost opposite the National Art Gallery, sitting high on a hillside street overlooking the Tagus.

There's no sign. You go past an old iron gate, ascend a flight of stone steps past trailing ivy and rugged walls. You enter York House itself through a garden cloister, where guests congregate under gnarled trees. Owned and run by a Frenchwoman, Madame Andrée Goldstein, York House is knowingly furnished with flair. Each bedroom is tastefully finished with antique beds, soft mattresses, and a liberal use of 18th- and 19th-century pieces. Almost all of the bedrooms contain private baths.

All year round the charge is 770$ ($30.03) per day for two persons, including all your meals. Single rooms with bath and full board go for 400$ ($15.60) daily. Preference is given to those requesting full board.

Everything is homelike. In the public rooms antiques are used: inlaid chests, coats of armor, carved ecclesiastical paintings and figures, ornate ceramics, gilt and bronze chandeliers. The former monks' dining hall has deep-set windows, large niches for antiques — and, best of all, a combined French and Portuguese cuisine. Guests gather in the two-level lounge for before or after-dinner drinks under a beamed ceiling, in a setting of ecclesiastical sculpture, 17th-century paintings, decorative torchiers, and church candlesticks made into table lamps.

Madame has recently acquired additional space, a former town house at #47, down the street, adjacent to the museum. Here you can book larger, more luxurious rooms, with abundant closet space and tiled private bathrooms. Only breakfast is served here, though main meals are provided back at the convent. Singles are 329$ ($12.83), with breakfast; doubles, 456$ ($17.78).

Estalagem do Cavalo Branco (The White Horse Inn), 146 Avenida do Almirante Gago Coutinho (tel. 72-61-21). To stay here requires a sense of adventure, humor, and a love of the fantastic. This former villa on a dignified residential boulevard leading to the airport has been taken over by Frederico de Eca Leal, a collector of Iberian antiques, a gourmet, and an interior decorator. He offers not only inexpensive rooms, but excellent meals in an unusual setting.

The bedrooms are individually decorated in a theatrical way, using bright colors and occasional antiques. A group of rooms on the lower level is for use in an emergency only, but generally the better rooms—up and down short flights of steps are quite comfortable and never boring. A personal favorite is the amusing attic room, with red walls and black furniture. For full pension, two persons in a room with bath pay 680$ ($26.53) daily, the tariff dropping to 520$ ($20.28) in a room without bath. Taxes and service are included.

Dining at the inn is festive in one of its series of midget rooms, crowded with antiques. One dining room has oak furniture against a background of opera red walls and gilded cherubs. If you're dropping in just for dinner, the cost of a table d'hôte, including both fish and meat dishes, is 110$ ($4.29). Every surface downstairs seemingly is covered with bric-a-brac, gilded torchiers, painted wooden chests, and window swags. On the stairway rests a clock collection, and in the open-beamed bar is a fireplace and an assemblage of more than 100 decorative oddments.

Residência América, 47 Rua Tomás Ribeiro (tel. 55-79-74), was dubbed a luxury pensao by the government a quarter century ago when it opened in the upper part of an eight-story corner building. The Picoas Metro stop is in front of the entrance. In an atmosphere of 1950s modern, but one, nevertheless, of comfort and utility, many a tourist has saved a pocketful of escudos.

All the compact centrally heated bedrooms with built-in furnishings contain private baths. In high season, preference is given those requesting full or half board. In a double, the full-pension rate for two ranges between 670$ ($26.13) and 731$ ($28.51) daily. Taking all their meals here, singles are charged from 350$ ($13.65) to 423$ ($16.50). Taxes are included.

The meals—good and hearty—are provided in the air-conditioned, top-floor dining room into which the sun pours through a wall of glass. All in all, the América sits in a handy location, just minutes from the Praça Marquês de Pombal, and is tended by a friendly helpful staff.

5. The Budget Range

Residência Pax, 20 Rua José Estêvao (tel. 56-18-61). With a facade of shiny marble at the entrance, it rises five stories high with tiers of bedroom balconies. Overlooking a shady street, it lies about five minutes from the Avenida da Liberdade, reached from the nearby Anjos Metro stop.

Owner Jacqueline Frey, a Swiss woman, learned about hotel life in her hometown, Basel. She has insisted that each of her 30 rooms possess a good contemporary style and comfort. Her rooms are done in a restful modern, with grained woods, simple fabrics, and warm colors. Most of the rooms open onto private balconies, and all contain private baths. Singles (available only from November 1 until May 1) rent for 225$ ($8.78), and doubles go for 380$ ($14.82) year round, these tariffs including both tax and breakfast.

The reception area is nicely decorated, and on another floor is an airy lounge where you can entertain or have breakfast.

Capitol Hotel, 24 Rua Eça de Queirós (tel. 53-68-11), is a fine little bargain, just minutes from the top of the Avenida da Liberdade and the Praça Marquês de Pombal. It nestles on a quiet street, away from busy boulevards, and opens onto a wedge-shaped park with weeping willows and oaks.

Attracting budgeteers, the Capitol places the emphasis on good, roomy chambers with private baths, all of which are furnished in a restrained, utilitarian fashion. The more expensive rooms open onto private balconies. Singles pay 305$ ($11.90) nightly; doubles, 460$ ($17.94), including breakfast and taxes. If you stay a minimum of three days, you're entitled to lower en pension rates.

Hotel Excelsior, 172 Rua Rodrigues Sampaio (tel. 53-71-51), enjoys a setting one block from Marquês de Pombal Square, at the entrance to Edward VII Park. Right off the upper regions of Lisbon's major boulevard, it is newly built, with 90 good-sized bedrooms, each with its own private bath.

Most of the rooms contain a small sitting area, with a combination desk and dressing table. For a single, the maximum rate is 250$ ($9.75), increasing to 340$ ($13.26) for the most expensive double. Breakfast and taxes are included in the tariffs. In a room with shower, but no tub, the tariffs are considerably reduced. In addition to the air-conditioned, wood-paneled bar, with bamboo planters for semi-tropical foliage, there's a spacious dining room, which has large view windows, and serves all three meals.

Residência Imperador, 55 Avenida 5 de Outubro (tel. 515-57), not far from the center, provides rooms with private baths for 175$ ($6.83) to 230$ ($8.97) in a single; 250$ ($9.75) in a double. The front entranceway, designed in Portuguese marble, is barely large enough to set down one's suitcase. However, the bedrooms and upper lounge are adequate in size. Opening onto balconies, the front bedrooms face a tiny private garden. The rooms themselves are contemporary in concept, neatly planned with built-in beds and simple lines. Muted colors are used on the walls and in the fabrics.

The residência has only one owner, A.T. Carvalho, who provides personalized service. On the top floor is an airy public room and terrace, with a glass front and cork floors, where breakfast is served. Trams 1 or 21 and the Metro (Saldanha station) can whisk you into the city.

Borges Hotel, 108 Rua Garrett (tel. 36-19-51), has undergone a face-lifting, but its tariffs are still old-fashioned. The beehive reception area is as crowded as the 19th-century coffee house next door, A Brasileira, the traditional gathering spot for the Portuguese literati. On the second floor of the Borges, the dining room partially escaped the contemporary treatment, its paneled walls and crystal chandeliers intact.

The 85 bedrooms and 12 suites have been refurnished in a semi-contemporary manner, with traditional draperies and counterpanes. All of the rooms have private baths or showers, the doubles ranging from 285$ ($12.12) to 410$ ($15.99), the singles going for anywhere from 200$ ($7.80) to 280$ ($10.92). Breakfast, taxes, and service are included. The location is persuasive, in the Chiado district, minutes from some of Lisbon's best-known restaurants and fado clubs, as well as the shops of Baixa.

Hotel da Torre, 8 Rua dos Jerónimos (tel. 63-62-62), is in a suburb of Lisbon, Belém, near an estuary of the Tagus. As such, it is suitable primarily for those who want to be in the belt of Lisbon's "museumland." The modest inn rises three stories, and is furnished in a regional style. Doubles with breakfast peak at 410$ ($15.99), though singles are charged 260$ ($10.14). The air conditioning is confined to the public rooms and the wood-paneled bar with its black plastic lounge chairs. Regional food is served in the provincial restaurant.

Residencia Caravela, 38 Rua Ferreira Lapa (tel. 53-90-11), is a 48-room, three-star hostelry near the American Embassy. Although modest in appointments, each of its accommodations comes complete with private bath or shower, central heating, and telephone. Singles are charged 190$ ($7.41), the tariff increasing to 240$ ($9.36) in a double. Breakfast is extra. The bedrooms are small. In fact, the entire hotel is compact and intimate. Reproductions of French furniture in the hallways add a touch of style.

READERS' HOTEL SELECTIONS: "**Pensao Brasilia**, 29 Rua Alexandre Herculano (tel. 59-213), is a find, although I may not have been the first to discover it. Four of us occupied two doubles, one with a full private bath, one with a wash basin and bidet, for a total cost of 260$ ($10.14), service included" (Mrs. Cecilia F. Brenner, Lakewood, N.J.). . . . "I stayed at the **Don Sancho I**, 202-3 Avenida da Liberdade (tel. 486-48) for $5.50 (U.S.) a night, with breakfast and bath included. The medium-sized rooms were very clean. The location's about three blocks from the American Embassy and near airline offices" (Albert B. Trim, New York, N.Y.).

Having secured suitable lodgings in the Portuguese capital, we move to a survey of its restaurants in all price brackets.

Chapter V

THE RESTAURANTS OF LISBON

1. The Deluxe Trio
2. The Medium-Priced Range
3. Less Expensive Restaurants
4. The Budget Range
5. Seafood on the Left Bank
6. The Foreign Colony
7. The Special Spots
8. Hard-Core Budget

LISBON OFFERS A WIDE RANGE of dining places, headed by such famous restaurants as Aviz and Tavares. The cuisine in these establishments is of a very high standard, ranking justifiably with leading places in other European capitals. Here, you'll encounter the best of Portuguese dishes, intermixed with the classics from Italy and France. In such establishments, a knowledgeable maître d'hôtel and a wine steward are at your elbow to guide you toward wise culinary decisions.

But you needn't pay high prices for top-quality food in Lisbon and its environs. There are many noteworthy regional restaurants, offering Portuguese cooking, even foreign viands, at various price levels—ranging from a simple beer and steak tavern, to a formal town-house-style dining chamber, to a modern cliffside restaurant with a panoramic view.

Aside from the recommendations contained within this chapter, you may also want to consider having your evening meal at one of the fado cafes (see our suggestions in Chapter VIII).

Portuguese friends often confide that it takes two hours for their countrymen to dine—"One hour to talk, another to eat."

1. The Deluxe Trio

Restaurante Aviz, 12-B Rua Serpa Pinto (tel. 32-83-91), is Portugal's poshest restaurant, a visual reminder of the city's glorious past. Known for its topnotch gourmet cuisine to prime ministers, exiled kings, and Mr. and Mrs. John Doe of Kansas City, the Aviz is a dearly loved treasure. What is now the Aviz was saved from the demolition of the famed hotel of the same name, once—in the pre-Ritz days—the only deluxe hotel in Lisbon. Salvaged from the ruins was the nucleus of the hotel staff, including the maître d'hôtel Anibal Espirito Santo Silva, and the chef Joao da Cruz Ribeiro. The bartender Tony Fadda is also part owner.

You ascend a staircase into celestial elegance. While drinks are served in the foyer lounge, menu selections are made. The ambience is that of a private club with mahogany paneling, tufted black leather chairs, green marble columns, and crystal. The hotel staff brought not only parts of the torn down establishment with them—including all the elaborate silver, a meat trolley, and the wall torchiers—but the secrets of the kitchen as well.

Aviz turns out many specialties, so making decisions is difficult. For an unusual beginning, try espadon fumé (smoked swordfish), for 96$50 ($3.76). This is served with quartered lemons wrapped in tulle tutus. An alternate choice might be a creamy vichyssoise at 35$ ($1.37). For a main course, the following dishes are recommended as exciting treats: entrecôte au poivre (pepper steak), 100$ ($3.90); fettucine (ribbon-thin egg noodles) alla Bolognese, 75$ ($2.93); and suprême de volaille Bolognaise (an elegant chicken suprême), 95$ ($3.71). For dessert, fine offerings include a small orange soufflé for 45$ ($1.76) and bananas flambé with kirsch for the same price. To the charge quoted will be added the local tax and service charge, plus a 25$ (98¢) cover.

Your table must be reserved in one of the trio of intimate dining rooms, preferably the larger green and gold chamber, with its ornate bronze and frosted glass, globed chandelier, and circular display of specialty foods (foie gras de Strasbourg, chilled cooked pears, cheese, and decorative flowers). The Aviz (closed Sundays) offers two evening settings, at 8 and 10. The last orders are taken at 2 p.m. for lunch, 10:30 p.m. for dinner. Your bill will be presented in an enclosed gold embossed leather folder on a silver tray.

Clement Freud went looking for the "best restaurant in Europe"—and when he arrived at the Aviz discovered he'd found it.

Restaurante Tavares, 37 Rua da Misericórdia (tel. 32-11-12), is a gilt and crystal world under a glass bell. This slice of the past offers a palace-style setting and a superb cuisine. White and gold paneled walls, three chandeliers, freshly arranged table roses, Louis XV armchairs—all keep intact the spirit of the 19th century.

Actually, Tavares was originally a cafe—dating from 1784 when a man known as O Talao founded it. When the two Tavares brothers died in the 19th century, half a dozen waiters formed a partnership and took over the restaurant. It is still owned by a combine of waiters, who continue its high standards. It is the oldest restaurant in Lisbon, attracting many diplomatic and government heads, as well as the literati.

Drinks are served in the petite front salon, where you can plan your meal. Fernando Lopes, the wine steward, aids you in your selection (he tries to provide a pleasant wine and does not push the most expensive bottles). Perhaps Carvalho Ribeiro Ferreirniepoort, one of the owners, will take your order.

A beginning might be crêpes de marisco, at 85$ ($3.32), or a vichyssoise, costing 30$ ($1.17). A main course selection might be the sole in champagne, 110$ ($4.29), a real delicacy, or tournedos Grand Duc, 110$ also. Many continental dishes are scattered throughout the menu, including the classic scallops of veal Viennoise, 85$ ($3.32). However, the restaurant nearly always serves sardines and salted codfish—so secure is it in its reputation.

For a wine, perhaps you'll try Colares Reserva Tavares 1960, costing 80$ ($3.12) and hailing from the wine caves of Tavares. To complete your meal, why not try the chef's dessert specialty, a high-rise soufflé for 55$ ($2.15), followed by a café filtro?

The Ritz Grill Room, 88 Rua Rodrigo da Fonseca (tel. 68-41-31), is in the Ritz Hotel, overlooking the terrace and the Park of Edward VII, but thankfully set apart from the main hotel lobby.

Before you make your selection, scan the daily specialties. The onion soup goes for 65$ ($2.54), and the melon of the season, with a slice of pungent Chaves ham, for 80$ ($3.12). True to its name, the room features grills, two of the favorites being the mixed grill Ritz with potatoes, 120$ ($4.68), and côte de beef for two persons, 280$ ($10.92). Among the fish entrees are grilled turbot at 120$ ($4.68) or a mixed fish fry at 130$ ($5.07). A pastry trolley will be brought to your table, with a choice of cake costing 40$ ($1.56) per portion. For a finish, try filtered coffee at 20$ (78¢). Service and taxes are included in the prices, but a cover charge of 30$ ($1.17) is added.

The Ritz Grill can become a habit hard to break, even on short stays in Lisbon. It opens at 7:30 p.m.

2. The Medium-Priced Range

Varanda do Chanceler, 7-A Largo do Chanceler (tel. 86-62-86), lies in the oldest part of the city and is associated with a building dating from 1625. However, its interior is modern—an entire wall of glass, allowing nearly every diner a view of the Tagus and its ships. With white walls, it seems more like a sun-filled patio, with red tablecloths and white wall torchiers.

A good choice when en route to the top of the Alfama, the air-conditioned restaurant because of its view makes a good luncheon choice. On every table you'll find a bouquet of roses, plus an appetizer of pâté and caviar.

There are nearly 20 starters from which to choose, ranging from sopa de mariscos (shellfish soup) for 30$ ($1.17), to a shrimp cocktail at 70$ ($2.73). A house specialty is lagosta gratinée (lobster of the house), 200$ ($7.80). Less expensive offerings include baked fish, 70$ ($2.73). Perhaps the most popular dish is partridge, at 80$ ($3.12), or duck in orange sauce, 75$ ($2.93). For 180$ ($7.02), two persons can order a châteaubriand flambé. To dine the Portuguese way, you can ask for a slice of serpa cheese at 30$ ($1.17), then finish with a dessert such as Chanceleres for the same price. There is also a daily special costing 150$ ($5.85), which, on the days we were last there, consisted of a sopa leonesa, filetes de crème, almond tart, wine, and coffee.

Gambrinus, 25 Rua das Portas de Santo Antao (tel. 32-14-66). Its stature among Lisbon's leading restaurants is justified. Intimate dining rooms are clustered around an open blue-tiled kitchen, where expert chefs in starched white hats prepare delicious meals, using large copper pots and a charcoal grill. The location is a breeze for those who want to dine in the heart of the city, off The Rossio, near the railway station, and on a little square in back of the National Theatre.

You can have your meal while sitting on leather chairs in the rear under a cathedral-beamed ceiling, or else select a little table beside a fireplace upon the raised end of the room. All is dominated by a skillfully made, impressionistic tapestry along one wall. There is also an alcove with a stained glass enclosure—all primitively modern. The walls of the back room are sedate with paneling, not unlike a sophisticated country lodge. For before dinner drinks, a front bar beckons.

Although there is a diversified à la carte menu, don't fail to check the especialidades do dia. The soups are good—everything from Andalusian gazpacho at 40$ ($1.56) to sopa de cebolo (onion soup) for the same price. Fish dishes range from conha com mariscos à thermidor (conch with shellfish) for 88$ ($3.43) to robalo (bass) à minhote at 116$ ($4.52). A Germanic meat dish, salsichas de Frankforte com choucroute (frankfurters with sauerkraut), costs 66$ ($2.57), and the specialty is rumpsteak Gambrinus, 124$ ($4.84). The restaurant offers elaborate desserts, such as a soufflé de baunilha (vanilla) at 50$ ($1.95), and crêpes suzette at 98$ ($3.82). Coffee with a 30-year-old brandy complements the meal perfectly.

Bodegon, Hotel Fénix, 8 Praça Marquès de Pombal (tel. 53-51-21), is a first-rate grill room attached to a hotel. You dine in a tavern setting, with beamed ceiling, tiled floors, wood-paneled pillars, warm Iberian colors of yellows and browns. Spanish engravings have been placed around the walls, and adjoining is a separate drinking bar.

For lunch or dinner, an 80$ ($3.12) set meal is featured, although some of the most popular house specialties include quail, partridge, and fresh salmon from the north of Portugal. The chef is known for smoking—try his smoked eel, smoked duck, or smoked swordfish. All year round you can order cultivated oysters, though they are at their best after October.

Among the à la carte selections are salmao grelhado (grilled salmon), 90$ ($3.51); lasagne Bolognese, 30$ ($1.17); sopa de cebola (onion soup), 20$ (78¢); calamares (squid), 50$ ($1.95); and paella à la Valenciana, 90$ ($3.51). For dessert, try crêpes suzette for two, 80$ ($3.12).

Comodoro, 20-23 Praça D. Joao de Câmara (tel. 358-14), resembles a businesspeople's club at lunch, a supper club in the evening. Between 11 p.m. and 3:30 a.m., upstairs, it changes character completely and is enlivened by music for dancing. By then, its conservative mien has disappeared entirely. The dining room is decorated with wood paneling, old prints of clipper ships, an enlarged photostat of the seaport of Lisbon's past, ships' lanterns, and a display of silver football trophies won by the waiters and kitchen staff.

The cuisine of the house is highly respected, as is the attentive service. A starter might be crème de mariscos (shellfish soup) for 18$ (70¢), or you might prefer a choice of about 21 hors d'oeuvres, priced according to what you select. Main dishes include the chef's specialty, lobster thermidor, but the price tag on that entry is 190$ ($7.41) at the least, usually more. Less expensive fare includes ameijoas (clams) en cataplana, 70$ ($2.73); filetes linguados (sole) suchet, 85$ ($3.32); and paella, 90$ ($3.51). Our special favorite is bife de lombo Comodoro, beef in a brown wine sauce with frankfurters, ham, french fried potatoes, spinach, and green beans, going for 90$ ($3.51). There is also a daily special for 75$ ($2.93) that includes a soup, a meat or fish dish, dessert, bread, and wine.

Pabe, 27A Rua Duque de Palmela (tel. 53-56-75), is the Portuguese name for pub, and that's what this cozy English-style place is. Convenient to the Praça do Pombal, the pub has done its best to emulate English establishments. There's a soft red carpet on the floor, mugs hanging over the long bar, a beamed ceiling, coats of arms and engravings of hunting scenes around the walls. Two saloon-type doors lead into a wood-paneled dining room, where you can sup on meat specially imported from the U.S. A châteaubriand for two has a 250$ ($9.75) tab. If you prefer local fare, start off with a shrimp cocktail for 75$ ($2.93), then Portuguese veal liver for 85$ ($3.32), or a supremo de galinha, which is white chicken with mushrooms, 80$ ($3.12). Finish with sherbet for 30$ ($1.17). The Pabe is closed on Sundays, and the crowd tends to be upper-class Portuguese and resident Yanks and Britons.

Sancho, 8A Travessa da Gloria (tel. 36-97-80), is a cozy rustic-style place just off the Avenida da Liberdade, close to the Praça da Restauradores. After passing a pleasant bar, you enter a dining room with red plush draperies over the windows, a beamed ceiling, a fireplace, and leather and wood chairs. A second adjoining room is equally pleasant. The walls are stuccoed, flowers are placed all around, and paintings hang on the walls. In summer the Sancho is air conditioned. A fish gratinée soup costs 20$ (78¢); a cream of shellfish, 18$ (70¢); robalo (bass) al forno, 62$ ($2.42); slices of turbot, 60$ ($2.34); veal scallopine, 75$ ($2.93); fried chicken, 50$ ($1.95); bife na frigideira, 66$ ($2.57); house tart, 22$ (86¢); crêpes suzette, 55$ ($2.15); a mousse, 14$ (55¢). Also good are the paella at 60$ ($2.34) and the swordfish, 56$ ($2.18).

Telheiro, 10A Rua Latino Coelho (tel. 53-40-07), means "The Roof" in Portuguese, and it's a bistro-like place not far from the Sheraton Hotel. The ceilings are beamed, and you sit on wooden chairs with heart shapes carved out of their backs. The friendly waiters are clad in scarlet waistcoats. Peppers hang from the chandeliers. Pâté, butter, and rolls are placed on your table before you even order. Specialties are the gazpacho, 15$ (59¢); mussels, 55$ ($2.15); turkey, also 55$; leitao (suckling pig), 70$ ($2.73); and the fried fresh tuna fish, 55$ ($2.15). For dessert, try the rum omelette, 40$ ($1.56), or a honey ball, 15$ (59¢).

Escorial, 47 Rua Portas de S. Antao (tel. 36-37-58). You can dine here with Spanish flair. Although right in the heart of Lisbon's restaurant district, this Spanish-owned establishment combines classic Spanish dishes with an inviting ambience. The dining room walls are paneled in rosewood, with frosted globe lighting. Around the scarlet-clothed tables, modern armchairs have been placed, stemmed glasses lined up, and napkins rolled like a Roman scroll.

The menu is in English (always look for the course of the day). An order of onion soup with cheese goes for 48$ ($1.87); a bisque of shellfish for 38$ ($1.48). Excellently prepared fish dishes include baked whiting with clams or a mixed fry, both 98$ ($3.82). A meat specialty is marinated pork cutlets served in a clay dish, and the chef does a good stroganoff, both again 98$ ($3.82). Desserts include a choice of tarts at 36$ ($1.40).

One touch indicates why Escorial is a fine dining room. Your brandy glass is flamed to just the right temperature before a drop of liqueur is poured. Senhor José Costa has assembled an admirable staff. Such things pay off, as Escorial attracts an interesting crowd from Lisbon, Estoril, and Cascais.

3. Less Expensive Restaurants

António Restaurante, 63 Rua Tomás Ribeiro (tel. 53-87-80), was created especially for Portuguese businesspeople who want a relaxing ambience and good food. A corner establishment, just a bit away from the din of central traffic, it is a refreshing oasis with blue and white glazed earthenware tiles. In fact, the color scheme of blue and white prevails, with a blue free-form ceiling, blue linen tops over white cloths, even crisp blue jackets on the waiters. Pewter service plates and fresh flowers set the taste level.

The menu's in English. You can start with a cream of tomato soup or shellfish soup for 12$50 (49¢). Orders of fish, garnished with vegetables, include filets with tomato sauce, 55$ ($2.15), or baked sole, 78$ ($3.04). Among the meat dishes, try an order of breaded chicken with spaghetti, 55$ ($2.15), or pork with clams, in the Alentejana style, 70$ ($2.73). Chicken de churrasco (barbecued) is another favorite at 55$ ($2.15). The dessert list is extensive, with even a banana split, 25$ (98¢).

The owner/manager of the restaurant, Antonio Oliveira, came to Lisbon in search of work from Viseu (in the north of Portugal), when he was 17 years old. He especially recommends his acorda de marisco, a stewlike, breaded dish of shellfish and eggs, which is a treat at 72$ ($2.81).

Restaurante Leao d'Ouro, 105 Rua I de Dezembro (tel. 36-94-95), stands beside the Estaçao do Rosso, the railway station best described as Victorian Gothic. The atmosphere of a large, old tavern prevails—high brick arches, a beamed ceiling, and a pictorial tile, depicting Portugal's liberation from Spain in 1640.

Food prices are keyed to the sparse Portuguese purse. You can start your meal with a rich-tasting soup, such as crême de camarao (cream of shrimp) for 12$ (47¢), or sopa Alentejana (made with bread and garlic, among other ingredients) for 11$ (43¢). Among the meat dishes, try pork chops prepared in the Alentejana way, 52$ ($2.03), or filet mignon, 75$ ($2.93).

A fowl specialty, if featured, is frango de churrasco, barbecued chicken. If one person orders it, the price is 50$ ($1.95). For dessert, try the pêssegos (peaches), the skin like the wall of a reservoir holding in all those juices. The price? Only 12$ (47¢).

Bonjardim, 10 Traverssa de Santo Antao (tel. 32-43-89), quite rightly deserves the enthusiastic approval of a Boston traveler: "I was given the names of eight inexpensive restaurants, including Bonjardim, to try out in Lisbon during my five-day stay. I ended up trying only two of them, as I took the rest of my meals at Bonjardim, sampling a different dish for lunch and dinner every day."

Manuel Castanheira, who owns and manages the restaurant, along with his handsome son, caters mostly to families, providing wholesome meals that fit most budgets (no main dish costs more than 60$ ($2.34). So successful has been their operation that they've taken over a building across the street, where the same menu is offered.

In the main restaurant, the second-floor air-conditioned dining room is in the rustic Portuguese style, with a beamed ceiling and a tile mural depicting farm creatures. The noonday sun pours in through seven windows. The street-floor dining room, with an adjoining bar for pre-meal drinks, has walls of decorative tiles accented by bunches of garlic and peppers along with a wooden oxen yoke.

During your dinner the aroma of fat chickens roasting to a golden brown on the charcoal spit can only persuade you to try a hen yourself. An order of this house specialty, frango no espeto, costs 55$ ($2.15), with a side dish of french fries going for 10$ (39¢). The cook also knows how to bake hake in the Portuguese style, for 55$ ($2.15). An alternate dish is pork, fried with clams, also 55$. For dessert, you can order a cassata at 12$ (47¢). The Bonjardim is open seven days a week from noon to 2 a.m.

Restaurante Agricola da Quinta da S. Vicente, 144 Telheiras de Cima (tel. 79-02-11), is an overgrown, once-isolated farm on the edge of the Lumiar district of Lisbon, away from the river. It's snowballed into a Portuguese family tradition to congregate here, and the weekends find many an informal wedding party gaily celebrating with continuous toasts with steins of beer or wine.

There's a huge dining room with a mosaic-decorated bar at one side, a walk-through garden, and a copper-hooded fireplace. Prices are inexpensive. Typical and delicious is the frango na pucara, chicken in an earthenware pot, and the frango (chicken) à S. Vicente is the specialty of the house. Both are 60$ ($2.34) per person. Among the game selections, coelho (rabbit) à cacadora stands out at 55$ ($2.15). Many diners begin their meal with a selection of mariscos (shellfish)— especially the ameijoas à espanhola (Spanish-style clams) at 55$ ($2.15). For dessert, why not try one of the native Portuguese cheeses, such as queijo serra, for 20$ (78¢)? A fresh fruit salad goes for only 15$ (59¢).

The restaurant is run by the sons of Francisco Rodrigues de Alemaida, who bring in an orchestra for dancing on Saturday and Sunday evenings from 9 p.m. to 1 a.m. Closed Tuesdays. Ask for the wine of the house, as the sons make their own. The Quinta is best reached by taxi or private car. You head up what at first appears to be a narrow village street, passing tree-shaded picnickers along the way.

Well-meaning Lisbon friends advise that "Americans won't like this place—it's too Portuguese." We think they're wrong!

Taverna do Infante, 124 Rua de Belém (tel. 63-13-76), stands in the suburb of Belém, whence the Portuguese launched their voyages of discovery. The tavern makes a good choice for a luncheon stopover if you're visiting the museums in the district. But dinner is even more attractive, if you don't mind driving out from the city. You dine at a candlelit table on the second floor under a beamed ceiling. The waitress brings out a large portion of a regional soup for 10$ (39¢). You can then proceed to beef Taverna, the chef's specialty, at 63$ ($2.46). If you prefer fish, the trout is reliable at 50$ ($1.95). We've also enjoyed the shishkebab, also 63$. Desserts average around 17$ (66¢). There are only 10 tables, and service tends to be slow.

O Funil (The Funnel), 82-A Avenida Elias Garcia (tel. 76-60-07). You have to be Portuguese to know about this place. It specializes in "cozinha Portuguesa," and does the cooking so well and so inexpensively that a line forms at the door, and it's hard to get a table. You enter into a street-floor tavern with crowded tables. But chances are you'll be directed to the lower level, where you can wait at the tiny bar while a table is made ready. The Funnel is owned by three men who offer their "vinho da casa" in three different sizes of pitcher. If you'd prefer a bottle, then we'd recommend the red Valpacos at 26$ ($1.01). Featured dishes include clams (ameijoas) at 78$ ($3.04) and roast pork at 65$ ($2.54). Also recommendable is the swordfish at 55$ ($2.15). The almond tart at 17$ (66¢) is a tasty dessert.

Toni dos Bifes, 50-E Avenida Praia da Victoria (tel. 73-60-80), is an old Lisbon standby where hungry Portuguese and foreigners have been going for years to get a good, inexpensive, and copious meal. Near the Monumental cinema, the restaurant has a plain but pleasant decor, with a counter on one side of the dining room and small tables on the other. Some tables and chairs are placed outdoors as well, in French-cafe style, with a glass enclosure. You begin with small portions of pâté and butter and toast, bread and roll, and then you can launch into the homemade tomato soup, 10$50 (41¢), or maybe a seafood omelette for 48$ ($1.87), followed by an entrecôte steak, 58$ ($2.26). Other specialties include the bacalhau (cod), 58$ ($2.26); pork Alenteijo style, 60$ ($2.34); bife de atum grelhado (grilled tuna fish), 55$ ($2.15); and breaded veal, 66$ ($2.57). Finish with a melon with ham, 30$ ($1.17), or a peach melba, 27$50 ($1). Bananas and cream cost 11$ (43¢), pineapple au kirsch, 27$50 ($1), and a rum apple, 21$ (82¢).

If Toni's is too crowded, try the next door **Picoas,** 10 Rua das Picoas, a friendly modern place with a similar counter and tables arrangement. Entrées run 45$ ($1.76) and 55$ ($2.15) for fish dishes and 45$ (1.76) and 65$ ($2.54) for the meats.

4. The Budget Range

O Paquito, 52A Avenida Conde de Valbom (tel. 76-64-23), has become a popular spot for in-the-know Lisboans, who either congregate at the bar in the front of the restaurant or sit at candlelit tables in the dining room. The decor is modern plastic, but discreetly so. There is soft piped-in music and pink carnations on the tables. You can start with a special salad for 23$ (90¢), or marisco soup, 17$ (66¢). This may be followed by cherne na parrilha (grilled turbot), 50$ ($1.95); an entrecôte steak, 95$ ($3.71); or a tournedos, 63$ ($2.46).

Pavilhao Bucelas, Parque Mayer (tel. 338-05), is tops for local color. It's tucked away in the Parque Mayer entertainment world, walled off from the Avenida da Liberdade, with its five variety show theaters, games of chance, rifle ranges, and kewpie doll prizes. This típico restaurant is owned by Xico Carreira, a bon vivant who was once a cowboy in the suburbs of Lisbon where bulls were raised for fighting. Nowadays, he owns his own bull-breeding ranch.

At his regional restaurant, bullfighters and aficionados attend, seeking typical Portuguese fare, well prepared and served in generous portions. Along one wall is an assemblage of bullfight memorabilia, such as posters and photographs of matadors. The restaurant's non-touristy, with its long bare tables, crude squat stools, bottles of wine, and brown ceramic platters.

The waitress will place a wicker basket containing crusty homemade bread of stone-ground flour on your table. A soup here costs 5$ (20¢). Meat dishes, such as pork chops, go for 70$ ($2.73) to 90$ ($3.51); an excellent filet of sole is 50$ ($1.95); and swordfish costs 50$ also. Less expensive is an omelette for 25$ (98¢). Flan (caramel pudding) is 17$ (66¢). The Bucelas also place a few tables outside for those interested in al fresco dining!

At the Pavilhao Bucelas, you can obtain the rare agua-pé, a combination of wine and water fermented together. It's delicious and can intoxicate quickly.

Dona Maria, 7 Largo do Regedor (tel. 349-82), is a rapid step away from the Teatro Nacional Dona Maria II at The Rossio. Go here for completely unpretentious Portuguese cuisine. The restaurant itself—popular with bullfight aficionados—is on the second floor of the building flanked by the fire department on one side, one of Lisbon's top restaurants, the Gambrinus (mentioned earlier) on the other. Inside, the dining room is informal, with a Spanish-style decor. A bas-relief of an Iberian village adorns the wall under a ceiling frieze of primitively painted flowers. The manager, Benigno Casal Amoedo, is proud of his good food.

Considering the quality of the cooking, the low prices many astonish you. For only 12$ (47¢), you can order a healthy-sized bowl of black bean soup, really a Brazilian specialty. The fish courses are a meal unto themselves: a specialty is bacalhau à Braz, dried codfish fried with potatoes, eggs, and onions, for 49$ ($1.91).

Meat courses start at 49$ ($1.91), the price for pork chops. Favorite main dishes include ribs of beef in the style of the province of Tras-os-Montes, also 49$. Desserts are numerous, with a rice pudding costing only 9$ (35¢). A typical Portuguese dessert is orange pudding, 12$ (47¢). Dona Maria will offer a second person a reduction if two order the same dish. Closed Sundays.

Novo Dia, 4D Rua Dom Antao de Almada, off the Largo de Sao Domingos, is most centrally located in the economy restaurant belt of Lisbon. It's owned by Alberto Sena da Silva, a doctor of economics, who offers Portuguese dishes at low prices in an atmosphere evoking Lisbon's past as a seaport. Behind its ornate tiled facade is a compact air-conditioned dining room with four groups of stone arches, blue and white decorative azulejos walls, and wrought-iron chandeliers casting soft lights over the starched linen tablecloths.

First courses include such soups as crème de mariscos (cream of shellfish) or caldo verde (cabbage and potato), a big bowl of either one going for 5$50 (22¢). The best buys are the servings for two, listed under the pratos do dia (plates of the day): ameijoas à espanhola (Spanish-style clams in a savory sauce), 60$ ($2.34); linguado grelhado (grilled sole), 60$ ($2.34); carne de porco Alentejana (pork in the Alentejana style), 50$ ($1.95). Desserts such as flan (caramel custard) cost 6$ (23¢), a chocolate mousse, 8$ (31¢).

For further local color, visit the fruit market and grocery directly across the street. Note the displays of cheese, wine, coffee, and tea—all casting an aromatic spell.

Pessoa Restaurante, 14 Rua de Santa Justa, is a super-economical place for Portuguese cooking on a street of low-budget restaurants. Also owned by Alberto Sena da Silva, he seems to be a master of creating fine food for economical prices. Much to our good fortune, he likes to share his enthusiasm for regional cuisine with others.

The atmosphere of Pessoa is tavern-style on two floors, with thick arches, walls of black and white tiles, simple tables lit by crudely ornate wrought-iron lanterns, plus an open brick fireplace where steaks and fish are broiled.

If you dine in the air-conditioned upstairs, the food is sent up on a trusty old dumbwaiter. For only 6$ (23¢), you can get a good-sized bowl of soup, such as a crème à Carolino. For a second course, a house specialty is fried swordfish, 55$ ($2.15). Another is filetes de linguado (filets of sole meunière), 60$ ($2.34). The menu is extensive: on our most recent visit we counted about

75 main dishes offered. Desserts are simple, however, with flan (caramel custard) going for 5$ (20¢).

Bonjardim, run by the previously mentioned restaurant of the same name, now has a nearby self-service cafeteria at 41 Rua do Jardim do Regedor. Sample dishes: seafood soup, 9$ (35¢); roast chicken with trimmings, 36$ ($1.40); garoupa fish à Bretone, 35$ ($1.37); and mousse, 9$ (35¢). The decor is simple, plastic, and efficient. The location is near The Rossio.

Rio Grande, 55 Rua Nova do Carvalho, is a popular restaurant near Lisbon's red light district. The no-frills large cellarlike dining room is patronized by the locals, who order a "cold cuts omelette" for 29$ ($1.13); fresh sardines for 36$ ($1.40); and swordfish, 40$ ($1.56). There are lots of other fish specialties, such as Spanish clams for 50$ ($1.95), or for those splurging, shrimps from Mozambique.

5. Seafood on the Left Bank

Floresta do Ginjal, 7 Ginjal (tel. 27-00-87), overlooks the waterfront on the left bank of the Tagus in Cacilhas. You dine on some of the best cooked fish dinners in the area, while overlooking the river life and the hills of Lisbon. Floresta is reached by ferry boat, either a small one costing 2$ (8¢) from Black Horse Square or a larger one for 1$90 (7¢) from Cais do Sodré. You can buy tickets right on the boat—someone comes around to collect the money. You can try to park your car in Black Horse Square, the cost being 3$ (12¢) for four hours.

The approach to the two-leveled dining room is by way of a long staircase, the walls covered with varieties of decoratively placed sea shells. Owned by José Alves de Melo and his sons for more than 40 years, the restaurant draws a thriving family trade from right bank Lisboan families, especially on Sunday afternoons.

While there is a complete menu of meat and fowl dishes, the fish sets the pace. A shellfish soup goes for 10$ (39¢), but the fishermen's stew or caldeirada at 55$ ($2.15) is a meal in itself. Another main course might be fried eels at 60$ ($2.34) or turbot meunière at 50$ ($1.95), although fowl fanciers will be attracted to the spit-roasted chicken for 53$ ($2.07). A dessert favorite is manjar de principe, made of eggs and almonds, 12$ (47¢).

A few steps further down the quay in Gijan are two restaurants for those on a tighter budget. Both are simple family places, with no frills.

At the **O Grande Elias,** next to the Floresta Restaurant, you can have a complete meal for only 60$ ($2.34), including bread, wine, soup, a dish of eggs, fish, or meat, followed by cheese, fruit, or a dessert. Further down the street, you come to **Gonçalves,** featuring a good oceanside view from the upstairs part, with a tourist menu for 75$ ($2.93). Downstairs is a large dining room which seats eight at each table. À la carte entrées go for 45$ ($1.76) to 70$ ($2.73).

6. The Foreign Colony

Michel, 5 Largo de Santa Cruz do Castelo (tel. 86-43-38), is a good bistro-styled French restaurant, with plenty of atmosphere and a hard-to-beat location right on the corner of a pocket-sized plaza in the Alfama. The restaurant's a remake of three buildings: a barber shop, blacksmith's shop, and a wine tavern, all renovated and decorated in a tastefully rustic manner. Antique wood chests are used for coffee tables in the tavern portion, and a refectory table holding desserts stands in the walk-in fireplace. The skylight is canopy covered, and the walls contain everything from violins to zithers to stirrups and ceramics.

Star performer is the chef-owner, Michel, a youthful, energetic host with a keen eye for food preparation and service. Moroccan born, Michel was trained in cooking in Southern France. Now he has his own Julia Child-style cooking show on Lisbon television. At his restaurant he not only provides delicious food, but seductive background music from a balladeer. The menu includes such items as French onion soup at 35$ ($1.37)—crusty with freshly baked cheese on top. Specialties include carré d'agneau Persillé (milk-fed lamb cooked in the oven) at 210$ ($8.19) and fondue bourguignonne, 260$ ($10.14) for two persons. The dessert specialty is crêpes suzette, 165$ ($6.44) for two persons. Closed Sundays.

Portas do Sol, 86 Rua de S. Tomé (tel. 86-16-33), is the leading French bistro restaurant of Lisbon, above the Alfama on a belvedere plaza. It's almost next to the Fundaçao Ricardo do Espírito Santa Silva and the Museum of Decorative Art.

Two arched windows open onto a bar-lounge, where most guests gather for an apéritif. The dining room invites with its rough white plaster walls, hand-carved tables, and high-backed leather chairs. Even the cloths are handmade, a good background for deep blue floral dishes and ruby-red glasses. The kitchen is ruled over by a Frenchwoman, who, with the help of her family, turns out excellent dishes.

The main course might include a steak au poivre at 80$ ($3.12), or veal kidneys in a smooth, light-tasting cream sauce, 60$ ($2.34). To finish your meal, you may choose fresh banana flambé, 40$ ($1.56). After coffee, you can visit the boutique, then stroll over to the belvedere for a view.

Restaurante "A Gondola," 64 Avenida de Berna (tel. 77-04-26), is where you can order some of the most reasonably priced and authentic Italian dishes in Lisbon. It's in its own orbit, outside the central hub of the city. True to the Italian custom, it offers not only an inside dining room, but a patio for al fresco meals.

You start off with a choice of seven different items, such as thin slices of smoked Chaves ham placed over a sun-ripened melon, 60$ ($2.34), or liver pâté, 40$ ($1.56). For your second course there are at least eight entrées—including, for example, filets of sole meunière, 80$ ($3.12). Your meat course to follow might include any of the Italian dishes, such as ravioli, 60$ ($2.34), or cannelloni, also 60$. Topping off the meal are fruit and dessert, perhaps a homemade cake. You can have quite a banquet in a pleasant, restful setting. In July, August, and September, the restaurant closes at 4 p.m. on Saturdays.

Xangai (Shanghai), 20B Avenida Duque de Loulé (tel. 573-78), is an outstanding Chinese restaurant near the American Embassy. An authentic cuisine is served here on green and pink plates imported from Macao. The setting is an impersonal modern one, with Oriental touches provided by the black and scarlet tasseled lanterns, the blue carpet, and lacquered screens.

As in most Chinese restaurants, dishes are best shared. Outstanding among the soups are bird's nest at 29$ ($1.13). Among the main dishes are hot and sweet shrimps at 65$ ($2.54); chicken and almonds, 52$ ($2.03); pork with green peppers and bamboo shoots, 50$ ($1.95); duck and pineapple, 60$ ($2.34); and shrimps with soy sauce, 63$ ($2.46). Especially tasty is a beef dish in an oyster sauce for 45$ ($1.76).

Desserts feature an apple dipped in an egg batter and fried, then served with a sprinkling of sugar, 20$ (78¢). Be sure to order a pot of delicate jasmine tea, with blossoms floating on top.

Restaurante Macao, 37A Rua Barata Salgueiro (tel. 588-88), is centered in the swankier section of Lisbon, and is the oldest Chinese restaurant in the city. The dining room is highlighted by red pagoda pillars and bright tasseled lanterns that lend a certain authenticity. Fernando O, the bright multilingual son of the owner, was born in Macao. He now manages the restaurant.

The menu is big, each dish numbered and translated into English. Both Peking and Cantonese cuisine are featured. Soup specialties include shark's fin at 30$ ($1.17). Egg roll is 22$ (86¢). Dishes personally sampled and preferred include sweet and sour fish, 45$ ($1.76); lobster in a sauce (prices vary daily); a king-sized prawn with lobster sauce, 85$ ($3.32); boneless fried chicken and walnut chicken, both 60$ ($2.34); and Cantonese duck, 70$ ($2.73). Nearly 10 choices of dessert are offered, including a fried apple at 25$ (98¢) or fried bananas for the same price. The Macao is open from noon to 3:30 p.m. and 7 to 11:30 p.m.; closed Sundays.

7. The Special Spots

SHELLFISH, STEAKS & BEEF: Cervejaria Ribadouro, 155 Avenida da Liberdade (tel. 494-11), is one of the typical shellfish and beer emporiums in central Lisbon, midway along the city's major boulevard at the corner of the Rua do Salitre. There's a minimum of decor in this tavern-style restaurant, as the management thus far has steered clear of touristy gimmicks.

Instead, the emphasis is on the varieties of fish offered. You select from more than 50 fish and meat dishes, highlighted by the crustaceans and "sea fruit" recommendations. Outstanding are sea fruit sailors' style—that is, in a marinade sauce—costing 120$ ($4.68). You can dine lightly as well, particularly at lunch, ordering such plates as shrimp omelette for only 35$ ($1.37).

Many diners often follow fish with a meat dish. If so, a good choice is sautéed veal cutlets with mushrooms, 65$ ($2.54). However, only those who've been trained for at least 25 years on the most mouth-wilting of Indian curry should try the sautéed pork cutlets with piri-piri, the latter made with red hot peppers from Angola. A wedge of Portuguese cheese "from the hills" goes for 15$ (59¢) and finishes off the meal nicely.

Cervejaria da Trindade, 20-B Rua Nova de Trindade (tel. 32-35-06), is a combination of a German beer hall and a Portuguese tavern—the oldest of them all, owned by the brewers of Sagres beer. Here you can order tasty little steaks and heaps of crisp french fried potatoes for 38$ ($1.48) per person. The meat is garnished with a dollop of country butter and a slice of aromatic lemon. Many of the Portuguese prefer bife na frigideira—that is, steak with a mustard sauce and a fried egg accompaniment, all in a clay frying pan. The tavern also features shellfish, which come from private fish ponds, and the house specialties are ameijoas (clams) à Trindade, 55$ ($2.15), and the giant prawns. To go with your main course, a stein of beer costs 6$ (23¢). For dessert, a good selection is a slice of queijo da serra (cheese from the mountains) and coffee. This restaurant was formerly a convent and later on a brewery. Its walls, which resisted the 1755 earthquake, are tiled with Portuguese scenes, such as one depicting a sunburst, a cornucopia of fruit, tropical birds, a gentleman holding a 17th-century stein. Meals are served in the inner courtyard on sunny days.

Cervejaria à Brilhante, 103 Rua Portas de Santo Antao. Go here if you enjoy seafood with beer. Lisboans from every walk of life stop off for a stein of beer and mariscos. Opposite the Coliseu, the tavern is decorated with stone arches, wood-paneled walls, and pictorial tiles depicting sea life. You can dine either at the bar or at marble tables.

The front window is packed with an appetizing array of king crab, oysters, lobster, baby clams, shrimps, even barnacles. And they aren't cheap. The price changes every day, depending on market quotations, and you pay by the kilo. Among the fixed-price items, a steaming bowl of shellfish soup is 14$ (55¢); an order of baked codfish, 55$ ($2.15); a filet of sole, 70$ ($2.73); a fresh fruit salad, 14$ (55¢).

READER'S SELECTION: "We bumped into a restaurant called **Cervejaria Inglesa,** 42 Rua das Portas de St. Antao, very near the center (tel. 32-41-88). There we had a delicious seafood meal for two for only 100$ ($3.90)" (Jerry Rosen, New York, N.Y.).

CHEESE AND WINE: Au Bon Mariage, 4-B Largo do Contador-Mor (tel. 86-07-27), is the only cheese and wine bistro in Lisbon. Nestled in the Alfama, near the base of St. George's Castle, this art-nouveau-styled establishment has become a rage among Lisboans. Inside, a musical comedy atmosphere prevails, the waiters rushing by in pistachio-colored jackets. Vibrant birthday-cake colors prevail on several levels, under arched and coved ceilings. You select your cheese from a crowded buffet server, each variety ranging in price from 25$ (98¢) to 75$ ($2.93) a helping. Along with a wide selection of crusty bread and crackers, wine is available by the bottle. The most festive dish is a cheese fondue for 175$ ($6.83). No other food is served. Don't miss the community washbowl—a handsome fluted brass bowl with ornate spigots—half hidden behind low-swinging doors.

8. Hard-Core Budget

Policia, 127 Avenido Donde de Valdom. À la carte dishes might be a mushroom omelette, 28$ ($1.09); cozido portuguesa, 67$ ($2.61); or rabbit with mushrooms, 68$ ($2.65); even breaded pork chops, 73$ ($2.85). A flan costs 11$ (43¢). Decor consists of a tiled floor and walls, bullfight posters, and slowly revolving ceiling fans. Everything is clean and homey. Closed Sundays.

Organizacoes Correia, 10C Rua das Picoas (tel. 437-23), is an eye-popping budgeteer's paradise. A favorite with students and impecunious artists, it features a four-course meal for 30$ ($1.17) or 40$ ($1.56). There's no menu, and no choice: you just eat what is being made that day, but the food is good and filling. Coming in from the tree-lined street, you walk down a couple of steps to four smallish rooms. There's a counter where you pay your chosen amount and are given a ticket. When the waiter serves you, you give him the ticket. Despite this being a rock-bottom budget place, the decor is pleasant, with low ceilings, nine tables in each of the cozy rooms, a tiled floor, and iron lanterns. When we were last there, the menu consisted of a soup, followed by grilled white fish with gravy, then a breaded veal cutlet with salad, plus wine and bread. The Correia is open for lunch and dinner, but is closed Sundays.

VEGETARIANS OF THE WORLD, UNITE!: Pensao Vegetariana, 112 Rua Rodrigues Sampaio (tel. 443-20), is the private world of Gilda dos Santos Lima, an enthusiast for natural foods and the vitamin and strength-building qualities of the not-so-lowly vegetable. She's happy with her vegetables, a veritable Mrs. Wiggs of the cabbage patch. Her miniature restaurant rests on the top (sixth) floor of a centrally located building.

Her pensao is pilgrim spartan, a wall motto freely translated as "Give us God and bread." It costs 70$ ($2.73) for an outside guest to have either a filling lunch or dinner here. In addition to her well-prepared vegetables, she offers homemade bread and croquettes packed with healthy ingredients. Her Italian salad is made with fresh green beans, cabbage, turnips, carrots, onions, potatoes, and olives. She uses vegetable or olive oil only, never cooking with butter, although it's on the table for those requiring it.

Her dining room is fresh and quiet, with only eight petite tables. During the week businesspeople come here for a light vegetarian lunch. Sunday is a different matter. At that time, Gilda feeds only her roomers and likes to sit around with her shoes off to rest her feet.

Reached by a small elevator, the Pensao Vegetariana offers simple, virtuous living—a healthy (no smoking allowed) atmosphere.

THE COFFEE HOUSES OF LISBON: How can one go to Lisbon without visiting one of the traditional coffee houses? It's like a trip to England without four o'clock tea, or to Munich without a stein in a beer hall. To the Portuguese, the coffee house is an institution—a democratic parlor where they can drop in for their favorite beverage, abandon their worries, relax, smoke a cigarette, read the paper, write a letter, chat with friends about tomorrow's football match or last night's lover.

The coffee house in Portugal is revered, although the older and more colorful ones with their turn-of-the-century charm are rapidly being replaced by the 20th-century world of chrome and plastic. According to the Portuguese, coffee from such places as Timor and Angola is the best in the world. They may be right, although its powerful flavor may not please the palate of percolator or freeze dried devotées.

One of the oldest coffee houses in Lisbon is **A Brasileira**, 102-A Rua Garrett (tel. 368-792), in the Chiado district. It's a 19th-century emporium, a favorite gathering place (today and yesterday) for the literati, who sit on its leather chairs and banquettes, sipping coffee from demitasse on tiny marble-topped round tables against a background of framed mirrors. A newspaper vendor wends his way through the crowd.

Outside, the street speaks of its past associations with men of letters. Garrett, a romantic dandy of the 19th century, was one of Portugal's leading poets (the street is named after him). The district itself—the Chiado—was named for another poet. On the square near the cafe a statue honors António Ribeiro, a 16th-century poet. Yet another poet, Bocage of Setúbal, used to frequent this coffee house. When once accosted by a bandit, he is said to have replied, "I am going to the Brasileira, but if you shoot me I am going to another world."

A demitasse of coffee—a bica—costs 2$50 (10¢), including a tip, a small amount to pay for the privilege of savoring another era.

SNACK BARS, RITZ-STYLE: **Monumental Snack Bars**, 77-C Rua Castilho, is a three-level dining establishment within the Ritz Hotel compound, although it has a separate entrance facing the Park of Edward VII. It wasn't along ago when it was an innovation for Lisboans to be served meals at a counter, but they are taking to it enthusiastically—enough so that they stand behind stools waiting for a vacant spot.

While the same basic menu is used on each floor, there is a slight difference in offerings. The top, or third floor features some Indian and Chinese dishes, while the lower level "bar" offers Italian specialties, including lasagne, 45$ ($1.76) and pizza, 55$ ($2.15).

On the separate and lengthy dessert menu, you'll find 16 varieties of fruit salad, six kinds of cheese, seven different cakes, tarts, and puddings, and seven kinds of ice-cream delicacies, everything from "Volcano" at 15$ (59¢) to "Himalaya" at 25$ (98¢). And don't worry if the waiter doesn't speak English—the menu has photos of the dishes, so just point. The snack bar opens at noon and closes at midnight.

Apolo 70 10 Avenida Julio Diniz (tel. 77-68-34), near the bull ring, is a self-contained unit that includes everything from an interior sidewalk cafe, to a discotheque, to a leather shop, to a cinema. Wander for an hour or two among the 38 shops, making purchases at a teenage boutique, getting your photograph blown up to poster size, or having your hair styled by experts. On the lower level is a pet shop, hobby shop, and a restaurant that vaguely evokes a merry-go-round. You can order a set meal for 70$ ($2.73). Main courses include a hamburger at 35$ ($1.37), a typical Portuguese fish stew at 40$ ($1.56), a shrimp or minestrone soup for 6$ (23¢). Ever had a banana mousse? Try one here for 12$ (47¢). Open till 12:30 a.m.

Galeto is another cafeteria—this one at 14 Avenida de la Republica (tel. 53-39-10). Downstairs is a plastic-style restaurant, serving some Brazilian specialties. Otherwise you can order bits of steak on a barbecued skewer for 75$ ($2.93); a fried sole, 68$ ($2.65); a mixed salad, 25$ (98¢); and rice pudding, 10$ (39¢). The special attraction here is the ice cream, a plate going for 18$ (70¢).

THE ENJOYMENT OF PORT: **Solar do Velho Pôrto**, 45 Rua Sao Pedro de Alcantar (tel. 32-33-07), is an institute cum club devoted exclusively to the drinking and enjoyment of port in all its known flavors. The choice is staggering, with close to 100 wines to choose from. The wine institute is near the Bairro Alto with its houses of fado. In the rear of a large building, it offers a quiet and relaxing atmosphere, the feeling enhanced by an open stone fireplace.

Owned and sponsored by the wine merchants of Porto, it displays many artifacts related to the industry. But the real reason for dropping in here during the day is for its lista de vinhos—you can have a glass (cálice) of extra seco (dry) for anywhere from 10$ (39¢) to 40$ ($1.56).

READERS' RESTAURANT SELECTIONS: "One inexpensive restaurant should be recommended—the **Progresso**, 2 Rua Barata Salgueiro, where the three of us could eat an evening meal for about $2.50 (U.S.) each, including wine and dessert. We ate several meals there, ordering

chicken, fish, and some sort of fried steak. All of it was clean and very tasty. Ask for José Ricardo da Costa, who speaks enough English for you to get by" (J. H. Arensman, Harrisburg, Ill.).
... "A good restaurant is **Restaurante 111,** 111 Rua dos Remedios in the Alfama. The interior is decorated in red and black, with rustic wood on the walls and candles flickering at your table. Roast cabrito (kid) is superb at 120$ ($4.68) for two. Mateus rosé wine is 65$ ($2.54), and fresh fruit in wine costs 35$ ($1.37). It was one of the best meals we had in all of Lisbon" (W. Michael Sharpe, Windsor, Ontario, Canada).

Not all the best restaurants or hotels are in Lisbon, as you'll soon see in the chapter coming up.

Chapter VI

ESTORIL, CASCAIS & SINTRA

1. **Estoril**
2. **Cascais**
3. **Oitavos**
4. **Guincho**
5. **Queluz**
6. **Sintra**
7. **Mafra Palace**
8. **Ericeira**
9. **Vale do Lobos**

THE ENVIRONS OF LISBON are so intriguing that many fail to see the capital itself—so lured are they by the siren call of **Guincho** (near the westernmost point in continental Europe), the roar from the **"Mouth of Hell,"** the soft muted song from Lord Byron's "glorious Eden" at **Sintra.** Another day could be spent drinking in the wonders of the famous library at the monastery-palace of **Mafra** (Portugal's El Escorial), dining in and touring the pretty pink rococo palace at **Queluz,** or enjoying a shore dinner at the Atlantic beach resort of **Ericeira.**

However, the chief magnet remains the **Costa do Sol,** that string of beach resorts—such as **Estoril** and **Cascais**—that form the Portuguese Riviera on the northern banks of the mouth of the Tagus. In fact, if you arrive in Lisbon when the sun is shining, the air balmy, you should consider seeking lodgings along this cabaña-studded shoreline. So near to Lisbon is Estoril that it's easy to dart in and out of the capital on sightseeing jaunts or fado sprees, while ensconced at a base in a hotel by the sea. An inexpensive electric train leaving from the Cais de Sodré in Lisbon makes the run frequently throughout the day and evening, ending its run in Cascais.

The sun coast is sometimes known as A Costa dos Reis, the coast of kings, because of all the deposed royalty who have settled there—everybody from exiled kings, to pretenders, marquises from Italy, princesses from Russia, and baronesses from Germany.

These aristocrats may live simply, perhaps a virtual recluse in an unpretentious villa, in the manner of Princess Elena of Roumania (Magda Lupescu); or they may insist on rigid court ambience, as does Umberto, the one-month king of Italy in 1946. Forced into exile when a plebiscite went against the monarchy, Umberto is well settled in Portugal. "He spends his days cataloguing family medallions, art works and books, and playing with grandchildren," or so wrote Charlotte Curtis.

Tending his cows in "baggy trousers and muddy boots" in Sintra is the Count of Paris, the pretender to the throne of France. A descendant of Louis Philippe, he was the son of the Duke of Guise. In 1969, another pretender, Don Juan, the Count of Barcelona, was short-changed the Spanish throne in favor of his son, Don Juan Carlos, named by Generalísimo Franco as his successor. The older Don Juan is the son of Alfonso XIII, the former king of Spain who was forced into exile in 1931. At one time, the Count of Barcelona was an officer in the British Navy and is today a noted yachtsman. Other nobility includes Joanna, the former Queen of Bulgaria, and the Infanta Dona Maria Adelaide de Braganza, sister of the Portuguese pretender.

The riviera is a microcosm of Portugal. Take the ride out on the train, even if you don't plan to lodge there. Along the way, you'll pass pastel-washed houses, with red-tiled roofs and facades of antique blue and white tiles; luxuriant vegetation such as rows of canna, pines, mimosa, and eucalyptus; swimming pools; and in the background green hills studded with villas and chalets.

ON THE WAY TO ESTORIL: Leaving Lisbon by electric train, our first stop along the Sun Coast is . . .

Oeiras

In the 18th century, this ancient town was considered one of the most beautiful spots outside of Lisbon. On the coastal road, about eight miles from the capital, it was selected by the Marquês de Pombal as the site of his petunia-pink country estate. The prime minister, of course, was the one who rebuilt Lisbon after the 1755 earthquake.

For many years, Pombal's palace housed art works belonging to the Calouste Gulbenkian Foundation. Now that the foundation has its own sparkling museum in Lisbon, the estate is closed to the public and guarded by the military.

Most visitors head for Oeiras for surf and sandy beaches, anchoring in at the following medium-priced motel:

WHERE TO STAY: Continental Holiday Motel, Estrada Marginal (tel. 243-11-86), is the kind of seaside-resort-style motel that most North Americans will readily appreciate and understand. Unequaled is its prime position, sandwiched between the road to Estoril and long strands of beach along the rugged coastline. It's such a complete recreational zone that one may never go farther afield, preferring to swim in its free-form pools built into the rocks, with flagstoned terraces for sun-soaking.

Each of its cottages has its own front terrace, opening either onto the garden of flowers and pines or else onto an ocean view. The Continental is a self-contained colony, with a large-scale self-service restaurant offering inexpensive meals, the Leopard Bar, a post office, a laundromat, and a host of recreational facilities, including boating, water skiing, mini-golf, and a children's playground under the pines.

In a typical unit the space includes a sitting area, an adjoining sleeping section with single beds, a separate shower and bath, a kitchen with a refrigerator, and a carport. Some of the rooms contain balconies with two beds. Maid service is provided, as are linens and kitchen utensils. In high season, the rate in a double is 300$ ($11.70), 240$ ($9.36) in a single, plus a 10 percent surcharge. An additional person sharing the room pays 60$ ($2.34). From October 15 to March 14, 50 percent reductions are granted.

A short drive farther up the coast delivers us to . . .

Carcavelos

On the road between Lisbon and Estoril, this seaside town boasts the longest stretch of beach along the Costa do Sol. Often considered its gateway, it commands a view of the white Manueline-style Tower of Belém farther back.

Carcavelos was noted for its fortress, S. Juliao, which once held prisoner so-called left-wing radicals during the Miguelite wars. The fortress, with its pale yellow walls and curious turrets is of a unique design that is attributed to the theories of Sebastien Le Prestre de Vauban, a French engineer.

The resort lies about 13½ miles outside of Lisbon and is easily reached on the electric train from the Cais do Sodré. Even if you don't go to Carcavelos, you may want to sample some of its full-bodied wine, praised by the Duke of Wellington.

The finest medium-priced accommodation there is provided by the following recommendation:

Hotel Praia-Mar, Quinta do Junqueiro, 16 (tel. 247-31-30). Everywhere you look there is a commendable blend of the best of contemporary architectural and furnishing design with Portuguese provincial. The all-glass walls, the wood paneling, the stark plaster, are perfect foils for the assemblage of antiques and reproductions. The more expensive bedrooms facing the sea have terraces with garden furniture, ideal for sun-tanning or breakfast.

In the rooms themselves, old-style carved Portuguese beds, high wooden chests with black marble tops, intricate high-backed chairs, black oak end tables, handmade rag rugs tastefully adorn the rooms. The baths, one with every bedroom, offer plenty of soft towels and fixtures such as bidets. In high season, from March 1 to October 31, rates depend on the view and whether you have a terrace. In a single, the tariff ranges between 410$ ($15.99) and 580$ ($22.63) daily; for a double, anywhere between 450$ ($17.55) and 620$ ($24.36).

In the main lounge, islands of streamlined modern groupings of furniture—black leather and teak—abound. An adjoining bar contains antiqued mirrors and art nouveau sculpture, opening onto a small patio with a fountain. There's even a boîte, as intimate as a pillbox, for discotheque dancing. A top-floor bar, paneled in walnut, invites lounging on its sleek brown and black armchairs. The vast, but personalized, dining room crowns the Praia-Mar, offering a panoramic view of the sea from almost every table.

The hotel is set back from the ocean and coastal road. Although many clients like to trek down to the public beach, others relax around the free-form swimming pool with its sun terrace. The electric train stop to Lisbon or Estoril lies about a two-minute walk from the entrance to the hotel.

Coming up, the "King" of the Costa do Sol.

1. Estoril

This chic resort along the Portuguese Riviera has long basked in its reputation as a playground of kings. Fading countesses arrive at the railway station, monarchs in exile drop in at the Palácio Hotel for dinner, the sons of assassinated dictators sunbathe by the pool—and an international joie de vivre pervades the air.

Once Estoril was a figment of somebody's imagination, a vision of Fausto Figueiredo, the founding father of the deluxe Palácio and the Casino. Before the First World War, Fausto Figueiredo envisioned hundreds of people strolling through the marble corridors and down mosaic sidewalks to the ocean as he gazed out over scrub pines and sandy hills.

Before the Second World War, Estoril was firmly entrenched in the resort sweepstakes. As Nazi troops advanced across Europe, many collapsed courts fled to Estoril to wait out the war in a neutral country. Word arrived daily from resistance movements, and hopes rose of regaining now-lost thrones.

The **Parque Estoril,** in the center, represents magnificent landscaping, a sub-tropical setting with the plants swaying in the breeze. At night when it's floodlit, fashionable guests go for a stroll. The palm trees studding the grounds have prompted many to call it "a corner of Africa." At the top of the park sits the **Casino,** offering not only gambling, but international floor shows, dancing, and movies.

Across the railroad tracks is the beach, where some of the most beautiful women in Europe sun themselves on the peppermint-striped canvas chairs along the Tamariz Esplanade. The atmosphere is cosmopolitan, and the beach is sandy, unlike the pebbly strand at Nice. If you don't want to swim in the ocean, you can check in at an oceanfront swimming pool for a plunge instead.

To the east is **S. Joao do Estoril,** which also boasts a beach and many handsome private villas. Most visitors go here to dine and dance at **A Choupana** (refer to our nightlife recommendations).

FOR GOLFERS: In the foothills of Sintra, a three-minute drive from the Casino, lies the **Clube de Golf do Estoril.** An attraction for international sportsmen, it offers a fairway set against a vista of pine and mimosa. The quality of the course is so acclaimed—one of the finest in Europe—that it is selected for international championship matches. Both a nine-hole and an 18-hole course are offered. Guests play from around 7:30 a.m. till sunset daily. On weekdays, you'll pay a 200$ ($7.80) green fee; 300$ ($11.70) on weekends and holidays. For 18 holes, a first-rate caddie charges 65$ (2.54), 45$ ($1.76) for nine holes. You can also rent clubs and a locker.

Estoril lies 15 miles west of Lisbon and is reached by an electric train from the waterfront Cais do Sodré. By private car, Estoril is approached either by the coastal road or an inland route.

A DELUXE HOTEL: Palácio Hotel, Parque Estoril (tel. 26-04-00), is legendary as a retreat for exiled royalty and as a center of World War II espionage. It scarcely seems possible that so much old-world elegance could have accumulated since 1930; but fast-breaking events, tumultuous happenings, and thronging international society telescoped its development and its prestige until it now has acquired a lustrous patina.

Its founding father was Fausto Figueiredo, and his descendants still own and run the hotel today. At its début, the Palácio received the honeymooning Japanese Crown Prince and his new bride. In time, other royalty would follow: Umberto of Italy; Don Juan, the Count of Barcelona. In World War II when people had escaped with a case of jewels and the clothes on their back, diamonds and rubies and gold were accepted instead of money.

The reception rooms are Pompeian, with sienna-colored marble pillars, bold bands of orange, and handmade carpets. Ideal for a tête-à-tête are the series of intimate communicating salons, with Wedgwood blue and white friezes on pilasters and walls, draped crystal chandeliers, and high arched windows with silk draperies. In the classic central drawing room, with black and white marble checkerboard floors, groups of antique furnishings are arranged for guests to have after-dinner coffee.

Dining is an event in one of the stateliest rooms along the Riviera. That jeweled choker or string of pearls, even the princess, is for real! The wine steward has a real working knowledge of his country's wines, quickly learning your tastes. A delicious four-course table d'hôte meal costs only 200$ ($7.80). Built off the grand salon in the southern wing, the Grill Room has access to the street for the general public. Quietly elegant, it features à la carte service in intimate surroundings.

The bedrooms are traditional with fine furnishings, such as an occasional brass bed, always a desk, a marble-topped chest, and twin wardrobes. Bedside buttons summon a maid or valet, but somehow the staff has a radar-understanding of when you need fresh towels. The baths are large and marble-faced, with bidets and heated racks. In high season, the singles rates range from 457$ ($17.82) to 612$ ($23.87); the double tariffs from 674$ ($22.29) to 889$ ($34.67), service and taxes included. Or you can occupy one of the modern, luxurious, furnished duplex poolside suites, all air conditioned, and pay 1,109$ ($43.27) for two. Full pension ranges from 1,354$ ($52.81) to 1,569$ ($61.19); 1,874$ ($73.09) in a suite.

Starting early in the morning, guests gather at the poolside terrace, overlooking the pool which is encircled by a reflection pool. A buffet luncheon is served on your chaise lounge or at a table beside a garland hedge of bougainvillea. The hotel itself opens onto the side of Estoril Park—capped by the glittering new Casino; the beach is only a short walk away. Golfers are given a free temporary membership in the local professional course at Estoril. Seven clay surface championship tennis courts are right next door to the hotel. Three courts are floodlit for nighttime playing.

THE MEDIUM-PRICED RANGE: Hotel Alvorada, 3 Rua de Lisboa (tel. 26-00-70), opened its doors late in 1969 to provide Spanish parador living on a small scale, opposite the Casino and the formally styled Estoril Parque. Just a three-minute trek from the sands, it is recommended to those desiring skillfully styled bedrooms and a walk-in private kitchenette, complete with refrigerator and cooking utensils.

Each room is furnished like a studio, with an open iron grill screen between the sleeping and dining sections. The highest tabs are for the rooms with views of the sea and park. In high season, the rate in a single is 300$ ($11.70); 340$ ($13.26) to 375$ ($14.63) for a double. Some of the above rooms are virtual suites and include a twin-bedded room, a sitting area, bath, kitchenette, and balcony. Four persons can book a super suite with two bedrooms for 540$ ($21.06), and 100$ ($3.90) for each extra bed.

The public rooms are personalized and well conceived. Off the reception area, the drinking lounge is decorated with modern Portuguese paintings and provincial-style furnishings. Meals are provided in the top-floor panoramic beamed-ceilinged dining room with its roof terrace—a setting enhanced by Portuguese artistry.

Hotel Cibra, Estrada Marginal (tel. 26-18-11), was built next door to its glamorous neighbor, the Palácio. Its nine floors with walls of glass soar high, about half of the rooms boasting good-sized balconies overlooking a view of the water and the Casino with its formal gardens. Only a minute or so from the seafront and the electric train station, it is in the center of Estoril's boutique district.

The upper-floor dining room provides unobstructed vistas of the sea and the nearby hills studded with luxurious villas. On many evenings a white-capped chef stands proudly in front of his specialty display table. In the marble-floored lounge and drinking bar, a good sense of contemporary design prevails, with plenty of museum-like space. Soft tufted leather chairs are gathered around marble-topped tables.

The bedrooms are not only trim, utilitarian, and uncluttered, but many have sitting areas, with wooden grained pieces. French doors open onto balconies in most of the rooms. All have shiny tiled private baths with a shower. Half pension in high season, June through September, is 395$ ($15.41) in a single, 655$ ($25.45) in a double.

Hotel das Arcadas, 1 Arcadas Parque (tel. 26-27-91), offers one of the most convenient ways of living in Estoril. It's not only inexpensive, but puts you in the bull's eye center of holiday activities. The two-story, arcaded, and crescent-shaped buildings are in different sections, flanking the entrance to the formal garden leading to the Casino. Near the beach, both series of rooms lie over boutiques selling antiques, sports apparel, handicraft items, and souvenirs.

A hidden bonus is the hotel's ownership by the neighboring deluxe Palácio. By staying at Das Arcadas and paying low rates, you can enjoy the facilities next door, including a swimming pool. At Das Arcadas there are no public rooms, lounges, or restaurants, although the rooms have fully equipped kitchenettes, private bathrooms, and verandas facing the park and the sea.

A large room for one or two, with a private bath and kitchenette, goes for 287$ ($11.19). If you decide to rent a suite, the daily rate is 449$ ($17.51) for one or two persons. Breakfast can be brought to your terrace for 17$ (66¢). Each of the rooms enjoys a personalized decoration, with parquet floors, marble-topped chests and tables, and simple decorative accessories.

Lennox Country Club, 5 Rue Infante de Sagres (tel. 26-04-24), is a private hillside villa now converted into a small hotel. It has a special appeal for those interested in golf—a great course almost next door—as well as for those interested in lounging—a circular garden swimming pool completes the perfect setting. Guests from Britain, America, and the rest of the world relax here, taking their meals, reveling in dips in the heated water, sunbathing, and enjoying the rock garden with its beds of red and gold cannas, banks of geraniums, and orange and purple bougainvillea.

Owners Brodie and Vera Lennox have chosen a friendly staff to watch over their domain. They train the staff well, seeing to it that flowers are put on the tables daily, that the tea is brewed correctly.

The bedrooms are named after famous golf clubs of Britain, and there's a pictorial tile plaque at the entrance that is reportedly Mr. Lennox's family tartan. Even the cozy sunroom is imbued with a Brigadoon theme, with liberal use made of the tartan. The living rooms are strictly family-style, with floral prints on the furniture and windows. Antique chests and old clocks intermingle with painted Portuguese chests. After dinner guests play bridge in a small sitting room, or gather for drinks, making out their own tabs!

Some of the bedrooms in the main villa have towers, with view windows. The less expensive accommodations are in the tuck-away guest annex in the garden. All the rooms are individually furnished in a homey fashion, with soft inner-spring beds, flower prints, comfy armchairs, and tiled baths or showers. The minimum rate for demi-pension is 450$ ($17.55) per person.

Estalagem Claridada, 14 Rua Mouzinho de Albuquerque (tel. 26-34-34), is a hillside villa near that of the Count of Barcelona. Liverpool-born Dorothy Habbick and her Scottish husband George welcome you in one of their 10 bedrooms, many of them decorated with antiques or traditionally styled reproductions. All accommodations have private baths. The half-pension tariff for two persons goes for 550$ ($21.45) in high season. At other times one person need pay only 360$ ($14.04) for the same arrangement. Some of the rooms contain terraces as well. Guests

CASCAIS 67

That Cascais is growing is an understatement. It's leapfrogging! At one entrance to the resort, someone penciled in the word City after Cascais. Although not officially recognized as such, it is well on its way. Apartment houses, new hotels, and the finest restaurants along the Costa do Sol draw a never-ending stream every year.

However, the life of the simple fisherman still goes on. Auctions—called a lota—at which the latest catch is sold still take place on the main square, except a modern hotel has sprouted up in the background. In the small harbor, rainbow-colored fishing boats must share space with pleasure craft owned by an international set which flocks to Cascais from early spring until autumn.

The tie that Cascais has with the sea is old. If you speak Portuguese, any of the local fishermen—with their weather-beaten faces—could tell you that one of their own, Afonso Sanches, discovered America in 1482, that Columbus learned of his accidental find, stole the secret, and enjoyed the subsequent acclaim.

Cascais lies only four miles west of Estoril, 18 miles from Lisbon proper. It's reached by the electric train which begins its run at the Cais do Sodré waterfront station, ending it in the center of town, across from the famous Fim do Mundo (End of the World) restaurant. The cost of a one-way, first-class seat is 15$ (59¢). Trains leave every 15 minutes.

Many visitors, both foreign and domestic, drive out to Cascais on a road-clogged summer Sunday to attend the exciting bullfights at the **Monumental de Cascais,** an impressive ring just outside the "city" center. A restaurant, **O Guizo,** has been installed underneath the spectator seats—so you can make plans to dine there before or after watching an exciting corrida.

The most popular excursion outside of Cascais is to the **Boca do Inferno** (Mouth of Hell). Reached by heading out the highway to Guincho, then turning left toward the sea, the Boca deserves its ferocious reputation. However, if you should arrive when the sea is calm, you'll wonder why it's called a caldron. At their peak, thundering waves sweep in with such power and fury that they have long ago carved a wide hole or boca in the cliffs. The Mouth of Hell can be a windswept roar if you don't stumble over too many souvenir hawkers. Take a bus from Cascais Station for 2$50 (10¢).

THE TOP HOTELS: Estoril Sol, Parque Palmela (tel. 28-28-31), is a luxury skyscraper holiday world, perched on a ledge, with the coastal highway and electric train tracks separating it from the beach. It represents a dream come true for its late owner José Teodoro dos Santos, a self-made personality, who originally arrived in Lisbon with less than a dollar in his pocket. He also built a new Casino at Estoril, and his work is now being continued by his children, headed by his son-in-law, Dr. Manuel Telles.

A modern land of resort living has been created: a gymnasium, an olympic-sized pool for adults, a smaller one for children, tennis courts, a complete sauna, facilities for horseback riding, water skiing, a shopping arcade, a garage and service station, and public rooms large enough for a great invasion of sun-seeking visitors.

The result was that the air-conditioned Estoril Sol ended up as the largest hotel in Portugal, with 400 bedrooms and suites overlooking the sea or the hills beyond. It boasts the largest dining room on the Costa do Sol, the most spacious main lounge (a traffic cop would be helpful here!), the greatest number of bars (five in all), the most expansive veranda on the peninsula, and a beach reached by an underground passageway.

Already the roster shows such check-in names as Gloria Swanson, Omar Sharif, Melina Mercouri, Juliette Greco, and Prince Rainier and Princess Grace. Even Zsa Zsa Gabor has made one of her famous exits here! The designers have furnished the public rooms and bedrooms in a modified Miami Beach style. The more expensive rooms have sea views and balconies. Naturally, every room has a complete tiled bath with gadgets.

Single rooms range in price from 360$ ($14.04) to 545$ ($21.25); doubles, from 510$ ($19.89) to 775$ ($30.17). Lunch or dinner costs 170$ ($6.63), and a continental breakfast is 43$ ($1.68). All taxes are included.

Estalagem Albatroz, 100 Rua Frederico Arouca (tel. 28-28-21). The wandering albatross, of course, is a bird noted as a master of gliding flight, capable of staying air-borne on motionless wings for hours on end. What an appropriate symbol for what is perhaps the most delectable treasure on the Costa do Sol! Whether you're seeking food, lodgings, or both, the inn is your "good luck" choice.

Positioned out on a ledge of rocks, it is screened from the road by a garden. A neoclassic villa, it was built as a luxurious holiday retreat by the Duke of Loulé, then acquired in the 19th century by the Count and Countess de Foz. Sometime in this century it was converted into an inn, and in time received such guests as Anthony Eden, Cary Grant, Chief Justice Warren Burger, the Duke and Duchess of Bedford, Claudette Colbert, William Holden, Amy Vanderbilt, and the former Queen of Bulgaria.

Your bedroom will either overlook the sea (you can hear the surf pounding on the rocks at night) or a quiet garden. The bedrooms are enjoyably furnished, with many comfortable pieces (all 16 rooms have private baths). There's a liberal sprinkling of good antiques throughout the chambers, plus paintings, bric-a-brac, and other decorative accessories collected from the corners of the earth. The prices of rooms fall into three categories, based on location, size, and view. Two persons can stay here and have full board (the food is one of the reasons for booking at the inn) for 870$ ($33.93) to 1,030$ ($40.17), including service and taxes. A room and breakfast for two ranges in price from 360$ ($14.04) to 520$ ($20.28). In a single, the cost of full board is 510$ ($19.89) to 620$ ($24.18).

In a small waterside garden, you'll find some white busts on pilasters, set in the midst of greenery—much admired by two former guests, Prince Rainier and Princess Grace. For a preview of the food, refer to our dining section in Cascais.

Hotel Cidadela, Avenida 25 de Abril (tel. 28-29-21). Architecturally and decoratively, this hotel is a citadel of high taste. Elegantly furnished in a restrained way, spacious in concept—both in its private and public rooms—and gracious in its reception and amenities—it is emerging as the sleeper of the Sun Coast. Many Riviera-bound guests have deserted their old favorites for this 1970s-style holiday rendezvous.

Although you can reserve a first-class room, built into the central block with balconies, the Cidadela will also place you in womblike comfort in one of its twin-bedded, terraced suites, or else in one of its apartment-like duplexes, the latter usually sheltering a ménage of anywhere from three to six persons. Priced at from 450$ ($17.55) to 850$ ($33.15) (during peak season), a regular double is tastefully furnished, the white walls becoming foils for the vibrant plaids. The range in tariffs depends largely on the view. Preferable are rear rooms, sheltered from the noise of traffic.

Two wings of rooms and duplexes face a garden with a large open swimming pool, partially edged by a wading pond. The duplexes are as complete as an apartment: a living room, dining room, and a fully equipped kitchenette on the lower floor, with a staircase leading to the upstairs bedrooms—two or three each—with private baths. Each floor opens onto verandas with garden furniture. For four persons, these suites rent for 1,400$ ($54.60); and the regular suites, when occupied by two, go for 1,100$ ($42.92). Service and taxes are included.

The three major public rooms are pleasantly decorated—the main living room with low modern groups of furniture in various primary colors. In the good-sized dining room, the sturdy armchairs, upholstered with primitive Portuguese fabric, seat many pleased diners desiring top quality cooking. You can take all meals here for 275$ ($10.73) extra per person. However, nearby is a supermarket for those wanting to whip up their own concoctions.

The intimate bar is done in lipstick red with gray-blue armchairs and "medievalesque" helmets and breast plates. On the premises are a garage, a boutique, a hairdresser, plus a concierge skilled at arranging boating and fishing trips, tennis games, a day at the golf course, horseback riding, or a ticket for the bullfight. The hotel divorces itself from the hustle-bustle of summering Cascais, and is reached by heading out on a tree-shaded avenue—past restaurants, boutiques, and nightclubs.

Our heartiest praise to the manager, Luís Faria de Carvalho, for his high-styled Cidadela.

THE MEDIUM-PRICED RANGE: Hotel Baía, Estrada Marginal (tel. 28-10-33), sits on what many consider the best spot in Cascais. Its harborfront balconies (a premium at regatta time) and terraces are almost on the Praia da Ribeira, where fishing boats and yachts tie in. Built in 1962 at the hub of the resort, the hotel was constructed of rugged terracotta brick, rising four stories high and offering private sun balconies with 66 of its 85 bedrooms. The lower level, especially the sidewalk cafes, have blossomed into the social center of Cascais.

Informality reigns inside the baía (bay). The rooftop terrace is large, good for sunbathing, and commands a view over the bay of Cascais.

The bedrooms are comfortably furnished in a modern style, all with private bath, telephone, radio, and glass doors opening onto balconies. In a single, the tariff is 261$ ($10.18), including breakfast; for a double, 387$ ($15.09) with breakfast. For full board, two persons pay 720$ ($28.08), taxes and service included.

In a 1973 renovation program, all public rooms were improved: the lounge is now larger and more comfortable and the restaurant air conditioned.

THE BUDGET RANGE: **Albergaria Valbom,** 14 Avenida Valbom (tel. 28-58-01), is right in the center of Cascais, providing 45 modern, comfortable rooms. There is little decor to speak of, but the prices are most attractive: single rooms cost 230$ ($8.97), dropping to 160$ ($6.24) in off-season. Doubles cost 331$ ($12.91) in season, 235$ ($9.17) in the winter. Breakfast is additional. No other meals are served.

Nau Hotel, 14 Rua Dra. Iracy Doyle (tel. 28-28-61), is a comfortable island of modernity in the main stream of "village" life, opposite the train station, next to a garage. What it loses by not having surrounding gardens, it makes up for with its all-purpose rooftop sun terrace. Here, in the midst of semi-tropical plants, guests can take breakfast or sunbathe. Its second floor, with one entire wall of glass, holds the main lounge, the Portalo Restaurant, and the Convez Bar. The walls of Portuguese cork, sturdy leather and brass-studded chairs give a nice touch to the dining room; but even more decorative is the food display arranged daily by the chef.

The 57 bedrooms are charming and cleancut. Against a background of utter simplicity, a skilled use is made of Portuguese pine and a dado with built-in headboards—accented by black-and-white checked fabrics. Each room has its own tiled bath and balcony. A single rents for 235$ ($9.17); a double for 335$ ($13.07). For half pension, one person pays 370$ ($14.43) daily; two persons, 605$ ($23.60). The tariffs are reduced from November 1 through March by 25 percent. The hotel takes its name, Nau, from a 15th-century sailing vessel dating from the days of Vasco da Gama.

WHERE TO DINE: Outside of Lisbon, this sprawling resort offers the heaviest concentration of high-quality restaurants in all of Portugal. Even if based in the capital, you should trek out to Cascais to sample the viands—both Portuguese and international dishes. Once you've tasted cognac-simmered lobster, mint-flavored shellfish soup, stuffed cuttlefish, shrimp pâté, even baked Virginia ham and southern fried chicken, you may become a total refugee from your hotel dining room.

Regrettably, from the customer's—not the owner's—point of view, many of the restaurants in Cascais tend to be overcrowded in summer, as they are so popular and quite reasonably priced. However, since many are excellent, press on to the next recommendation if you can't find a seat at your first choice. What follows is a wide-ranging survey of the best of the lot, in all price ranges.

The Top Choices

Estalagem Albatroz, 100 Rua Frederico Arouca (tel. 28-28-21), is considered the finest and most elegant restaurant in Cascais. The dining room is in the oldest part of the villa, built originally as a holiday retreat for the Duke of Loulé. Against a background of antiques, many celebrities have taken rooms here just so they can enjoy the cuisine. Portuguese and international cooking are featured.

On the à la carte menu, house specialties include cherne (turbot) à la marinière, 85$ ($3.32), and canard à l'orange, also 85$. Dessert choices such as crêpes suzette, 70$ (2.73), are offered. The wine cellar is varied and well stocked. Start your meal in the green room, a favorite of guests who enjoy its cozy ambience near the sea.

Fim do Mundo, Avenida Valbom, at the corner of Rua Sebastiao José Caravahlo e Melo (tel. 28-02-00). At the end of the electric train run from Lisbon, Senhor Barreto's The End of the World restaurant reigns supreme in Cascais' center. Drawing a steady stream of foreign visitors and international celebrities, it turns out a cuisine that packs in discriminating diners elbow to elbow. First, the ambience is pleasant: walls of Portuguese tiles, a stone fireplace, deeply set windows, and a rustic-style tavern where the bartender will mix your favorite drink. Second, all the food is freshly prepared. The specialty is shellfish: lobster curry, grilled lobster, lobster thermidor, prawn curry, even clams Portuguese-style. The British *Observer* labeled it "an excellent place for a shellfish orgy." For the above-mentioned dishes, the tabs change daily, depending on market quotations, but they are almost always expensive. A less expensive regular that wins many friends is the chef's English-style steak-and-kidney pie, 65$ ($2.54).

Other dishes are so good that even the most inveterate restaurant shopper will want to return again and again—perhaps to sample the calf's kidney with bacon grilled on a spit, 60$ ($2.34); the tournedo Portuguese-style, 70$ ($2.73); or the filets of sole with banana, 65$ ($2.54). For dessert, why not try Fim do Mundo cake with cream, 35$ ($1.37)? In season, Douro oranges or Sintra strawberries are unbeatable. Open from noon to midnight, and head waiter Antonio Ribeiro makes you feel at home at all hours.

Restaurante do Pescador, 9 Rua das Flores (tel. 28-20-54). The name, The Fisherman; the lane, The Street of Flowers; and the proximity to the fish market may lead you to expect a simple cafe. But after you've smacked your lips at its caldeirada de lagosta com frango, you'll know differently. This savory concoction, on which the tab fluctuates daily, is made with fresh lobster and tender chicken, simmered in a base sauce of cognac and rum with the natural juices, then served in a crockery pot.

The decor is tavern-style, with hand-hewn beams, iron lanterns, cork and wood paneling, lobster baskets, ships' models, smoked fish and meats, and strings of garlic, red pepper, and onions. Everything sets the mood for fine eating. An appetizing table in the front displays a mouth-watering selection of prepared foods, fruit, wines, and cheeses.

Featured, of course, are the fish dishes. Even if you decide to forego the house specialty, you may not want to pass up sopa marisco (shellfish soup) for 25$ (98¢), which is prepared with a savory tomato base and flavored with a sprig of mint. Another recommendation is mixed fish grill for 70$ ($2.73). Finally, another Portuguese dish is a fish soufflé, also 70$.

The owner Ramiro Lueiano Pinto has his own nursery at G᠁ ᠁o, near the Cabo Raso Lighthouse, where his collection of lobster, crayfish, and other mariscos are tended to. Attracted to his Fisherman are a host of well-known personalities, entertainers such as Juliette Greco, Jerry Lewis, and Peter Lawford. The cafe serves till midnight.

The Medium-Priced Range

Reijos Restaurant, 35 Rua Frederico Arouca (tel. 28-03-11). First, you should be warned that it's likely to be crowded, and that you'll either have to wait for a table or abandon all hope in high season. This intimate, informal bistro is that good! The fine foods of two countries—the United States and Portugal—are combined on the menu, and the result is altogether pleasing. An American citizen, Ray Ettinger, who is a purser for a transatlantic airline, has teamed up with a Portuguese, Tony Brito, pooling their talents in the running of this successful enterprise. Often, Mr. Ettinger brings in hard-to-get items by airplane.

At times, to the homesick Mr. Ettinger, nothing is more delectable than such Stateside specialties as a hamburger (at lunch only), 30$ ($1.17), or baked Virginia ham at 65$ ($2.54); with cole slaw, 20$ (78¢). Other popular items include lobster thermidor at 120$ ($4.68); beef stroganoff, 55$ ($2.15); pepper steak, 75$ ($2.93); and shrimp curry, 75$ also. From Macao, two Chinese dishes are prepared at your table: beef with green peppers at 60$ ($2.34) and shrimp and cucumbers at 70$ ($2.73). Lunch is served from 12:30 to 3:30 p.m.; dinner, 7-11 p.m. (telephone first). The service from the young staff is excellent.

Restaurante "O Batel," 4 Travessa das Flores (tel. 28-02-15), fronts the fish market. It's giving the better restaurants of Cascais quite a scare, as it is real competition! Styled as a country inn, it doesn't overdo with touristy gimmicks. The atmosphere is semi-rustic, with rough white walls and old beamed ceilings. The light filters in through bottle glass onto a collection of fishing boat models. A display indicates the ingenuity of the chef, his wares enhanced by a basket of figs, plums, peaches, and fresh flowers.

The prices are reasonable—and that, balanced with the superb viands, explains why the tiny tables are filled at every meal. Lobster thermidor and lobster stewed in cognac are the house specialties, but the price on these items changes daily. For something less expensive, we recommend Cascais sole with banana, 75$ ($2.93); lobster and chicken stew for two, 280$ ($10.92); and a real savory dish, clams with cream, 80$ ($3.12). For openers, you can try oysters on ice with lemon, 35$ ($1.37). To complete your meal, if you're still hungry, such desserts as pineapple with Madeira wine, 30$ ($1.17), and crêpes suzette, 75$ ($2.93), are offered. Wine tip: order a Casal Mendes rosé, a cool choice.

Restaurante Gil Vicente, 22-30 Rua dos Navegantes (tel. 28-20-32). This is the kind of bistro you usually find on a back street in a town along the Côte d'Azur. Set on the rise of a hill above the harbor, it was converted from a fisherman's cottage. Both the cuisine and the ambience reflect the mood of its owner, who sees to it that excellent dinners are served at candlelit tables. Lunch isn't offered, but dinner is likely to extend until the early hours of the morning.

The name of the tavern, Gil Vicente, honors a 16th-century writer who is sometimes considered the father of Portuguese drama—a virtual Iberian Shakespeare, if you will. In spite of his lyricism, the decor of the restaurant is simple—a setting of plaster walls, an old stone fireplace, windows recessed with pots of greenery. To spice up matters, an ornate iron washstand has been adapted for condiments, and the walls contain heads of old iron bedsteads, now gaily painted.

You're likely to be won over by the cooking (pâté, crêpes, shellfish, or grilled chicken and steaks)—and the reasonable tariffs. To whet your appetite, try the assortment of hors d'oeuvres, 40$ ($1.56); the pâté maison, 35$ ($1.37); or the bisque of shellfish, 25$ (98¢). At least three main dishes hit the mark every night: sole coebert, 60$ ($2.34); escalope Cordon Bleu, 65$ ($2.54); and grilled steak with mushrooms, also 65$. Among the sweets, you can settle for a fruit salad or a chocolate mousse at 15$ (59¢), or a banana flambé at 25$ (98¢).

The John Bull (Britannia Restaurant), 4-A Largo Luís de Camoes (tel. 28-01-54). With its black-and-white timbered Elizabethan facade and an owner nicknamed Kim, you'd expect a wedge of Merrie Old England. But it's merely a mock-up, and the owner Mr. Couto is Portuguese. However, he's imported many of the trappings from England to create—or rather to re-create—the atmosphere. The restaurant is open from noon to 4 p.m. and from 7 p.m. to midnight.

In the street-floor pub, the John Bull, you can order an iced pint of lager. The setting is appropriate—wood paneling, oak beams, a fireplace, crude tavern stools and tables, pewter pots, and ceramic jugs.

The meals at the second-floor Britannia Restaurant feature a medley of English and Portuguese, even American, dishes. A rarity on any Portuguese menu is American southern fried chicken, 58$ ($2.26), and T-bone steak at 90$ ($3.51) is another familiar Yankee favorite. For English tastes, specialties include calf's liver, bacon, and french fries, 66$ ($2.57). A winning dessert is a homemade cake for 19$ (74¢), or vanilla ice cream for the same price.

O Guizo, Praça de Toiros (tel. 28-34-34), is built right into the lower tier of the Cascais bull ring. Not by accident, it is a favorite choice with both Portuguese and Spanish matadors, who often meet their friends here, celebrating victories or cheering themselves up after defeats. The restaurant is colorfully styled with bullfight memorabilia, cart wheels, blue plates, brightly hued oxen tassels, and copper pieces. The atmosphere is enlivened with tablecloths in red, turquoise, and yellow—around which red cowhide-covered chairs are placed.

The chef proudly proclaims that he prepares "the real Portuguese food," as opposed to the standard restaurant fare. The menu changes daily, but examples of what he means are provided by such dishes as soup du jour at 12$ (47¢) or a rich-tasting chicken and rice soup, 25$ (98¢). Leading off the grandes especialidades of the house is bacalhau (salted codfish) que nunca chega, 50$ ($1.95). Other dishes include a beef with cognac, 70$ ($2.73), and a roast veal, 55$ ($2.15). For dessert, select the cake of the house at 15$ (59¢), or a pudding made of eggs and coconut for the same price. Youthful Joaquim Caetano, who owns the restaurant, especially recommends the sautéed pork with rice to his American friends. In the evenings, there's often dancing to records, sometimes as late as 3 a.m., although the restaurant usually closes at midnight. Lunches are served only on Saturdays and Sundays.

Salinha Saloia, 14C Rua da Palmeira (tel. 286-61-17), is a cozy, bistrolike place with candles and flowers on all tables, and a rustic Portuguese decor. The charming surroundings are completed by topnotch meals. Best here is the açorda de marisco (grated peasant bread, baked with a raw egg, spices, and seafood) for 70$ ($2.73), or a charcoal-broiled chicken, 55$ ($2.15). Another good selection is the ham and melon, 25$ (98¢), a perfect beginner.

Farta Pao, Estrada da Malveira, was originally a barn that has been converted into a restaurant—an ideal setting for country dining. The name of the restaurant means more you cannot eat. The large barnlike dining room has two huge open fireplaces, tiled floors, and rustic ornaments such as pitchforks, strings of garlic, hoes, and pots. Lighting is provided exclusively by kerosene lamps and candles. Outside is a terrace with more tables for al fresco dining.

You can start off your repast with a seafood soup for 45$ ($1.76), almost a meal in itself. Grilled sea bass goes for 55$ ($2.15), but the specialty is sargo da roca (white sea bass) which costs 80$ ($3.12) for two people. A huge veal steak for two is 100$ ($3.90). You can finish off with an orange pudding at 15$ (59¢). The house wine goes for 30$ ($1.17) a bottle. To find the Farta Pao, take the road to Malveira da Serra for about four kilometers, then turn left down a short dirt road when you see the sign on the right reading Cacos Velhos.

Snobissimo, 12 Rua Xavier Palmerim (tel. 28-21-25), is an art nouveau dream come true. It is a fun place for drinks and meals. The restaurant is so packed full of curious items and decorations that it takes half the evening just to look at everything. One room is a complete library; another has its walls covered with photographs of habitués. Within its rooms, on two floors, is a wealth of old mahogany, marble, and overscaled art nouveau sculpture. An aged bronze cash register clanks out your payment. Upstairs is a fabulous fin de siècle cocktail lounge and bar, with huge bronze statues, cartoons and photos of celebrities. One table is actually made out of an old roulette wheel. The owner, Paulo Guilherme, is an interior decorator.

Visit the Snobissimo any time between 6 p.m. and 3 a.m. Whiskey costs 60$ ($2.34); beer, 20$ (78¢); and soft drinks, 15$ (59¢). As for meals, onion soup goes for 30$ ($1.17); a special salad,

45$ ($1.76); creamed trout, 60$ ($2.34); and tournedos, 80$ ($3.12). For dessert, have the crêpe martiniquaise, 30$ ($1.17).

The Budget Range

Frango Real, José Frederico Ulrich (tel. 28-21-68), is a family affair. In honor of its namesake, Royal Hen, you are greeted at the door by an aroma of crusty, tender chicken turning a golden brown on a charcoal-fired spit. Manuel Caeiro Garcia heads the family management, assisted by his sister. Together they have created a rustic-style inn, with a trio of dining rooms (we prefer the one on the right with latticed ceiling and hand-hewn beams). For a plate of six sardines, you'll pay 40$ ($1.56). But the real reason for coming here is to order Frango Real assado no espeto (spit-roasted chicken) for 70$ ($2.73).

Game is also a specialty of the chef, particularly his perdiz de escabeche (partridge in a marinade) at 102$ ($3.98). For dessert, standard choices, always good, include a chocolate mousse at 14$ (55¢). An 8$ (31¢) cover is assessed.

Estribinho, Largo das Grutas (tel. 28-19-01), is a success story. This rustic tavern, offering some of the best, yet least expensive food in Cascais, is the fulfillment of the dream of one of two partners, Cezar Pereira and Fernando Jorge da Cruz Antunes. Originally, Senhor Pereira had gone to America to seek his fortune, becoming a marine captain in World War II, seeing action in Japan. Later, he returned to his home country to create this little restaurant, which surrounds his guests with Portuguese symbols of good country eating.

Hanging from the ceiling are garlands of onions, strings of peppers, pigtails of garlic, smoked sausages, pineapples, and glass steins. There's a rough wooden dado, with many nooks for intimate dining. Offering two levels, it's just off a little square to the right of the leading movie house of Cascais.

The menu is extensive. A soup of the day is always featured at 10$ (39¢), and you can try the chef's delicacy, shellfish soup, for 10$ also. A good main dish is the tournedos, 55$ ($2.15). The meat and poultry dishes are served with vegetables. The shellfish, especially the freshly gathered clams at 60$ ($2.34), are also well recommended. Each day a special sweet is offered, costing 15$ (59¢). For a change of pace, why not try the house sangría? The Estribinho is open most of the time: from 8 a.m. until 4 a.m.—a fine choice for off-hour snacks.

Costa Azul, 3 Rua Sebastiao José de Carvalho e Melo (tel. 28-11-40). The "Blue Coast" is likely to attract the natives of Cascais, not just the tourists. A blackboard standing out front announces the special regional fare of the day. The restaurant is usually crowded with hungry diners, and it may be difficult to get a table. All the typically Portuguese trappings are here, including pineapples, pigtails of garlic, and sprigs of bay leaf hanging from the ceiling. Often featured are clam soup at 14$ (55¢); pork Alentejano, 65$ ($2.54); and bacalhau (cod) à Costa Azul, 55$ ($2.15). Closed Tuesdays.

READERS' RESTAURANT SELECTIONS: "Os Doze Restaurante, 71 R. Frederico Arouca (tel. 28-53-34), offers some of the best food in Portugal. We especially like the appetizer—avocado stuffed with shrimp sauce—and the oxtail soup was also out of this world. My husband and I feel whatever your selection you'll find it well prepared and delicious. The service is good also, as is the selection of wines. If you have trouble making up your mind, the proprietor Mr. Baptista will make it up for you. He's a gem and makes everybody comfortable. The cavern-like restaurant is small, with a lounge in front. Port-oysters cost 40$ ($1.56); pâté, 23$ (90¢); turtle soup, 20$ (78¢); poached sea bass, 70$ ($2.73); chicken curry, 65$ ($2.54); pork chops, 65$ also; and a chocolate soufflé, 50$ ($1.95). It's closed Wednesdays" (Mr. and Mrs. James Borsil, Chicago, Ill.).... "In Cascais, we found a great family-style, family-run restaurant where our family of four ate soup, salad, and main course featuring meat or fish and potatoes or rice, with very good house wine, for under $12 (U.S.), including tip. People come from Lisbon to dine there at luncheon (1-3 p.m.) and dinner (8-10 p.m.). It is always crowded, so one should arrive about 12:45 or 7:45 so as not to have to wait for a table. The cafe is at **30 Rua de Bela Vista** (tel. 28-12-15). The owner is Ilidio Pereira, and the restaurant is staffed by what I gather to be four generations of Pereiras, and all of them, like the proprietor, are very friendly. The restaurant is on a street right behind the movie theater, and one of the sons speaks English if you need help in translating the menu" (Milo Gwosden, Palo Alto, Calif.).

3. Oitavos

Restaurante de Oitavos, Estrada do Guincho (tel. 28-92-77), is reached by a winding road. You arrive at a restaurant and teahouse on a plateau with a view of the coast. In the background loom the hills of Sintra. The restaurant is in the modern style, designed with glass walls to show off the view. The cuisine features regional fare. You might begin with a shrimp cocktail at 50$

($1.95), or perhaps grilled sardines at 25$ (98¢). For a main dish, it's best to stick to the fish dishes. Sole is prepared in an interesting number of ways, costing 80$ ($3.12). Frango (chicken) à piri-piri at 60$ ($2.34) is the "hottest" item on the menu. Among the desserts, the most lavish is a banana flambé at 25$ (98¢).

4. Guincho

Guincho means caterwaul, screech, shriek, yell—the cry that swallows make while darting among the air currents over the wild sea. These swallows at Guincho are to be seen year round, unlike their fickle fair weather counterparts at San Juan Capistrano, California. Sometimes at night, the sea—driven into a frenzy—howls like a wailing banshee—that, too, is guincho. The settlement itself is near the westernmost point on the European continent, known to the Portuguese as **Cabo da Roca.** The beaches are spacious and sandy; the sunshine incandescent; the nearby promontories, jutting out amidst white-tipped Atlantic waves, spectacular. The windswept dunes are backed by wooded hills, and to the east the Serra de Sintra is silhouetted upon the distant horizon.

The **Praia do Guincho** draws large beach crowds each season. However, it's wise to keep in mind the advice of Jennings Parrott, writing in the *International Herald Tribune:* "If you are caught up by the current, don't fight it. Don't panic. The wind forces it to circle, so you will be brought back to shore." A local fisherman, however, advises that you take a box lunch along. "Sometimes it takes several days to make this circle." The undertow is treacherous, be forewarned!

Guincho lies about four miles from Cascais, about six from Estoril. To reach it, you have to either drive or take a bus from Cascais for a fare of 12$ (47¢). One of the primary reasons for coming to Guincho is, of course, to sample its excellent seafood restaurants, described below. One can try, for example, the crayfish-sized, box-jawed lobsters known as bruxas, which in Portuguese means sorcerer, wizard, witch doctor, even a nocturnal moth. To be totally Portuguese, you must also sample the barnacles, called percêbes, meaning to perceive, to understand, to comprehend. After devouring these creatures, many foreign visitors fail to comprehend or perceive their popularity with the Portuguese. The fresh lobsters and crabs are cultivated in nearby shellfish beds, themselves a fascinating sight.

If you're staying over at one of the recommendations described below, the night calls of the "sirens" may enchant and enrapture you.

THE UPPER BRACKET: Hotel do Guincho (tel. 285-04-91) is a remake of a 16th-century fortress, standing on a rocky coast, not far from Cabo da Roca. Orson Welles once stayed here, fascinated by the mist and the surging roar of waves as they dashed against the stone cliffs.

You enter through a cloisterlike arcaded courtyard, with a four-sided balcony and four stone water wells. The one-time arsenal that once quartered troops now has de luxe bedrooms, all with private baths. The individualized bedrooms echo the castle's various architectural features: arched, deeply set windows, stone or plaster walls, plus an intelligent combination of antiques or reproductions. The charge is from 595$ ($23.21) to 665$ ($25.94) in a single, from 850$ ($33.15) to 950$ ($37.05) in a double.

There are several lounges, each richly decorated. To dine, you enter a spacious ocean-view room, with hand-embroidered draperies, high-backed chairs, and an overscaled antique armoire. The food and service are excellent. Lunch costs 170$ ($6.63); dinner 290$ ($11.31).

THE MEDIUM-PRICED RANGE: Estalagem Muchaxo, Praia do Guincho (tel. 285-0221), was begun more than 30 years ago as a simple straw hut set up on rugged wave-dashed rocks, with the father of the present owner selling brandy and coffee to the fishermen. Gradually, the senior Muchaxo started to cook for them. In time, beach-loving Germans discovered the place, and eventually even royalty, such as ex-king Umberto of Italy, arrived wanting to be fed.

Nowadays, the new has absorbed the old, although the straw shack remains to please traditionalists. António Muchaxo and his sons operate this over-blown hacienda, placing emphasis on the rustic blended with a mild dose of the contemporary. The estalagem is rectangular-shaped, with windows of bedrooms overlooking either the courtyard or the nearby coast and hills. At one side, thrust out onto rock walls, is a swimming pool with terraces and diving boards.

After a day of swimming guests gather in the châlet-style living room to warm themselves at the huge raised stone fireplace. They use a natural stone milling wheel as a coffee table and relax in rattan chairs brought in from Madeira.

There's a choice of two dining rooms, one modern, the other with bamboo ceiling, staccato black and white covered tables, and hand-painted provincial furniture. People drive from miles around just to sample the Muchaxo culinary wares, highly praised by such discriminating Iberian travelers as James A. Michener, author of *The Source, Hawaii,* and, of course, *Iberia.*

The adventurous will begin their meals with barnacles, 60$ ($2.34), described previously. The house specialty is lobster, Barraca style, for 245$ ($9.56), although an order of grilled sea bass is decidedly less expensive at 85$ ($3.32). A game dish worth recommending is partridge Barraca style, 95$ ($3.71). However, unless your throat is lined with asbestos, avoid ordering the chicken with piri-piri sauce—made with hot peppers from Angola. One diner is said to have fainted after tasting this concoction! An excellent finish to a meal here would be banana fritters, 20$ (78¢).

Those who want to anchor in will find a choice of 24 rooms in three price ranges—the most expensive directly overlooking the sea, the middle price group with side views of the ocean, and the cheapest facing the blue-green hills on the horizon. A single ranges from 300$ ($11.70) to 370$ ($14.43) nightly; a double from 435$ ($16.97) to 540$ ($21.06). Two persons can stay here, taking all their meals, for 975$ ($38.03) to 1,080$ ($42.12) per day. All rooms have private baths, telephones, and central heating.

Each bedroom is unique, though most of them have basic stark white walls with beamed ceilings. Original use is made of provincial hand-painted furniture and accessories. Carved ox yokes serve as headboards for the beds, and the floors are spotted with black and white calfskin rugs.

A BUDGET INN: **Mar do Guincho Estalagem,** Praia do Guincho (tel. 28-90-51). While this modern inn—also known as Mestre Zé—contains relatively inexpensive bedrooms, its success stems from its superb kitchen. With the help of his brother, the owner Joaquim Pereira Cardoso started the business many years ago in a crude straw hut. Today he can look with pride at a plaque from *Holiday* magazine, honoring his establishment as one of the most outstanding in Portugal.

The stone inn is simple, uncluttered—rather starkly modern—set on a low cliff, with its bedrooms and dining room facing the pounding surf. From the à la carte menu, you can order freshly made shrimp soup for only 10$ (39¢). Oysters are difficult to obtain, but when they appear on the menu, they go for 8$ (31¢) apiece.

Shellfish is the house specialty, although the prices are beyond the means of many diners. However, you can order shrimp, barnacles, stuffed crab, and grilled lobster. The sweet-tasting, freshly caught clams—served in their natural state—can be a smooth compromise at 60$ ($2.34). Meat eaters will find an excellent pork Alentejano for 90$ ($3.51). A wide range of fruits from the Portuguese heartland is offered for dessert, along with such sweets as queijadinhas de amêndoa, a kind of almond cheese cupcake, 4$50 (18¢).

If you're staying over, you should take the full-pension plan: 280$ ($10.92) to 290$ ($11.31) in a single, 487$ ($18.99) to 500$ ($19.50) in a double. Slightly cheaper rooms are available sans sea view. The bedrooms contain private baths and balconies, but there are no social lounges. If you're tempted to stay here, you'll dine well, living informally in casual attire, sunbathing, playing in the surf, and falling asleep listening to the constant rhythm of the surf breaking on the rocks below your balcony.

Back in Lisbon, we strike out this time on quite a different excursion:

5. Queluz

On the highway to Sintra, just 9½ miles from the capital, Queluz shimmers in the sunlight—a brilliant example of the rococo in Portugal. An evocation of the 18th century is effected by the faded cotton candy decoration, inspired in part by Versailles.

Pedro III ordered its construction in 1747, and the work dragged on until 1787. The architect Mateus Vicente de Oliveira was later joined by French decorator and designer Jean-Baptiste Robillon. The latter was largely responsible for the planning of the garden and lakeland setting, through which the promiscuous queen Carlotta Joaquina—with her beet-colored nose jutting forth—raced to her next indiscretion.

A fire in 1934 destroyed a great deal of Queluz, but tasteful and sensitive reconstruction has restored the light-hearted aura of the 18th century.

The topiary effects, with closely trimmed vines and sculptured box hedges, are highlighted by blossoming mauve petunias and red geraniums. Lavender, purplish-red porphyry, and pink are the colors on the palette. Fountain pools on which lilies float are lined with blue azulejos (earthenware tiles), reflecting the muted facade, the statuary, and the finely cut balustrades.

Inside, you can wander through the dressing room of the Queen, lined with painted panels depicting a children's romp; stroll through the Don Quixote Chamber (Dom Pedro was born here and returned from Brazil to die in the same bed); pause in the Music Room, complete with a French grande pianoforte, an 18th-century English harpsichord, and a gilded sacrificial patera; and stand in the mirrored throne room adorned with glittering crystal chandeliers. In the way that the Spanish use La Granja, the Portuguese still hold state banquets here.

Festooning the palace are all the eclectic props of the romantic era—the inevitable chinoiserie panels (these from the Portuguese overseas province of Macao); Florentine marbles from quarries once worked by Michelangelo; Iberian and Flemish tapestries; Empire antiques; indigo blue ceramics from Delft; 18th-century Hepplewhite armchairs; porcelains from Austria; carpets from Rabat; Portuguese Chippendale furnishings; and wood pieces (jacaranda) from Brazil—all of which are of exquisite quality. When he visited Portugal, former President Eisenhower was housed in the 30-chambered Pavilion of D. Maria I, as was Queen Elizabeth II on another occasion. These storybook chambers, refurbished by the Portuguese government, are said to have reverberated with the rantings of the grief-stricken mad monarch Maria I, who, it is alleged, had to be strapped to her bed at times.

The admission to the palace is a well-spent 5$ (20¢); the hours from 10 a.m. to 5 p.m., except on Thursdays when it is closed. From Lisbon, you can visit Queluz by a train departing from the central station at The Rossio.

DINING IN AN 18TH-CENTURY KITCHEN: Cozinha Velha (Old Kitchen), Palácio Nacional de Queluz (tel. 95-02-32). If you have only two or three meals in all of Portugal, take one of them here. Once it was the kitchen of the palace, built in the grand style; now it has been converted into a colorful dining room that finds favor with gourmets, royalty, and the average tourist seeking a romantic setting for a fine dinner.

The entrance is through a miniature garden patio. The dining room is like a small chapel, with high stone arches, a walk-in free-standing fireplace, marble columns, and the original spits. Along one side is a 20-foot marble chef's table that's a virtual still life of the culinary skill of the chef—augmented by baskets of fruit and vases of semi-tropical flowers. You sit on tall ladderback chairs in a setting of shiny copper, oil paintings, and torchiers. And the skillfully trained waitresses are costumed in regional dress.

Fortunately, meals are served seven days a week (luncheon, noon to 3 p.m.; dinner, 7:30 to 10). The 160$ ($6.24) table d'hôte is excellent and includes soup (such as creamed vegetable made with the rich essence of locally grown produce), a fish dish (perhaps sole meunière), followed by a meat platter, then dessert.

From the à la carte menu, you can order such house specialties as a tournedó à Cozinha Velha, 115$ ($4.49); filet mignon Béarnaise, 100$ ($3.90); or spit-roasted pork-the way a former king liked it—for 85$ ($3.32). Choosing an appropriate dessert from the trolley requires the wisdom of Solomon.

6. Sintra

"It is indeed a fairytale setting and gives one the feeling that this is where Sleeping Beauty must have rested all those years." These were the words of a publicist singing the praises of Sintra. Writers have been doing that ever since Portugal's greatest poet Luís Vas de Camoes proclaimed its glory in "Os Lusíadas" (The Portuguese).

Lord Byron called it "glorious Eden" when he and his companion John Cam Hobhouse included Sintra in their grand tour of 1809. Subsequently, English romantics thrilled to the description in the poet's autobiographical "Childe Harold."

Picture a town on a hillside, decaying "birthday cake" villas covered with azulejos coming loose in the damp mist hovering like a veil over Sleeping Beauty. What would Sintra be without its luxuriant vegetation? It's all here; camellias for melancholic romantics, ferns behind which lizards dart, pink and purple bougainvillea crawling over garden trelliswork, red geraniums sitting out on wrought-iron balconies, eucalyptus branches fluttering in the wind, lemon trees studding the groves, succulent strawberries weighing down plants in the surrounding countryside, and honey-sweet mimosa scenting the air.

Be duly warned: there are those who visit Sintra, fall under its spell, and stay forever!

Sintra is one of the oldest towns in the country. When the Christian Crusaders captured it in 1147, they fought bitterly against the Moors firmly entrenched in their hilltop castle, the ruins of which remain today.

The town, 18 miles from Lisbon, is on the northern slope of the granite Sintra Range. A 45-minute train ride from the neo-Manueline-style railway station at The Rossio in Lisbon will deposit you here. Visitors staying in the Costa do Sol hotels can make bus connections at both Cascais and Estoril. Sintra is also visited on many organized tours departing from Lisbon, although this latter method allows no time for personal discovery—which is essentially what Sintra is all about.

Of its many residents today, the best known is the Count of Paris, the pretender to the throne of France. Now aging, he is seldom seen in Sintra itself. Writing in the *New York Times,* Charlotte Curtis noted: "He is a gentleman farmer whose dairy supplies the best tables in Lisbon. On a good day, he may be found in his barn, milking the cows."

THE SIGHTS: The specific sights of Sintra are set forth below, but the task of selection is difficult. Byron put it well: "Ah me! What hand can pencil guide, or pen, to follow half on which the eye dilates."

Opening onto the central square of the resort town is the:

National Palace of Sintra

Until 1910 this was a royal palace. Its last royal inhabitant was Queen Maria Pía, the Italian grandmother of Manuel II, the last king of Portugal. Much of the palace was constructed in the days of the first Manuel the Fortunate.

Outside, two conically shaped chimneys tower into the sky, forming the most distinctive landmark on the Sintra skyline. Long before the arrival of the conquering Christian Crusaders under Afonso Henriques, this was a summer palace of Moorish sultans, filled with dancing harem girls who performed in front of bubbling fountains. Although the original was torn down, the Moorish style of architecture was incorporated in latter day versions of the palace. The entire effect is rather a conglomeration of styles, with Gothic and the original Manueline predominant.

The glazed earthenware tiles or azulejos lining many of the chambers are among the best you'll find in Portugal. Joao I, one of the founding kings, was fond of the Swan Room. Joao was the father of Henry the Navigator and the husband of Philippa of Lancaster.

It is said that one day the English Queen came upon her king embracing one of the ladies of the court. Apparently, she did not hold a grudge against him for this one indiscretion, but it grew into a court scandal of which the king became painfully aware. Hoping to end speculation and save his wife further embarrassment, he called in his decorators and gave them a secret mission. The room was locked. When the doors were finally opened to the ladies of the court, they marched in, only to discover that the ceiling was covered with magpies. The symbol of the chattering birds scored a point, and a new subject of gossip was discovered. Guides now call the salon the Chamber of the Magpies.

The Room of the Sirens or Mermaids is one of the most elegant in the palace. In the Heraldic or Stag Room, coats-of-arms of aristocratic Portuguese families and hunting scenes are depicted. From most of these rooms, wide windows look out onto attractive vistas of the Sintra mountain range. Tile-fronted stoves are found in the Old Kitchen, where the feasts of yore were held, especially game banquets in the reign of Carlos I, the king assassinated in 1908.

The palace is rich in paintings and Iberian and Flemish tapestries. But it is at its best when you wander into a tree and plant-shaded patio and listen to the water of a fountain. Perhaps the young king Sebastiao sat here lost in the dreams of glory that would one day take him and his country on an ill-fated mission to North Africa—a mission that would cost him his life.

As you approach the palace, you can buy a ticket at the kiosk on your left. The cost is only 5$, one of the best investments you'll make in all of Portugal. Visiting hours are daily from 10 a.m. to 5 p.m., except on Thursdays when it is closed.

The Pena Palace

Towering over Sintra, this palace appeals to special tastes. From its perch on a plateau about 1,500 feet above sea level, it stands like a medieval fortress on one peak, looking at the ruins of the old Moorish castle on the opposite hill. Part of the fun of visiting it is the ride up the verdant winding road, through the Praque da Merendas.

At the top you come upon a form of Wagnerian fantasy, perhaps something the mad Bavarian, Ludwig, would have constructed. This castle in the sky was called a "soaring agglomeration of towers, cupolas, and battlemented walls" by *National Geographic*. The inspiration behind it was Ferdinand of Saxe-Coburg-Gotha, the husband of Maria II.

Of course, Ferdinand needed a German to help him build this fantasy. While dreams of the Middle Ages danced in his head, the Baron Eschwedge arrived. You can still see a sculptured likeness of the Baron by looking out from the Pena at a huge rock across the way. Romantically, the architect fancied himself a soldier, armed with a halberd.

In the early 16th century, Manuel the Fortunate had ordered a monastery built on these lofty grounds for the Jerónimos monks. Even today you can visit a cloister and a small ogival chapel that the latter-day builders decided to preserve.

Crossing over a drawbridge, you'll enter the palace proper, whose last royal occupant was Queen Amélia. On a long-ago morning in 1910, she clearly saw that monarchy in Portugal was drawing to an end. Having already lost her husband and her soldier son two years before, she was determined not to lose her second offspring, the king Manuel II. Gathering her most precious items and only the small family heirlooms that could be packed quickly, she fled to Mafra where her son was waiting.

Behind she left Pena Palace and was not to see it again until 1945, when she returned to Portugal under much more favorable conditions. Pena has remained much as Amélia left it, and that is part of its fascination; it emerges as a rare record of European royal life in the halcyon days preceding World War I.

For an entrance fee of only 5$ (20¢), you can visit the palace daily from 10 a.m. until 5 p.m., except on Tuesday when it is closed.

Pena Park was designed and planted in a four-year span beginning in 1846. Again, Ferdinand was the controlling factor behind the landscaping. What he achieved was one of the most spectacular parks in Portugal, known for the scope of its plant and tree life. For an eye-opening vista of the park and the palace, you can make the ascent to **Cruz Alta.**

Forming the third member of the palace-castle triumvirate is . . .

The Moorish Castle

The fortification—the Castelo dos Mouros—had been around for a long time when Scandinavian Crusaders in 1147 besieged and successfully captured it from its Moorish occupants. It was built sometime between the 8th and 9th centuries at a position 1,350 feet above sea level. The consort of Maria II, Ferdinand, the German responsible for Pena Palace, attempted restoration in the 19th century, but was relatively unsuccessful.

To reach its decaying ramparts, you take a path that's a 10-minute walk. The path branches off from the road Parque de Merendas (a small sign points the way). There's a parking area for your car, and a guide will send you off in the right direction. Once you're there, the view is spectacular.

The following and final sight within Sintra is missed by too many visitors —and what a pity! It's one of the gems.

Monserrate

One Englishman, Francis Cook, between 1846 and 1850 set out to make Lord Byron's dream of a glorious Eden even more of a reality. Bringing in landscape artists and flora from everywhere—from Africa to Norway—he planned a botanical garden, the rival of which is not to be found either in Spain or Portugal.

The garden scales the slope of a hill—paths cut through to hidden oases— and you need to give it the better part of an afternoon. Walking back is rough on all but seasoned hill scalers. However, it's worth the descent.

At the bottom, Cook built his **Palácio de Monserrate.** It seemed that in his Eden, only a Moorish temple would do. But when Cook died, Monserrate faced a troubled future. An English manufacturer purchased the property and set out virtually to destroy Cook's dreams. He began by selling the antiques in the Palácio, and it's said that he made so much money on the sale that he was paid back for all the cash he sank into Monserrate. He wasn't satisfied. When news leaked out to Lisbon that he was going to subdivide the park and turn it into a housing development of villas, the government belatedly intervened— and well that it did. When you see Monserrate, you'll surely agree that it belongs to all the people, preserved and well-maintained.

Lilies float on cool fountains, flowers scent the air, ferns scale the hillside, northern spruce grows tall, and flora from Africa thrives as if it were in its native habitat. Charging no entrance fee, the park is open from 10 a.m. to 7 p.m.

One final stopover—lying outside of Sintra—merits exploration:

Convento de Santa Cruz dos Capuchos

Dom Alvaro de Castro ordered that this curiously structured convent be built for the Capuchins in 1560. Cork was used so extensively in its construction that it is sometimes known as the cork monastery.

You walk up a moss-covered path, like a wayfarer of old approaching for his dole. Ring the bell, and a guide—not a monk—will appear to show you in and out of the miniature cells. The convent is in a secluded area, 4½ miles from Sintra.

It appears forlorn, forgotten. At its finest hour, it probably wasn't too lively. The Capuchins who lived here—perhaps eight in all—had a penchant for the most painstaking of detailed work. For example, they lined the walls of their monastery with cork bark tiles and seashells. They also carved a chapel out of rock, using cork for insulation.

When making toilets or "refrigerators," they displayed ingenuity. A hospital was even installed into the most cramped of quarters. Their monastery is perhaps the coziest in the world. Outside, one of them found time to fresco an altar in honor of St. Francis of Assisi.

In 1834, they left suddenly; but fortunately the curiosity they left behind wasn't destroyed by vandals. The convent can be visited today without an admission charge, though it's customary to tip the guide who shows you through.

DINING IN AN 18TH-CENTURY STYLE: Hotel Palácio de Seteais, Seteais, Sintra (tel. 293-3200), is Portugal's most romantic dream palace converted into a hotel. Lord Byron worked on "Childe Harold" in the front garden. The palace is approached via a long private encircling driveway, past shade trees, a wide expanse of lawn, yew hedges, and the silhouette of the building itself. The stone-built architecture is formal, dominated by an arched entryway.

Seteais looks older than it is, having been built in the late 18th century by a Dutch Gildemeister. It was subsequently taken over and restored by the fifth Marquis le Marialva, who sponsored many receptions and galas for the aristocrats of his day.

The palácio is on the crest of a hill, with most of its drawing rooms, galleries, and chambers overlooking the lower formal terraces, flower garden, and a vista toward the sea. Upon entering there is a long galleried hall, a dramatic staircase, with white and gilt balustrades and columns, leading to the lower-level dining room, drinking lounge, and garden terraces.

Along the corridor are museum-caliber tapestries, groupings of formal French, Italian, and Portuguese furniture, and a hand woven decorative carpet. On the left is a library and an adjoining music room, furnished tastefully with period pieces.

The main drawing room is an achievement, with its blend of antiques dominated by a fine mural extending around the cove and onto the ceiling. Large bronze chandeliers with crystal add to the luster. The guest book reads like a Who's Who: glowing comments from Nelson Rockefeller, Richard Nixon, Gloria Swanson, Claudette Colbert.

However, don't just drive up to the entrance and expect to be given shelter. There are only 18 rooms (almost all with private bath), so advance reservations may be needed. Housed in beautiful rooms furnished with antiques or reproductions, you'll pay from 465$ ($18.14) for one person to 660$ ($25.74) for two, breakfast, service, and taxes included. The inclusive rate goes from 825$ ($32.18) for one person to 1,380$ ($53.82) for two.

Lunch or dinner is special, and it's possible to come here just for your meal. In summer, the tables are graced with low clusters of pink or blue hydrangea from the garden and each is set with stemware and silver.

The set meal of 180$ ($7.02) consists of four courses, with dishes such as turbot in a cream sauce browned in the oven with spinach. The hors d'oeuvres are among the best, especially the crayfish and fish mousse. The dessert trolley is intriguing—pastries with light rich cream blended with a flaky crust and fruits. After-dinner coffee is taken on the adjoining terrace and loggia or else in the dining room.

As is obvious, the Palácio de Seteais wins our warmest, unqualified praise. The palace is under the able direction of Alberto de Vasconcelos.

Galeria Real, Rua Tude de Sousa, in Sao Pedro de Sintra (tel. 98-16-61), is a unique mixture of antique galleries and an 18th-century-style restaurant. The Galeria Real is one of the most impressive looking places in Portugal. On the ground floor is a cocktail lounge as well as eight shops crammed with antiques, busts, and paintings. Going up a balustraded staircase, you come to further antique shops and a sumptuous restaurant, lorded over by Francisco Correia. The main dining room has a hand-painted, beamed ceiling, tiled floors, small wooden frame windows, flowers on each table, carved wooden chairs, and candles. All this is a perfect setting for unhurried dining in a royal fashion. Each day there is a special menu for 136$50 ($5.32) for lunch and dinner which might start with a cream of tomato soup or a melon cocktail, followed by a filet of sole or a queijada de bacalhau (a codfish soufflé which is a specialty of the house). The final course might be veal cutlets or a steak, followed by assorted desserts. A la carte entries include sole for 75$ ($2.93); or tournedo Galeria Real, 88$ ($3.43). Good are the chicken shishkebab and the espeteda de frango, both 88$ also.

BUDGET HOTELS AND RESTAURANTS: Central Hotel, 35 Largo da Rainha D. Amélia (tel. 98-00-63), should be given a heavy check with your pencil if you prefer a charming family-owned-and-operated village inn offering personalized accommodations and good food. The hotel opens onto the main square of Sintra, facing the National Palace.

The owner Laura de Jesus Raio, along with her son and daughter-in-law, have created a homelike inn. The facade is inviting, with decorative blue and white tiles and an awning-covered front veranda with dining tables.

The interior, especially the bedrooms, reflects the English background of the owners (they lived in Surrey, near London, for seven years and have accumulated some excellent antiques). Each room is furnished individually, with a reliance on fine old pieces—polished woods, inlaid desks, and lots more. The baths, one to nearly every room, are well designed, with tiles and happy colors.

The cost for one person in a room with bath is 200$ ($7.80) nightly, increasing to 260$ ($10.14) for two. You'll be charged 25$ (98¢) for breakfast, 110$ ($4.29) for a complete luncheon or dinner. The most economical way is to order all of your meals for only 760$ ($29.44) full pension for two.

The restaurant of the Central offers a choice of dining on the veranda overlooking the village, or in one of the large interior rooms. The cooking is primarily Portuguese, with such main courses featured as escalopes of veal in a Madeira sauce, 65$ ($2.54); veal cutlet Milanese, 65$ also; beef Portuguese, 65$; and châteaubrian for two, 110$ ($4.29). A traditional dessert, homemade caramel cup custard, goes for 15$ (59¢).

A set meal is also offered for 110$ ($4.29). One typical repast included an omelette with kidney sauce, followed by a white fish dish with a salad, then roasted veal, a cake, fruit, coffee, and a half bottle of the regional wine.

To quote the Senhora, with her snowy white hair and sweet face, "My son says I'm everyone's mother—and wants me to refrain. But I say, I am this way."

Estalagem da Raposa, 3 Rua Alfredo Costa (tel. 980-465), formerly was a private home which belonged to an old Sintra family. It's been run as an inn for the last quarter of a century. It's centrally located, within walking distance of the railroad station. The house is set back from the street in a fenced and flowered yard.

The inn is owned by a Lisbon family and is under the able attention of Mrs. Margarita Araujo, who speaks French and English. A charming woman, Mrs. Araujo makes you feel at home immediately. She keeps a careful eye on the housekeeping and upkeep of the 10 high-ceilinged rental units. Rooms all have tile baths, and they're furnished with old-fashioned pieces that are homey and comfortable.

Singles are 170$ ($6.63) daily; doubles, 260$ ($10.14). A single person in a suite is charged 210$ ($8.19); two persons, 300$ ($11.70). The maid who keeps the rooms in spotless condition is polite, and she runs right up with a ring of keys to open your door the moment she hears you on the carpeted stairs.

7. Mafra Palace

This baroque chef d'oeuvre of precision craftsmanship is an ensemble of discipline, grandeur, and majesty. At the peak of its construction, it is said to have employed a working force of 50,000 Portuguese men. A small town was built just to house the huge corps, the cream of the crop of a small nation's working force.

Its master model was El Escorial, that Daedalian maze constructed by Philip II outside Madrid. Mafra's corridors and complex immurements may not be as impressive, nor as labyrinthine, but the diversity of its contents is amazing. The end product was 880 rooms, housing 300 friars, who could walk through 5,000 doorways, stare out of 2,500 windows.

That devout king of "peace and prosperity," Joao V, seemingly couldn't sire an heir, and court gossips openly speculated that he was sterile. One day he casually mentioned to a Franciscan that if he were rewarded with an heir, he would erect a monastery to the order. Apparently, the Franciscans—through what the king considered "divine intervention"—came through. Joao produced his heir, and Mafra was born, the work actually beginning in 1717. Originally, it was to house 13 friars, but that figure rapidly mushroomed into 300, as the Franciscans had a population explosion uniquely their own!

It is said that Mafra—13 years in the making—was built with gold and diamonds pouring in from the new colony of Brazil. Seeing it now, and considering building methods in those days, one wonders how such a huge task was ever completed in so short a time.

Its more than 110 chimes, made in Antwerp, can be heard from a distance of 12 to 15 miles when they are played at Sunday recital. Holding the chimes are two towers which flank a basilica, capped by a dome that has been compared to that of St. Paul's in London. The inside of the church is a varied assortment of chapels, 11 in all, expertly crafted with detailed jasper rerердос, bas-reliefs, and marble statues from Italy (the musculature of St. Sebastian is awesome!).

In the monastery is found the pride of Mafra—a 35,000-volume library with tomes two and three hundred years old, many gold leafed. Viewed by some more favorably than the world-famed library at Coimbra, the room is a study in gilded light, decorated in what has been called grisaille rococo. In the Museum of Religious Art, the collection of elaborately decorated vestments is outstanding.

Following the omnipresent red Sintra marble, you enter the monks' pharmacy, hospital, and infirmary—the beds sans mattresses. Later, you can explore the spacious kitchens and the penitents' cells, with the flagellation devices used by the monks.

The summer residence of kings, Mafra was home to such members of Portuguese royalty as the banished queen Carlotta Joaquina. In addition to his love of painting, Carlos I, the Braganza king assassinated at Black Horse Square in 1908, was also an avid hunter. In one room, he had chandeliers made out of antlers, upholstery of animal skins. His son, who ruled for two years as Manuel II, spent his last night on Portuguese soil at Mafra, fleeing with his mother Amélia to England.

You can wander through the trompe l'oeil-ceilinged audience room; through the sewing room of the mad Maria I; the music room of Carlos. Throughout the apartments hang decaying tapestries, taking their place in a setting of antiques, ceramics, and silverware.

The charge for admission is 5$ (20¢); the hours from 10 a.m. to 5 p.m. From Sintra, you can make bus connections to Mafra, about 25 miles from Lisbon.

8. Ericeira

Just 32 miles from Lisbon and a quick 13 miles across the countryside from Sintra, this fishing village nestles on the Atlantic shore. Its narrow streets are lined with brilliant whitewashed houses, accented by bright pastel-painted corners and window frames. To the east, the mountains of Sintra appear on the horizon.

The sea has been giving life to Ericeira for 700 years and continues to do so today. Not only do the fishermen pluck their food from the sea, but it is the sea, especially the beach, that lures streams of tourists every summer—adding a much-needed shot in the arm to the local economy. Along the coast lobsters are bred in cliffside nurseries (serraçao)—any place in Ericeira, especially at the Hotel Turismo da Ericeira, lagosta is la specialité de la maison!

In 1584 Mateus Álvares arrived in Ericeira from the Azores, claiming to be the king Sebastiao (The Desired One), who was killed (some say disappeared) on the battlefields of North Africa. Álvares and about two dozen of his chief supporters were finally executed after their defeat by the soldiers of Philip II of Spain; but he is today remembered as the King of Ericeira. It wasn't until an October day in 1910 that the second monumental event occurred at Ericeira. From the harbor, the fleeing Manuel II and his mother Amélia set sail on their yacht to a life of exile in England. The House of Bragança—monarchy itself—had collapsed in Portugal.

For such a small place, there are quite a few sights of religious and historic interest in Ericeira. The **Church of Sao Pedro** (St. Peter) and the **Misericórdia** (charitable institution) both contain rare 17th- and 18th-century paintings. The **Hermitage of St. Sebastiao,** with its Moorish designs, would seem more fitting in North Africa. Rounding out the ecclesiastical ring is one more hermitage, this one dedicated to **St. Anthony.**

The chloride-rich spring waters (radioactive) of **Santa Maria** are popular with health-spa enthusiasts. But it is the crescent-shaped sandy **Praia do Sol** that is the favorite of Portuguese and foreign visitors alike. Ericeira maintains bus connections with both Sintra and Lisbon (you can also take the train from Lisbon to Mafra, where bus connections can be made).

9. Vale do Lobos

This often forlorn-looking "Valley of the Wolves" is a popular Sorrento Secreto for lovers, or a place where soccer players like to rest and recuperate between matches at its only hotel. The immediate environs are peaceful and tranquil, the gentle wooded hills rolling into the distance.

Some 12½ miles north of Lisbon, the Vale is reached via Queluz and Belas, heading in the direction of Sabugo before turning off to the right. At a spot some 1,000 feet above sea level, in a tree-studded valley, the following establishment was erected.

A BUDGET HOTEL: Vale do Lobos Hotel, Vale do Lobos, Sabugo (tel: 29-28-43). This one-time private villa was converted more than 12 years ago into a country inn-hotel, created expressly for those seeking a tranquil retreat. Wedding receptions are held here—there's even a honeymoon suite so couples won't have far to go! Lovers of nature enjoy the garden walks, the open-air swimming pool surrounded by flagstone terraces, and the pathways lined with blue and pink hydrangeas and red geraniums.

The bedrooms themselves, 30 in all with private bath, are small, but quite comfortable and attractive, with old-fashioned provincial-style furniture (high headboards, for example). The tariff for a single room ranges from 120$ ($4.68) to 160$ ($6.24). For a double the price jumps from 165$ ($6.44) to 300$ ($11.30), depending on the size of the room and the view. With full board, a single person pays from 328$ ($12.80) to 364$ ($14.20); two persons, 560$ ($21.84) to 620$ ($24.18).

There are a number of cheerful lounge rooms—homelike, very Portuguese. Dining here is enjoyable—three walls of windows overlooking the garden and its trellis of purple bougainvillea. Many drive all the way out from Lisbon on an excursion to sample the good-tasting home cooking. A table d'hôte is offered, including, say, caldo verde (a potato and cabbage soup), then a fish dish, a mixed salad, perhaps Valencian paella, a dessert, and the fruit of the season, all costing only 85$. You don't have to be a guest of the hotel to drop in for dinner.

Now that we've seen, sampled, and eaten our way through the environs, we'll return to Lisbon.

Chapter VII

THE SIGHTS OF LISBON

1. The Alfama
2. Belém
3. Museums and Galleries
4. The Churches of Lisbon
5. A Bullfight Spectacle
6. Other Sights

IN LISBON IT'S STILL a case of the frame competing with the picture. Although the Portuguese capital offers many worthwhile attractions, its Lorelei environs echo a siren call that few can resist. Many guests end up using Lisbon only as a base, while venturing forth during the day to Lord Byron's "variegated maze of mount and glen" at Sintra, to the sandy beaches along the Portuguese Riviera (Estoril and Cascais), to the monastery and royal palace at Mafra, even as far north as the fishing villages of Nazaré or Fátima where three shepherd children claimed to have seen a vision of the Virgin Mary on May 13, 1917.

One reason Lisbon gets overlooked is that enough time isn't budgeted for it. One or two days simply isn't adequate for Lisbon and the environs. A minimum of five days is needed. Another reason is that the attractions of Lisbon remain relatively unknown. Seemingly, every stone in Rome has been documented or recorded by someone. But in talks with literally dozens of visitors, the question most often asked is, "What does one do in Lisbon?"

This chapter hopes to answer that question, specifically with regard to sightseeing. If your time is limited, and you can cope only with the musts, then you should explore (1) the **Coach Museum**, (2) **Jerónimos Monastery**, (3) the **Alfama** and the **Castle of St. George** (for the view if nothing else). At least two art museums, although not of the caliber of Madrid's Prado, merit attention: (1) the **National Art Gallery** and (2) the **Gulbenkian Center for Arts and Culture.**

These sights are rated for those in a hurry. Readers who enjoy more leisure time can visit the **Fundaçao Richardo do Espírito Santa Silva** and watch reproductions of antiques being turned out, decaying tapestries repaired, books gold-leafed; or you can see the gilded royal galleys at the **Naval Museum;** or wander through the **fish market;** or explore the arts and crafts of a **Belém folk museum,** and lots more.

More importantly, the Lisbon voyager will discover—just by walking its streets—a city unique in the world, a capital that extended its power across continents.

LISBON: SIGHTSEEING 87

At the entrance to the castle, visitors pause at the "Castle Belvedere." The Portuguese refer to this spot as their ancient window overlooking the Alfama, the Serras of Monsanto and of Sintra, the Ponte 25 de Abril spanning the Tagus, Commerce Square, and the tiled roofs of the Portuguese capital. In the square stands an heroic statue—sword in one hand, shield in the other—of the first king, Afonso Henriques, who freed Lisbon from its Moorish conquerors.

Inside the castle grounds, you can stroll through a setting of olive, pine, and cork trees—all graced by the appearance of a flamingo. In bad weather when rain is sweeping the city, you'll focus on a cannon and think of the massacres that must have occurred on this blood-soaked hill. On a fair day, you'll perhaps notice that only the willows weep or the oleander dazzles. Swans with white bodies and black necks glide in a silence shattered by the blood curdling scream of the rare white peacock.

In the one building remaining of the former royal palace—known as The Alcáçova—you can see Roman and Islamic tombstones. For a more detailed survey, borrow a pair of binoculars. Open every day from 9 a.m. till sunset, the castle may be visited without charge.

THE CATHEDRAL (SÉ): Even the tourist literature admits that the Cathedral is "not very rich." Characterized by twin towers flanking its entrance, it represents an architectural wedding of Romanesque and Gothic. The facade is severe enough for a medieval fortress, and like many European cathedrals, it has had so many different architectural fathers that it is truly a stylistic bastard. And then the devastation caused by the earthquakes of 1344 and 1755 didn't help either.

At one point in its history, the site of the present Sé was allegedly used by the Saracens as a holy mosque. When the city was captured by Christian Crusaders—led by Portugal's first king, Afonso Henriques—the structure was rebuilt. That early date in the 12th century makes the Sé the oldest church in Lisbon.

Inside are housed many treasures, such as the font where St. Anthony of Padua is said to have been christened in 1195. A notable feature is the Gothic chapel of Bartolomeu Joanes, constructed in the 14th century. Other interesting sidelights include a crib by Machado de Castro (the Portuguese sculptor of the 18th century who did the equestrian statue on Black Horse Square); the sarcophagus of Lopo Fernandes Pacheco, dating from the 14th century; and the original nave and aisles.

To visit the sacristy and cloister requires a guide and a 2$50 (10¢) admission ticket. The cloister, built in the 14th century by King Dinis, is of ogival construction, with garlands, a Romanesque wrought-iron grill, and tombs with inscription stones. In the sacristy are housed marbles, relics, valuable images, and pieces of ecclesiastical treasure from the 15th and 16th centuries.

Whether you're Catholic or not, you may want to attend a service here—if for no other reason than to see the scarlet red robes of the priests—a miniature medieval pageant. If viewed in the morning, the stained-glass reflections on the floor evoke a Monet painting.

At Largo da Sé, the church may be visited from 9 a.m. till 6 p.m. Although within walking distance of Black Horse Square, it can be reached by taking streetcar 28 (Estrêla) or 11 (Graça).

Facing the Cathedral is:

SANTO ANTONIO DA SÉ: St. Anthony of Padua was born in 1195 in a house that stood on this spot at Largo de Santo António da Sé. In the crypt, a guide will show you the alleged spot where the saint was born. The original church was destroyed by the earthquake of 1755, and the present building was designed by Mateus Vicente in the 18th century.

Although buried at Padua, Italy, this itinerant Franciscan monk remains the patron saint of Portugal. The devout come to this little church to light candles under his picture. He is known as a protector of young brides.

As a saint, he also has a special connection with the children of Lisbon. To erect the altar at the church, the children of the Alfama built miniature altars with a representation of the patron saint on them to raise money.

June 12 of every year is designated as St. Anthony's Day—a time of merry making, heavy eating, and drinking. In the morning there are street fires and singing, climaxed by St. Anthony's Feast on the following day.

2. Belém

At Belém, where the Tagus (Tejo in Portuguese) meets the sea, the caravels were launched on their missions: Vasco da Gama to India; Ferdinand Magellan to circumnavigate the globe; Dias to round the Cape of Good Hope.

Belém emerged from the Restelo—that point or strand of land from which the ships set sail across the Sea of Darkness. As riches, especially spices, poured back into Portugal, Belém flourished. Great monuments, such as the Belém Tower and Jerónimos Monastery, were built and embellished in the Manueline style.

In time the royal family establish.... summer palace here. Much of the character of the district came about when wealthy Lisboans began moving out and erecting town houses. For many years Belém was a separate municipality, eventually, however, becoming incorporated into Lisbon as a parish.

Nowadays it's a major target for sightseers, as it's a virtual monument-studded museumland.

For most visitors, the first sight is:

THE TOWER OF BELÉM: This quadrangular tower on the Avenida Marginal is a monument to Portugal's Age of Discovery. Erected in the Manueline style between 1515 and 1520, the tower is the most classic landmark in Portugal, often used on documents and brochures as a symbol of the country itself.

It has been called a symbol of Portugal's great military and naval past. Erected in the reign of Manuel the Fortunate, the tower stands on or near the spot where the caravels set out.

Architect Francisco de Arruda blended a potpourri of styles: Romanesque, Gothic, even Moorish—all flavored by the Manueline style, characterized by such devices as twisting ropes of stone. The coat-of-arms of Manuel I rests above the loggia, and balconies grace three sides of the monument. The stone crosses along the balustrade of the loggia symbolize the Portuguese Crusaders.

However, the richness of the facade fades once you're inside. Gothic severity reigns. A few antiques are there, including a 16th-century throne graced with finials and an inset paneled with pierced Gothic tracery. To go inside, you'll cross over a drawbridge and enter through a Renaissance-style doorway. The tower is open daily from 10 a.m. to 5 p.m. (in summer from 10 a.m. to 7 p.m.); an admission ticket costs 5$ (20¢).

Wax dummies model a full range of Portuguese naval uniforms, from one worn at a military outpost in Mozambique in 1896 to a model as late as 1961. A special room is devoted to the interior of master cabins. The most outstanding is the stateroom of the royal yacht of Carlos I, the Braganza king assassinated at Black Horse Square in 1908. It was on this craft that his son, King Manuel II, and the queen mother, Amélia, escaped to Gibraltar, following the collapse of the Portuguese monarchy in 1910.

Historical exhibits include a letter from Lord Nelson (Bronte Nelson), dated October 24, 1799, earnestly desiring "that your Excellency will not think of quitting Malta till I have a proper force to relieve you." A large map traces the trail of Brito Capelo and Roberto Ivens through the African continent in 1884-1885.

The Naval Museum also honors some of the early Portuguese aviators. Displayed is the aquaplane Santa Cruz, the first aircraft to cross the south Atlantic. The date was March 30, 1922 ("Aventura Magnifica" hailed the press), and the pilot was Gago Coutinho. The flight was from Lisbon to Rio de Janeiro, with stopovers en route. Also displayed is a 1917 airplane, the first one used by Portuguese aviators, containing bicycle wheels.

The museum charges 7$50 (29¢) for admission every day except Wednesdays when it's free (children, eight to 16, pay half price). Known as the Museo de Marinha, it is open daily, except Mondays, from 10 a.m. to 5 p.m.

Annexed to the museums, the Calouste Gulbenkian Planetarium is open Wednesday, Saturday, and Sunday. Admission is 10$ (39¢).

Those too rushed to see the above-mentioned attractions somehow find time for:

THE COACH MUSEUM: Visited by more tourists than any other attraction in Lisbon, the Coach Museum at Belém's Praça Afonso de Albuquerque is considered the finest of its type in the world. It's housed in what was originally an 18th-century riding academy connected to the Belém Royal Palace.

Around the turn of the century, Queen Amélia, wife of the painter king, Carlos I, founded the museum. Amélia, however, fled to England with her son Manuel II upon the collapse of the monarchy.

The coaches stand in a former horse ring, and most of them date from the 17th to the 19th centuries. Drawing the most interest is an opulently decorated trio of gilded baroque carriages once used by the Portuguese ambassador to the Vatican at the time of Pope Clement XI (1716). Also displayed is a 17th-century coach in which the Spanish Hapsburg king, Philip II, journeyed from Madrid to Lisbon to see his new possession.

Other coaches include the processional chariot of "Our Lady of Cabo," the coach of King Joao V, of Queen Maria Ana de Austria, as well as Queen Maria's berlinda. Portuguese and foreign harnesses and trappings—all the gala livery—are also exhibited.

On the second floor, the collection includes saddles (an "amazon" one for Maria II), 17th- and 19th-century costumes and uniforms, festively decorated livery, some 17th-century stirrups, and a portrait of Queen Amélia. The portrait gallery belonged to the House of Braganza, which collapsed in 1910. Pictured are such notables as Maria I and a host of minor royalty.

The museum is open from 10 a.m. to 5 p.m. daily, except Mondays and holidays. During summer it is open from 10 a.m. to 6:30 p.m. It charges 5$ (20¢) admission, except on weekends, when it's free.

Opening onto the Avenida Marginal is:

THE MUSEUM OF POPULAR ART: Nowhere are the folk arts and customs of the Portuguese displayed more dramatically than here. Regional crafts and costumes are grouped according to provinces. The walls are painted by contemporary artists—some of the best in Portugal—including Manuel Lapa and Thomaz de Mello. Their work is supplemented by enlarged photographs of the people of the provinces, each region of which maintains its separate personality.

From the fertile Minho district in the northwest (considered by many the most beautiful part of Portugal) and from the slopes of the Douro Valley (where grapes for port wine are grown) comes a collection of sun clocks, ceramic plates and pottery, a Matósinhos chest, a 19th-century bride's hat, musical instruments, and hand-painted harnesses used for oxen.

Trás-os-Montes, in the severe mountains of the northeast, is represented by an exhibition of fire blowers, masks, spinning wheels, black earthenware (which you can purchase along the roadside if you travel there), and a large handmade rug collection.

In the museum, it's a short trip from Trás-os-Montes to Southern Portugal and the Algarve, the region that evokes the landscape of North Africa. Displayed are the line-cut chimneys from Loulé (in shops you can buy miniatures of these), a water cart, cork objects, palm baskets, and fishing nets.

The Beira room reproduces the interior of a country house of Monsanto, once voted the "most Portuguese village in Portugal." Blacksmith artifacts, ox harnesses, hand-embroidered linen bedspreads, boats from Aveiro, and wicker and straw baskets round out the offerings.

The central tourist district of Estremadura and the plains and pasturelands of Ribatejo are represented by dogs of the hearth, painted dolls from Estremoz, a pilgrimage cart from Elvas, fishermen's "popcorn" sweaters from Nazaré, cork sculptures, and a wax dummy modeling the garb of the campino. This Ribatejo cowboy is really a herdsman who looks after the bulls on the plains.

The museum is open daily, except Mondays, from 10 a.m. to 5 p.m. and charges 1$50 (6¢) admission, except on Thursday and Sunday when it's free. Buses 12 and 14 go there.

If you have a car, drive up to **Restelo Chapel** before heading back to Lisbon. It was at this point that priests held masses, praying for the success of such epic voyages as that of Vasco da Gama. A chapel in the Manueline style stands on the spot today. A belvedere overlooks the Tagus, offering good views of Belém Tower and Jerónimos Monastery.

3. Museums and Galleries

Although most of the museums of Lisbon are at Belém, two major attractions are found in the city: the National Art Gallery and the Gulbenkian Center for Arts and Culture, described below. For a survey of yet two more museums—the St. Roque gallery of ecclesiastical art and the Archaeological Museum in the ruins of the Carmo Church—refer to "The Churches of Lisbon," immediately following.

NATIONAL ART GALLERY: The country's greatest collection of paintings is housed in this art gallery. However, there is much to see, and many notable paintings, including "The Temptations of St. Anthony" by Hieronymus Bosch, are sheltered inside.

At 95 Rua das Janelas Verdes, the museum is open from 10 a.m. to 1 p.m. and from 2:30 to 5 p.m. every day, except Mondays (on Thursdays and Saturdays until 7 p.m.). A 5$ (20¢) entrance fee is charged except on admission-free Saturdays and Sundays.

An important part of the museum, and actually its oldest building, the Church of the Carmelite Convent of Sto. Alberto, should be visited. It constitutes an exhibition of sculpture, painted and gilt carved wood, and glazed tiles (azulejos) of the 16th, 17th, and 18th centuries, with which the chapel is decorated.

In the 15th century Nuno Gonçalves did a series of panels for the Convent of S. Vicente de Fora. Not only was the polyptych the masterpiece of Gonçalves, but it has remained the most celebrated of all Portuguese art works. It depicts a red-robed and scarlet-hooded saint (whose body was said to have been carried to Lisbon by ravens) holding a Bible, and surrounded by about 60 people.

Another notable painting is a "Salomé" by Lucas Cranach, showing the curiously attired creature holding the disembodied and open-eyed saint's head on a plate. Also attributable to Cranach is a "St. Catherine."

Other memorable works are by Velázquez, Anthony Van Dyck, Sir Joshua Reynolds, Gustave Courbet, Andrea del Sarto (a self-portrait), Magnasco (a Venetian scene standing on an easel), Pieter Breughel ("Charity Works"), Memling, Murillo, Joos Van Cleef, Dürer ("St. Jerome"), Hans Holbein ("Virgin and Saints"), Zurburán (an entire salon), Poussin, Pontormo ("Alessandro di Medici"), and Frei Carlos, a well-known painter of the Flemish-Portuguese school (first half of the 16th century).

The collection of antique jewelry is remarkable. Gil Vicente created a custodia or monstrance for the Jerónimos Monastery at Belém in 1506 with the first gold that Vasco da Gama brought back from the East. Exceptional also is a processional cross once used at the Monastery of Alcobaça. The Germain brothers created a famous 18th-century silver plate weighing at least a ton—a gift for Joao V, a Portuguese king.

The outstanding sculptor of the 18th century, Machado de Castro, is well represented. Other exhibits include a collection of rare china, both Oriental and European; an exhibition of old Portuguese ceramics; rare antiques, some dating from the 15th century; Flemish tapestries; 16th-century Persian carpets; a rich assemblage of vestments; Italian polychrome works; and, open since 1974, the Patiño Room, lined with 18th-century French-designed Rocaille boiseries from the Paar Palace in Vienna, and decorated with furniture and a Savonnerie carpet of the same century.

GULBENKIAN CENTER FOR ARTS AND CULTURE: Lisbon's newest museum—inaugurated in 1969—is also one of its best. The Armenian oil tycoon Calouste Gulbenkian willed to the Foundation an outstanding collection of art, considered by many to be among the best in the world in private hands.

This multi-million-dollar center was erected on what was formerly the private estate of the Count of Vilalva. At 45 Avenida da Berna, it is open on Tuesday, Thursday, Friday, and Sunday from 10 a.m. to 5 p.m.; from 2 to 8 p.m. on Wednesday and Saturday. The museum closes on Mondays. Except on admission-free weekends, the entrance fee is 5$ (20¢).

Gulbenkian, a long-term art connoisseur, purchased some of his most notable acquisitions from the Hermitage at Leningrad, a feat requiring almost super-human negotiating skill.

Some of the best-known paintings displayed are Rembrandt's "Figure of Age"; Rubens' "Portrait of Helena Fourment"; and Renoir's "Portrait of

Madame Claude Monet Lounging." Other outstanding works include Guardi's scenes of Venice; Gainsborough's "Portrait of Mrs. Lowndes-Stone"; Anthony Van Dyck's "Portrait of a Man"; Degas' "L'homme et le pantin," plus a self-portrait; Mary Cassatt's "Motherly Care"; and Monet's "The Break-up of the Ice."

The displays also include 15th- and 16th-century French antiques; gold and silver tea service and candelabras; René Lalique glassware and jewelry; and Luca della Robbia ceramics. In the Egyptian wing, the bronze cats are exceptional, as are many of the Greek and Roman exhibitions, including a head attributed to Phidias from the 5th century B.C.

The museum also has a rich collection of art of the Middle East, particularly ceramics and textiles of Turkey and Persia.

MUSEUM OF DECORATIVE ART: Once a private palace belonging to a banker, this Alfama museum is devoted to the decorative arts. Many of the furnishings inside date from the 17th and 18th centuries. The museum stands at the Largo das Portas do Sol, one of the most attractive belvederes in Lisbon.

You are conducted through by a guide every day except Monday, from 10 a.m. to 1 p.m. and from 2 to 5 p.m. (on Sundays, only from 1-5 p.m.). The admission charge is 5$ (20¢), except on Sundays when it's free.

Run by the Fundaçâo Ricardo do Espírito Santo Silva, the museum displays the banker's rich collection of art objects, tapestries (many Flemish ones), rare Oriental china, engravings, and a crystal and silverplate collection. One exhibit is a rare Flemish tapestry dramatizing the sea route of Vasco da Gama to India.

In one room young Portuguese girls with nimble fingers and keen eyesight work long hours repairing decaying tapestries. Many museums in Europe as well as art connoisseurs such as the Rockefeller family send their tapestries here for these girls to work on. Between sewing sessions, they rest their eyes on Photoplay-type pictures of American movie stars, which they plaster on the walls.

A visit to this Azurara Palace is usually followed up by a tour of the famous **Fundaçâo Ricardo do Espírito Santo Silva,** 90 Largo das Portas do Sol. This is really a factory—but what a factory! Naomi Barry exclaimed, "Every other nook and cranny of the palace is an atelier humming with a kind of activity that has almost disappeared from the world."

In the two dozen workshops, you'll find wood-carving experts, iron forgers, metal engravers, expert Arraiolos carpet weavers, silversmiths, and bookbinders who work in gold leaf and can reproduce with accuracy characteristic bindings from the 16th century up to the romantic period.

One of these workshops was responsible for the restoration of Madame Du Barry's library at Versailles. Many of the furnishings in the suites at the Ritz and at the Palácio de Seteais at Sintra were reproduced in the workshops here.

Whatever you want reproduced, including anything you see at the palace, can be turned out. However, money and time should be no object.

MUSEUM OF CONTEMPORARY ART: Don't expect anything at this museum to be very contemporary or very exciting. Still, for the art connoisseur, especially one with traditional tastes, it displays works of leading romantic Portuguese painters of the late 19th and early 20th centuries.

The gallery is an old museum, dating from 1911 when it was probably considered avant-garde. Some of the paintings, such as a portrait that Sousa

Lopes did of his mother, are intriguing. The Porto-born sculptor Teixeira Lopes is represented by several works, but you'll see better examples of his style if you visit his home city.

Occasionally, a foreign piece—such as a Rodin bronze—will creep in, or else a rare nude by Sousa Pinto. Perhaps the most famous painter represented is Columbano, who lived from 1856 to 1929. The gallery offers an entire room filled with his canvases, chiefly his portraits. Other works are by José Malhoa, Velozo Salgado, Carlos Reis, and Eduardo Malta.

At 6 Rua Serpa Pinto, the museum is open daily except Monday, from 10 a.m. to 5 p.m., and charges 5$ (20¢) for entrance except on admission-free weekends. Buses 12 and 27 from Praça Pombal, or Bus 14 from Praça Figueira will take you there.

THE MILITARY MUSEUM: This museum was built on the site of a naval shipyard, which existed in the reign of Dom Manuel I (1495-1521). Later a founder was erected, producing gun powder for the ships sailing on their missions of maritime discoveries. A fire damaged these buildings, and the 1755 earthquake destroyed them completely.

King Joseph I (1750-1777) ordered the construction of new buildings and an additional arms warehouse. The present building, therefore, was not at all planned as a museum. For that reason, paintings by Portuguese masters from the past three centuries coexist with beautiful tiles and pieces of gilt carved wood. These are but a backdrop, of course, for bronze cannons of various periods and light arms of artistic and historical value. One of the cannons is from Diu, weighs 20 tons, and bears Arabic inscriptions. Some iron pieces date to the 14th century.

Light weapons—various guns, pistols, and swords—are displayed in cases. One of the prize exhibits is a gorget worn by Francis I, king of France. Other exhibits include the swords of King John I and Nuno Álvares Pereira, both of the second half of the 14th century. Yet another display is a two-hand sword once belonging to Vasco da Gama.

The museum is at Largo do Museu de Artilharia, in front of the railway station of Santa Apolónia, a short walk from the Terreiro do Paço.

The Military Museum is open daily, except Monday, from 10:30 a.m. to 5 p.m., charging 7$50 (29¢) for admission. That fee drops to 5$ (20¢) on Sundays.

RAFAEL BORDALO PINHEIRO MUSEUM: Rafael Bordalo Pinheiro was a ceramist and caricaturist in the 19th century, and this museum at 382 Campo Grande honors his memory. Actually, it's the most esoteric museum in Lisbon and is of little interest to the average North American visitor—unless he finds himself on a rainy day in the city with nothing else to do.

But if one knew more about Pinheiro's day—that is, 19th-century Portuguese life—if one knew the scandals of the literati, then the kindly artist could be more appreciated. In his caricatures he poked fun at some of the most distinguished men of his day.

Pinheiro's crustacean and reptilian ceramics are of interest, perhaps intentionally bordering on caricature. Search out the portrait that Columbano, the outstanding Portuguese painter who died in 1929, did of Pinheiro.

You can visit the museum (no entrance fee) any day, except Monday, from 11 a.m. to 5 p.m.

4. The Churches of Lisbon

"If you want to see all of the churches of Lisbon, you'd better be prepared to stay here for a few months," the guide told a tourist. What follows is the pick of the litter.

THE PANTHEON CHURCH OF ST. ENGRACIA: Generations came and went, but it looked as if St. Engrácia would never be built. The old church that stood on this spot was wiped out in the earthquake of 1755, but workmen in the 18th century started the task of rebuilding in the baroque style. The job bogged down, and it wasn't until the 1960s that the church was finally completed.

The effect today is austere, befitting a Pantheon of such heads of state as Sidónio Pais, assassinated in 1918, and the general, António Oscar de Fragoso Carmona. The latter was president of Portugal from 1928 until his death in 1951.

The church, built with four square towers, also contains memorials to such personages as Henry the Navigator; Luís Vas de Camoes, author of "Os Lusíadas"; Almeida Garrett, the 19th-century romantic poet; Vasco da Gama; and Pedro Alvares Cabral, the explorer who discovered Brazil.

CARMO CHURCH (THE ARCHAEOLOGICAL MUSEUM): Standing in its ruins today, you can only imagine the glory of this former convent of the 14th century. On the morning of November 1, 1755, the church was crowded for All Saints' Day. The roof cracked and buckled. It was the Lisbon earthquake. When the debris was cleared, only a Gothic skeleton remained. For some reason, the Carmo Church was never reconstructed.

Silhouetted against the Lisbon sky are the chancel, apse, and the Great Door, a section of which has been converted into an **Archaeological Museum.** The meager treasures inside include a Roman sarcophagus, a numismatic collection of rare medieval coins, a window removed from the Jerónimos Monastery at Belém, some skeletons resting under glass, and a few 16th-century tombs. The museum is at Largo do Carmo, best reached by taking the Santa Justa elevator from the Street of Gold below. The hours are from 2 to 5 p.m. daily, except Monday. Entrance fee is 5$ (20¢).

ST. ROQUE CHURCH AND MUSEUM: Go here to see a fabulous collection of baroque-style silver sculpture. For example, a pair of silver and gold torchiers, designed by Gagliardi, weighs about 840 pounds—one of the finest in the world. Among the treasures is gold embroidery dating from the 18th century. The church itself was built in the mid-1500s in what has been called Jesuit-style architecture.

The museum adjoins the church and is usually visited first. Among the treasures—aside from those already mentioned—is a vestment said to have been worn by the Pope 200 years ago in the sacrament of St. John's Chapel in Rome. Most of the religious art came from Italy in the reign of Joao V. Specific gems include a Gigli-designed chalice, an iconograph of St. Ignatius, portraits from the 16th century (notably one of the wedding ceremony of Manuel the Fortunate, another an unflattering rendition of pudgy Catherine of Austria).

In the church itself—under a painted wood ceiling—is one of the best known chapels in Lisbon, that of St. John the Baptist. It was built in Rome in the 18th century, completely dismantled, then shipped to Lisbon and reassembled in its entirety, with alabaster, lapis lazuli, and other materials. Joao V ordered the chapel and was intrigued with the mosaics in marble that resemble an oil painting.

In the sacristy are paintings depicting events in the lives of Jesuit saints.

The church and museum at Largo Trindade Coelho may be visited from 9 a.m. to 6 p.m. daily, except Mondays, for a 5$ (20¢) admission fee. No charge on Sundays. Take bus 37 from The Rossio.

ST. VINCENT OUTSIDE THE WALLS: In this Renaissance church, the greatest names and some forgotten wives of the House of Braganza were placed to rest. It's really a Pantheon. Originally a convent from the 12th century, the church was erected between 1582 and 1627. At that time it was outside the walls of Lisbon, although the sprawling city has long ago incorporated it. On the morning of the earthquake of 1755, the cupola fell in.

The Braganzas, one of whom is still a pretender to the throne of Portugal, assumed power in 1640. This one family then ruled until 1910, when the Portuguese monarchy collapsed and King Manuel II and the queen mother, Amélia, fled to England.

The body of Manuel II was subsequently returned to Portugal following his death. Amélia, the last queen of Portugal, died in 1951 and was also entombed here. Her husband, Carlos I, the painter king, and her son, Prince Luís Felipe, were both killed by an assassin at Terreiro do Paço in 1908. Their bodies were also interred here.

Aside from the royal tombs, one of the most important reasons for visiting St. Vincent is to see its azulejos (the glazed earthenware tiles), some of them illustrating the fables of La Fontaine. Although we suspect no one's officially counted them, their number is placed at one million. In the sacristy the architect chose Portuguese marble to line the walls and combined it with jacaranda wood from Brazil. Look for a curious ivory statue of Christ, carved in the former Portuguese province of Goa in the 18th century.

The church, at Largo de S. Vicente, may be visited only from 10 a.m. to 6 p.m. for a 5$ (20¢) admission.

CHURCH OF MADRE DE DEUS: One of the outstanding characteristics of Portuguese churches is the architectural device of lining the walls with azulejos, glazed earthenware tiles. Delft blue and white usually predominate in the color scheme, crowned by baroque carved gilt wood, framing a rich collection of 17th- and 18th-century oil paintings. The small sacristy is lined with polychrome azulejos (Portuguese work), and there you can also see the retable of Sta. Auta, of the 16th-century Flemish school. For some of the finest azulejos decoration, visit this former convent—founded by Queen Leonor in 1509.

Near the riverside, at 4 Rua Madre de Deus, it is open from 10 a.m. to 1 p.m. and from 2:30-5 p.m. every day, except Mondays, and charges no admission. Generally, a guide will conduct you on a tour of the precincts.

5. A Bullfight Spectacle

Bullfighting in Portugal was once the sport of noblemen. Today, the art form still draws a crowd, although the "aristocrats" are now the spectators.

Unlike the Spanish, the Portuguese do not kill the bull—a prohibition decreed in the 18th century by Prime Minister Marquis de Pombal, following the death in the sport of the son of the Duke of Arcos.

Critics in the last few years have been mounting an attack against this limitation. A Lisbon commentator Jaime Saraiva was quoted in the press: "A bullfight without a kill is a great lie; it is not serious."

However, Marvine Howe wrote: "With the elimination of the death stroke, the Portuguese bullfight lost most of its excitement only to become one of the most beautiful equestrian displays in the world."

At the start of the corrida, the matadors parade in, attired in their "suits of light," based on the same style worn in the 18th century. They are followed by cavaleiros, the men who fight the bull on horseback, eventually placing darts in his neck.

Trailing are the moços de forcado, a team of tacklers who grapple with the bull—some in face-to-face combat! The forcados wear olive-colored trousers separated from their gold jackets by a red sash. Their calves are covered with white stockings, and traditionally a green cap, trimmed in red, rests on their heads (many of the tacklers have now abandoned this garb).

When the trumpet sounds, the cavaleiro and the bull enter the ring. The horseman and his steed race toward the bull, swerving just in time to avoid a head-on collision. As he passes the animal, the cavaleiro thrusts three or four darts into his neck.

Before the fight ends, a phalanx of eight tacklers advance toward the bull, the leader shouting: "Eh, Touro! Eh! Touro!" Using nothing but their bare hands, the forcados tackle the bull. For many, this is the most exciting aspect of the game. However, the horns are padded with leather bandages known as emboladas.

You can attend one of these pageants from Easter until around mid-October. The 8,500-seat **Campo Pequeno** (reached on the Metro) in Lisbon is the largest ring in the country, and usually presents fights on Thursday and Sunday afternoons in season. These corridas and the names of the stars (or lack of them!) are announced well in advance, so your hotel concierge can be of help to you (many arrange tickets).

Another major bullring is the **Monumental de Cascais**, at Cascais, the resort lying west of Estoril on the Costa do Sol. You can take the electric train from Lisbon which ends its run in Cascais; from the station, an inexpensive taxi will take you to the bullring itself, just outside the center of town.

When a major star isn't appearing, the average price for one of the best seats is 120$ ($4.68) to 150$ ($5.85)—that is, in the sombra (shade) section. For sombra y sol, you'll pay around 70$.($2.73), and your seat will be in the shade for half of the fight, in the sun for the remainder.

6. Other Sights

Those sights in and around Lisbon that could not be categorically listed elsewhere are highlighted below. Certain of these attractions reveal much about the nations' natural resources, geography, climate, inhabitants, and life style, and it is the knowledge of these things that make you far more than just a tourist passing through. For example:

THE SPECTACLE OF THE MARKET: The big market of Ribeira Nova is as close as you can get to the heart of Lisbon. Near the Cais do Sodré, where trains are boarded for the Costa do Sol, an enormous roof shelters a collection of produce stalls, where you'll see, in its native state, the produce you'll be eating later at one of Lisbon's finest restaurants.

Foodstuffs are brought in each morning in bulging wicker baskets filled with overscaled carrots, cabbages big enough for shrubbery, stalks of bananas. Some of the produce arrives by donkey; some of it by truck; some balanced on top of the heads of Lisboan women in the Mediterranean fashion—all from yesterday's field. The rich soil produces the juiciest of peaches, the most aromatic tomatoes.

"Seeing eye" fishing boats—many believed to have been based on Phoenician designs—tie up at the dock at dawn with their catch. The fish are deposited on long marble counters: cod, squid, bass, hake, swordfish. Soon the varinas (fishwives) take wicker baskets of the fresh catch, balancing them on their heads, and climb the cobbled streets of the Alfama or the Bairro Alto, selling the fish from door to door.

At the market itself, mounds of vegetables, fruit, and fish are hovered over by hearty, friendly, outgoing Portuguese women gaily clad in voluminous skirts and calico aprons. On cue the vendors begin howling out the value of their wares, stopping only to pose for an occasional snapshot.

Adjoining the market, away from the river, cutstone streets are flanked with shops selling inexpensive Portuguese clothing. The best buy—if you can locate one—is a distinctively styled cape from the Alentejo district. In three tiers, these capes are often capped with red-fox collars.

Finally, we know of no better way to cap your Lisbon sightseeing adventure than by heading to:

THE GREENHOUSE: The Portuguese call it their Estufa Fria. It's in the handsomely laid out Edward VII Park, named after Queen Victoria's son, to commemorate his three trips to Lisbon. Against a background of streams and rocks, the tropical plants grow in such profusion that some writers have called it a "sylvan glade." It is even more than that, so luxuriant is its growth that it evokes a rain forest.

The park itself lies at the top of the Avenida da Liberdade, crowned by a statue of the Marquis de Pombal, with his "house pet," a lion. There's a 2$50 (10¢) admission charge to the greenhouse, which is open from 10 a.m. to 6 p.m.

JARDIM ZOOLOGICO: The Zoological Garden, with a collection of some 3,500 animals, enjoys a flower-filled setting in the 65-acre Park of Laranjeiras, about a 10-minute subway ride from The Rossio, on the Estrada de Benfica. The Children's Zoo, with its miniature houses in small gardens, is exceptional. There are also a small train, rowboats, a roller skating rink, elephant and pony rides, films, and puppet shows presented on Sundays. It's open from 9 a.m. till sunset. Admission is 10$ (39¢) for adults; 5$ (20¢) for children 5-10. Take buses 15, 31, 41, or 46 from The Rossio.

BRITISH CEMETERY: Up the Rua da Estrêla at one end of the Estrêla Gardens lies the British Cemetery. It's famous as the burial place of Henry Fielding, the English novelist (*"Tom Jones"*) and dramatist. A sick man, Fielding went to Lisbon in 1754 for his health, and the story of that trip is narrated in the posthumous tract, *"Journal of a Voyage to Lisbon."* Reaching Lisbon in August, he died two months later. A monument was erected in 1830, honoring him.

READER'S RECOMMENDATION: "For a good view of the harbor and a place to sip a drink leisurely, go to the **Parque Eduardo VII, Esplanada in Topo.** The drinks are cheap, and there is food available, although it didn't look too inviting. The strangest part of it was that there weren't any other tourists there during our visit. You can sit outside under umbrellas on top of this nice hill and just look. A lot of students were there with their books studying" (Mrs. Bob Lowdon, Fort Worth, Tex.).

Chapter VIII

NIGHTLIFE IN AND AROUND LISBON

1. The Fado Clubs
2. The Capital After Dark
3. Estoril by Night
4. The Clubs of Cascais

UNLESS YOU HAVE experienced the nostalgic sounds of fado—the songs of sorrow—you will not know Portugal. Certainly not its soul. The fado is Portugal's most vivid art form; and no visit to Lisbon should be planned without at least one night spent in a local tavern, where this traditional folk music is heard.

Originating in the lowly dock area, fado rose to embrace the hearts of the Portuguese people. A rough translation of fado is fate, from the Latin fatum, meaning prophecy. The quintessence of saudade, fado usually tells of unrequited love, jealousy, a longing for days gone by. As one expert put it, it speaks of "life commanded by the Oracle, which nothing can change."

Fado found its earliest fame in the 19th century with Maria Severa, the beautiful daughter of a gypsy who took Lisbon by storm, singing her way into the hearts of the people—and especially the heart of the Count of Vimioso, an outstanding bullfighter of his day. Legend has it that she is honored by present-day fadistas who wear a black-fringed shawl in her memory.

In this century the most famous exponent of fado is Amália Rodrigues, introduced to American audiences at an unheralded appearance in the 1950s at the New York club, La Vie en Rose. She was discovered while walking barefoot and selling flowers on the Lisbon docks, near the Alfama. Fado is also sung by men.

Clutching black shawls around themselves, the female fadistas pour out their true emotions, from the tenderest whisper of hope to a wailing lament of life's tragedies. As they sing accompanied by a guitar and a viola, they seem to lose all contact with the surrounding world—standing against a black gas street lamp, without benefit of theatrical spots, make-up, or other scenery—just standing there. They seemingly outdo the Rhine's Lorelei in pulling you into their world of tenderness and fire.

Even though a great deal of the enjoyment is derived from understanding its poetic imagery, a knowledge of Portuguese is not essential. The lyrical power, the warmth of the voices, the personality of the singer can go a long way in communicating.

Don't go to hear fado and plan to carry on a private conversation. It's considered very bad form. Most of the authentic fado clubs are clustered near each other in either the Bairro Alto or else in the Alfama, between St. George's Castle and the docks, and you can "fado hop" between these two typical quarters.

Alfama-bound hoppers can ask the taxi driver to deliver them to the **Largo do Chafariz,** a small plaza a block from the harbor, and Bairro Alto devotées can get off at the **Largo do S. Roque.** Most of our recommendations lie only a short walk from either of these squares.

The cafes offer regional Portuguese dinners, though it's customary to go and order drinks only (usually a two-drink minimum). The music begins between 9 and 10, but it's much better to arrive after 11 p.m. Many of the clubs stay open till 3 a.m.; others till dawn.

1. The Fado Clubs

Lisboa à Noite, 69 Rua das Gáveas (tel. 36-85-57). Electricity fills the air—the tempestuous Fernanda Maria is about to make her first appearance of the evening. Tossing down a shot of whiskey offered by a waiter, she stands quietly, tensely clutching her back shawl. Then she comes forward, pauses, scans the audience, and pours forth all the fiery intensity of fado. You, too, may fall under her spell. Success has come to Fernanda—she owns the club.

The 17th-century-style setting is rustic yet luxurious (once this Bairro Alto club was a stable). Creating its present ambience are thick stone-edged arches, heavy hand-hewn beams, blue and white tiled walls, a round well with its original bucket, a collection of old engravings, antique guns, and pewter and copper. When it's cold scented eucalyptus logs crackle in a high fireplace. In the rear is an open kitchen and charcoal grill, with an assemblage of spices, sausages, garlic pigtails, and onions hanging from the beams.

House specialties include dry codfish Fernanda Maria flambé, 105$ ($4.10), and steak Lisboa à Noite flambé, 170$ ($6.63). A soup Alentejana at 25$ (98¢) can begin your meal. Minimum is 150$ ($5.85).

Taverna do Embuçado, 10 Beco dos Curtumes (tel. 86-08-16). Just a short stroll from the docks where she sold flowers as a girl, Celeste Rodrigues (Amália's sister) stands like a Greek tragédienne. She knows the meaning of tragic loneliness, as revealed in her voice. In the soft light, she is an earthy, yet classic, beauty.

This old-world tavern in the Alfama section is a temple of fado in a setting of oak beams, a huge walk-in fireplace, and wide arches. Against one wall stands a wooden chest, an antique ecclesiastical carved figure, and an ornate silver candelabrum. The cafe is owned by a singer, Joao Ferreira Rosa.

It's possible to order drinks only (a two-drink minimum). For whiskey or rum, you pay 80$ ($3.12) per drink. Many elect to dine here, ordering green soup for 50$ ($1.95), followed by the house specialty, bife à Embuçado, 140$ ($5.46), finishing off with a freshly mixed fruit salad for 40$ ($1.56).

To get to this club let a taxi driver deposit you at a nearby plaza. Usually there's a uniformed attendant on the spot, ready to escort you down the alley on a two-minute walk to the club.

"A Severa," 49-57 Rua das Gáveas (tel. 36-40-06). Good food and careful selection of fadistas make this the perennial favorite. Before he became President, Mr. Nixon selected it for a night on the town with his wife, leading a congolike line between the tables, warbling the refrain, "Severa . . . Severa . . . Severa." Every night top singers—both male and female—appear at the Bairro Alto nightspot, accompanied by guitar and viola music. Alternating are folk dancers who perform in regional costumes. In a niche you'll spot a statue honoring the club's namesake, Maria Severa, the legendary gypsy fadista of the 19th century. After midnight tourists seem to recede a bit in favor of loyal Lisbon habitués, who request and sometimes join in on their favorite fado number.

The club is owned by Julio Barros and his wife Maria José. He keeps everything running smoothly out front, and she takes care of the kitchen, turning out regional dishes based on recipes from the north of Portugal. For dinner don't miss chicken cooked and served in a clay pot for 110$ ($4.29) per person. Her green cabbage soup goes for 35$ ($1.37). Another house specialty is stuffed squid, 95$ ($3.71), as well as steak of the house, fried in a clay dish, for the same price. Closed Thursdays.

Restaurante Machado, 91 Rua do Norte (tel. 36-00-95), has won the test of time—and is today one of the favored fado clubs of Portugal. In days of yore you could spot perhaps Edward G. Robinson or Vittorio de Sica listening to the incomparable Amália Rodrigues. Alternating with its fadistas are folk dancers—whirling, clapping, singing their native songs in colorful costumes. The evening dinner hour starts at 8, and the doors don't close till 3 a.m. when the last fadista aficionado trails out humming his favorite song.

Dinner is à la carte, and the cuisine is mostly Portuguese, with any number of regional dishes. House specialties include chicken in a pot, 85$ ($3.32); stuffed squid, 90$ ($3.51); steak Machado, 95$ ($3.71); roasted baby goat, 95$ also; and pork with clams, 90$ ($3.51). A simple dessert to follow might be almond cake made with nuts from the Algarve, 35$ ($1.37). You pay a minimum of 86$ ($3.25).

Guests often join the singers and folk dancers, carrying arched garlands of flowers, as they parade around the crowded tables, singing the "Marcha do Machado."

Parreirinha da Alfama, 1 Beco do Espírito (tel. 86-82-09). Seemingly, no fadista worth her shawl hasn't sung at this old-time cafe—just a one-minute walk from the dockside edge of the Alfama. It's fado and fado only that enthralls here—not folk dancing. You can order a good regional dinner beginning early, but it's suggested that you go toward the shank of the evening ... and stay late! It's open all night. In the first part of the program, the fadistas get all the popular songs out of the way, then settle in to their own more classic favorites.

Drinks average around 80$ ($3.12) for hard liquor, half that for soft drinks. You can order a filling dinner for 210$ ($8.19), and the menu includes specialties from nearly every region of Portugal. The atmosphere is self-consciously taverna, with all sorts of Portuguese provincial oddments along with photos of famous people who've been here. One can forgive the too cute reproduction of a village, with its mock doors and windows. However, the singers selected by the management are first rate.

O Faia, 48-56 Rua da Barroca (tel. 36-93-87), is an antiga adega, the domain of the fadista Lucília do Carmo. When she makes her entrance, you'll recognize her as a star. Her alternating singers set the scene like a Greek chorus. A popular male fadista, Carlos do Carmo (Lucila's son), and singer Moniz Trindade entertain at O Faia. Between numbers, regionally attired folk dancers perform on the stage.

The club is in the heart of the Bairro Alto—a lower-level tavern restaurant with coved ceilings, thick arches, and murals of Old Lisbon. There's a minimum of 115$ ($4.49) per person. The cuisine here combines international with Portuguese dishes. Fado music commences at 10 p.m., and lasts till around 3 a.m. Open every night except Sundays.

Viela, 14 Rua das Taipas (tel. 32-72-56), is also frequented by fado devotées. It presents its showcase of fado in a down-to-earth atmosphere, feeling no need to rely on frills or stylish decor. It offers a quartet of alternating fadistas, who stand against a lamp post, singing their refrains.

Hopefully, Sergio will perform on the night you drop in. A cult surrounds this dynamic fadista. A youthful man, he casts everyone under his spell, singing directly to every table. Often the guests know every line by heart, even joining in at times.

The Viela is in a hidden-away cellar on a narrow street, not far from the Avenida da Liberdades. You can order two or three drinks, fulfilling your minimum of 100$ ($3.90), which includes service and taxes. The music starts at 11 p.m. and lasts until 5 a.m. The later you go, the better. Closed Sundays.

O Poeta, 22 Travessa de San Miguel (tel. 86-85-52), is a showcase for Maria da Fé, a Portuguese recording artist and fadista. Newer than the clubs recommended previously, it is air conditioned. Madame da Fé performs against a backdrop of a Lisbon photo mural. Portuguese floor shows are staged nightly between 10 p.m. and 3 a.m. The minimum is 100$ ($3.90) which, incidentally, is the cost of the average drink.

2. The Capital After Dark

Fado outshines other nighttime entertainment in Lisbon. However, for a change of pace, we've included suggestions for most tastes: vaudeville houses; nightclubs for conventional drinking and dancing; and discotheques for those of limber limb.

On a more cultural note, opera and ballet buffs may want to attend a performance at the **Teatro Nacional de Sao Carlos,** at Largo de Sao Carlos, created in the 18th century and booking top companies from different countries. The season begins the latter part of January, extending through June. In addition, there are several theaters presenting plays from autumn through spring—but only in Portuguese. Recitals and concerts are held at various places in Lisbon, especially The Greenhouse in Edward VII Park. Motion pictures are shown in their original language. To obtain information on any of the above, consult a copy of *What's On in Lisbon,* available at most newsstands, although your hotel concierge is also a good bet for information, since one of his duties is reserving seats.

THE DISCOTHEQUES: Ad Lib, 28 Rua Barata Salgueiro, is a posh discotheque dreamed up by a clique of chaps who wanted an elegant place to have a bash. On the top floor of a modern building, it doesn't call attention to itself with a sign outside. A uniformed attendant at the formal entrance checks on the intercom system to weed out undesirables. If you're well groomed and not drunk, you stand a good chance of scaling the citadel; even so, it's wise to telephone in advance (56-17-17).

Upstairs, you'll enter a penthouse with a bar on one level, tables and a dancing area on another. A plant-filled terrace provides a view of Lisbon by night. The decor is that of the East, with fine stone Buddhas from Macao, mirrors, and candles in red bowls. Playing the newest continental and American records is a disc jockey. There's a minimum of 150$ ($5.85), with whiskey costing around 75$ ($2.93) per drink; soft drinks, 30$ ($1.17).

Carrousel, 77 Rua Castilho, lives up to its position in the Ritz compound, overlooking Edward VII Park. Entered via a private doorway, it caters to well-heeled post-25 couples out for a night on the town. A carousel theme is suggested by stripes of red, white, and blue against walls of black infinity. Off center a disc jockey flips and plays an eclectic collection of international recordings.

The club is good for sound. The Carrousel imposes an 88$50 ($3.45) minimum, with Scotch or rum and Coca-Cola going for 73$ ($2.85), rye for 70$ ($2.73). Although the doors open at 10:30 p.m., no one seems to appear until after midnight. Once there, couples often stay till 3:30 a.m., squatting on grasshopper chairs, sipping, dancing, or gazing at the "man in the moon" and the simulated stars. Closed Sunday.

O Caruncho, 2 Rua Alexandre Ferreira, in the Luminar suburbs, rocks to recorded music in a converted stable. The oldest discotheque in Lisbon, Caruncho in Portuguese means dry rot. Nevertheless, it has its steady friends, who dance on a center medallion under a wagon-wheel chandelier. Hanging red lanterns make everyone a most unusual color. Open nightly at 10, the discotheque charges 60$ ($2.34) for drinks until it shuts down at 3:30 a.m. Better have your own transportation or you'll never make it back to the center of the capital.

THE NIGHTCLUBS: Maxime, 57 Praça da Alegria (tel. 35-366), is Portugal's leading nightclub, offering continental entertainment as well as folk dancing and fado. Its entrepreneurs have tried to carve a niche as an international showplace with the sexiest show in Lisbon, which is staged at 1:30 a.m. and again at 3 a.m. Frankly, it's keyed to the Portuguese cork farmer or olive grower who wants to be mildly titillated and amused at some of that alleged Paris-London-New York show biz glamor.

The early part of the evening starts at 8:30 for dancing, the second part at 10 p.m. and midnight, when a showcase of Portuguese folklore dances and fado is presented, the performers regionally garbed. The minimum charge is 138$ ($5.38) per person, and you can order dinner from a menu that includes such dishes as steak Maxime, 80$ ($3.12); a châteaubriand for two, 200$ ($7.80); and banana flambé, 35$ ($1.37).

O Porao da Nau, 1 Rua Pinheiro Chagas (tel. 51-501), is a nightclub with a fine combo for dancing. The action takes place in the hold of a simulated Portuguese man-of-war of the 15th century. You descend to the lower levels at the centrally located Residência a Ponte. You get the feeling that the gangplank will be lifted, the sails hoisted.

Around a circular marble dance floor is a musician's area, with tables set on different levels. The walls are planked, the main beams time aged, and there's a gun collection, rope railings, an early map charting Portuguese possessions, a spherical globe, and a finely carved wooden figure used on the bow of a sailing vessel. The combo provides rhythm for dancing, backed up by on-the-beam vocalists. A minimum of 101$ ($3.94) is charged, including service. At 5 a.m. you're tossed overboard!

Frou-Frou, Campo Grande, is a cafe in a large park in the suburbs of Lisbon. A circular theater, it's decorated in the traditional style. Folkloric shows, offering guitar music, fado singing, and regional dances are presented nightly at 11. One bar is at the reception entrance, the other in the dining room. The least expensive way to patronize Frou-Frou is to order a drink at one of these bars. You pay only for the drinks you consume. Otherwise, you're charged a minimum of 325$ ($12.68) in the dining room. Of course, for that minimum you get a full dinner and at least five libations. If you consume that much drink, you may end up in the show. Between acts patrons dance to live music.

MUSICAL REVUES—PORTUGUESE-STYLE: Just off the Avenida da Liberdade, in the **Parque Mayer**, is a cluster of vaudeville and music halls each offering a revista, a Portuguese revue similar in some respects to Spanish zarzuela. In the park are a few restaurants and Coney-Island-style fun and chance stalls, where Lisboans throw darts and win dubious prizes. Here you can feel the entertainment pulse of the people, seeing everything from popular singers to fadistas to acrobats to ballet dancers.

You may be happily surprised to find that the average orchestra seat at one of these revues is offered for about 50$ ($1.95), depending on the performance. However, you can sit in the peanut balcony, taking along a bag of hot roasted chestnuts, for 15$ (59¢). Hours of performances vary, so check at the box office or with your hotel concierge. Often there are two shows nightly: one at 8:45; the last one at 10:45. On Sundays and most holidays, matinée performances are at 4 p.m.

Especially recommended is the **ABC Theatre**, offering big-time fado and popular Portuguese singing stars, skits, dancers, acrobats, and comedians. The **Capitol**, charging from 30$ ($1.17) to 100$ ($3.90), is the largest, staging musical revues with songs, dancing, and skits, varying its program with light concerts and orchestral music. **Maria Vitoria** presents topnotch vaudeville artists, pop singers, guitarists, fadistas, and acrobats. And finally, the **Teatro Variedades** features slapstick tragedy, popular entertainment, the wailing lament of fado, and the Ballet International.

A BAWDY CRAWL ALONG THE DOCKLAND: Remember those movies of Mediterranean port cities, showing red neon lights flashing, drunken sailors staggering down labyrinthine narrow streets, a mixed bag of human flotsam unmatched since Jean Genet wrote of his "whores, thieves, pimps, and beggars." These rip-roaring scenes live on in Lisbon, in the little streets near the dock area, where sailors hang out at bars named after western American states: Arizona, California, Texas.

The most popular—occasionally drawing some of the slumming Ritz and Palácio crowd—is the **Texas Bar**, 21 Sao Paulo, a gusty tavern under a bridge. A singer and seedy combo are suspended from the ceiling, usually warbling a Portuguese version of an old country and western hit.

If you're a single man (if you're a single woman, stay away!), you'll be surrounded on entering by the widest assemblage of Gravel Gertie lookalikes this side of Barcelona or Marseilles. "Speak English?" is the typical query. One young man—trying to escape—answered a resounding, "No, Svenska." But a girl was found who spoke lilting Swedish. The Texas Bar accommodates all!

When the fleet's in—and some fleet from some port is likely to be in all the time—this waterfront hotspot can be very rowdy.

For much tamer fare, we strike out for nighttime fun along the Costa do Sol.

3. Estoril by Night

GAMBLING: The **Casino** (tel. 264-521) at Estoril is the glamor-hub for international society. Occupying a position on the rise of a hill, it opens onto the formal gardens of the Parque Estoril which sweep toward the water. The glass walls suggest an international museum of modern art, and enclose an inner courtyard, with tiled paths, a fountain and pool, and borders of lilac-colored petunias and red carnations.

ESTORIL BY NIGHT 107

Off the main lobby are various bars, a nightclub, a motion-picture theater, an art gallery, and groups of boutiques. The five-star magnet, of course, is the Casino itself, which accepts your mad money between 3 p.m. and 3 a.m. (passport required). An adjoining salon is for one-arm bandits. In the main room you can take your chance at roulette, French bank, chemin-de-fer, baccarat, blackjack/21, craps, and slot machines. A tourist pass is given for 30$ ($1.17).

Other diversions include the **Grand Salon Restaurant,** really a supper club offering a limited 230$ ($8.97) dinner for light eaters, beginning at 9 p.m. Many prefer to go for drinks only, paying a minimum of 120$ ($4.68); 140$ ($5.46) on Saturdays. The extravaganza stage show commences at 11:30 p.m. On the arena stage, leggy, feathered, and bejeweled showgirls strut their wares to good advantage in billowing trains and bespangled bras. Another cabaret-style show begins at 1 a.m. in the **Wonder Bar,** where the house minimum is also 120$ ($4.68); 140$ ($5.46) on Saturdays.

A small movie theater shows films daily, the matinée costing 25$ (98¢), the nighttime showing 32$ ($1.25). It's the same on weekends and holidays. There's also an art gallery selling contemporary paintings, and a few boutiques offering women's apparel and souvenirs.

DINING AND DANCING: **A Choupana,** on the coastal road at S. Joao do Estoril (tel. 26-30-99), is the best supper club along the Costa do Sol. It offers a good sound for dancing nightly in a setting on the edge of a cliff, with views of lights from fishing boats and ocean liners, the sound of the surf, and the sight of sunsets. A Choupana—which means hut or shack in Portuguese—is the territory of five partners. One rules in the kitchen, winning bravos from such an élite crowd as South American embassy officials, the Spanish royal family, the Count of Paris, even actors such as Ray Milland and Raymond Burr.

The main room is on two levels, with enough waterside window space to provide everyone with a good seat. On the bill of fare, you can order such delicious dishes as partridge stewed in a casserole, 82$ ($3.20); duck with orange sauce, 110$ ($4.29); and a mixed grill Choupana, 95$ ($3.71). Two exceptional fish dishes are lampreys, Portuguese style (only in season), 100$ ($3.90), and a Marseillaise-style bouillabaisse, 90$ ($3.51). In season, strawberries from Sintra at 50$ ($1.95) make an exciting finish.

Last but not least is the topnotch trio. Music for dining begins at 9:30 p.m.—for dancing at 10 p.m.—and continues until closing at 3:30 a.m. It's possible to order drinks only, for which you'll pay a minimum of 65$ ($2.54).

Frolic, Parque Estoril, stands opposite the Casino. It is both a discotheque and a first-class restaurant. If you want dinner, you can go early—at least from 7 p.m. on. Featured are such items as châteaubriand at 81$ ($3.16); sole meunière with prawns at 80$ ($3.12). If you're just in the mood for dancing, the best hours are between 11 p.m. and 3:30 a.m. You're charged a minimum of 75$ ($2.93). Whiskies are priced at 40$ ($1.56).

A FORTRESS DISCOTHEQUE: Forte Velho (Old Fort), Sao Pedro Cadaveira, S. Joao do Estoril, is where the very young meet in a very old setting. On the sea, the discotheque was ingeniously conceived by José Dias Pegado, who captured a 17th-century fortress built on a cliff above the ocean. It's built of solid rock and offers a central room with fireplace and walls papered with magazine cutouts—all dominated by a hanging metal fish casting reflections from the psychedelic spotlights.

Dancing is to records only, and there's an adjoining bar with stools and cozy banquettes, ideal for hand-holding couples. For a change of pace, drinks are carried out on the terrace to the parapet, where imbibers gasp at the steep drop to the surf below. The fun commences at 10 p.m., although it doesn't really warm up till around midnight. The Old Fort rides the crest until closing at 3:30 every night, year round. You pay a minimum of 50$ ($1.95) during the week, 70$ ($2.73) on weekends; for scotch, the price is 50$ ($1.95), only 25$ (98¢) for beer or soft drinks. Foreign women are welcomed on their own.

A FADO BAR IN ESTORIL: Bar Galito, Estrada Marginal, is handy for those who want an easy and inexpensive evening of fado, without having to make the trek into Lisbon. Within sight of the Hotel Cibra, it is near the station and next door to the Banco de Alentejo. Inside, it consists of two adjoining rooms, the gap bridged by fadistas and their guitarists. The decor is contrived taverna, with brass-studded leather chairs and crude stools. There's a house minimum of 60$ ($2.34) after 10:30 p.m., and it's a friendly and pleasant place—easy to while away an hour.

The most popular bar at press time was the **Pickwick Pub,** 3 Avenida Biarritz. The Pickwick is decorated like an old English pub, complete with carpeted floor, mugs hanging over the bar, and plenty of cozy nooks and crannies where you sit in subdued lighting. Soft music is provided from a disc jockey sitting in an adjoining room. You can play darts, have light meals, and while away a couple of hours chatting with the locals and foreigners. It's open from 2:30 p.m. until midnight (later in summer). A pint of English ale goes for 30$ ($1.17), a half pint for 20$ (78¢).

A BOITE AND BAR IN MONTE ESTORIL: Ronda, 3 Avenida Sabóia. Discotheque addicts are fickle, flitting from one hot spot to another, then on to the next even before the season is over. Apparently, one exception to the rule is this perennially popular modern boîte. Perched on a hill above the coastal highway in Monte Estoril, it offers an unobstructed view of the Bay of Cascais, and a smartly and comfortably outfitted interior in red. It provides the latest recorded music for dancing. The records start spinning at 10 p.m. There is an 80$ ($3.12) minimum. You pay 30$ ($1.17) for a beer, 65$ ($2.54) for whiskey, plus taxes. Open nightly, it closes at 3:30 a.m.

Ray's Cocktail Bar & Lounge, 25 Avenida Sabóia, in Monte Estoril, is popular with American expatriates, many of whom make it their private club. It's a souped-up decorator extravaganza that belongs to a New Yorker in exile who is known simply as Ray. Inside, you're likely to find a completely catholic assemblage of elements—a fátima hand from Tangier, a glass ruby-colored newel post finial, chandeliers dripping with crystal, an ostrich fan (in black, no less), antique benches, provincial chairs, plus a heterogeneous mixture of modern art. Everyone seemingly enjoys Ray's drinks (many enjoy quite a few of them!), and his minimum is a modest 15$ (59¢). Most strong drinks cost 45$ ($1.76). Hovering everywhere at once, even joining in a bit of the juicy gossip of the day, Ray is the perfect host. He is at home from 6 p.m.

4. The Clubs of Cascais

The **Van Go-Go,** 9 Travessa Alfarrobeira, is a chic playground. Modestly hidden in a corner stone building, it was transformed from a simple fisherman's cottage into a discotheque. A doorman inside carefully evaluates those who would cross the threshold, using some inner radar we don't understand. If you are seemingly well-behaved and not on the prowl, then you'll be given the green light to go inside.

Behind its facade, you'll encounter a hip young crowd similar to the one at Juan-Les-Pins. On the inside, a seductive atmosphere is created by the black glass walls, and the customers can rock and roll. You pay 100$ ($3.90) as a minimum, with beer priced at 30$ ($1.17), whiskey and rum drinks at 80$ ($3.12). The Van Go-Go opens its doors year round at 10 p.m., closing at 3:30 a.m.

Palm Beach, Praia da Conceiçao, is a hillside discotheque with a rather swank atmosphere—again with a doorman to weed out undesirables. As of this writing, the Palm Beach is riding the crest of the wave along the Costa do Sol, drawing a young, fun-loving crowd that's well-mannered enough to please the management. The club is positioned below the coastal road, its wide windows overlooking the Bay of Cascais. You lounge comfortably on banquettes and chairs when not dancing on the mini-sized floor. The atmosphere is informal—not dressy—and only records are played. The minimum is 160$ ($6.24), with beer costing 30$ ($1.17), and hard drinks 60$ ($2.34) to 80$ ($3.12).

Borsalino, 19 Rua Visconde da Luz (tel. 286-43-81), is a hub for an international crowd of young people, who drop in any time between 4 p.m. and 3:30 a.m. for drinks and talk. The excitement is generated partly by the head bartender, Luís Eduardo, and partly by the atmosphere itself. Art nouveau reigns. On quiet nights you're likely to find some twosome playing chess at one of the tables. You pay 10$ (39¢) for soft drinks; 15$ (59¢) for a pint of beer; 30$ ($1.17) for gin or vodka, and 35$ ($1.37) for a regular whiskey.

Arreda, 3 Rua Alexandre Herculano (tel. 28-38-64), is a showcase for male fadista Gulio Ribeiro. "I'm just an amateur," he confesses. However, we know he's been singing for 16 years. He takes special care to capture the nuance of the words and music of fado. His somewhat hard-to-find fado house is off-the-beaten path. The decorations are regional. Sometimes late at night he invites his friends to join him in fado singing. The atmosphere is spontaneous. The Arreda is open daily from 10 p.m. till 3:30 a.m. The price of one whiskey—that is, 65$ ($2.54)—is the only admission you have to pay.

Rolls-Royce, 6-B Travessa Fonso Sanches, is sometimes known as the R.R. Club. It's the latest craze in Cascais among discotheque dancers. Because of the blasting sound track, the atmosphere is supercharged. To get in, you're charged a minimum of 120$ ($4.68), including service and tax. The average whiskey costs 75$ ($2.93). The Rolls-Royce runs every day.

Beyond Lisbon and the Costa do Sol lies a series of one-day trips from the capital, previewed in the two chapters coming up.

Chapter IX

SOUTH OF THE TAGUS

1. Azeitao
2. Sesimbra
3. Portinho da Arrábida
4. Setúbal
5. Palmela

THE WIDOW AND THE SPINSTER, the rheumatic and those plagued with "the vapors"—the bulwark of Victorian England's 19th-century continental travelers—crossed the Tagus by boat and headed for the scenic wonders on the left bank of Lisbon.

Chances are, under one arm, they carried a gold-leafed copy of a work by Robert Southey, England's Poet Laureate. After all, this Lake poet, a much-traveled gentleman, did more than anyone to publicize the glories that awaited his countrymen on the other bank. He virtually made the trek famous when he wrote: "I have never seen such a sublime panorama as the Arrábida Mountains afford, which, constantly changing as we go our way, offer us new beauties at every turn."

Nowadays, the narrow isthmus south of the Tagus is fast booming into a major attraction, beefed up by foreign visitors who seemingly have never heard of—nor could care less about—what the son of an unsuccessful linendraper had to say about the district's natural beauties.

Behind the upsurge of interest is the Ponte 25 de Abril, the longest suspension bridge ever erected in Europe. It has speeded traffic and development to the area, and now it is possible to cross the Tagus in minutes, then head rapidly across good roads through pine groves to the vertexes of the triangle known as "The Land of the Three Castles": Sesimbra, Setúbal, and Palmela. Of course, traditionalists still prefer taking the ferry from Black Horse Square in Lisbon, docking in Cacilhas.

The isthmus—long cut off from the Portuguese capital—is wild, rugged, lush, and productive. The groves are heavy with the odors of ripening oranges and vineyards known for their grapes used to make muscatel. With craggy cliffs and coves in the background, the crystalline waters of the Atlantic are ideal for swimming and skin-diving, or fishing for tuna, swordfish, bass, whatever.

Sandy beaches double as the sites of fish auctions and leisurely sunbathing (some of the skimpy suits worn by North European beauties make aging black-shawled Portuguese varinas cross themselves). Further up from the sardine-canning center of Setúbal, the coastline roughens where the Serra of Arrábida meets the sea, resulting in an abundance of caves, grottos, and precipitous crags.

The land possesses vivid reminders of its past, reflected in Moorish architectural influences, Roman ruins and roads, heritages from the Phoenicians, and Spanish fortresses. Mighty castles and humble fishermen's cottages alike shook on a November day in 1755 when the earthquake brought Lisbon to her knees. Signs of that catastrophe are still evidenced in the ruins of the hamlet of Palmela, and the lonely walls of Coina Castle.

The strip of land plummets toward the sea, stretches along for miles of sandy beaches, and rolls through fertile vineyards. It's a place of contrasts, natural beauty, and history.

Its proximity to Lisbon (Setúbal is only 25 miles from the capital) makes it possible for a one-day excursion. But its unusual inns and low tariffs mark it as a place where the dollar-wise reader will want to linger.

1. Azeitao

This sleepy village lies in the heart of quinta country. In Portuguese, a quinta means a farm, villa, or country house. At its most meager, it is a simple farmhouse surrounded by lands. At its best, it is a mansion of great architectural style filled with art decorations. Azeitao boasts the best!

It is said that King Manuel I started the concept of quintas in the early 16th century when he built the **Quinta de Bacalhoa** at Vila Fresca de Azeitao. The king's mother once lived there. In time it was taken over by the son of Afonso de Albuquerque. At one point in its history, the building was owned by the Braganzas, eventually falling into disrepair, as many of its decorations—specifically its antique tiles—were carted off by vandals.

Before World War II, the mansion was purchased by an American woman who worked for years restoring it as much as possible to its original condition. The architecture is characterized by loggias, pavilions, half-moon domes that suggest a Moorish influence, and a trio of pyramided towers. One of the panels of 16th-century azulejos (tiles) depicts an innocent Susanna being hotly pursued by lecherous Elders. Some architectural critics have suggested that the palace itself betrays the first buds of the Renaissance in Portugal. Even though it is a private residence, you can sometimes obtain permission at the gate lodge to visit the topiary gardens.

On the other hand, the second 16th-century mansion, **Quinta das Torres**, can not only be visited, but you can stop over for a meal or even spend the night (see below). The third palace was erected at Vila Nogueira de Azeitao by the Dukes of Aveiro in a classically Renaissance style.

Azeitao makes a good base for trekkers, especially those who want to scale the limestone Serra of Arrábida by foot. Others settle for long walks through scented pine woods or silvery olive groves. To cap your day, you can order some Azeitao cheese and a bottle of local muscatel. The village lies 9½ miles north of Setúbal, 15½ miles south of Lisbon.

THE BUDGET RANGE: Quinta das Torres, 5 Estrada Nacional, Azeitao (tel. 228-00-01), is a 16th-century baronial mansion, which up until recently used only candlelight and kerosene lamps to illuminate its stately rooms at night. It's been kept intact on purpose for those desiring to live quietly—stepping back in time. It has been owned by the same family for many generations, and the present descendant, Dr. Bento de Sousa, perpetuates the old traditions.

The estate is approached through large gates and along a tree-lined driveway. Gradually, a pair of square peaked towers framing the entrance terrace comes into view. Ten bedrooms, all with private baths, have been set aside for paying guests. Each is quite different, ranging from smaller chambers to a ballroom-size suite dominated by princess-style brass beds, with a higher tester and flouncy soft ruffles. Some of the rooms have high shuttered windows, time-mellowed tiled floors, antique furnishings, vases of fresh flowers, oil lamps, and niches with saints or madonnas. The half-board rate for two persons ranges between 445$ ($17.36) and 630$ ($24.58). In a suite, the half-board rate for two is 680$ ($26.53) daily.

The dining room of the Quinta has a coved ceiling, a tall stone fireplace where log fires are lit on chilly evenings, plus elaborate scenic tiles depicting "The Rape of the Sabine Women" and "The Siege of Troy." The rich-tasting, heavy cuisine is well recommended, and a meal will cost around 120$ ($4.68). The windows open onto a pool where white swans glide by. Luncheon is often served near a tree-bordered ornamental fish pond filled with carp and containing a domed cupola. A five-minute walk through an olive grove leads to a large spring-filled pool where guests dip and sunbathe.

2. Sesimbra

To the Portuguese, Sesimbra used to be a closely guarded secret. With justification, it is considered one of the most unspoiled fishing villages in the country. True, the hill-scaling Hotel Do Mar has opened up, attracting a steady stream of international visitors; but the varinas and fishermen still go about their time-honored task of plucking their livelihood from the Atlantic.

Against a backdrop of rocky cliffs, sardines, shellfish, whiting, and the scabbard fish—with its whip-shaped body and daggerlike teeth—lie stretched out on the sandy beach. When the fleet comes in, the day's catch is auctioned at a lota. Donkeys carry boxes laden with sea fruit, and saffron-colored nets are hoisted up into the sun to dry.

Far down the beach, beyond the boat-clogged harbor, is the 17th-century **Fortress of St. Teodosio,** built to fortify the region against the pirates who plagued and plundered, carting off the most beautiful women and young girls.

A walk along the ruined battlements of the five-towered **Castle of Sesimbra** reduces the village to a nearly immobile miniature. The Castle was captured from the Moors in 1165 and rebuilt following the 1755 earthquake, which sent sections of its crenelated walls tumbling to the ground. Enclosed within is a church and a meager archaeological display of artifacts removed from the ruins.

More recently, Sesimbra has been enjoying popularity as an angling center, attracting swordfish hunters. The resort lies about 19 miles south of Lisbon, 17 miles west of Setúbal. Sesimbra is connected by bus to Lisbon. You can also get to Sesimbra by taking the ferry from Terreiro do Paço wharf for a fare of 1$80 (5¢), then a bus from Cacilhas for 17$ (66¢).

THE TOP HOTEL: Hotel Do Mar (tel. 229-326) is one of the most unusual self-contained beach resort hotels south of the Tagus—a beehive construction of luxury units spreading from a high cliff to the water below. Its architectural concept is perhaps the most creative of any hotel in Portugal. The passageways are like continuous art galleries, with good contemporary paintings and especially prized ceramic plaques and sculpture, and the main lobby houses a glassed-in aviary with tropical birds. The year-round hotel was the creation of three brothers, one of whom did the interior design. He is to be congratulated, especially for such features as creating an "undersea" boîte beneath the pool, and turning it into a haven for snug discotheque life. During the day, one can soak up sun at the beach or at the circular swimming pool.

The 120 bedrooms are stacked up adobe fashion—each with its own bath and private terrace, with a view of the ocean and gardens sweeping down the hillside. Furnishings are streamlined and well selected; the rooms airy, with breakfast being served on an outer flower-filled terrace. Full pension for two costs 780$ ($30.43) or 1,120$ ($43.70), depending on the size of rooms and time of year. Singles with all meals are 572$ ($22.31) and 810$ ($31.59), taxes included.

There are two dining rooms: one circular self-service, operating in summer, the other, on an upper ledge, warmed with wood-grained paneling and overlooking the sea. If you're stopping off on a day trip from Lisbon, you can order a luncheon for 125$ ($4.88). The before-dinner gathering point is a rustically styled bar; after-dinner guests congregate in a living room, with a white wall fireplace, and islands of red and black chairs and tables on Chinese red floors. The concierge will arrange for everything from fishing to hairdressing appointments. The hotel operates transfer services.

3. Portinho da Arrábida

The limestone Arrábida Mountains stretch for about 22 miles, beginning at Palmela and rolling to a dramatic end at Cape Espichel on the Atlantic. At times the cliffs and bluffs are so high that you must seemingly peer through clouds to see the purple waters of the Atlantic below.

A Swiss botanist once said the mountain range contained "the most amazing flora to be seen in Europe." The foliage that rims the cliffs and the surrounding areas is lush, sub-tropical, and wide ranging—everything from holm oaks, sweet bay, pines, laurel, juniper, cypress, araucaria, magnolia, lavender, myrtle and pimpernels. It's a riot of color and fragrance carpeting the mountains.

The Serra is riddled with numerous caves and grottos, the most famous of which is the **Lapa de Santa Margarida.** Of it, Hans Christian Andersen wrote: "It is a veritable church hewn out of the living rock, with a fantastic vault, organ pipes, columns, and altars."

Perched on a hillside like a tiara over Portinho da Arrábida, the **New Convent** dates from the 16th century. You can go to the gate and ring for the caretaker, who may or may not show you around the precincts.

Plummeting down to the sea, you arrive at Portinho da Arrábida itself, at the foot of the Serra. This is a favorite oasis with many families from Lisbon who rent little multi-colored cottages on the beach. Portinho da Arrábida—which can be approached from either Setúbal or Sesimbra—lies about 23 miles south of Lisbon. By public transportation, you must make bus connections in Sesimbra.

A BUDGET INN: Estalagem de Santa Maria da Arrábida (tel. 208-05-27). The restaurant part of this hill-hugging inn was carved out of the remains of a fort. Below the coast road, it practically meets the sea. With its stone walls, pots of red geraniums, and all-glass walls along the oceanside, it forms a setting for some of the most inexpensive, but savory, viands south of the Tagus. To dine here, it's more economical if two persons order the same main dish. For example, a platter of caldeirada à Estalagem, the fish stew of the house, costs 65$ ($2.54) for two persons. There are at least two dozen fish dishes from which to choose, including grilled sea bass, 65$ ($2.54) for two, and grilled red mullet, 80$ ($3.12) for two. You can order an Azeitao tart or pie for 65$ ($2.54), but you should try the special cheese of the district (Azeitao) for 20$ (78¢).

Owned by Sergio Gama, the sleeping part of the estalagem is about a five-minute walk away, along a circuitous cliffside road. The inn is a white stucco building, erected above the road, with stepped terraces allowing the better rooms to have private patios. There are no lounges, except for the casual front one with garden furniture. The bedrooms are well kept, and the beds are decorated with either mahogany inlays or white iron curlicues. Usually you're greeted with a pungent aroma from the highly-waxed parquet floors. The tariffs are based on the view and the plumbing—rooms with full bath are more expensive than those with just a bidet and wash basin (each of the latter has the use of a clean hall toilet and shower). Two persons can stay here, taking half pension, at prices that range anywhere from 320$ ($12.48) to 380$ ($14.82) daily. The inn is open only from March 1 to October 31.

4. Setúbal

On the right bank of the Sado River, 25 miles south of Lisbon, lies one of Portugal's largest and most ancient cities, said to have been founded by the grandson of Noah. Motorists often include it on their itineraries because of an exceptional inn, the **Estalagem de S. Filipe,** installed in a late 16th-century fort overlooking the sea (see below).

Setúbal is known as the center of Portugal's sardine industry and for the production of the most exquisite muscatel wine in the world. As far back as the days of the Romans and the Visigoths, the aromatic and hearty grapes of this region were praised by connoisseurs.

Orange groves (a delicious jam is made from the fruit), orchards, vineyards, and outstanding beaches (a popular one, **Praia da Figueirinha**) compose the environs of Setúbal. And the white pyramidal mounds you see dotting the landscape are deposits of sea salt drying in the sun, another major commercial asset of this seaside community.

Many artists and writers have come from Setúbal, none more notable than the 18th-century Portuguese poet Manuel Maria Barbosa du Bocage, a forerunner of romanticism. At the Praça do Bocage, a monument honors him.

Across the Sado is the sand-dune-studded isthmus of **Tróia.** Ruins of Roman villas on the bank and occasional discoveries of Phoenician remains indicate a once-thriving port. Excavations began on the ruins in the mid-19th century, uncovering part of what was known to be Cetobriga, a city dating from the third and fourth centuries. A ferry or a launch will take you over and back. If the pursuit of antiquity isn't enough, you can relax at one of the beaches.

In Setúbal is the late-15th-century **Church of Jesus,** an example of the Manueline style of architecture. Of particular interest are the ornate decorations on the main doorway and the Arrábida marble columns. Each of the latter is actually three columns twisted together like taffy to form a cable or rootlike effect. Somehow they don't seem to hold up the vaulted ceiling, but give the illusion of appendages grown down to the floor.

Raymond Postgate wrote that the columns "look as if they had been twisted and wrung by a washerwoman," and Hans Christian Andersen recorded that the monument was "one of the most beautiful small churches that I have ever seen." The church has been heavily restored, the latest wholesale renovation in 1969-70. Adjoining is the unpretentious **Town Museum,** housing some early 16th-century Portuguese paintings, as well as some Spanish and Flemish works, coins, shards, and other artifacts from the sandy pit of Tróia. The church-museum is at the Praça Miguel Bombarda, off the Avenida 22 de Dezembro.

To reach this port, where windmills still clack in the countryside, roosters crow, and the "girls of the sardines" speak Portuguese with a seemingly Arabic accent, take the ferry from Lisbon to Barreiro. There, you can board a train for the rest of the way.

For accommodations, Setúbal offers two possible choices: one a hilltop castle, another a partially restored 16th-century convent. Modern hotels cater to more conventional tastes. If you're passing through for the day, the recommended luncheon stopovers are the Estalagem de Sao Filipe or the Club Naval Setúbalense.

THE MEDIUM-PRICED RANGE: Estalagem de Sao Filipe, Castelo de Sao Filipe (tel. 238-44). This fortress-castle, dating back to 1590, was built by an Italian architect who came to Portugal during the ill-fated reign of the young king Sebastiao. The builder gave it a crowning perch on a hilltop overlooking the town and the harbor. You wind your way up a curving mountain road, passing through a stone arch, by towers to the belvedere. Rooms that once were for the soldiers and the governor have been tastefully and richly furnished with antiques and reproductions. In earlier days there were guns and ammunition, but they have given way to soft beds and ornate Portuguese crafted headboards. The walls of the chapel and the public rooms contain tiled dados, depicting scenes from the life of S. Filipe and the life of the Virgin Mary.

The bedrooms are individually treated, each with its own personality. They are reached via what seems like miles of plant-filled corridors, up wide worn stone steps. Singles range from 200$ ($7.80) to 235$ ($9.17); doubles from 280$ ($10.92) to 330$ ($12.87).

Dining is pleasant, sitting in Windsor-style armchairs. Six alcoved windows open onto a panoramic view. Against a background of tiled dado, a primitive tapestry and photostated engraving, an à la carte luncheon or dinner, including many fish specialties, is served. Most guests take this meal when they stop over on a day trip from Lisbon. The clients seem to gravitate to the medieval-style drinking lounge, with its coved and arched ceiling, pierced copper hanging lanterns, tiled bar, and husky brass-studded armchairs. The sitting rooms are also intimate, with tiled walls, antiques, bowls of flowers, engravings, chests, and copper artifacts in the niches.

THE BUDGET RANGE: Hotel Esperança, 220 Avenida Luísa Todi (tel. 251-51), is Setúbal's modern hotel, standing on the harbor boulevard named after the famous singer. There are two pleasant living lounges, but the hub of city life is the canopy-covered cafe in front, with its umbrella-shaded tables. While sampling the regional viands at the top-floor dining room, you'll have a view of the Sado River and the boats in the harbor.

The bedrooms, 76 in all, each with a tiled bath and shower, are restrained and contemporary, with wood tones and soft fabrics. The tariff in a single ranges between 150$ ($5.85) and 220$ ($8.58); in a double, from 200$ ($7.80) to 300$ ($11.70).

Quinta de S.·Joao, 18 Rua Almeida Garrett, is installed in a half-restored 16th-century monastery. Behind high walls, it sits on a street honoring Portugal's romantic poet of the 19th century. The convent was first used by nuns in 1529, and the granddaughters of Joao II came here. Neglected for centuries, it had been handed along to various proprietors before it came into the healing hands of Rafael Emidio Croner Torres and his wife. He is a collector of antiques—in fact, has an antique shop in the city (we suspect he uses the convent to store surplus pieces). The long and arduous task of restoration has begun.

First, he furnished the bedrooms well and installed a bath with each one of them. The rooms vary in size and convenience, but they are all reached via long narrow flights of stairs, along many corridors. The price of a single ranges between 140$ ($5.46) and 200$ ($7.80); the tariff in a double graduating from 240$ ($9.36) to 350$ ($13.65). Those who prefer to live here as master of the quinta should consider suite No. 106 (one night it accommodated nine guests). The cost hovers around 350$ ($13.65) for a party of four. Your parlor will have a red velvet settee and matching chairs, a grandfather clock, and several chandeliers dripping with crystal.

Breakfast is the only meal served—family-style at a long refectory table on one side of the loggia of the inner cloister. There's a cozy living room, with a valuable inlaid desk, open fireplace, time-mellowed chests, and a Victorian settee and chairs. Everything seems to open onto the cloister, with its overgrown and untidy garden, planted with plum trees, flowers, vegetables, wisteria, all growing around an aged carriage. In the chapel, tiled walls depict scenes from the life of John the Baptist, including one of Salome asking for his head.

WHERE TO DINE: Restaurante Naval Setúbalense, 300 Avenida Luísa Todi (tel. 236-74), is especially noted for its tempting array of acepipes (hors d'oeuvres). In a creaky, once-private home, you dine in the old-fashioned living room. Favored by many Portuguese navy officers, the restaurant offers excellent food at low prices. The proprietor Laureano Rocha came from Vigo, Spain, nearly a half century ago.

For only 110$ ($4.29), he offers a well-prepared four-course meal, beginning with a selection of 18 hors d'oeuvres, including "whatever the best things are on the market that day." The best things are likely to include "knives" (a particular kind of shellfish), oysters both stuffed and natural, curried rice, two kinds of sardines, squid, garbanzos, and a type of black-eyed pea known as "the man with two faces." The second course always includes fish—perhaps sole or turbot—followed by beef with french fried potatoes and green beans, then cheese and dessert. It's the best food buy in Setúbal. The service is polite and the ambience is homelike, enhanced by walls covered with contemporary paintings.

From Setúbal, it's only 5½ miles north to:

5. Palmela

The village of Palmela lies in the heart of a wine-producing region, in the foothills of the Arrábida Mountains. It is famous for its fortress, from which at a vantage point of 1,200 feet, you'll be rewarded with one of the most extensive and varied views in all of Portugal. Over sienna-hued valleys and vineyards heavy with grapes, one sees the capital to the north, the estuary of the Sado to the south.

The position of **Palmela Castle** has long been a strategic point in securing control of the lands "south of the Tagus." It was from Palmela that Afonso Henriques, the first king of Portugal, drove out the Moors and established his new nation's domination in the district. The fortress itself was built in the 12th century, and was, in its day, a splendid example of medieval military architecture. It is further believed that the Celts founded a castle on the spot in 300 B.C.

Shades of 1755 still haunt the once-mighty fortress today. Its stones—covered with saffron-colored moss—are dislocated from their foundations, and gaping cracks appear in the walls. Indeed, the denizens of Palmela claim that much of their little hamlet was constructed with pieces of the fortress.

Of special interest is the Roman road discovered behind the Castle by archaeologists. It is the only such road to be unearthed in Portugal, and makes for speculation as to its relationship with the Roman beach colonies of Tróia, off Setúbal. You can scale the hill to the Castle any time of the day.

The tourist circuit belt between Óbidos and Nazaré unfolds in the next chapter.

Chapter X

ESTREMADURA

1. Obidos
2. Caldas da Rainha
3. Berlenga Islands
4. Alcobaça
5. Aljubarrota
6. Sao Martinho do Porto
7. Nazaré
8. Batalha
9. Fátima

THE BLACK-SHAWLED WOMEN of Nazaré traced against the darkening sea . . . the phenomenon of Fátima . . . the sedate charm of the antique town of Óbidos . . . the curative waters of Caldas da Rainha . . . the jagged granite islands of Berlenga . . . the rolling plains near Alcobaça . . . the sandy beaches along the way.

The first flowers of empire bloomed in these lands north of Lisbon hundreds of years ago, and the beauty has not been diminished by time. Like the once-white limestone of Battle Abbey (Batalha), this land has been gilded in the sunlight of the passing years.

Estremadura is a land of contrasts. Stories—apocryphal, real, and living—still inspire the burial hall of kings, empty niches never filled, and broad squares and green plains where man's faith has been restored and his fate decided. Deaths and royal intrigues, castles rising in the air—all are woven together, the warp and woof inextricably bound up in the whole fabric.

The Atlantic smashes the coast at Guincho, while further up it can hardly muster a ripple in the snug cove of Sao Martinho do Pôrto. These coastal regions are teeming with seafood: nursery-bred lobster, shrimp, crabs, squid, tuna, barnacles, and albacore. The sea is never far from any spot in Estremadura. From many a village's bastion, its shimmer can be seen, a reminder of the source of the land's bounty. In the many examples of Manueline architecture, especially at Batalha, the tie with the sea remains unbroken. The basic nautical designs—ropes, cables, armillary spheres, seascape effects—acknowledge the debt.

If it is impossible for you to spend several days exploring Estremadura, you can dip into it on one-day trips from Lisbon: first to Óbidos, 58 miles from Lisbon; then to Alcobaça, 67 miles from Lisbon; on to Nazaré, 81 miles from Lisbon; back to Batalha, 73 miles from Lisbon; and finally, a stop at Fátima,

87 miles from the capital. Traveling to these five major targets will take you through the heartland of Estremadura.

1. Obidos

Years after Afonso Henriques drove the Moors out of Óbidos, the poet king, Dinis, and his saintly wife Isabella of Aragon passed by the battlemented walls of this medieval borough and were struck by its beauty. The Queen likened the village to a jewel-studded crown, with its extended walls and gleaming plaster-faced houses. Anxious to please, Dinis made her a present of this gemlike village ribboned by a defensive wall. A tradition was established. Instead of giving precious stones, Portuguese royal bridegrooms presented Óbidos to their spouses—and it didn't cost them a penny. And what Queen could complain at getting such a gift?

Entered through a tile-coated gatehouse, Óbidos rises on a sugarloaf hill, above a valley of vineyards. Its mellow golden towers, its ramparts (rebuilt in the 12th century and subsequently restored), and its crenelated battlements contrast with bright white houses and the rolling countryside where windmills clack in the breeze.

Inside its confines, you will have traveled back hundreds of years. The narrow streets are either cobbled or made of roughly hewn flagstones. Green shoots lodge in the crannies of the walls, and vines climb the sides of tile-roofed houses. A loom hums in a candlelit vaulted workshop. A living piece of history.

In the baroque **Parish Church of Santa Maria**, Afonso V, at the age of 10, exchanged marriage vows with his beguiling cousin, only 8. Inside, the church is lined with remarkable blue and white azulejos (tiles). Pause long enough to admire a Renaissance tomb and the paintings of Josefa of Óbidos, a 17th-century artist. In the Chapel of St. Lawrence are contained relics of saints' hands.

The castle has been converted into a tourist inn (pousada). From its ramparts you can bask in views of Estremadura—the scene so unspoiled one can imagine Afonso Henriques' retinue marching over the hills.

Save some time for browsing through the shops, searching out thick-woven fabrics, regional rugs (both hand and machine made), raffia and hand-made bags, and the local lace.

This well-preserved national monument village lies 59 miles north of Lisbon. Trains leave Rossio Station in Lisbon.

In accommodations you have a choice of a converted castle, a convent, or a hostelry outside town.

THE BUDGET RANGE: Pousada do Castelo (tel. 951-05). This Manueline-trimmed stone palace lodged on the ramparts of the walls of Óbidos is firmly rooted in Portugal's history, and today—with the supervision of the government—it is one of the best run pousadas (tourist inns) in the country. Reached via twisting cobblestone streets through the village, the entrance is through a thick Gothic archway. You ascend further, into a wide sunny forecourt, and up a grand stone stairway to the main hall.

There are several well-furnished lounges, but regrettably, only six bedrooms. Three of these contain private baths, the occupants of the others making use of corridor plumbing. Most wayfarers stop off just for the day, partaking of the 100$ ($3.90) luncheon or dinner. Try for a table near one of the view windows. The dining room is in the Portuguese quinta style—almost grand, yet nicely primitive, with old oak beams, tiled dado, a fireplace, wrought-iron chandeliers, and leather chairs. If you're not staying at the pousada, call ahead for summertime dining reservations.

The fortunate few snare the rooms, enjoying the character of the bedchambers, furnished with antiques or fool-the-eye reproductions. Deeply set windows have tiny monk ledges, where you can squat to enjoy the view of the surrounding countryside. Homelike cretonne fabrics cover the beds, and a few rooms contain desks with brass church lamps, armchairs and ecclesiastical wall plaques.

For demi-pension, the single rate ranges from 190$ ($7.41) to 260$ ($10.14), increasing to anywhere from 330$ ($12.87) to 430$ ($16.78) for two persons. Fellow guests gather in one of two drinking lounges for sundown libations.

Estalagem Do Convento, Rua Dom Joao Ornelas (tel. 952-17), is an old village nunnery turned inn. Outside the town walls, it is owned by a French woman, Suzanne Balivet, who doubles as a professor in Lisbon when she's not an innkeeper in Óbidos. On weekends, she's here full-time. The reception lounge is surely the tiniest on the Iberian peninsula, with a fireplace, 17th-century chest, torchier, and a pair of gilt angels. She has utilized her Gallic ingenuity in furnishing the 13 rooms, employing furniture to complement the structure. Although the beds are old, the mattresses are new, and tiled bathrooms have been sneaked in. The bedchambers open off rambling corridors with chests and benches large enough to hold the trousseaux of a dozen brides. The cost for one person is 235$ ($9.17) with breakfast; a double, with sitting room and breakfast, is 345$ ($13.46).

Since this is primarily an inn, and the food is French-delicious, it's wisest to pay the extra 220$ ($8.58) for three meals a day. Guests from outside are welcomed as well, and can order a 110$ ($4.29) table d'hôte or else specialties from the à la carte menu, including French onion soup, pepper steak, and crêpes suzette. The dining room decor consists of heavy black beams, an open corner stone fireplace, and a brick oven. On sunny days, guests dine on the rear patio, in a garden with a moldy stone wall and tangerine and orange trees. In addition to a bar with hand-hewn beams, there's a living room with leather armchairs, old paintings, an 18th-century desk, and a brass-studded chest dated 1827. A curiosity is the converted wine cellar, now an intimate boîte with a petite dance floor and imported recordings. Minimum is 50$ ($1.95).

About 3½ kilometers out of Caldhas on the road to Óbidos is a pleasant hostelry called **Mansao da Torre** (tel. 952-47). You drive under a stone archway down an entry some 100 feet long and come to a hacienda-type building, flanked by a large stone tower. Inside, there's a foyer with a large painting of Portuguese galleons, an old clock, model sailing ships, and two globes on a chest. There are only six rooms, but they have a homey charm about them. A double with breakfast costs 300$ ($11.70), and singles go for 200$ ($7.80). In the rear is a pleasant ranch-style bungalow, where some of the rooms are located. The Mansao is open all year.

2. Caldas Da Rainha

After a bad night's sleep, the sister-queen of Manuel the Fortunate one day set out from Óbidos to Batalha. Passing through a small village en route, the rheumatic Leonor is said to have seen peasants bathing in fetid pools off the side of the road. When told of the therapeutic value of these springs, she had her ladies in waiting clear the area to protect her modesty. A screen of fabric was draped around her, and she descended—partially dressed—into a foul sulphur bath.

So great was her relief from her long-suffering ailment that she returned to Caldas da Rainha again and again—in fact, hocked her personal wealth in rubies and gold jewelry (many gems given to her by her deceased husband, The Perfect Prince, Joao II), to construct a hospital and an adjoining church. The chapel, **Nossa Senhora do Pópulo,** was built at the dawn of the 16th century in the Manueline style—then at its apex—and is graced with a well-executed landmark belfry. Inside are handsome 300-year-old glazed earthenware tiles in buttercup yellow and marine blue. Today, a classic green bronze statue of Leonor stands at Largo do Conde de Fontalva; and the town has been a spa ever since—enjoying a particular chic in the 19th century.

Caldas da Rainha is also noted for its ceramics—especially the "cabbage leaf" designs on soup tureens and accompanying bowls. Inside the town and outside along the road to Alcobaça, you can stop at many roadside stands and purchase these ceramics at far cheaper prices than you'd pay in Lisbon. However, you'll have to carry them back to the capital with you and arrange shipment there. These primitively painted reproductions of cabbage, fruit, shellfish, and lizards are made from the local clay, and many of them—especially the reptilian and crustacean specialties—evoke the designs of the famous ceramist and caricaturist Rafael Bordalo Pinheiro. He had a studio at Caldas da Rainha during its heyday as a 19th-century resort.

Caldas da Rainha is also a thriving market town, the activity centering on the Praça da Republica where you'll see what surely must be the world's largest cabbages. Women with weather-beaten faces sell wild hares in the shop stalls, and at day's end, trudge wearily home. In winter men in fur-trimmed coats walk around clutching red hens, much to the pleasure of camera-snapping tourists.

The town is some 60 miles north of Lisbon, and is usually visited after Óbidos, four miles away.

3. Berlenga Islands

The Berlenga Islands—granite rocks set in the Atlantic—are an island hideaway. Eight miles out in the ocean, a medieval fortress once stood sentinel over the Portuguese coastline.

Drawn especially to the isles in summer are skin-divers and fishermen, intrigued by the undersea fauna, the long-finned tunny (albacore), jack fish, and varieties of marine crustaceans. Equipment is available at Péniche, 57 miles north of Lisbon. From this port town—jutting out into the Atlantic like a tongue—a launch goes to the Berlenga Islands. The trip—likely to be rough over choppy waters—takes about an hour.

You can visit the islands just for the day, exploring on your own, and returning in the late afternoon. The launch leaves Péniche weekdays at 10:30 a.m., coming back at 6 p.m. On Sundays, the ferry departs twice in the morning —at 9:30 and again at noon—returning at 4 and 6 p.m. If the sea is bad, the ferry schedule is altered or abandoned.

4. Alcobaça

At the apex of its power in the Middle Ages, this Cistercian monastery was one of the richest and most prestigious in Europe. Begun around 1152, it was founded to honor a vow made by Portugal's first king, Afonso Henriques, should he be victorious over the Moors at Santarém. Alcobaça, at the confluence of the Alcoa and Baça Rivers, was built to show his spiritual indebtedness to St. Bernard of Clairvaux, who inspired (others say goaded) many Crusaders into battle against the infidel.

Today, the monastery—in spite of its baroque facade and latter-day overlay—is a monument to simplicity and majesty. Somehow a sense of other worldliness pervades as you walk down the 350 foot long nave. Tall chalk-white clustered columns, like trees, hold up a vaulted ceiling nearly 70 feet high.

The transept of Alcobaça shelters the Gothic tombs of two star-crossed lovers, the Romeo and Juliet of Portuguese history. They were Pedro the Cruel and the ill-fated Spanish beauty, Inês de Castro, his mistress and (later perhaps) his wife. The work of an unknown sculptor, their sarcophagi (though damaged) are considered the greatest pieces of sculpture from 14th-century Portugal.

The oval-faced Inês is guarded and protected by angels hovering over her. Her tomb rests on sculpted animals with human faces—said to represent the assassins who slit her throat. Pedro captured two of them, personally ripping out and eating their hearts. Inês was buried at Alcobaça during a torchlight parade, following a ghoulish ceremony in which her decaying body was exhumed. The king had his courtiers kiss her rotten hand and honor her as "the queen of the realm." Around the tomb are panels depicting scenes from the Last Judgment.

Pedro hoped to rise on that day of Resurrection to greet Inês emerging from her sleep of centuries. On a wheel of fortune at his tomb, a sculptor, following his mandate, carved the words: ate o fim do mundo, meaning until the end of the world. Guarded over by angels, his feet nestled on a dog, Pedro was buried in a tomb supported by lions, symbols of his timeless rage and vengeance.

There is much to see at Alcobaça, certainly the Cloisters of Silence, with their delicate arches, favored by Dinis, the poet king. He sparked a thriving literary colony at the monastery, the monks busily engaged in translating ecclesiastical writings. But aside from the tombs and cloisters, the curiosity is the kitchen, through which a branch of the Alcoa River was routed. As in most Cistercian monasteries, the reason for a flowing brook was one of sanitation. Chroniclers have suggested that the friars fished for their dinner in the brook, later washing their dishes in it. In the huge chimneyed pit, five or six steers or oxen were roasted at the same time. A six-ton marble table resting here would probably have accommodated Gargantua and Pantagruel.

In the dining room are found niches where the monks prayed while the hierarchy ate. In honor of an old tradition, Queen Elizabeth II was feted at a luncheon here. In front of the dining room is a fountain, where Portuguese girls wet their fingers, putting the water to their cheeks. The old women of the village predict that by so doing the young girls will soon get married.

Finally, in the 18th-century Salon of Kings are niches with sculptures of some of the rulers of Portugal (many fell from their resting places and were damaged in the 1755 earthquake). An air of melancholy is lent to the scene by the empty niches left waiting for the rulers who were never sculpted. The tiles in the room depict, in part, Afonso Henriques' triumph over the Moors.

After your visit, you can explore the nearby market, said to sell the best fruit in all of Portugal, especially succulent peaches grown in surrounding orchards originally planted by the Cistercian monks. Many stalls also sell the blue and white pottery of Alcobaça.

Trains depart from Lisbon's Rossio Station, 67 miles away.

5. Aljubarrota

Against a backdrop of mountain scenery, the extensive green fields on the Aljubarrota plateau are considered "the birthplace of Portugal." Between Alcobaça and Batalha, on August 14, 1385, near the village of Aljubarrota, Portuguese independence was secured. Joao I, the founder of the Aviz dynasty, and his young captain, Nuno Álvares—fortified by scythe- and shovel-bearing peasants and some English archers—defeated the Castilian sea of soldiers.

A story of the battle itself relates how during the heat of conflict the king and his army were consumed by thirst under a blazing sun. He vowed that never would a voyager pass this way again without access to water. Today, outside of the village, a small chapel offers a pitcher of fresh water in a niche in honor of that ancient commitment.

But a far better way of refreshing yourself is at the following roadside inn in:

THE BUDGET RANGE: Estalagem Do Cruzeiro (The Inn of the Cross), 1 Estrada Nacional (tel. 421-12), is a privately owned roadside inn, a favorite of wayfarers heading north and a luncheon stopover. When they came this way, Prince Rainier and Princess Grace of Monaco pre-selected it for a royal luncheon. It sits on the brow of a hill, with views of the orchards and surrounding countryside, the construction typical of a Portuguese villa.

Dressed in regional clothing, the waitresses set the mood by placing a basket of hot homemade corn bread, round balls of the local cheese, and ripe olives on your dining table. The table d'hôte meal costs 110$ ($4.29). The dinner always begins with soup, follows with say, caldeirada mista à Nazaré (mixed fish stew), then a meat course, fruit and dessert (usually a sweet country pudding or cake). Hopefully, you'll be there in July or August during the peach season—the fruit is tree-ripened and lusciously juicy.

For overnight stopovers, there are rooms at many prices. The most expensive are the doubles on the top floor—each with a balcony and private bath costing 240$ ($9.36) for two. Singles go for 125$ ($4.88) and 155$ ($6.05), with bath. The furnishings are in the old style, with high wooden headboards.

6. Sao Martinho do Porto

This seaside village nestles between pine-covered foothills and the ocean. Its main attraction is an almost landlocked sandy beach, brightly scalloped into the terrain. The waters are calm and clear, the days gently descending from May to October.

For many Sao Martinho do Porto makes a good base for touring: Óbidos is 12½ miles away; Alcobaça, 11; Fátima, 28; Batalha, 22; and Caldas da Rainha, 9½. It is 72 miles by rail from Lisbon, and only a short run north to the fishing village of Nazaré. A coastal road skirts the village, and buses run regularly into Nazaré.

In hotels, there is the following recommendation:

The Budget Range
   Parque Hotel, Avenida Marechal Carmona (tel. 981-08), is old-fashioned and gracious, set in its own small private garden. Ideal for families who want to live pleasantly and inexpensively near the beach, it is surrounded by trees, with summer furniture set out for periods of relaxation. It's especially favored by economy-minded English tourists, who like an atmosphere of large-sized bedrooms and homey furniture.

Open only from the first of June to the first of October, it has installed private baths in 29 of its 44 bedrooms. Full board for two persons ranges from 423$ ($16.50) to 501$ ($19.54).

You dine in a turn-of-the-century hall, with an elaborate ceiling and an old chandelier. The food is well prepared and served, the portions generous. In all, the hotel is a world of polished floors, well-scrubbed rooms, and old-style servants. At an outside terrace with a bar, guests dance to records. On the grounds are two tennis courts.

7. Nazaré

What strikes one immediately about the people of Nazaré is their self-containedness. The inhabitants of Portugal's most famous fishing village live in a unique, tradition-bound, ageless world. Many have never been to Lisbon; indeed, many have never left their village, except perhaps to make the pilgrimage to nearby Fátima.

The people remain insular, even though their village blossoms into a resort in summer. White tents filled with international visitors dot the crescent-shaped beach. Yet the natives go about their time-honored tasks, perhaps pausing to pose for camera fans. Nazaré was originally discovered by writers and painters; but in the 1960s seemingly everyone arrived.

Don't expect stunning architectural styles or historic sights. The big attraction is its people and their boats. Claiming descent from Carthaginian and Phoenician ancestors, many of the natives of Nazaré are characterized by aquiline noses and dark brows—a gentle, hard-working folk whose classical features are marked and lined by sad, yet noble, countenances.

The clothes of the villagers are patch quilts of sun-faded colors. The rugged-looking men appear in rough woolen shirts and trousers, patched in kaleidoscopic rainbow hues, resembling Scottish plaid. Although the origin of this apparel remains unknown, one explanation ventured is that the fishermen picked up the designs from Wellington's troops who passed this way during the Napoleonic wars. On their heads, the men wear long woolen stocking caps, in the dangling ends of which they keep their valuables—a favorite pipe, even a crucifix.

The women are mostly barefooted, wearing embroidered handmade blouses and pleated skirts also made of plaid woolens patched many times. It is customary for the women to don black as a traditional sign of mourning—black tasseled shawls, black capes or cowls; whereas, the unmarried girls of the village are traditionally attired in seven petticoats. The government has made it illegal to count these petticoats, as many tourists were fond of doing in the 50s.

The boats of the fishermen are Phoenician in design—elongated, slender, and decorated in bold colors. Crudely shaped eyes often appear on the high knifelike prows, eyes supposedly imbued with the magical power to search the deep for fish and to avert storms. Powered by oars, the boats contain lanterns for the dangerous job of fishing after dark. During the gusty days of winter, or at high tide, the boats are hauled in and lined up along the waterfront promenade.

While the men are at sea, the women wait—passing their time mending nets, drying sardines on the beach, perhaps nursing children, darning socks, or sewing patches on articles of clothing. At sundown they squat in circles, waiting on the somber shore. When their men come in, the business of sorting out the fish begins. The women trudge up toward the shoreline with heavy baskets balanced precariously on their heads. Some hang nets to dry in the night air; some slice entrails from the silver bodies upon the beach; others chase away pestering children . . . and some wait.

Nazaré is divided into two sections, the fishing quarter and the Sítio, the latter being the upper town which is almost exclusively residential. Near the beach, you'll find handicraft shops, the markets, restaurants, hotels, and pensions. The main square opens directly onto the sea, and narrow streets lead to the smaller squares, evoking a Medina in a Moorish village. Simple shops hang objects outside their doors, indicating what they sell (for example, a carved wooden cow head indicates the butcher shop). At the farthest point from the cliff and square are the vegetable and fish markets, where auctions are held.

Jutting out over the sea, the promontory of the Sítio is awesome, a sheer drop to the ocean and the beach below. It is reached either by a funicular or else a goat-steep cobblestoned pathway. At the Sítio the Virgin Mary supposedly appeared in 1182. A young horseback-riding nobleman, Faus Roupinho, was pursuing a wild deer, but dangerously neared the precipice, shrouded in mist. The fog lifted suddenly to reveal the Virgin and the chasm below. In honor of this miracle, the nobleman built the Chapel of Memory. Today, near the spot, you can go inside the 18th-century structure honoring that long-ago event.

About eight miles from Alcobaça, Nazaré lies 82 miles north of Lisbon. From the capital, take the three hour train ride to the nearest station of Valado, where bus connections into Nazaré can be made. Coaches depart from Lisbon's Rossio Station.

In accommodations, Nazaré offers the following:

TWO MODERN HOTELS—BUDGET RANGE: Hotel Da Nazaré, Largo Afonso Zúquete (tel. 463-11). Such moderno as this hotel offers is a contrast to the fishing village. Six streamlined floors of contemporary design are set on a tiny plaza, a two-minute walk from the waterfront and beach. The facade is a sun-reflecting white and yellow, with a private balcony and all-glass picture windows for the front bedrooms. A rooftop terrace for the sun-lounging life puts the beauty of Nazaré and the clifftop Sítio in your lap.

The dining room underneath also opens onto window walls peering out over the village housetops, the rugged cliffs, the harbor where tomorrow's sardines are being hauled in. The dining room (open to the public in general) serves fish dishes. The set lunch for 110$ ($4.29) includes a soup course such as Alentejana gazpacho, followed by grilled sardines, then a meat selection—perhaps pork in the style of the Algarve. Assorted cakes from the dessert trolley pass by, topped by a choice of seasonal fruit. On the à la carte menu, the specialties on which the tab changes daily include lobster thermidor, grilled crab, shrimps, natural clams, or clams in a savory sauce.

Those staying over will find functional but well-furnished bedrooms, some with carpeting in the famous Nazaré plaid design. The tariffs vary according to the size and view, with doubles ranging from 275$ ($10.73) to 325$ ($12.68), and singles going for anywhere from 200$ ($7.80) to 230$ ($8.97). Breakfast is 25$ (98¢). You'll also find the full-pension prices a bargain. Importantly, the hotel provides parking places in space-starved Nazaré. There is both a main-floor lounge and a duet of drinking bars—all brightly modern, with bold solid color schemes, a nautical tapestry, murals, and paintings of the local fishermen. It's open all year.

Hotel Praia, 39 Avenida Vieira Guimaraes (tel. 464-23), is the leading competitor. An 80-bedroom, six-floor hotel, it is decorated in a contemporary style, all rooms equipped with private bath, the front ones opening onto the ocean. It is well positioned, opposite the Mercado (open market) and only a three-minute walk to the sandy beach where the fishing boats and bathing cabins lie. Touches of the village spirit abound in the decor. A room-long photo mural of the Phoenician-inspired fishing boats rests in the dining room. Even the colors of the lounge furnishings—cardinal red and spring green—match some of the sea-going craft.

The bedrooms are streamlined with Nordic-inspired furnishings. Depending on the size and the view, a single ranges from 120$ ($4.68) to 255$ ($9.95), a double from 175$ ($6.83) to 370$ ($14.43). The cuisine is recommended, the 135$ ($5.27) table d'hôte meal bountiful and the fish dishes fresh.

AN OLD-FASHIONED INN: Pensao-Restaurante Ribamar, 9 Rua Gomes Freire (tel. 461-58), is a genuine old-fashioned village inn, with a traditionally styled dining room at its core. It's exactly on the water, with most of its rooms opening onto a balcony seat from which guests watch the beaching of the sardine-filled boats. Or you can watch (without being caught staring) the multi-petticoated women or the tasseled stocking caps of the men.

Even if you're passing through just for the day, you may want to try a regional meal in the oak beamed dining room. A table d'hôte is offered for 72$ ($2.81), and includes specialties such as cream of shellfish soup, fish stew (caldeirada) in the Nazaré style, and roast kid. The atmosphere is genial, with ornate tiles, forest green chairs and draperies, and stark white cloths.

A twisting stairway in the rear leads to the old-style bedrooms, down halls of muted cream, with rattan baskets of pine cones on each landing. Some rooms are simple, perhaps too much so for the average traveler. But they are maintained immaculately; the beds are good; the linen fresh. Only 11 of the 28 rooms contain private baths. Two persons can stay here, taking all three meals, at prices that range from 410$ ($15.99) to 530$ ($20.68) per day. The full-board rate in a single without bath ranges from 225$ ($8.78) to 275$ ($10.73) per day. All taxes are included.

WHERE TO DINE: Mar Bravo, 67 Praça Sousa Oliveira (tel. 461-80). Of the dozens of restaurants and pensions in this bustling village, one of the best and most popular is Mar Bravo, on the corner of the town's busy square overlooking the ocean. The decor is simple tile, with a huge photo of the Nazaré beach covering the back wall. A complete meal costs only 60$ and consists of soup, followed by a fish or meat dish, bread, and wine. There's a menu in English. À la carte specialties are bass caprice for 50$ ($1.95); fish stew Nazarine, 50$ also; or charcoal-grilled pork, 50$. Dessert might be a soufflé for 40$ ($1.56), a fruit salad for 18$ (70¢), or an orange pudding for 10$ (39¢). Even on rainy winter Sundays, the restaurant attracts many locals, which is the best proof of the pudding (or the caldeirada!). Upstairs is a second dining room, with an oceanside view. Connected with the Mar Bravo is a three-star pension called the **Pensao Madeira**, simple but adequate.

8. Batalha

The founder of the House of Aviz, Joao I, vowed on the plains of Aljubarrota in 1385 that if his underequipped and outnumbered army defeated the powerful invading Castilians, he would commemorate his spiritual indebtedness to the Virgin Mary. The result: the magnificent Battle Abbey, Batalha. Designed in the splendid Gothic-Manueline style, it appears as an imposing mass of steeples, buttresses, and parapets when approached from its western facade. Although much restored, it is a jewel case of fine cut gems in stone.

The western porch—ornamented by a tangled mass of Gothic sculpture of saints and myriad figurines—is capped by a stained-glass window of blue, mauve, and amber. The hue of the limestone has supposedly changed through the ages; today it is a light burnished beige, similar to the color of the facade of the Convent of Christ at Tomar. Napoleon's irreverent Gauls used the stained-glass windows for target practice, turning the nave into both a latrine and a bordello.

In the Founder's Chapel, completed in 1435, Joao I and his English queen, Philippa of Lancaster, daughter of John of Gaunt, lie in peaceful repose, their hands entwined. Near that of his parents is the tomb of Prince Henry the Navigator, whose fame eclipsed their own even though he never sat on the throne, but spent a great part of his life at the School of Navigation at Sagres, on the southern coast of Portugal. Henry's sculpted hands are clasped in prayer. Three of the other princes are also entombed here under a ceiling resembling snow crystals. The Royal Cloister—considered by many the most outstanding feature at Batalha—is attributed to Afonso Domingues. These cloisters reveal the beginnings of the nautically oriented Manueline architecture. (Still a second cloister, called the Meditation Cloister, dates from the 15th century.)

The magnum opus of the monastery is the Chapter House—a square chamber whose vaulting is an unparalleled example of the Gothic style, bare of supporting pillars. When originally built by a French architect, it collapsed, but a Portuguese redesigned it and slept under it for eight days to prove its soundness. The two tombs of Portugal's Unknown Soldiers from World War I are guarded by sentinels and the glow of an eternal flame. In one part of the quadrangle is the Unknown Soldiers Museum, housing gifts to the fallen warriors from the people of Portugal and from other countries, including a presentation from Maréchal Joffre. Beyond the crypt are the remains of the old wine cellars.

The filigree designs ornamenting the coral-stone entrance to the seven Unfinished Chapels is stunning. The Capelas—under an inconstant "sky ceiling"—are part of one of the finest examples of the Manueline style of architecture, a true extravaganza in stone. It seems a pity that construction was abondoned here so that workers and architects for Manuel I could help build his Monastery at Belém. Originally, the chapels were ordered by Dom Duarte, the son of Joao I, but he died before they could be completed.

Outside in the forecourt, a heroic statue was unveiled in 1968 to Nuno Álvares, who fought with Joao I on the plains of Aljubarrota. Batalha stands 73 miles north of Lisbon, reached by taking a train to Valado where bus connections are made to Batalha.

READER'S RESTAURANT SUGGESTION: "Just right of the bus stop where you are dropped off in Batalha is an excellent restaurant—**Casa de Vitoria**. It is a small local place with plenty of color. The food is good and very cheap. A meal of chicken, french fries, sliced tomatoes, house wine, and fruit costs around $2.50 (U.S.) each" (W. Michael Sharpe, Windsor, Ontario, Canada).

9. Fátima

This is a world-famed pilgrimage site. Thorny bushes, dwarfed holly, gnarled and twisted olive trees, a stray oak—the terrain around Fátima is wild, almost primitive, with an aura of barren desolation hanging over the countryside. But if you should go on the 13th of May or the 13th of October, the drama that unfolds is remarkable. Beginning on the 12th of each of those months, the roads leading to Fátima are choked with pilgrims traveling in donkey-pulled carts, on bicycles, or in automobiles. Usually, however, they go on foot—some even walking on their knees in penitence. They camp out till day breaks. In the central square itself—larger than St. Peter's in Rome—a statue of the Madonna passes through the crowd. In the breeze 75,000 handkerchiefs flutter, like thousands of peace doves taking flight.

Then, as many as are able crowd in to visit a small slanted-roof shed known as the Chapel of the Apparitions. Inside stands a single white column marking the actual spot where a small holm oak had once grown. It is alleged that an image of the Virgin Mary appeared over this oak on May 13, 1917, when she is said to have spoken to three shepherd children. The oak has long ago disappeared, torn to pieces by souvenir collectors; many of its fragments now rest in the homes of peasants where they are viewed as sacred religious relics. The oak that now stands near the chapel existed in 1917, but was not connected with the apparition. The original chapel constructed here was dynamited on the night of March 6, 1922 by skeptics who suspected the church of staging the so-called miracle.

While World War I dragged on in Europe, the trio of devoutly faithful children—Lúcia de Jesus and her cousins, Jacinto Marto and Francisco—claimed they saw the first appearance of "a lady" on the tableland of Cova da Iria. Her coming had been foreshadowed in 1916 by what they would later cite as "an angel of peace," who is said to have appeared before them.

Though attempts were made to suppress their story, news of it spread quickly—eventually generating worldwide enthusiasm, disbelief, and intense controversy. During the July appearance, the lady was reported to have revealed three secrets to them, one of which prefigured the coming of World War II, another connected with Russia's "rejection of God." The final secret—recorded by Lúcia—was opened by church officials in 1960, but they refused to divulge its contents.

Acting on orders from the Portuguese government of the time, the mayor of a nearby town threw the children into jail and threatened them with torture, even death in burning oil. Still, they would not be intimidated, sticking to their original story. The lady was reported to have made six appearances, the final one on October 13, 1917, when the children were joined by an estimated 70,000 persons who witnessed the now famous Miracle of the Sun. The day of October 13 had broken to pouring rain and driving winds. Observers from all over the world, many of them journalists and self-professed atheists, testified that at noon "the sky opened up" and the sun seemed to spin out of its axis and hurtle toward the earth. Many at the site feared that the Last Judgment was upon them. Others later reported that they thought the scorching sun was crashing into the earth and would consume it in flames. Many authorities—and certainly the faithful pilgrims—agreed that a truly major miracle of modern times had occurred. Only the children reported seeing "Our Lady," however.

In the influenza epidemic that swept over Europe after World War I, both Francisco and Jacinto died. The oldest among them, Lúcia, is still alive, living as a Carmelite nun in a convent at the university city of Coimbra. Lúcia returned to Fátima to mark the 50th anniversary of the apparition. The Pope flew in from Rome.

A cold, white, pristine Basilica in the neoclassic style was erected at one end of the wide square. If you want to go inside, you may be stopped by a guard if you're not dressed to suit him. A sign posted outside reads: "The Blessed Virgin Mary, Mother of God, appeared in this place. Therefore, women are asked not to enter the sanctuary in slacks or other masculine attire."

Outside of Fátima, in the simple and poor village of Aljustrel, you can still see the houses of the three shepherd children.

Fátima lies 36 miles east of Nazaré and about 88 miles north from Lisbon. A train from the capital arrives near Fátima. From the rail station, coaches connect with the pilgrimage site itself.

When you arrive, everything at first seems to be either a souvenir shop, a pension, or a hotel. But in accommodations, Fátima is disastrously equipped on the days of the major pilgrimages (it's virtually impossible to secure a room unless you're reserved months in advance). Those visiting at other times of the year may find the following recommendations suitable:

THE BUDGET RANGE: Hotel de Fátima, Cova da Iria (tel. 972-51), is a leading hotel, rated three stars by the government. Many of its 69 rooms and nine suites overlook the sanctuary itself. The ever-increasing invasion of pilgrims to the shrine forced the hotel to enlarge, branching out into a new part. All rooms have natural wood furnishings in the provincial Portuguese style, with private baths, central heating, and telephones. The building has three floors, served by two elevators. For half pension the price for two persons is 520$ ($20.28), taxes included. On the main floor is a cozy little sitting room with a brick fireplace, a reception lounge, a large sitting room, plus a dining room where you can order a four-course table d'hôte luncheon or dinner for 110$ ($4.29).

Estalagem "Os Três Pastorinhos," Cova da Iria (tel. 972-29), is translated as the Inn of the Three Shepherd Children. The building is designed in a holiday style, with its most recently added bedrooms opening onto private balconies overlooking the sanctuary.

About half of the bedrooms are furnished in a semi-modern—though not overly stylish—way, and the others are more traditionally designed. All of them contain private bath, though one group offers showers instead of tubs and is cheaper. One person pays from 140$ ($5.46) to 210$ ($8.19) for a room with bath; two persons are charged from 195$ ($7.61) to 295$ ($11.51). Breakfast is an additional 23$ (90¢). Two can stay here on full-board terms for 645$ ($25.15) per day. If you're just passing through, you can come in for a multi-course meal costing 100$ ($3.90). The lounge and dining room open onto raised sun terraces, edged with pots of flowering plants.

Hotel Pax (tel. 974-12) is modern, perched atop a hill near the shrine. It is only rated as two stars, but for quality and comfort it should certainly be three. Among its many facilities are a large souvenir shop; a clean, large though ascetic dining room; and simple but comfortably appointed rooms. The hotel has its own chapel as well as a small bar. A single is 160$ ($6.34); a double, 220$ ($8.58). Lunch or dinner by itself is 100$ ($3.90). Complete pension for two runs 260$ ($10.14).

Domus Pacis Hostel, adjacent to the sanctuary grounds (tel. 972-00), can be seen from miles around because of its towering blue-colored Byzantine cupola. It is a hotel with a story. Twenty-seven years ago, Monseignor Colgan, an American from Plainfield, N.J. (who died in 1972) founded an organization called the Blue Army to promote Fátima. The organization runs this 55-room hotel as well. Among the facilities are a large conference hall seating 500, a Byzantine chapel containing the "Our Lady of Kazan" icon which the organization bought two years ago for a million dollars, a small bar, and a no-frills restaurant. At the entrance to the building is a large white statue of the Virgin, with a golden crown on her head and a rosary in her right hand. Rooms at the hotel (also known as Pilgrim House) cost 90$ ($3.51) for a single, 140$ ($5.46) for a double, and 180$ ($7.02) for a triple. Most rooms, by the way, have only a shower. Full pension for three people costs 600$ ($23.40). Special rates are given for groups of more than 15 persons. To get to the hotel, follow the Blue Army signs posted all over town.

Pensao-Restaurant Zeca is a modern, clean hotel set in a large garden at the entrance to town and serving the best food in Fátima, with the biggest portions. You sit in a friendly dining room with picture windows facing a garden, wood and tile wall decorations, cloth napkins, and table-cloths. On our last visit we had a table d'hôte meal for only 80$ ($3.12), which included a bowl of freshly made vegetable soup, a huge portion of veal scallopine (three cuts!) with french fries and spinach, topped by mushrooms and cooked in wine, and a large portion of custard. A la carte specialties are a mixed salad, 15$ (59¢); a sausage omelette, 25$ (98¢); and fish and meat dishes, 55$ ($2.15).

You can stay in a modern room here (only 12 available) for 250$ ($9.75) in a double with bath; 180$ ($7.02) for single with bath. Breakfast costs 20$ (78¢) extra.

Chapter XI

THE ALGARVE

1. Sagres
2. Lagos
3. Portimao
4. Praia da Rocha
5. Silves
6. Armaçao de Pera
7. Albufeira
8. Praia de Quarteira
9. Vilamoura
10. Vale do Lobo
11. Faro
12. Sao Brás de Alportel
13. Olhao
14. Monte Gordo

IN THE ANCIENT MOORISH town of Xelb (today called Silves), a handsome and sensitive Vizier is said to have once lived. During one of his sojourns into northern lands, he fell in love with and won the hand of a beautiful blonde-haired Nordic princess. Marrying her, he brought her back to the Algarve.

Soon the young princess began to pine, finding no solace in the Moor's rose castle. Her young husband finally learned, after much coaxing, that his new bride's melancholy came from her longing for the snow-covered hills and valleys of her native land.

Issuing a decree, the Vizier demanded that thousands of almond trees be planted throughout his realm. From that day on, pale white almond blossoms have blanketed the Algarve in late January and early February. The sight acted as an anodyne to the heart of the young princess. On seeing the blossoms, she found she could finally fulfill her marital duties and lived happily ever after in her Vizier's sun-drenched kingdom with its sweet-smelling artificial winters ... or so the story goes.

The maritime province of the Algarve, often called the Garden of Portugal, is the southwesternmost part of Europe, its coastline stretching a distance of 100 miles, all the way from Henry the Navigator's Cape St. Vincent to the border town of Vila Real de Santo António, fronting a once-hostile Spain.

Called Al-Gharb by the Moors, the land south of the serras (hills) of Monchique and Caldeirao remains a spectacular anomaly that seems more like a transplanted section of the North African coastline. The temperature in winter averages around 60 degrees Fahrenheit, increasing to an average of 74 in summer. During the day the sky is a pale blue, deepening in the evening to a rich cerulean. The countryside abounds with growth: almonds, lemons, oranges, carobs, pomegranates, and figs—the latter sending their branches crawling across the ground like the tentacles of an octopus. The road from Lagos to Sagres is lined with giant geraniums.

Expanses of sun-drenched golden sands contrast harmoniously with sinuous-scored rock passageways that open up into high-ceilinged grottos and sea caves with natural pillars supporting ponderous arches above inrushing waters. The variety of the coastline provokes wonder: sluggish estuaries, sheltered lagoons, low-lying areas where the cluck of the marsh hen rises into the air, long sandy spits, pine woods breaking upon a pounding surf, and promontories jutting out into the white-capped aquamarine foam.

Even though most of the towns and villages of the Algarve are more than 150 miles from Lisbon, the great earthquake of 1755 was felt here as well. Entire communities were wiped out; however, there remain many Moorish (even Roman) ruins. In the character of its fret-cut chimneys, mosque-like cupolas, and cubist houses, a distinct Oriental flavor still prevails.

The market places in the shaded arcades of Algarvian villages sell esparto mats, copper work, pottery, and almond and fig sweets, sometimes shaped like birds and fish. Through the narrow streets comes the fast sound of little accordions pumping out the rhythmical corridinho.

Many small fishing villages dot the Algarvian coast, their names tongue twisting: Carvoeiro, Albufeira, Olhao, Portimao. The black dress of the varinas (with embroidery on their apparel, a flower-studded hat on their head), the healthy ruddy faces of the "bullfighters of the sea," the fishing craft—all create a living bridge with tradition in a land known to Phoenicians, Greeks, Romans, Visigoths, Moors, Christians, and now foreign tourists of every hue.

A NEW RIVIERA: Clearly, a new Riviera is in the making.

The accommodation outlook is one of exceptional—though government-regulated—growth. New construction is planned so as not to spoil the natural beauty of the coastline (Spain's Costa del Sol is a painful nightmare for what can happen with an unchecked hotel boom).

Excellent accommodations are provided in nearly all price levels, the list topped by five luxury hotels (two of which have their own 18-hole championship golf course). The hotels—scattered along the coast from Monte Alvor to the Vale do Lobo—have reciprocal meal arrangements. Others are at Praia dos Três Irmaos, Praia de Rocha, and Albufeira.

Budgeteers seek out bargains in the pensions and estalagems, some of them in converted mansions and villas. The government owns two pousadas—one on the sea at Sagres, the other in the mountains (Sao Brás de Alportel). In July and August the Algarve peaks in popularity.

The flight from Lisbon to the Algarvian airport at Faro takes about 30 minutes. There are daily flights all-year-round leaving Lisbon, with two daily return flights also. You can go by one of three daily trains. Take the ferryboat at Black Horse Square in Lisbon, disembarking at Barreiro on the opposite bank of the Tagus, where Algarve-bound trains can be boarded. Three times a week, there's an only-first-class special run. A daily motorcoach also leaves from Barreiro to the Algarve, and a drive in your own rented car takes about five or six hours.

ALONG THE WAY—SINES: On the somewhat barren route from Lisbon to the Algarve, attractions are rare. However, 99 miles south of the capital—almost exactly midway between there and Cape St. Vincent—sits the little fishing village of Sines. The side road to the promontory of Sines runs through a land swept by sea breezes. Along the 11-mile route from the cutoff point at Santiago do Cacém, pine forests rise along the horizon, the scent from the resin-filled barrels permeating the air.

The origin of Sines is lost. Many of the natives, like those at Nazaré, trace their ancestry to the Phoenicians. The village sits upon the crest of a high inclined surface, its little houses—trimmed in cobalt blue—blending into the sky. Below the residential district, a natural rock looms over the tiny harbor. Off the coast is a small island, Pessegueiro, on which the crumbled ruins of a fortress remain.

Vasco da Gama was born at Sines in 1469, and his house—long ago torn down—has been reconstructed in the original style. Even the local cinema is named after the great explorer. Anglers are attracted to Sines because of the bass and swordfish. Sand dunes rise along the extensive beaches, which are private, remote, seldom sharing their tranquil beauty with the Algarve-bound motorist.

SANTIAGO DO CACEM: On the main road to the Algarve, the village of Santiago do Cacém—dedicated to St. James—is crowned by the ruins of a castle built by medieval knights upon the foundation of a Moorish fortress. At the castle walls there is a fine view of the sea and the cypress-studded countryside, from which a low hum and clack of windmills can be heard.

Two Pousadas

Algarve-bound vacationers or returning suntanned tourists like to stop off for a luncheon at the **Pousada de Sao Tiago**, Estrada Nacional (tel. 59). This salmon-pink hilltop villa is approached via a climbing road through pine and fir trees, seemingly like a private estate. Guests walk around the terraced garden or take a dip in a pool surrounded by lawns and rows of cypress trees, plus a classic piece of sculpture in a coved niche.

In the chalet-styled dining room (or on a wide terrace where tables are set under an arbor of magenta bougainvillea), you can order a four-course table d'hôte luncheon for 100$ ($3.90), including a hobnail glass carafe of the local wine and crusty homemade bread. First, you get a bowl of soup from the tureen, fish caught that day at Sines, meat with vegetables, then seasonal fruit. You can take coffee in the lounge in front of a 15-foot inglenook, sinking into the soft sofa. This combination lounge and dining room is decorated in the provincial style, with a collection of handmade ceramic figures and jugs.

Seven bedrooms are furnished comfortably with antiques or good reproductions. All contain hot and cold running water, with easy access to toilets and baths in the corridors. Single rooms rent for only 70$ ($2.73); doubles, 95$ ($3.71).

Continuing south, we come upon the **Pousada Santa Clara**, opened in 1971, at the Barragem Marcello Caetano of **Santa-Clara-a-Velha** (tel. Saboia 53), overlooking the large lake and dam of the rio Mira. The charming pousada is a most convenient stopover on the Lisbon-Sagres road to the Algarve. There are six pleasant double rooms with bath. One person pays 95$ ($3.71); two persons, 145$ ($5.66). Full pension for one is 280$ ($10.92); for two, 520$ ($20.28). If you stop for just a meal, the tab comes to 100$ ($3.90). Breakfast is 17$50 (68¢).

READER'S SELECTION: "A truly wonderful pensão more than filled my needs, the **Pensao Esperança**, Largo Presidente Carmona. The basic rate for a single was 75$ ($2.93), and even though I had full board for only a day, I got a truly marvelous reduction: for a room for two nights, one breakfast, two dinners, and one lunch, I paid 275$ ($10.73). The food was some of the best I had in Portugal: huge portions, filling soups, really tasty steaks, veal, and fish. The basic set lunch or dinner was soup, bread, two more filling fish and meat courses, with fruit to follow, and this was 75$ ($2.93), including wine, unlimited bread, and service. My room here was simple and spotlessly clean. The bar of the pensao was friendly, with cheap, good coffees and alcoholic drinks" (J. Barrie Jones, Paylersbury, Northamptonshire, England).

1. Sagres

At the extreme southwestern corner of Europe, Sagres is a rocky escarpment jutting out into the Atlantic—the ocean beating itself into a aquamarine froth upon the steep cliffs. It was here that Henry the Navigator, the Infante of Sagres, "dreamed dreams no mortal ever dared to dream before." He also proved that they could come true, launching Portugal and the modern world upon the seas of explorations. At Sagres, Henry, son of Joao I and Philippa of Lancaster, established his School of Navigation.

He died (1460) before the great discoveries of Columbus and Vasco da Gama, but those explorers owed a debt to him. A virtual ascetic, he assembled the best navigators, cartographers, geographers, scholars, sailors, and builders he could muster, infusing them with his rigorous devotion and methodically setting Portuguese caravels upon the Sea of Darkness.

Today, at the reconstructed site of his windswept fortress upon Europe's "Land's End" (nicknamed that after the narrowing westernmost tip of Cornwall, England), you can see a huge stone compass dial which he is alleged to have used in the naval studies pursued at Sagres.

At a simple chapel here—restored in 1959-60—sailors are said to have prayed for help before setting out into uncharted waters. To the left of the chapel is the villa where Henry lived (inquire at the Tourist Office nearby if you want to visit the interior). On what is believed to have been the site of the School of Navigation, a youth hostel has been installed. In the Auditorium of Sagres, a film is shown daily, depicting the story of Henry the Navigator; the English language version (it costs 5$) is shown at 3:45 daily.

Three miles away is the promontory of **Cape St. Vincent.** The Cape is so named because, according to legend, the body of St. Vincent arrived mysteriously here on a boat guided by ravens. Others claim that the body of the patron saint—murdered at Valencia, Spain—washed upon the shores of Lisbon. A lighthouse stands here today. Sea gulls glide upon the air currents; and, on the approach, a few goats graze on a hill where even the trees are bent from the gusty wind.

Both the Cape and Sagres (especially from the terrace of the pousada), offer a view of the sunset. To the ancient world, the Cape was the last explored point, although in time the Phoenicians pushed beyond it. Many mariners thought that when the sun sank beyond the Cape, it plunged over the edge of the world. To venture around the promontory was to face the demons of the unknown.

Sagres lies 174 miles south of Lisbon; from Lisbon's Terreiro do Paço (Black Horse Square), you can take a ferry across the Tagus to Barreiro. From there, it's possible to make connections with the Southern Line Railway on its run to Lagos. At Lagos, buses ply back and forth between that town and Sagres. The accommodations at Sagres are limited, but good.

A MEDIUM-PRICED HOTEL: Hotel da Baleeira (tel. 64-212) is a first-class "Whaleboat." It enjoys a ship's bow position, spread out as it is above the tiny fishing port, with boats tied up in the harbor. Rising on the crest of the hill like a building on the North African coast, it affords a view of the shoreline. Even its angular salt-water swimming pool is thrust out on a ledge, surrounded by a flagstone terrace. It's almost like swimming in the ocean, only you are perched high on a cliff. The largest modern hotel on this land projection, it offers 105 bedrooms and three suites, all with private baths and sea-view balconies.

The hotel has nearly doubled the number of its bedrooms in recent years, although the older ones are quite small (as are the baths) and are furnished with dated modern pieces. The bedrooms are on the lower level. In high season, you pay 680$ ($26.53) for full pension for two persons; 425$ ($16.58) for one person.

If you're exploring the Algarve, and are in Sagres just for the day, you can stop off and order a 110$ ($4.29) luncheon or dinner in a dining room cantilevered out toward the sea, with everyone getting view seats. The chef has his own private lobster tanks (no frozen lagosta here); and the meals are well prepared and served in an efficient manner.

The atmosphere is that of a private world, as the hotel has its own sandy beach, car park, hairdresser, cocktail lounge, and mini-boîte operating only in summer and featuring dancing to records, plus a combo imported on weekends.

THE BUDGET RANGE: Pousada do Infante, Ponta da Atalaia (tel. 64-222), seems like a one-time monastery built by ascetic monks who wanted to commune with nature—the rugged beauty of the rocky cliffs, the pounding surf, the sense of the infinity of the ocean. The glistening white-painted government-owned tourist inn with a tiled roof is spread out along the edge of a cliff, protruding rather daringly over the sea. It boasts a long colonnade of arches with an extended stone terrace set up with garden furniture, plus a second floor of bedrooms with private conies.

The public rooms are generously proportioned, gleaming with marble, and decorated with unusually fine tapestries depicting the exploits of Henry the Navigator. Large gold velvet couches flank the fireplace with tall brass floor lamps. In the dining room, the walls are lined with azulejos (tiles), and in the corner rests a cone-shaped fireplace with a mounted ship's model. Sitting in Portuguese provincial chairs, guests can order the traditional bargain luncheon or dinner of the pousadas, costing 80$ ($3.12), and including homemade bread, homemade soup from a tureen, a fish course, meat with vegetables, and dessert.

There are 15 bedrooms and each has a private tiled bath, and is furnished with traditional pieces. You pay only 220$ ($8.58) for a double room, 155$ ($6.05) for a single. It's best, however, to take the full-pension tariffs, a real saving at 590$ ($23.01) for two, 340$ ($13.26) for one.

Have a pre-dinner drink on the terrace, and watch the ocean-going vessels make their way around the point, heading for faraway ports of call.

2. Lagos

What the Lusitanians and Romans called Locobriga, and the Moors knew as Zawaia, was to become, under Henry the Navigator, a private experimental shipyard of caravels. Edged by the Costa do Ouro (Golden Coast), the Bay of Sagres at one point in its epic history was big enough to allow "407 warships to maneuver with ease."

An ancient port city (one historian traced its origins back to the Carthaginians three centuries before the birth of Christ), Lagos was well known by the sailors of Nelson's fleet. From Liverpool to Manchester to Plymouth, the sailors spoke wistfully of the beautiful, green-eyed, olive-skinned women of the Algarve. Eagerly, they set into port, looking forward to drinking the heady Portuguese wine and carousing.

Actually, not that much has changed since Nelson's day, and few go to Lagos wanting to know of its history. Rather, the mission is to drink deeply of the pleasures of table and beach.

In winter, the almond blossoms match the whitecaps on the water, and the climate is warm enough for sunbathing.

In town, the **Flea Market** sprawls through narrow streets, the vendors selling such articles as rattan baskets, earthenware pottery, fruits, vegetables, crude furniture, cutlery, knitted shawls, and leather boots.

Less than a mile down the coast, the hustle-bustle of market day is forgotten, as the rocky headland of the **Ponta da Piedade** (Point of Piety) appears. This beauty spot is considered by many the best on the entire coast. Dotted among the colorful cliffs and secret grottos carved by the waves, are the most flamboyant examples of Manueline architecture.

LAGOS

Much of Lagos was razed in the 1755 earthquake—at which time it lost its position as the capital of the Algarve. Today, only ruins remain of its former walls of fortification. However, traces of the old are still to be discovered on the back streets. On the Rua Silva Lopes, just off the waterfront, sits the 18th-century **Igreja de Santo António** (Church of St. Anthony). Decorating the altar are some of the greatest rococo gilt carvings in all of Portugal. Begun in the 17th century, they were damaged in the earthquake, but subsequently restored. What you see today represents the work of many artisans—at times, each of them seemingly pursuing a different theme.

Attached to the church is the **Museu Regional de Lagos,** containing replicas of the fret-cut chimneys of the Algarve, three-dimensional cork carvings, 16th-century vestments, ceramics, 17th-century embroidery, ecclesiastical sculpture, a painting gallery, weapons, minerals, and a numismatic collection. An oddity is a sort of believe-it-or-not section, displaying among other things an eight-legged calf. In the archaeological wing are Neolithic artifacts, along with Roman mosaics found at Sagres, fragments of statuary and columns, and other shards of antiquity from excavations along the Algarve. Charging an admission of 5$ (20¢), the museum is open daily, except Monday, from 9:30 a.m. to 12:30 p.m. and from 2-5 p.m. Telephone: 623-01.

In the old **Customs House** on the Praça Infante, Dom Henriques stands as a painful reminder of the Age of Exploration. The arcaded slave market—the only one of its kind in Europe—looks peaceful today, but under its four Romanesque arches captives taken from their homelands were sold to the highest bidder. The house opens onto what is today a peaceful square, dominated by a statue of Henry the Navigator.

Lagos is 21 miles east of Sagres, 164 miles south of Lisbon and 49 miles west of Faro. To reach it by rail from Lisbon, take the ferryboat at Black Horse Square across the Tagus to Barreiro. There, connections to Lagos can be made on the Southern Line Railway.

In accommodations it is well stocked, beginning with our favorite:

THE UPPER BRACKET: Hotel de Lagos, 1 Rua Castilho (tel. 620-11), is a 20th century castle with its own ramparts and moats (two swimming pools). This first-class hotel crowns a hill at the top of Lagos, so no matter which room you're assigned, you'll have a view, even if it is one opening upon a sun-trap courtyard with semi-tropical greenery. The main room evokes a hacienda atmosphere, with a background of bone white plaster walls, enlivened by sunny colors. Guests gather here in one of the clusters of soft built-in sofas set on carpets. In a corner logs burn in a fireplace in chilly weather. Excellent meals are served in an expansive harbor-view room, decorated in wood paneling and shades of burnt orange.

A few bedrooms with patios are on the ground level, but most of them are on the upper six floors—each containing a private bath. The rooms both single and double, even the suites, offer a choice of standard and deluxe. In high season (June through September), demi-pension for one person ranges from 296$ ($11.54) to 366$ ($14.27); for two persons, from 492$ ($19.19) to 732$ ($28.55). The average bedroom has a background of stark white walls contrasted with warm Oriental colors in shades of burnt orange, gold, lime, sun yellow, and bronze. The furnishings emphasize the slimline upholstered look, with most rooms opening onto a wedge-shaped balcony where you can order breakfast. Amenities include a boîte (the Zum-Zum Room), a poolside bar, two lounge bars, and complete air conditioning.

The hotel also features a beach club two kilometers away, with a heated saltwater pool, restaurant, snack bar, and mini-golf.

THE MEDIUM-PRICED RANGE: Hotel Sa Cristovao, Rossio de S. Joao (tel. 63-051), may have been a simple estalagem at one point, but that is now history. The rather modest beginnings have given way to an avant-garde stylishness, the interior seemingly inspired by a latter-day Frank Lloyd Wright. At the edge of town, almost within sight of the harbor, the hotel sits on a busy parkway junction of the coastal highway and the road to Lisbon. There is a rooftop solarium. Owned and run by Torralta C.I.F., the first-class hotel is maintained on a personal basis.

The bedrooms are inviting in their uncluttered design. Shafts of finely grained wood are used in a Mondrian fashion at the windows, beds, and headboards. The walls are likely to be sky blue, with deeper hued carpets and draperies. Each room opens onto a private terrace, and is priced according to size and placement. A single with bath is 180$ ($7.02); a double with bath, 240$ ($9.36).

Opening off the reception are several public lounges, the largest of which could win a prize for design. It uses natural pine slats for the ceiling, cube lighting, and pillars. One part on a lower level makes for intimate seating around a freestanding black fireplace. Before-dinner drinks are available in the cocktail lounge, which opens onto an inner patio with a fountain waterfall.

Hotel Meia Praia, Meia Praia (tel. 62-001), means halfway to the beach. Edging up to the ruins of an old fortress, this first-class hotel is for those who want sand, sun, and good food rather than an exciting decor. The hotel—containing 66 bedrooms, all with private bath—was built as the Greeks preferred: at a point where a hill begins its rise from the sea. Surrounded by private gardens, it fronts railway tracks and a wide sandy beach, four miles long. The guests play tennis on two professional hard courts, linger in the informal garden, where white iron outdoor furniture is scattered under the olive and palm trees, or loll by the large pools, one for adults, another for children. Non-guests pay 30$ ($1.17) for use of the pool. On tennis courts, guests are charged 30$ ($1.17) an hour; non-guests, 50$ ($1.95).

The oceanside bedrooms have balconies with partitions for sunbathing. The furnishings in the rooms are uncluttered, functional, and modern. The most expensive rooms have sea views and two balconies; the medium-priced rooms, a sea view and one balcony; and the cheapest rooms have no balconies and overlook the hills. For a full pension, a single pays anywhere from 309$ ($12.05) to 393$ ($15.33) nightly; two persons from 476$ ($18.57) to 641$ ($25). Across the entire all-glass front of the hotel is a combination dining room, lounge, and drinking bar.

The hotel is run by the Torralta group, and will probably be open all year.

Hotel Riomar, 81 Cándido dos Reis, (tel. 68-091), is a modern structure in the center of town. It has a pleasant downstairs lounge, a cozy bar, and a tasteful decor. Its 37 rooms are closed in the winter. A single with bath costs 245$ ($9.56), and a double with bath goes for 390$ ($15.21). Breakfast is included. The hotel gives substantial discounts when the tourist tide ebbs, as much as 40 percent on our last visit.

THE BUDGET RANGE: Casa de Sao Gonçalo da Lagos, 73 Rua Candido dos Reis (tel. 621-71). This exquisite pink town villa, with its fancy iron balconies, dates back to the 18th century. Until recent times, it was the private family house of a gracious English-speaking Portuguese lady, Julieta Ferreira Candelas Rocha de Abreu, who has consented to accept paying guests. At the core of Lagos, close to restaurants and shops, her antique-filled home is a near-undiscovered gem. Most of the public lounges and bedrooms turn, in the Andalusian fashion, to the inward peace of a sun-filled patio. Here, surrounded by bougainvillea climbing up balconies, guests order their breakfast—sitting under a red and white fringed parasol and enjoying the splashing and gurgling of the fountain.

All the furnishings are individualized: no bedroom is like another. Delicate hand-embroidered bed linens are color coordinated to the counterpanes and blankets, and you're apt to find period mahogany tables, silver candlesticks, chests with brass handles, inlaid tip-top tables, old desks, fine ornate beds brought from Angola, pewter and brass lamps, even crystal chandeliers. For one person, the daily cost ranges anywhere from 170$ ($6.63) to 210$ ($8.19); from 240$ ($9.36) to 295$ ($11.51) for two, taxes included. In the restoration of the house, modern amenities were added, so that each room contains a private bath. Breakfast, the only meal served, costs an additional 26$.

The luxury pension is in a rambling casa (house), with various stairways leading to corridors with fine old prints, engravings, and Portuguese ceramic bowls of flowers on aged hand-carved chests. Guests enjoy get-togethers in the large living room, with its comfortable armchairs drawn up around a fireplace. Here, again, the furnishings are personalized, with a preponderance of antiques, including an English spinet piano, a gilt Italian mirror and console, a statue of a saint, and bronze torchiers.

WHERE TO DINE AND DRINK: The **Bar Barroca,** Rua da Barroca, is a modern Portuguese tavern, dispensing healthy-sized drinks and regional meals. It's placed at the top of a slight incline and narrow street, close to the waterfront. The atmosphere is relaxed, conducive to dining and drinking. Guests dine under a high beamed ceiling. On a busy night, the tables in the rear or on the mezzanine are popular. Closed on Fridays in winter only.

The food is well prepared, the portions generous, the cuisine Portuguese. The chef's specialty is caldeirada Barroca, a hearty Algarvian fish stew (the price on this dish changes daily, depending on the seafood the cook buys at the lota). Others prefer bife Barroca, 70$ ($2.73), or the beef stroganoff, 50$ ($1.95). To begin your meal, try the caldo verde (potato and greens soup), 10$ (39¢).

"**Os Arcos,**" 32 Rua Dr. Oliveira Salazar, only a block from the fishing harbor, is a friendly restaurant and bar owned by an "Aussie" and a "Kiwi." The accent is on informality and good food. The menu changes daily, the prices depending on the produce offered and the season. Lunches of English fish and chips, homemade pies, and salads average around 40$ ($1.56) to 50$ ($1.95) per head, with dinners costing from 95$ ($3.71). Closed Sundays.

Pouso do Infante, 11 Rua Alfonso d'Almeida, is a pleasant tavern-type restaurant, with an iron chandelier, walls decorated with local craftwork, and rustic-type chairs painted green with straw seats. A vegetable soup costs 10$ (39¢); a shrimp cocktail, 40$ ($1.56); veal scallopine with spaghetti, 60$ ($2.34); sole with banana, 65$ ($2.54); chicken curry with rice, 60$ ($2.34); lamb in wine sauce, 65$ ($2.54); and almond cake, 10$ (39¢).

"**53**" is an English-run bar-restaurant, with a small bar, settees in front in a cozy style, where Lagos' English and American colony congregates in the evenings. You can have snacks such as beef curry with rice, 50$ ($1.95); chile con carne, 42$50 ($1.66); chicken with "chips" in a basket, 65$ ($2.54); homemade shepherd's pie, 25$ (98¢); or simply a ham and cheese sandwich, 15$ (59¢). A pot of tea goes for 15$ (59¢), and a scotch costs 17$50 (68¢). In the rear is an intimate restaurant and an outdoor patio where guests gather on summer evenings. The dining room is candlelit, and walls are decorated with sea shells, fishing nets, indirect lights, and bottles. Entrees include a large steak with potatoes, 110$ ($4.29); deep-fried scampi with french fries or salad, also 110$; king prawns, grilled, with french fries or salad, 110$; a soup of the day, 12$50 (49¢); and peaches and cream, 17$50 (68¢). Your hosts are Frank and Jean, who hail from Norwich, England.

Lagosteira, 20 Rua 1 de Maio, has long been a mecca for knowledgeable diners in Lagos. Its decor is simple, with tiles running up half of the wall, the rest painted in a deep maroon color. There's a small bar on one side. The Lagosteira features a set menu for 65$ ($2.54), which includes a vegetable soup, veal in wine, fruit or ice cream. Otherwise, order the fish soup, 17$ (66¢); clams Lagosteira style, 89$ ($3.47); sirloin steak, 69$ ($2.69); and mixed salad, 15$ (59¢). Best bets are the seafood, including fried filets of hake with tartar sauce, 49$ ($1.91). Flan is 15$ (59¢). The restaurant is open from noon till 2 a.m., except Mondays.

READER'S RESTAURANT SUGGESTION: "**A Gruta de Joao de Sousa e Castro,** 9 Rua do Ferrador (tel. 6-25-85). Of all the kind and warm Portuguese I've met and known, Don Joao is unrivaled. His warmth, goodness, and sincerity are indeed a rarity anywhere today. And it was this radiating kindness which came straight from the heart that drew us like a magnet over and over again for the ten days we spent here in Lagos. I cannot do justice to this gracious man by writing you about him, but only ask that your readers find out for themselves, as we did by visiting his little restaurant-bar. Gruta is Portuguese for cave, hence the caveman amid the pots and pans. But please don't expect a restaurant with a 'cavelike' amosphere—as there is none. This place is a small, simple, family-like restaurant, with some of the best food I've eaten in all my travels. We ate there daily and our bill for two (with soup, main course, fruit, and a liter of wine along with service) rarely came to more than 100$ ($3.90) to 120$ ($4.68). All of the main dishes are priced at 40$ ($1.56) to 45$ ($1.76). The fish especially is delicious! One can eat quite well for very little if you don't drink the way we do (I forgot that we usually had a couple of brandies)—hence, our bill was more than normal. Closed on Thursdays. But the most fantastic thing about the place—and I cannot emphasize this enough—is Don Joao!" (Mary Helen Hernandez, San Antonio, Tex.).

PRAIA DONA ANA: About a mile west of Lagos this tiny cove contains rock formations that appear as a painted desert in the sea and sand. The grottos, arches, caves, and grotesques have been carved and colored by the weather and water in subtle hues of reds, ochres, golds, and scarlets. An island at its mouth landlocks the lagoon where scarred cliffs—reflecting amber, burgundy, russet—plummet into the deep blue waters. This cove is a rare experience and one of the most scenic spots along the Algarve.

A Medium-Priced Hotel

Hotel Golfinho (tel. 63-001) is modern, built near the swimming cove of this idyllic little retreat. It's been such a success that more rooms have been added as well as a swimming pool. For those who enjoy sun and sea, it brings a sophisticated touch. The lounges and bar, though, have a starkly contemporary background which the nautical paraphernalia doesn't offset.

The bedrooms, each with a private bath, are in a restrained style, crisp and neat. Sitting terraces with rattan furniture are an added attraction. The prices vary according to the view, with a twin sea vista being the most favored. In high season, two persons are charged 720$ ($28.08) daily for demi-pension. For the same arrangement, one person pays 490$ ($19.11).

Meals are served by candlelight, casting shadows on the rough white plaster walls with large jewel-like inserts. At dinner, the tab for the table d'hôte is 160$ ($6.24) per person. There are two bars where guests congregate—one semi-paneled in pine is a focal point for expatriates who've built sea-view villas along the nearby cliffs.

3. Portimao

Go here only if you prefer the life of a bustling fishing port instead of a hotel perched right on the beach. Ever since the 1930s, Praia da Rocha, two miles away, has snared sun-loving traffic. But the Algarve is so popular in summer, that even Portimao is developing a base of tourists.

The wafting aroma of the noble Portuguese sardine permeates every street and cafe nook. As a fish-canning center, Portimao leads the Algarve, but doesn't top Setúbal in production. Still, for a change of pace, this town—on an arm of the Arade River—makes a good stopover center (it also has some fine dining recommendations). Stroll through its gardens, its shops (especially noted for their pottery), drink the wine of the cafes, and roam down to the quays where you will see sardines roasting on braziers. The routine activity of the Algarvians is what gives the town its charm. On its left bank the little whitewashed community of **Ferragudo** is unspoiled, but tame, with a castle.

In accommodations Portimao itself is limited, except for the following:

THE MEDIUM-PRICED RANGE: Hotel Globo, 26 Rua da Guarda (tel. 221-51), is an island of contemporary living in the heart of the old town. A first-class hotel, it is recommended for its cleancut, well-thought-out design. Snug modern balconies overlook the tiled rooftops crusted with moss. In 1967 the owner-manager Faustino Pereira de Carvalho imported an uninhibited architect to turn his inn into a topnotch hotel. Each of the 64 bedrooms, all with private baths, enjoys good taste in layout and furnishings. The decor is highlighted by parquet floors, matching ebony panels on the wardrobes, built-in headboards, living room chairs and tables, and a marble desk with a black stool. In high season, the half-board rate for one person costs 336$ ($13.10); for two persons, from 557$ ($21.72) to 627$ ($24.46).

On the ground floor is an uncluttered, well-furnished lounge, again with comfortable pieces in warm fabrics and woods. There is an adjoining lounge and bar, with a stylized cut-out mural of fine food and drink, neat zigzag table nooks, and a rich marble-topped bar.

Crowning the top floor is a dining room, the Aquarium. Encircled by four glass walls, permitting unblocked views of the harbor, ocean, or mountains, the restaurant is inviting, its tables set with crystal stemware and flowers. A set four-course menu costs 135$ ($5.27).

A MOTEL IN THE ENVIRONS: Motel Parque Algarvio, nine kilometers outside Portimao and one kilometer from Lagoa on the main highway (tel. 522-65), is good for overnighting on the route along the Algarve. There are 42 rooms furnished simply and functionally, each with a small terrace and plastic chairs. The rustic room has a vaulted roof, with tile-decorated walls. Prices are in the three-star range. The motel has a pleasant pool. A double with bath is 200$ ($7.80), which includes breakfast off-season. It's open all year.

THE BUDGET RANGE: The Dennis Inn & Bar, 10 Rua 5 de Outubro (tel. 24-273), is an English-Canadian compound staked out in a converted town villa, where friendly hospitality is generated. It's the fulfillment of a so-called retirement plan dreamed up by John and Ruth Dennis, who wanted a good life in a sunny climate. Mr. Dennis, a former experimental test pilot, runs the attractive ground-floor pub, which overflows into a flower-filled patio from May till October. Together they have furnished the villa's eight bedrooms (all containing private baths) with provincial pieces from Alentejo—freshly painted and decorated, uncommercial looking, very homelike. "We try to keep it in character," Mrs. Dennis says. She charges only 125$ ($4.88) per person for a room, including breakfast and tax.

The corridors and chambers have a collection of original Portuguese paintings. In addition, Mrs. Dennis runs the newly added snack bar, specializing in sandwiches and salads.

PORTIMAO 137

WHERE TO DINE: **Alfredo's Restaurant,** near the waterfront in Portimao, 10 Rua Pé de Cruz, fills an important gap along the Algarve: a topnotch restaurant operating outside of a hotel dining room. It is in the old tavern style, on the ground floor of a modern building. Against a backdrop of chalk-white walls, provincial artifacts are used decoratively, the new combined with the old. From the dining room, you can see an ornately tiled open kitchen, with a charcoal grill, crocks of lobster, baskets of mushrooms, cabbage, salad greens, even a glass case of fresh fish.

You dine on high-backed chairs with rush seats, where you can see the carved refectory table laden with cheeses, baskets of fruits, special desserts, and a tall scale. A candle in a brass holder is lit by the waiter, and you make your choice from an à la carte menu. Recommended are the fish soup at 16$ (62¢); ameijoas à Alfredo's, 85$ ($3.32); pescada (hake) à marinheira, 69$ ($2.69); and tournedos Rossini, 85$ ($3.32). Until you've tried the light and creamy chocolate mousse at 20$ (78¢), you haven't had a really super dessert in the Algarve.

Cesar, on the Rua do Pe da Cruz, a few feet from Alfredo's, is a fine choice for the budget. It's like a bistrot, with a counter-bar at the entrance containing an espresso machine, and then there are two rows of tables, with high-backed chairs. Soft lights adorn the green walls, as do plates and pictures. The daily specials might be an asparagus soup for 15$ (59¢); shrimp cocktail, 50$ ($1.95); or grilled steak, 52$ ($2.03). After dinner you can have your coffee and brandy in the small corner lounge in the back of the restaurant.

Lucio, 1 Largo Francisco A. Mauricio (tel. 24-292), is as simple as can be, but serves the best seafood in town at low prices. The rooms command a view of the port and the sea gulls circling the fishing boats, even a less-romantic gas station. The dining room is small, triangular in shape, with no frills, tiny tables, and tiled walls. This is where knowledgeable locals go, too. Fresh clams cost 90$ ($3.51); lagostas, 400$ ($15.60) a kilo; and shrimps, 280$ ($10.92) a kilo. A fried or grilled sole costs only 45$ ($1.76); sardines, 35$ ($1.37); and squid, 10$ (39¢).

A RESORT COMPLEX: Just a couple of miles outside of Portimao, on the coast, **Torralta Alvorbeach** (tel. 428) is a complex still in the course of expanding (telephone the Torralta Club International at 51-748) in Lisbon for more information before striking out for it). The facilities—both natural and man-made—are spectacular, including more than three miles of fine sandy beach, a nearby golf course, swimming pools, riding facilities, tennis courts, nautical sports, fishing, several bars and restaurants, including self-service snack bars.

Handsome are the self-contained and comfortably furnished studios, apartments, and villas. In studios and apartments, the cost for two persons in high season comes to 400$ ($15.60). Ranging upward, 14 clients are accommodated for 1,250$ ($48.75) daily. In-between possibilities range from four to six to eight persons. More expensive, the self-contained villas accommodate anywhere from five to 14, costing anywhere from 1,500$ ($58.50) to 3,000$ ($117) daily, these tariffs including water, gas, electricity, a change of linen, and daily cleaning on the premises. Breakfasts are 25$ (98¢), with a complete luncheon or dinner going for 110$ ($4.29).

EXCURSIONS FROM PORTIMAO: An excursion can be made from Portimao via a winding 15-mile road north to **Monchique, Foia,** high in the hills at an altitude of 2,700 feet. In Roman days the soldiers discovered this little spot and turned it into a spa.

Where to Stay and Eat

The **Estalagem Abrigo de Montanha** (tel. 92-131), is a small inn set in the midst of scenery like a botanical garden. With all those camellias, rhododendrons, mimosa, banana palms, and arbutus blooming, plus the tinkling waterfalls, you'd never believe the hot Algarve coast was only a couple of miles away. The inn has only six double rooms, but each is complete with bath. On chilly evenings guests gather before a fireplace in the lounge. In the attractive restaurant, good food is served. For one person, the daily rate ranges between 200$ ($7.80) and 380$ ($14.82), increasing to anywhere from 300$ ($11.70) to 500$ ($19.50) for two. If you want full pension, add 175$ ($6.83) to the tariffs. Otherwise, a main meal, if ordered separately, costs 90$ ($3.51). Breakfast is 25$ (98¢).

On the drive up this mountain region, several small restaurants specialize mainly in grilled chicken. **Ruxinol** (tel. 92-215), for example, is across the road from the hot mineral springs of Caldas (once an old Roman spa). It enjoys a colorful setting, with a large terrace and a spectacular view. Main dishes, such as sole, mullet, king prawns, lamb, and steaks, cost from 50$ ($1.95) to 85$ ($3.32). On the outdoor grill, barbecued suckling pig or lamb is cooked to order. Special Portuguese dishes can also be prepared if you telephone in advance. Closed on Tuesdays.

4. Praia da Rocha

This creamy yellow beach has long been the most popular seaside resort on the Algarve. The beauty of its rock formations led English voyagers to discover it around 1935. At the outbreak of World War II, there were only two small hotels on the "Red Coast," interspersed with a few villas, many built by wealthy Portuguese. Nowadays, Praia da Rocha is booming, as many have fallen victim to the spell cast by its shoreline and climate.

It is named "The Beach of the Rock" because of the sculptural formations of the rock—the most famous one suggesting bears, twin brothers, and a triumphal arch. Some have seen a "seaside cathedral," others "surrealistic sculptures." At the end of the mussel-encrusted cliff, where the Arade flows into the sea, the ruins of the **Fort of St. Catarina** lie, the location offering many views of Portimao's satellite, Ferragudo, and of the bay.

Praia da Rocha is endowed with accommodations in all price ranges, the leader of which is—

A CLIFFSIDE HOTEL: **Algarve Hotel,** Praia da Rocha (tel. Portimao 24-000), is strictly for those who love the glitter and glamor of the lush life. With a vast staff at one's beck and call, under the general direction of Jose Abreu, a guest is ensconced in luxury within an elongated block of rooms poised securely on the top ledge of a cliff. On a lower terrace is an overscaled kidney-shaped heated swimming pool (plus another one for children), with a sundeck cantilevered out over still another cliff, projecting above rugged rocks, caves, and a sandy cove.

The main lounge is like a sultan's palace: gold velvet chairs, Oriental carpets, brass and teak screens, antique chests, and sink-deep sofas set around a copper-hooded fireplace. The corridors are graciously styled, with white marble, patterned blue azulejos, carved figures and chests, plus lamps and stone slab consoles. The bedrooms have white walls, colored ceilings, intricately tiled floors, mirrored entryways, indirect lighting, balconies with garden furniture, and baths with separate showers, double basins, and heated towel racks. Everything is air conditioned and centrally heated. In a single, the full-board rate in high season is 1,070$ ($41.73); in a twin-bedded room, 1,750$ ($68.52). Costing more, of course, are three spectaculars—a decorator's tour de force in originality—the Yachting, Oriental, and Miradouro Suites.

In the formal dining room, with its waterside windows, chinoiserie ceilings and pillars, you can order a table d'hôte dinner for 200$ ($7.80). Two French chefs, with Brazilian backgrounds, provide gourmet-level meals on the à la carte menu. Buffet luncheons in season are served down by the swimming pool. A one-of-a-kind nightclub books top-flight entertainers (even Amália Rodrigues), in addition to their regular troupe of folk dancers. The club, charging about 50$ ($1.95) for the first drink, is like an Oriental grotto dug out of a cliff, with three stone walls and a fourth allowing for an oceanic backdrop.

Extra services include a sauna, hairdresser, barbershop, manicurist, laundry and dry cleaning, baby sitting, boutiques, and complete room service. There's even a social director who plans personalized activities such as fishing parties on the hotel boat (with seafood stews), games of bridge, barbecues on the beach, minigolf, volleyball, tennis competitions, plus water-skiing and deep-sea fishing.

THE MEDIUM-PRICED RANGE: The **Hotel Júpiter,** Estrada Marginal (tel. 220-41), is a spread-out, 10-floor structure, set starkly on the main avenue, with a swimming pool out front. A three-minute walk down the cliff-scaling stairway takes you to the sandy beach and surf swimming. The hotel's two lower levels consist of lounges, a bar, a nightclub, a four-lane bowling alley, TV and bridge rooms, a snack bar, dining room, hairdresser, and barbershop.

On the upper floors, 144 bedrooms are provided at four different price levels. The tariffs in single or double rooms are based on whether they are in or out of season. For full board, the price of a single ranges from 445$ ($17.36) to 530$ ($20.68); from 740$ ($28.86) to 900$ ($35.10) for a double. Every room is air conditioned, centrally heated, and equipped with private bath and balcony. The regular bedrooms are conservatively contemporary with harmonious color blendings of burnt orange and wood tones contrasted with cool white walls and picture windows.

The main dining room, carpeted in russet and forested with wood-paneled pillars, has warmth and dignity. You can order a well-prepared table d'hôte luncheon or dinner for 140$ ($5.46). On the lower level is a snack bar, with primitive painted panels. Adjoining is the Júpiter Night Club, a circular room featuring an inlaid dance floor depicting the days of the sun. A nightly floor show is presented, and an orchestra plays for dancing four times a week. The minimum is 60$ ($2.34).

THE BUDGET RANGE: Hotel Bela Vista, Praia da Rocha (tel. 240-55), is an old mansion built during the last century by a wealthy family as a summer home. Since 1934, it's been a special kind of hotel—ideal for those who respond to the architecture of the past. Rated first class, it's lodged in an oceanside position, atop its own palisade, with access to a sandy cove where you can swim. The villa is white, with an ornate tower and terracotta tiled roof—a coastal landmark spotted by fishermen bringing in their boats at sundown. It's flanked by the owner's home and a simple cliff-edge annex shaded by palm trees.

The attractive structure and its decorations have been preserved, although plastic modern furniture has been sneaked into the public lounges. The entry hallway has an art nouveau bronze torchier and a winding staircase, with walls almost covered with blue and white tiles. The azulejos decorations are on most of the lounge walls as well. Guests enjoy get-togethers around a baronial fireplace with a tiled facade. In the high-ceilinged dining hall are more tiled dados, plus high-backed carved chairs. Meals combine Portuguese cuisine with a continental flair.

The bedrooms—all with bath—are priced according to size, plumbing, view, and placement. Those facing the sea—the former master bedrooms—are worth the additional money asked. The main house is preferable to the annex. For full pension in high season, one person pays 480$ ($18.72); two persons from 800$ ($31.20) to 900$ ($35.10). Although each room has character, most of them contain tiled dados. Decorations vary from a tiled inset shrine of the Virgin Mary to crystal sconces.

PRAIA DOS TRÊS IRMAOS:

Go here for the beach—nine miles of burnished golden sand, broken only by an occasional crag riddled with arched passageways. Just west of the better known Praia da Rocha, The Beach of the Three Brothers has been discovered by skin divers who explore its undersea grottos and shoreside caves.

Its neighbor is the whitewashed fishing village of **Alvor**, where Portuguese and Moorish arts and traditions have mingled since the Arabs gave up their 500 years of occupation. Alvor was a favorite coastal haunt of King Joao II.

A new gambling casino has opened. Modest in size compared to the one at Estoril, it features roulette, blackjack, and craps. You pay 30$ ($1.17) for a two-day pass, 50$ ($1.95) for a week. A modern restaurant features an 185$ ($7.22) set menu for a four-course meal, and also offers floor shows at 11 p.m. and 1 a.m. Those going just for the show pay a 100$ ($3.90) minimum. Two other similar casinos operate in the Algarve, one at Monte Gordo, near the Spanish border, and another at Vila Mouro.

Staying in Praia dos Três Irmaos

Alvor Praia, Praia dos Três Irmaos (tel. Portimao 240-21). "You'll feel like you're loved the moment you walk in the door," said a well-dressed woman visitor from the Midwest. This citadel of hedonism seemingly has more joie de vivre than any hotel on the Algarve! Its position is perfect—as are the building, bedrooms, decorations, service, and food.

On a landscaped crest, the luxury hotel has many of its bedrooms and public rooms exposed to the ocean view, the gardens, and the free-form olympic-sized swimming pool. Gentle walks (or else an elevator) lead down the palisade to the sandy beach and the rugged rocks which rise out of the water.

The accommodations are quite varied—everything from a cowhide-decorated room evoking Arizona's Valley of the Sun, to típico Portuguese accommodations with provincial furnishings. Many of the rooms contain private balconies where guests take breakfast facing the backdrop of the Bay of Lagos. Open year round, the hotel in high season (June 1 to September 30) charges from 520$ ($20.28) to 725$ ($28.28) in a single, from 800$ ($31.20) to 1,145$ ($44.68) in a double, including a continental breakfast, service, and taxes. For half pension, 200$ ($7.80) per person is added to the bill. The rooms contain oversized beds, plenty of clothing space, a long desk and chest combination, and well-designed baths with double basins and lots of towels.

The hotel is so self-contained you may never stray from the premise! Inside, a wide domed air-borne staircase leads to a lower level, encircling a Japanese garden and lily pond. The main dining room is on two levels, with three glass walls so that every guest has an ocean view. The Maisonette Grill is considered separately as a restaurant recommendation (see below). Like an exclusive club, the main drinking lounge is equipped with deep-leather chairs and adorned with a cubistic modern ceiling.

The concierge will arrange for fishing excursions on the hotel's 14-ton hull boat, the *Caturra,* brought here from Holland. In addition, he can get you reduced green fees on a nearby 18-hole golf course. Other sports include horseback riding, water skiing, and tennis. On the lower level of the hotel are boutiques, a newsstand, hairdressers, and the "only authentic Finnish sauna in Portugal."

Dining in Praia dos Três Irmaos

The **Maisonette Grill,** Hotel Alvor Praia, Praia dos Três Irmaos (tel. 24201), takes its rightful place alongside other distinguished restaurants connected with luxury hotels, such as the Ritz Grill in Lisbon. It has become the smartest place for gourmet cuisine along the restaurant-poor Algarve coast. A great deal of the credit goes to the maître d'hotel Manuel Alves, who has transcended the rigid formalities of his trade, tossing aside the usual pomposity in favor of twinkling eyes and wide smiles. With a skilled eye and a quick hand, he makes the Grill his personal stage.

The Grill, in spite of its spaciousness, has an intimate aura, allowing you plenty of time to peruse the à la carte menu. You might begin your meal with chilled vichyssoise at 45$ ($1.76). Entrees include poached turbot in court bouillon for 100$ ($3.90), and a rib of beef, 222$ ($8.66) for two persons. The dessert menu has such delicacies as Rothschild soufflé, 60$ ($2.34), and crêpes suzette, 70$ ($2.73). All taxes are included.

MONTES DE ALVOR: The **Penina Golf Hotel,** Montes de Alvor (tel. Portimao 220-51), between Portimao and Lagos, was founded by a group of hotel entrepreneurs, the first deluxe hotel on the Algarve. Nowadays, of course, it's getting competition from the other luxury quartet. Golfing fans remain loyal to the Penina, however, as it is a major sporting mecca. An 18-hole championship golf course was designed by Henry Cotton between the hotel and the sea.

Most of the bedrooms contain picture windows and honeycomb balconies providing views of the course and swimming pool. The less expensive rooms open onto vistas of the Monchique hills. Rates vary considerably—for half pension, one person pays anywhere from 685$ ($26.72) to 728$ ($28.40); two people in a double are charged from 1,334$ ($52.03) to 1,414$ ($55.15) for half pension. The standard bedrooms are furnished in a pleasant style, combining traditional pieces with Portuguese provincial spool beds. The rooms are spacious enough for off-the-course relaxation, and contain good-sized beds and tiled baths. Based on double occupancy, top-floor rooms cost only 952$ ($37.13) for two, half pension. The golf is thrown in free.

Those not sunning themselves by the pool are transported to the hotel beach, with its own snack bar and changing cabins. The ground level of the Penina is devoted to changing rooms, lockers, and a golf school and shops. Other facilities include a sauna, billiard room, a beauty parlor, and a barbershop. Two hard tennis courts are offered. The main lounges have more practical comfort than style. Guests enjoy cocktails in the longest bar in the Algarve, then proceed to either the Grill Room or the dining room (table d'hôte meals in the latter) for a well-prepared repast, capped by dancing.

PRAIA DO CARVOEIRO: One of the beaches along the Algarve coast has been turned into an expatriate colony. Often a chic crowd of people settle here. If you're honored with an invitation inside one of the white-washed villas, don't be surprised to find, say, a couple of original Dufys on the walls. Lying about three miles south of the wine-rich town of Lagoa, the sandy beach nestles between two rock masses, creating a solarium. The shadows of the cliffs are cooling, the sea calm.

Incidentally, before venturing down to the little commune of Praia do Carvoeiro, you may want to stop off at **Lagoa,** on the main coastal highway. If you announce yourself at the door to the big warehouse here, chances are you'll be allowed to visit the wine cellars.

Dining in Praia do Carvoeiro

A Galeria, Estrada do Farol (tel. Lagoa 571-33), is a unique island of gourmet food, offered in the fishing village "living room" of the friendly, yet salty, Graydon M. Hough, a former New York school teacher. It's the so-called retirement scheme of Mr. Hough to cook and serve wonderful food to earn money "to feed my prized Russian wolfhounds." With a credo of "I've never put anything on the table I haven't tasted before," he operates his honey of a restaurant with flair and style.

Rolls-Royces, Jaguars, the carriage trade are drawn to his little villa—a parade of discerning visitors, as well as American and English expatriates who live in the nearby villas. In-the-know guests telephone several hours ahead to have special dishes prepared, although it's possible to drop in on short notice for pot luck. Still, you should phone first, as people have a way of knocking on the door even when Mr. Hough is sleeping.

He sets three tables in his pleasant living room—one in front of the sofa, another by the window, a third in front of the fireplace where he keeps gnarled knots burning slowly on cool nights. He provides American-style drinks, such as a double dry martini for 50$ ($1.95). You might even be given one free on your arrival—Mr. Hough's way of helping Americans cope with the dollar devaluation. Hot rolls pop out of the oven in the evening and are placed on your white tablecloth along with country-churned butter. Soups such as homemade fish and vegetable costs 30$ ($1.17). A tuna salad plate with french fries or chips costs 75$ ($2.93). Such classics as southern fried chicken at 80$ ($3.12) are usually available, although his repertoire is wide ranging (hopefully, you'll be there when he prepares moussaka). At the counter, he always keeps a homemade cake, perhaps banana layer, or a pie made with tart apples, to tempt you. Most dinner tabs, including an apéritif, a full course table d'hôte gourmet meal, the finest Dao Valley wine, brandy with coffee, service, and tax, come to about 180$ ($7.02). It's also possible to come by for tea or coffee with a sandwich or cake for 35$ ($1.37).

A short drive north from Lagoa takes you to:

5. Silves

When you pass through the Moorish-inspired entrance of this hill-side town, a strange feeling hovers in the air. Silves is unlike the other towns and villages of the Algarve. It lives in the past, recalling its heyday when it was known as Xelb, the seat of Moslem culture in the south before it fell to the Crusaders.

Christian warriors and earthquakes have been rough on Silves. But somehow the **Castle of Silves,** crowning the hilltop, has held on, although it's seen better days. Once the blood of the Moslems—staging their last stand in Silves—"flowed like red wine," as one Portuguese historian put it. The cries and screams of women and children resounded over the walls: decapitation was swift. Nowadays, the only sound you're likely to hear is the loud rock music coming from the gatekeeper's house.

The red sandstone Castle itself may date back to the 9th century. From its ramparts you can look down the saffron-mossed tile roofs of the village houses, down the narrow cobbled streets where roosters strut and scrappy dogs sleep peacefully in the doorways.

Inside the walls, the government has planted a flower garden, adorning it with golden chrysanthemums and scarlet bracteal poinsettia. In the fortress is a huge cistern through which water rushes and a deep well made of sandstone. Below are dungeon chambers and labyrinthine tunnels where the last of the Moors hid out before the Crusaders found and sent them to their deaths.

The 13th-century Gothic **Cathedral of Silves,** down below, is disciplined but foreboding. Its walls are cracked and split, and the evidence of decay and neglect hang over it. On the interior, it is bleak. The Christian architects who originally built it may have torn down an old mosque. Still in all, the Cathedral is considered one of the most outstanding religious monuments in the Algarve.

Outside the main part of town, near an orange grove (one of the local Silves boys will surely volunteer as your inexpensive guide), a lonely open-air pavilion shelters a 15th-century stone lacework cross. This curious ecclesiastical art work is two-faced—depicting a Pietà (the face of Christ is destroyed) on one side, the Crucifixion on the other. It has been declared a national monument of incalculable value.

WHERE TO DINE: If you're in Silves for lunch, then visit the English **Casa Velha de Silves** (tel. 423-74). On one recent occasion, two well-informed readers stopped off and reported they were served an excellent soup, an imaginative and tasty Spanish veal, and a "delightful banana-butterscotch-ice cream concoction—one of the best meals we had in Portugal," for $10 (U.S.). They added, "We found it more attractive than the sights of the town." Closed Mondays.

6. Armaçao de Pera

Squat fishermen's cottages make up the core of this ancient village. It rests almost at water's edge on a curvy bay that edges up to its Golden Beach, one of the largest along Portugal's southern coast. In the direction of Portimao are rolling low ridges, toward Albufeira rosy cliffs.

Once Armaçao de Pera was utilized by the Phoenicians as a trading post and stopping-off point for cruises around Cape St. Vincent. Near the center of the village is a wide beach where fishing boats are drawn up on the sands—a sight when a fish auction (lota) is held. The **Casino,** however, is dull—no gambling, only occasional dancing, and during the day women often come here with their embroidery.

While at the resort, you may want to walk out to the desolate **Nossa Senhora da Rocha** (Our Lady of the Rock), a Romanesque chapel on a 95-foot-high stone that sticks out into the ocean like the prow of a boat. Underneath are the cathedral-sized **Sea Grottos (Furnas).** To visit these, you have to call at the Tourist Office and make arrangements to go out in a boat, but they're certainly worth the effort. Unique in the Algarve, the sea caves are entered through a series of arches that frame the sky and ocean from the inside. In their galleries and vaults, where pigeons nest, the splashing and shouting reverberates in the upper stalactite-studded chambers.

The nearest railway station is at the village of Alcantarilha, five miles away.

THE UPPER BRACKET: Hotel Do Garbe, Armaçao de Pera (tel. 551-87), is a self-contained resort dominating the top of a cliff, with a sandy beach at its feet. Stone steps lead up through the terraced palisade to the hotel, built block fashion—its white walls, bedroom balconies, and public terraces shining in the summer sun.

The gracious public rooms—built on several levels—are modern, but warmed by a use of color and natural wood. In the main sitting room, with its open fireplace, furnishings are grouped with an eye to the sea view; likewise, the dining hall turns to the sea. If you're just passing through, you can order a luncheon or dinner for 150$ ($5.85).

The bedrooms combine Scandinavian and Algarvian features. Often a room will have stone and plaster built-in end tables and window seats; beds set on pine frames; an occasional white skin throw rug; a red parasol on a private patio; and leather-toned tile floors. Room rates vary according to placement, size, and view—the higher tariffs for one of the four luxury or nine junior suites. The high-season, full-board rate for one person ranges from 450$ ($17.55) to 550$ ($21.45); for two persons, from 760$ ($29.64) to 1,100$ ($42.92), taxes and service included.

From Armaçao de Pera, it's a 6½ mile drive east to:

7. Albufeira

This cliffside fishing village is the St. Tropez of the Algarve. The lazy life, sunshine, beaches, and cheap food make it a haven for young people and artists, although the villagers haven't quite made up their minds as to what they think of the invasion that began in the late 1960s. Some of them, however, open the doors of their cottages to those seeking a little tuck-away cell for a few escudos a night. Those without the money often sleep in a tent on the cliff, or under the sky.

The village itself retains characteristics more readily associated with a North African seaside community. Its streets are steep, the villas drunkenly staggered up and down the hillside. Albufeira rises above a sickle-shaped beach that shines in the bright sunlight. A rocky grottoed bluff separates the strip used by the sunbathers from the working beach, where brightly painted fishing boats are drawn up on the sand. Access to the beach is through a tunneled rock passageway.

In accommodations, the resort is well supplied—although the tariffs in many of the establishments are more suited to the middle-class pocket-book than that of the young people who favor the place so much. Outside of the village at the **Praia Maria Luísa** sits a Dutch-owned hotel—one of the finest on the Algarve—but for a luxury market only. We'll lead off with this recommendation, following with the lower-priced establishments in the village proper.

AN AVANT-GARDE LUXURY HOTEL: Hotel Balaia-Penta, Praia Maria Luisa (tel. 52-681). When you walk into the domed entrance hall, you might think you're in Manhattan's Guggenheim Museum, or maybe one of the leading department stores of Paris. Tiers of roughly hewn balconies rise sky high, making the Balaia-Penta the most exciting hotel—decoratively and architecturally—on the Algarve. The public rooms seem to flow one into another in an avant-garde style, with connecting passageways.

The architect, a Portuguese named Conceiçao Silva, designed the hotel like a $ sign, so as to give more rooms a view of the sea. His talented wife, Carmen Valente, did the interior decoration, using overscaled contemporary paintings on stark white walls. The large-scaled, colorful furnishings were selected by her.

Above the central core, corridors lead to 186 bedrooms and six super deluxe suites. The bedrooms are fashion-plate examples of taste; every room is uncrowded, with fine furnishings coordinated with simple textured fabrics, and often utilizing silk-screen hangings of fishermen. In high season, the rate in a single room is 700$ ($27.30), increasing to 900$ ($35.10) for two persons in a usually twin-bedded room (these tariffs include service and tax). Near the main building are 12 attractive bungalows, each having a three-bedroom suite—complete home with a kitchenette and private terrace, renting for 1,700$ ($66.30) daily for anywhere from two to six persons. Half pension is an additional 195$ ($7.61) per person daily.

The Dutch director René Moussault runs Balaia-Penta as if it were his own estate. To set the mood, he offers new arrivals welcoming cocktails. A tennis player, he is found on the courts almost daily. In addition, he has lined up a number of social and sporting activities arranged through the concierge—everything from donkey riding to water skiing to clay-pigeon shooting (an 18-hole golf course is nearby). Most guests, however, like to lounge by the heated swimming pool, enjoying a cold buffet luncheon.

The drawing rooms and salons are too numerous to itemize. The dining room, in blue and white, provides a stunning setting; whereas the grill relies on cardinal red linen and white carpeting, a background for dinner nightly (except Mondays). Also on the premises is a discotheque, featuring occasional fado and folklore entertainers. A whiskey costs about 60$ ($2.34).

The resort is four miles east of Albufeira, on about 40 acres of hilly land, encompassing a shoreline of rugged rock formations and a series of near-private coves for surf swimming.

THE UPPER BRACKET: Hotel Sol e Mar (tel. 52-121), has captured the prime position within the village itself. The leading first-class hotel in Albufeira, it deceives you with its two-story entrance on the upper palisade. You suppose you're entering a modern ranch-style inn. Not so! When you walk across the spacious, sun-filled lounges to the picture windows and look down, it's a six-story drop. Hugging the cliff are bedrooms and a wide stone terrace with garden furniture and parasols. On still a lower level is a sandy beach.

There are 74 bedrooms, only six of which are singles. Most contain private balconies, and a knowing decorator's touch is manifested. For example, the streamlined twins have overscaled black and white plaid covers, South American wooden headboards, locally painted seascapes, slimline armchairs, and plenty of wardrobe space. In high season, the half-pension rate is 480$ ($18.72) for two persons; 685$ ($26.72) for three; and 228$ ($8.90) in a single. Service and taxes are included in the rates.

Guests, a continental crowd with a sprinkling of Americans, enjoy the sunsets from the main living room. Diners take their meals in a two-level room. On the opposite side is a drinking lounge, bright and lively, and a room for card players. There is also a television room decorated with prints of uniformed soldiers. After dinner concerts are played on the electric organ till long past midnight.

During the day, guests take the elevator to the lower sun terrace, to find swimming, sunbathing, and the Esplanade Café, designed as a Portuguese tavern with Madeira stools, decorative tiles, hanging anchors and waiters in checked plaid shirts in the Nazaré style.

Every night except Mondays, guests dance at the O Pescador boîte to the latest records, paying a minimum of 30$ ($1.17) for drinks, including entrance, for non-residents.

THE MEDIUM-PRICED RANGE: Estalagem do Cêrro, Rua B (tel. 52-191), happily captures Algarvian charm, yet doesn't neglect all the contemporary amenities. It's appropriately named The Inn of the Craggy Hill, and is the inspiration of a young architect helped by the proprietor, an old Navy Commodore. An oldish, regional-styled building was joined to a more modern structure—maintaining its original character. They are connected by a two-story open solarium with lacy trailing vines. Making for a lush setting are the little patios, filled with waist-high geraniums, fig trees reaching across balconies, towers, and paved walks through spice and rose gardens.

The bedrooms, all with private baths, are regionally inspired—each maintaining its own character. The decorations include reed and rattan chairs, built-in window seats, esparto mat headboards, fireplaces (in some rooms), hanging basket lamps, handwoven draperies, tiled walls and niches. In high season, the single rate for full pension is 320$ ($12.48) to 350$ ($13.65); the double tab, 505$ ($19.70) to 600$ ($23.40). Seven suites are available and well worth the added cost—full pension for two is priced at 680$ ($26.52). Taxes are included in all tariffs.

The villa-sized dining room, built on several levels, with arched windows, parquet floors, and provincial reed chairs, provides good meals, combining regional Portuguese dishes with an international cuisine. Before and after dinner, guests gather in the little bar or in the lower level living room, with its armless leather chairs, wooden slat ceiling, and wall of decorative tiles.

Mar à Vista, Cerro da Piedade (tel. 52-154). From the crow's nest vantage point of this estalagem, you can gaze out over the rooftops of the village below—the beach dotted with bright tents for bathers. The rooftop dining room of this first-class inn, decorated in a provincial style with blond paneling, takes advantage of the view. Regional dishes are the fare, mixed with an international cuisine. Off the reception area, the petit salon blends hues of bronze, gold, and maroon, where guests may watch television if they wish. Still another place for guests to gather is the bar, whose muted tones of soft brown and amber panels, marble tables, and sofas create a pleasant ambience for drinks and conversation.

The rooms, 84 beds in all, mostly contain private balconies. The walls are hung with interesting prints; the furnishings, though not sumptuous, are typical and comfortable. On the half-pension plan, single rates range between 380$ ($14.82) and 415$ ($16.19); doubles between 430$ ($16.77) and 490$ ($19.11), including taxes.

Hotel Boa-Vista, Rua B (tel. 52-175). Built in the Algarvian style, and set high above the sea outside the village center, the Residence of the Good View offers two different modes of living: one in its amenity-loaded main building, another in its block of furnished efficiencies across the street. The style, the welcome, the high level of taste are set by an Englishman, Alfred Worth, the hotel's owner who once managed the well-known Santa Isabel in Funchal, Madeira. A special feature is a new temperature-controlled swimming pool with an encircling moat.

The decor of the reception and lounges exudes an easy sophistication. The view of the bay from the dining room complements the fine meals served, and in either of the two bars, the waiter will quickly learn your favorite drink. The rooms themselves open onto balconies, from which you can look down upon the whitewashed, orange-tile-roofed cottages to the bay below. The private baths are superb, in gray and white with marble. Leather banquettes and Carmen-red fabric add an attractive note. For half pension, a single person is charged 355$ ($13.85); two persons, 599$ ($23.36), taxes included.

For a real bargain, consider the nearby apartments, ideal for the family trade. Each of the 15 suites contains a kitchen, dining room, lounge, and balcony. Each can accommodate up to four persons and is furnished with twin beds, double settee, sofa, armchairs, refrigerator, stove, and marble-topped sink. The apartments range in price from 342$ ($13.38) to 495$ ($19.31), the cheaper rate for one person, the higher tariff for occupancy by four.

Vila Recife, up the hill from Sol e Mar, on the street leading into and out of town (tel. 52-047), is a luxurious old villa converted into a hotel. Many of its 23 rooms look down on a garden with palm trees where guests sip drinks in the evenings sitting on white metal lawn furniture, shaded by cool arbors and purple bougainvillea. There's also a large adjoining garden, plus an old-fashioned sitting room as well. The high-ceilinged bedrooms are homey, some commanding a view of the whole town. Upstairs is a terrace for sun-worshippers. A double with breakfast costs 180$

($7.02) in off season. Five rooms without bath go for only 150$ ($5.85) with breakfast. Singles without bath rent for 100$ ($3.90); with bath, 120$ ($4.68). The house is open all year.

THE BUDGET RANGE: Hotel Baltum, Avenida Eduardo Rios (tel. 52-106), is only a one-minute walk from the main beach strip. The hotel and its nearby annex are ideal for those who want modern accommodations at low cost. In the main building, the Baltum offers 26 rooms, each with central heating, private bath, telephone, and balcony (except for three rooms). Cozy sitting areas—furnished with armless leather chairs, blond coffee tables, and overstuffed couches—are available to those willing to spend a few more escudos.

The full-pension tariff ranges from 297$ ($11.58) to 317$ ($12.36) in a single; 605$ ($23.60) in a double. The provincial-style dining room, the sala de pantar, offers both Portuguese and international dishes. Meals cost 172$ ($6.71). The solarium-terrace with its little bar has music for dancing nightly.

The annex—called the **Anexo Baltum,** Rua Cândido dos Reis (tel. 52-306)—is in the center of the village, near the Cine Pax. The lobby is dominated by a circular staircase (the walls of which are carrousel-lined from floor to ceiling with decorative tiles). The rooms here are similar to those at the Hotel Baltum—being even newer, and equipped with showers instead of tubs. You'll have to do your soaking in the Atlantic! Some of the streamlined bedrooms have balconies, though others open onto an uninspired view of the central air shaft. The rates are slightly lower here than at the main hotel with singles going for anywhere from 100$ ($3.90) to 195$ ($7.61); doubles from 140$ ($5.46) to 240$ ($9.36), depending on the view and whether or not a sitting room is included.

WHERE TO DINE: Restaurante Alfredo, 9-11 Rua 5 de Outubro (tel. 150) serves what are really banquets, in an attractive atmosphere. The restaurant has enjoyed fame along the Algarve, although its former owner and namesake has now moved to a similarly named restaurant in Portimao. Just a minute's stroll from the market square, it is housed in an old building that looks as if it's always been an inn. It's full of atmosphere: crude wooden tables and chairs just made for leisurely drinking.

The restaurant's on the second floor—a heavily beamed room furnished with antiques, such as a grandfather's clock, a gilt mirror, faded oil paintings, and silver candelabra. There's an open fireplace with a pair of primitive cherub torchiers, plus a kitchen open to the full view of diners who watch their meals being grilled in a 10-foot-wide fireplace, or simmered in copper pots and pans.

To begin your meal, a shell dish of black olives, country pâté, and crusty bread, is set before you. On the menu you'll find cod, 60$ ($2.34); fish h ets, 60$ also; a mixed grill, 80$ ($3.12); tournedos, 85$ ($3.32); roast chicken, 50$ ($1.95); mixed salad, 15$ (59¢); and melon, 8$ (31¢). Alfredo's is open daily from noon to 3 p.m. for lunch; from 7 to 10 p.m. for dinner. It's closed Wednesdays.

"O Cabaz da Praia" (The Beach Basket), 7 Praça Miguel Bombarda, near the Hotel Sol e Mar, sits on a colorful little square, opposite a little chapel where village funerals are held! It's home base for an English couple, Jeanne and David Shean, along with their well-mannered and charming children, Christopher and Matthew. They migrated from their Surrey home to earn a living here where the sun shines eternally, and they have transformed a fisherman's cottage into a friendly place at which to order homemade meals. So inviting is the ambience, that it has lured guests from nearby hotels who have already paid for their meals en pension.

Mr. Shean has given the place a marine look, and set up tables on the waterview balcony. His wife, who has that gleaming English complexion and loveliness, prepares hot meals as well as wicker baskets stuffed with good things for the beach. Her specialty is an international cuisine, with emphasis on French cooking. Hopefully she'll have a soup made with tomatoes bought fresh at the open market; perhaps a savory broth of leeks. The cost is 20$ (78¢) a bowl. A favorite local dish is freshly caught Algarve sole, served with fresh vegetables for 85$ ($3.32), although you may prefer the daube de boeuf with buttered noodles, 65$ ($2.54).

Mrs. Shean notices that Americans "go a bundle" for her homemade cakes and pies, especially chocolate gâteau at 25$ (98¢) and lemon meringue pie at 30$ ($1.17).

Fernando, on the main square, with a large outdoor terrace, temptingly displays low-priced tourist menus. Entrees go from 50$ ($1.95) to 70$ ($2.73). There's a pleasant indoor dining room as well.

Oasis, Rua Largo Eng. Duarte Pacheco, right on the town's main square and opposite the market, is a favorite budgeteer's haunt, owing to its pleasant location, outside terrace, and low prices. À la carte items feature tomato soup, 8$ (31¢); filet of sole, 60$ ($2.34); and Alentejano pork, 55$ ($2.15). You can sit outdoors under shady trees, or indoors at candlelit tables.

A Ruina, Cais Herculano (tel. 520-94), sits right opposite the fish market. From the arcaded dining room, with its long wooden, candlelit tables, you can peer out at the fishermen mending their nets. Another cavelike room has more tables and a bar. The decor is simple and unpretentious, but the seafood is fresh. Specialties include grilled tuna for 50$ ($1.95). A tomato soup goes for 8$ (31¢); cutlets, 50$ ($1.95). Custard is 6$ (23¢); mousse, 7$ (27¢). The prices are posted behind the counter near the entrance.

Snack Bar O Isca, 10-12 Rua Candido dos Reis (tel. 52-075), despite its name, is really a pleasant little restaurant with a varied menu and no frills. Sea bass filets cost 38$ ($1.48); spaghetti Bolognaise, 40$ ($1.56); English-style liver, 40$ also; pork with clams, 50$ ($1.95); and a prawn omelette, 30$ ($1.17). There are high-backed wooden chairs set at tables and a bar on one side.

THE LOCAL PUB: **Sir Harry's Bar,** on the market square, is in the center of the village. Sir Harry (Warner) can be distinguished by his beaming smile and RAF-type mustache. His fashionable bar is a gravity point for any bloke who has abandoned his Cotswold tweeds for the lighter threads of the Algarve. Converts swear that Sir Harry's is their Algarvian "local." The bar itself merges the ambience of a black-and-white timbered village pub with the coziness of a Portuguese fisherman's cottage.

Beneath the low natural beams, a comfortable array of Savonarola chairs, crude tables, and wooden settles are found on two levels—divided by wrought-iron railings. The collection of rifles, steins, gleaming copper pots and pans, and earthenware water jugs provide the genuine ye olde touch. A bar of herringbone brick and timbers has heel-propping stools, attracting those drawn to the center of the action. Most drinks, such as a rum Coke, go for 50$ ($1.95). Hearty sandwiches are served as well. Open daily, year round.

8. Praia de Quarteira

With its miles of sand dunes, Quarteira may one day be billed as the Atlantic City of the Algarve, but that isn't likely to happen soon.

Between Albufeira and Faro, this once-sleepy fishing village used to be known only to a handful of artists who provided amusement for the local fishermen and their varinas. Now with the invasion of outsiders, the traditional way of life is upset.

Golfers who don't want to pay the high tariffs at Vale de Lobo or Vilamoura (both of which have 18-hole golf courses) can stay inexpensively in Quarteira at one of the accommodations listed below. The above-mentioned courses are only a 10-minute drive away, and Quarteira itself lies about seven miles from the Faro Airport.

Except for some dreary pensions, the accommodations include:

THE MEDIUM-PRICED RANGE: **Hotel Beira Mar,** Avenida Infante de Sagres (tel. 651-32). The latest building to grow up in Quarteira is a second-class, 51-bedroom hotel. It is functional, efficient, and has a fine location. With a single bound from the front entrance, a long-legged sprinter will land right on the sandy beach! All bedrooms contain immaculately kept private baths and sun porches, from which guests can see the Phoenician-inspired prows of the fishing boats 150 yards down the beach.

The rooms contain up-to-date furnishings, many utilizing decorative blue and white tile configurations. For a room plus breakfast, the single tariff is 275$ ($10.73); the two person tab, 350$ ($13.65). In off season, a single with bath is 90$ ($3.51); a double with bath, 120$ ($4.68). The lounges and reception make use of walnut-colored slat facings and ceilings. The brown tile floors, especially at the entrance, are highlighted by the whiteness of the walls and stark plaster pillars. Before-dinner drinks and evening get-togethers may be enjoyed in the hotel bar, walled with tiles of a golden-grain.

Hotel Toca do Coelho, Avenida Infante de Sagres (tel. 65-15-0), provides a modern seafront accommodation, with a wide sandy beach as its front yard. Recently reconstructed, it was thoroughly updated, each room provided with a private bath, central heating, telephone, and piped-in music. Half of the lodgings have over-sized glass doors opening onto private balconies. Full pension rates range from 270$ ($10.53) to 465$ ($18.14) in a single; from 480$ ($18.72) to 790$ ($30.81) in a twin, taxes included. Breakfast costs 30$ ($1.17). Lunch or dinner is 135$ ($5.27). The Portuguese bill of fare, incidentally, is excellent, with an emphasis on sea-fruits. Adding to the hotel's resort aura are a heated swimming pool; two solariums; an open-air, sea-view dining room, and two bars.

A HOLIDAY VILLAGE: Between Albufeira and Quarteira, in a delightful pinewood, the **Aldeia das Acoteias** is the most recently developed holiday village—designed in the typical Moorish style of the Algarve. For rent are fully equipped and furnished small studio apartments, bungalows, and large family villas. The resort is operated under the aegis of the **Touring Club of Portugal,** which accepts bookings at its main office in Lisbon at 231 Avenida Almirante Reis (tel. 71-91-81). The village offers a supermarket, restaurant, nightclub, and swimming pool. Golf and riding facilities as well are nearby. Apartments begin at 350$ ($13.65) daily for one person, increasing to 850$ ($33.15) daily for a party of four. Five clients can rent a bungalow at a cost of 1,000$ ($39); eight persons, at 1,200$ ($46.80); 10, at 1,400$ ($54.60). Breakfast costs 30$ ($1.17) in the restaurant, and the main meal, anywhere from 90$ ($3.51) to 120$ ($4.68). Add 190$ ($7.41) per person to the price of the room if you desire full pension. Included in the tariffs are beach facilities, a cleaning service, and babysitting.

Adjoining the fringes of Praia de Quarteira is:

9. Vilamoura

Although the remains of a Roman villa were discovered when builders were working on a marina, the history of this settlement is yet to be written. At a central point on the Algarve coast, only 11 miles from Faro Airport, Vilamoura is an expansive land-development project. Plans call for a city larger than Faro, a protected harbor sheltering 1,000 boats, and an interior lake linked with the bay and ocean by two canals. One can sum up the Vilamoura situation by comparing it to the weather of New England: "If you don't like it now, wait a minute!"

The **Vilamoura Casino** is the second of the Casinos do Algarve. It is close to the Vilamoura Golf Club. The casino features a gambling salon with roulette, blackjack, French banque, and baccarat. A separate salon is devoted to slot machines. Featured also is a 250-seat supper club, with two floor shows nightly.

Entrance to the slot machines is free, but a small entrance fee to the main gambling room is charged, beginning at 30$ ($1.17) for two nights. The casino is open from 5 p.m. to 3 a.m. every day of the year. Tourists must present their passports.

Projected are more than 100 hotels, but at the moment you'll have to make do with a fare more limited selection in:

THE MEDIUM-PRICED RANGE: **Vilamoura Hotel** and the **Clube Vilamoura** (tel. Quarteira 653-321). You're offered two excellent choices of accommodations at this Moorish-style country club, favored by golf enthusiasts who like to sleep, swim, and dine close to the links. You can select your room in either a first-class inn or else in one of the group of apartment bungalows, only moments from the 18-hole course.

The hotel itself features a cluster of cubistic rooms, built around a swimming pool and terrace. These rooms contain their own tiny patios, and all of them are equipped with freshly tiled baths.

The nearby apartment bungalows comfortably house anywhere from two to eight persons, the facilities including a foyer, living room, dining area, and kitchenette. Like the hotel, the architectural concept is Algarvian cubistic, and the furnishings are homelike, in a modified contemporary way. For two persons at the golf club, the high season cost of lodgings ranges from 410$ ($15.99) to 515$ ($20.09), the latter rate for a twin-bedded room classified as a superior suite. The single rate is 310$ ($12.09) daily, all tariffs including breakfast, service, and tax. In one of the terrace houses, two persons pay 385$ ($15.02) in a studio complete with kitchenette, telephones, and maid service. Four persons are housed for 750$ ($29.25); six persons, 880$ ($34.33). Full pension is an additional 250$ ($9.75) per person daily.

Motorists passing through for the day can stop off and enjoy an excellent meal at the golf club restaurant, where à la carte luncheons or dinners average 100$ ($3.90) to 120$ ($4.68) per person.

10. Vale do Lobo

The name Valley of the Wolf suggests some forlorn spot, set amid bleak terrain. Hardly likely! The Vale, west of Faro, about a 20-minute drive from the airport, is the site of an exciting new golf course designed by Henry Cotton, the famous British champion. Some of the holes are played by the sea, resulting in many an anxious moment when a shot may hook out over the water a precarious distance from the green. To play costs 250$ ($9.75) a day for visitors, 200$ ($7.80) a day for hotel guests. Recently another nine-hole course and a nine-hole par 3 course, a putting green, and driving range have been installed.

Reached through fig orchards, cork forests, and a valley of tufted pines, the seaside strongly evokes Carmel, California. Pale golden cliffs jut out over sandy beaches that stretch brilliantly in the distance until they evaporate into a faint haze.

A BRITISH-RUN DELUXE GOLF HOTEL: **Hotel Dona Filipa,** Vale do Lobo, Almansil (tel. 94-141). Forget everything you've ever known about British Trust Houses in England! With such touches as gold-painted palms holding up the ceiling, the Dona Filipa bears about as much resemblance to its tired old sisters back in the British Isles as Raquel Welch does to Dame Edith Evans. The grounds are unquestionably impressive, embracing 450 acres of rugged coastline with steep cliffs, inlets, and sandy bays.

The exterior of the hotel is comparatively uninspired, but a wonderful dimension was brought to the interior by Duarte Pinto Coelho, who worked on the Spanish Pavilion at the New York World's Fair. Green silk banquettes, marble fireplaces, paisley-covered pillars, Portuguese ceramic lamps, old prints over baroque-styled love seats—the flair is lush. Aside from a Chinese room for card playing, the most popular meeting point is the Gothic Bar, with its cathedral-like stools, wooden decorations, and matching floor and upholstery fabric in azulejos patterns.

There are 130 air-conditioned rooms—all with bath, most with balcony. Singles cost 720$ ($28.08); doubles, 1,030$ ($40.17). For full pension, add 375$ ($14.63) per person per day. A meal in the restaurant costs 200$ ($7.80). All prices include service, taxes, and golf green fees at the Vale do Lobo championship 27-hole golf course.

Dining is formal and gracious, with a knowledgeable maître d'hôtel and wine steward guiding you on your selections. At the beach is a discotheque, where the latest international records are played for dancing (occasionally, folk artists and fadistas perform).

A RESORT CENTER: **Quinta do Lago,** near Almansil, three miles west of Faro, is a sprawling 1,600-acre estate, which is selling private plots within it. The area will have a hotel, on which construction should start shortly. Already open are: a riding center, unquestionably one of the best in Southern Europe; a 27-hole golf course, designed by American course architect William F. Mitchell, and recognized among the top six in Europe; two tennis courts; **Pony's,** the Algarve's new, sophisticated discotheque; the luxurious **Casa Velha Apartamentos** (tel. 94-358), overlooking the seawater lake and provided with every modern comfort; and the superb **Casa Velha** restaurant (tel. 94-272), renowned for its fine food and impeccable service. Its dining room is built in a simple rustic style. You sit along divans with cushions. Adjoining is a swimming pool for those who want to take a dip into the water before plunging into the meal. It has recently been enlarged with a grill room and a pergola at the pool edge. Recommended are smoked swordfish with horseradish sauce, 95$ ($3.71); cataplana Algarvia for two, 200$ ($7.80); rack or saddle of lamb persillée for two, 300$ ($11.70); délices of sole Casa Velha, 115$ ($4.49); strawberry soufflé for two, 120$ ($4.68); crêpes Casa Velha, 60$ ($2.34); and fish soup du pêcheur, 45$ ($1.76). A chateaubriand for two costs 260$ ($10.14).

11. Faro

Flowers brought in from the countryside are plentiful. In the blue lagoon sailing enthusiasts glide by. A típico old quarter flanks the ruined ramparts that proved all too vulnerable in the past. At the yacht harbor starlings and sparrows flutter nervously, while children run noisily to the pastry shops to buy stuffed figs and almond cakes. Beyond the waterfront lie the tree-studded avenues and cobbled alleyways of the city.

FROM VALE DO LOBO TO FARO

Once loved by the Roman and later the Moor, Faro is the capital of the Algarve. Sit at a cafe sampling the wine, and you'll watch yesterday and today pass by. An old man walks ahead, pulling a donkey on which a parasol-shaded girl in a white dress is sitting. Brushing past is a German student in short pants, his white skin turned golden by the sun.

Faro is a hodgepodge of life and activity: it's been rumbled, sacked, and "quaked" by everybody from Mother Nature to the Earl of Essex (Elizabeth's old favorite).

Since Afonso III drove out the Moors for the last time in 1266, Faro has been Portuguese. On its outskirts a new international jet airport brings in thousands of visitors every summer. The airport has done more than anything else to speed tourism not only to Faro but to the Algarve in general, as jet planes make it possible to reach Faro from Lisbon in 30 minutes.

The most bizarre attraction is the **Capela d'Ossos** (Chapel of Bones), entered from the rear of the **Igreja de Nossa Senhora do Monte do Carmo do Faro,** via a courtyard. Erected in the 19th century, this chapel is completely lined with the skulls and bones of human skeletons—an extraordinary ossicular rococo. In all, it's estimated there are 1,245 human skulls.

The church itself, built in 1713, contains a gilded baroque altar. Likewise, its facade is baroque, with a bell tower rising from each side. Topping the belfries are gilded mosque-like cupolas, connected by a balustraded railing. The windows of the upper levels are latticed and framed with gold, with statues standing in each of the niches on either side of the main portal.

Other religious monuments include the old **Sé** (Cathedral), built in the Gothic and Renaissance styles (originally a Moslem mosque stood on this site); the **Church of St. Francis,** with excellent panels of glazed earthenware tiles in milk white and Delft blue, depicting the life of the patron saint; and the **Convent of Our Lady of the Assumption,** declared a national monument and noted for its Renaissance portal and cloister.

But most tourists don't come to Faro to look at churches, regardless of how interesting. Rather, they take the harbor ferry to the wide, white sandy beaches called the **Praia de Faro,** on an islet. The ride (available only in summer) costs 10$ (39¢) for a round-trip passage. The beach is also connected to the mainland by bridge, a distance of about 3½ miles from the town center. Once there, you can water ski and fish or just lounge in the sun, renting a deck chair and umbrella.

The accommodations, however, tend to be disappointing, except for the following recommendations:

THE UPPER BRACKET: Eva Hotel, Avenida da República (tel. 240-54), dominates the harbor, just as fortresses did centuries ago. The eight-floor modern hotel occupies an entire side of the yacht-clogged harbor, and provides direct sea views from most of the bedrooms.

Most of the public rooms are spacious and comfortable. Best part is the rooftop terrace and swimming pool, supported on 16 posts about 100 feet above ground level. With its view of the islands and lagoon, the top-floor restaurant serves well-prepared meals.

The air-conditioned bedrooms are restrained, furnished in harmonious colors. The bathrooms are tiled in black and white. In high season a single ranges in price from 190$ ($7.41) to 280$ ($10.92), with twin-bedded rooms going for 310$ ($12.09) to 450$ ($17.55) (with private balconies). For half pension, add 175$ ($6.83) per person. During the summer, there's activity in the nightclub on the ground floor, either with a small orchestra or records for dancing.

THE MEDIUM-PRICED RANGE: The **Hotel Faro,** Praça D. Francisco Gomes (tel. 220-76), is a first-class B hotel with 52 rooms (eight with shower) opening right onto the bustling harbor, a prime position. The lobby—a cool, tasteful, and contemporary design, with splashes of greenery —sets the tone: that is, all the conveniences but very little fanfare. The furnishings in the rooms are comfortable, though uninspired, and many contain balconies opening right onto the square and its bird concerts.

For full pension, you pay anywhere between 410$ ($15.99) and 480$ ($18.72) for one person, between 680$ ($26.53) and 810$ ($31.59) for two persons. Taxes are included. The least expensive rooms contain shower baths. The suites have a small sitting room with a bed sofa, suitable for a third person. In a light and spacious room, the restaurant serves French and Portuguese dishes complemented by a well-coordinated wine list. The bar provides drinks, which you can order from the mezzanine while surveying the scene below.

THE BUDGET RANGE: Hotel-Residência Lumena, 27 Praça Alexandre Herculano (tel. 220-28), is owned by London-born Roy Nadler. He has taken over an old mansion on a square shaded by jacaranda trees. For bed and breakfast, the Lumena charges from only 180$ ($7.02) for two persons, including tax.

Originally, this hotel was the town house of the reigning sardine family of Faro. Built at the edge of the sidewalk, with wrought-iron gratings at its windows, the Lumena offers 12 double rooms and two suites, each with private bath. The rooms are all shaped differently and furnished with pieces inherited from the casa. Throughout are antiques, carved chests, satin wood tables, painted dressers, and armoires. Many people come here for the village-like bar with its three-legged stools, old port barrels, painted chests, what-not cupboard of glassware, and other provincial furniture. Drinks and light snacks are also served in the courtyard at the rear which is shaded by grapevines.

WHERE TO DINE: Al-Faghar, 30 Rua Tenente Valadim (tel. 237-40), one flight up, has a cozy, well-furnished dining room with candles on the tables, local crockery and Portuguese plates, an elegant bar, and a romantic Moorish patio. It is English owned and run. A la carte dishes include vegetable soup with hot garlic bread, 17$50 (68¢); pâté de foie, 35$ ($1.37); fried filets of swordfish, 45$ ($1.76), or 32$50 ($1.27) for a half portion; tournedos Brétonne, 79$ ($3.08); or the chef's salad feast, 69$ ($2.69), which contains everything. Also good are the ham steak Hawaii, 69$ ($2.69), and the paupiettes de steak au poivre, 79$ ($3.08). Finish with brandied peaches and cream, 25$ (98¢). The restaurant is open noon to 3 p.m. and 7 to 11 p.m. Look for the six English and Portuguese flags hanging from the balcony.

Folclore, Rua Tenente Valadim, is one of several local restaurants in a narrow non-traffic street with tables set outdoors as on Seville's Calle Sierpes. The Folclore offers a shrimp cocktail for 50$ ($1.95); a special salad for 17$ (66¢); açorda de marisco, 50$ ($1.95); bife de atum, 45$ ($1.76); pork chops, 40$ ($1.56); and fruit salad with sherbet, 20$ (78¢). Nothing is extraordinary, but it's not bad.

FARO AFTER DARK:
The **Kon Tiki Nightclub,** Rua da Marinha, under the Hotel Faro, right off the harbor square, is considered the most elegant place in town. The table candles cast a dim, almost lurid, rose glow, reflecting off the white Moorish arches. The ceiling is low and dark, and the crude rattan and bamboo tables and low chairs are in the Polynesian style. Many are huddled in corners and secluded nooks, providing ideal spots for intimate conversations during breaks in discotheque dancing. There is no minimum, and drinks run around 60$ ($2.34) to 80$ ($3.12) for whiskey. Just off the harbor square, the Kon Tiki floats from 10 p.m. until 4 a.m.

Paddy's Bar, 1 Rua Oliveira Salazar, is snugly hidden in a lane. It is perhaps the friendliest bar in Faro, where meeting people is easy in a relaxed atmosphere, especially for those who like an occasional (or frequent) pint. The pub rooms are warmed by an open fire in winter, the knotty pine walls and rough oaken beams hung with 19th-century prints and a collection of brass stirrups from the British Isles. Settled in any one of a multitude of handsome leather chairs, you can enjoy a whiskey for 35$ ($1.37), a bottle of beer or a brandy for 10$ (39¢). Paddy's is open seven days a week.

A SIDE-TRIP TO LOULÉ:
Loulé, 9½ miles north of Faro, is a market town in the heart of the chimney district of the Algarve. If you ever thought that chimneys couldn't excite you, you haven't seen the ones here. From many of

the houses and cottages, these fret-cut plaster towers rise. You may even see one on the house of a very discriminating dog! They resemble fine lace work or filigree in stone; others are as delicately contrived as forms of snow crystals blown against glass.

In Loulé itself, you may want to visit the Gothic-style **Parish Church,** which was given to the town in the latter 13th century, and the Church of the **Misericordia,** looking like a wedding cake, especially its Manueline entrance. The town also contains the remains of a fortress-castle which Afonso III captured from the Moors.

12. Sao Brás de Alportel

Traveling north from Faro for 12½ miles, you'll pass through groves of figs, almonds, and oranges, through pine woods where resin collects in wooden cups on the tree trunks. At the end of the run, you'll come upon isolated Sao Brás de Alportel, one of the most charming and least known spots on the Algarve.

Far from the crowd on the beaches, it attracts those wanting pure air, peace, and quiet—a bucolic setting filled with flowers pushing through nutmeg-colored soil. Northeast of Loulé, the whitewashed, tile-roofed town rarely gets lively except on market days. Like its neighbor, Faro, it is noted for its perforated plaster chimneys. At the foot of the Serra do Caldeirao, the whole area has been labeled "one vast garden."

The big attraction at Sao Brás de Alportel is:

A HILLTOP BUDGET POUSADA: Pousada de Sao Brás (tel. 423-05) offers a change of pace from the seaside accommodations. The government-owned inn is a hilltop villa, with a crow's nest view of the surrounding serras. It's approached through a fig orchard in which stones have been painted with welcome in many languages. The fret-cut limestone chimneys perch over the potted plants and foliage of the grounds and an occasional antique wagon wheel—a sedate and tranquil scene.

Many visitors arrive just for lunch or dinner, returning to the coastline by night, but a knowing few remain for the evening. In the dining room, rustic mountain tavern chairs and tables rest on handwoven rugs. The soft sofa before the wood-burning fireplace is a perfect place for lingering over a cup of coffee. The 80$ ($3.12) table d'hôte dinner offers soup, a fish course, a meat dish, vegetables, and dessert. Pleasant waitresses in blue and white pleated aprons edged with lace serve you the savory soup from a steaming tureen. The cuisine is plain, but good—the portions generous.

After dinner you may want to retire to the beamed-ceilinged sitting room to watch the embers of the evening's fire die down. Then trundle upstairs, past the large ornamented tasseled donkey collar for a night's sleep in cozy beds in a room cooled by highland breezes. The bedrooms themselves are decorated in inventive regional styles (nine without bath, eight with). The full pension bill is 207$ ($8.07) without bath or 232$ ($9.05) with bath in a single: 355$ ($13.85) without bath or 395$ ($15.41) with bath for two.

In addition to Loulé and Sao Brás de Alportel, do see:

ESTOL AND MILREU: Two broken capitals and some fluted columns stand on ground blanketed by buttercups. In classical times, the Roman soldiers—seeing the gardens of the Algarve in spring—decided that a Temple of Venus was in order. **Milreu** was turned into a spa, and today numerous fragments, mosaics, baths, even water pipes are in evidence. Archaeologists have claimed that some of the ruins are those of a Christian church built in the 3rd century A.D., making it one of the earliest in the world. There is no admission, no guard—just a lonely field and an old deserted farmhouse adjoining.

From Milreu, you can see **Estói,** a former Roman town five miles from Olhao. Tourists are still greeted with interest around here; old women stare at them from behind the curtains of their little houses, but begging children are likely to follow them about. Estói is an unspoiled village, where women can be seen washing their clothing in a public trough. Its garden walls are decaying, its cottages well worn by the time and the weather.

In Estói is the 18th-century villa, the **Palácio do Visconde de Estói,** with a salmon-pink facade. It is made up of formal gardens, Italian marble statues, fountains, terraces, belvederes, and stairways rising by cypresses and patches of lavender.

13. Olhao

If you approach this fishing village by the road from Estói, you'll pass a small aqueduct, a creaking watermill, and sheep grazing in the fields. Along the way, gypsies trudge by, some riding in gaily painted carts pulled by mules (known as carrinhos de molas).

The Olhao appears—a living re-creation of a Georges Braque collage with all the skillful shading and color modulations of Cézanne. This is the famous cubist town of the Algarve, so long beloved by painters. The brilliant white blocks stacked one upon the other, with flat red tile roofs, and exterior stairways on the stark walls, evoke the aura of the casbahs of North African cities.

We hope that you'll be able to attend the fish market near the waterfront when a lota (auction) is under way. Olhao is also known for its bullfights of the sea, in which fishermen wrestle with struggling tuna trapped in nets and headed for the smelly warehouses along the harbor.

For the best view, climb **Cabeça Hill,** its grottos punctured with stalagmites and stalactites, or perhaps **St. Michael's Mount,** offering a panorama of the Casbah-like Barreta. Finally, for what is perhaps the most idyllic beach on the Algarve, take a 10-minute motorboat ride to the **Ilha de Armona,** a nautical mile away. Olhao itself is 6½ miles west of Faro.

Most tourists visit just for the day, although an estalagem is there for those wanting to soak up color.

THE BUDGET RANGE: Hotel Caíque, 37 Rua Dr. Oliveira Salazar (tel. 721-67). In a village hard pressed for suitable overnight accommodations or restaurants, this Kayak Inn is an easy winner. Open year round, its 40 bedrooms come equipped with private baths. The rooms are small and uninspired, but they're clean and comfortable. Prices are from 240$ ($9.36) for full pension for one; from 365$ ($14.24) to 390$ ($15.21) full board for two. To be quoted on pension terms, you must stay a minimum of two days.

Guests on full pension may have picnic lunches packed for day excursions at no extra charge. Also, the hotel provides a launch service to the beach on Armona Island, and will arrange fishing and sightseeing expeditions. The hotel also offers a lounge, a fine regional restaurant serving 90$ ($3.51) table d'hôte meals, a bridge room, a bar, solarium, and three sitting rooms—one on each floor. From the rooftop terrace is a view of the village.

TAVIRA: An Algarvian gem, sleepy Tavira sits like a town of the past century. It's approached through green fields studded with almond and carob trees, the latter producing a dry pod of hard seeds in sweet pulp (eaten by both man and animals). Sometimes called the Venice of the Algarve, Tavira lies on the banks of the Ségua and Gilao Rivers, which meet under a seven-arched Roman bridge. In the town square, palms and pepper trees rustle amidst the cool arches of the arcade.

A tunny fishing center, Tavira is cut off from the sea by an elongated spit of sand, the **Ilha de Tavira,** which begins west of Cacela and runs all the way past the fishing village of Fuzeta. On this sandbar, reached by motorboat, are two beaches: the Praia de Tavira and the Praia de Fuzeta. Others prefer to go to the beach at the tiny village of **Santa Luzia** about two miles from the heart of town.

Tavira is festive looking with floridly decorated chimneys topping many of the houses, some of which are graced with emerald-green tiles and wrought-iron balconies capped by finials. Many doorways are adorned with fret-work. The liveliest action, however, centers on the fruit and vegetable market on the river esplanade. The town lies about 19 miles east of Faro.

14. Monte Gordo

Monte Gordo is the last in a long line of Algarvian resorts, lying as it does directly west of the frontier town of Vila Real de Santo António. Its wide beach—one of the finest along the southern coast of Portugal—is backed by lowlands studded with pines. The resort lies at the mouth of the Guardiana River.

The fishing village goes on as before (except the varinas urge their sons to take to the hotels instead of the sea, fishing for tips instead of tunny). Wives in housecoats emerge from newly built houses to receive the best of the fresh catch from fishermen who ride bicycles through the streets delivering orders. The village is small, filled with squat houses predominantly colored robin's egg blue or coral.

For such a small resort, Monte Gordo is well supplied with hotels.

THE UPPER BRACKET: Hotel Vasco da Gama, Avenida Infante D. Henriques (tel. 321), is the most expansive and impressive modern hotel built at the eastern end of the Algarve. Its entrepreneurs know what their northern guests seek—lots of sunbathing and swimming. Although it enjoys a position on a long, wide, sandy beach, it also offers an olympic-size swimming pool with high-dive board, and nearly an acre of flagstoned sun terrace.

Inside is a high-ceiling oceanfront dining room, with additional tables on the mezzanine, plus several well-furnished lounges with many groupings of chairs for that quiet conversation. Other conveniences include two drinking bars, and a boîte where it's possible to dance to records or combos several nights a week.

While the hotel is geared to large groups, individual guests are welcomed as well. For full pension in high season, the rates range from 350$ ($13.65) to 580$ ($22.63) in a single, and from 680$ ($26.53) to 860$ ($33.54) in a double. The prices of the 182 rooms vary according to size and exposure. In all cases, the furnishings are excellent and conservative. Glass doors open onto balconies, and the baths are tiled.

Families who want to anchor in by the beach should consider booking one of the flats in the block of efficiency apartments overlooking the sea. For one of them (meals extra), two persons pay 380$ ($14.82); four persons, 610$ ($23.79); and six persons, 840$ ($32.76).

Just a block away, also overlooking the pine woods and ocean, is a small less expensive hotel owned by the Vasco da Gama (guests are allowed to use the facilities of the more expensive sister). Rated first-class B by the government is the **Hotel das Caravelas,** Monte Gordo (tel. 459). It's modern and simpler, with eight floors of rooms, and a roof terrace attracting sun seekers. Its 87 bedrooms have little balconies, private baths, and attractive and comfortable furnishings. For full pension, a single person pays from 348$ ($13.57) to 572$ ($22.31); two persons, 530$ ($20.68) to 714$ ($27.85). The dining room on the top floor opens onto a good view in many directions.

THE MEDIUM-PRICED RANGE: Hotel dos Navegadores, Rua Gonçalo Velho (tel. 451). Its glaring white facade belies the niceties found inside. All 103 rooms come with private baths and terraces, opening onto the pine woods and the sea, a short haul from the sands. The furnishings are inspired by provincial designs—most inviting, especially the black-cushioned rattan armchairs. There is a warm-water swimming pool. The half-pension rate for a single is 620$ ($24.18); for two people, 670$ ($26.13).

Black and gold ladderback chairs are foils for the creamy interior of the dining area, where fine international and regional dishes are served. What could better satisfy the sun-soaked bather than a chilled bowl of gazpacho, followed by an omelette with savory bits of smoked ham, then grilled mutton chops, and an iced bowl of fresh fruits? Dinners are even more elaborate. The chef doesn't believe in attracting weight-watching guests!

Albergaria Monte Gordo, Monte Gordo (tel. 524), was a popular estalagem that turned into a small, family-type hotel. A streamlined modern structure, it is open to the sky and sea, emulating a pueblo style of architecture. Directly across the road is a wide beach. All the bedrooms contain private baths. A double room with bath and terrace facing the sea costs 250$ ($9.75). Considerable reductions are granted in winter. The staff is friendly and young, the atmosphere informal. An added decorative touch in the public rooms are the primitive fabric and needlework hangings of Sylvia Ameida of Los Gatos, California. Especially interesting is one of orange and blue simulated tree trunks holding an intricate little bird's nest. The hotel restaurant serves well-prepared seafood, such as grilled hake or browned bream with anchovy filets.

On the premises a nightclub has a separate entrance beneath the esplanade. Here guests can dance to international records and to a four-piece combo on Saturday nights.

THE BUDGET RANGE: Pensao Residência Catavento, Rua Projectada (tel. 24-28), is the best bargain in Monte Gordo, rated by the government as a luxury pensao. This Inn of the Weathervane is owned by Manuel Dias and Fernando Lágaro, who maintain a simplicity and cleanliness that have won them many repeat customers. Their rooms are so pristine they're almost monastic. Room and breakfast for one is 130$ ($5.07) to 160$ ($6.24); for two, 195$ ($7.61) to 230$ ($8.97). Breakfast only is served.

Inside the Catavento, the walls are hung with wooden cutouts and atmospheric prints of fishing boats. The lounge is highlighted by two-tone wooden dado; and the breezy dining room serves a varied local and international cuisine. The beach is but a minute's walk from the front door, and for 15$ you're permitted the use of a shower, an umbrella chair, and the toilets there.

For a final stopover, about two miles east of Monte Gordo, there is—

VILA REAL DE SANTO ANTONIO: Twenty years after the Marquês de Pombal rebuilt Lisbon, after the great earthquake of 1755, he sent the architects and builders to Vila Real de Santo António where they re-established the frontier town on the opposite bank from Spain. Separated from its Iberian neighbor by the Guadiana River, Vila Real de Santo António offers a car-ferry between Portugal and Ayamonte, Spain.

Pombal's reason for wanting a town here was motivated by jealousy of Spain. It took only five months to build. Much has changed, of course, although the Praça de Pombal remains. An obelisk stands in the center of the square, which is paved with inlays of black and white tiles radiating like rays of the sun, and filled with orange trees.

A long esplanade, the Avenida da Republica, lines the river, and from its northern extremity, you can view the Spanish town across the way. Gaily painted horse-drawn carriages take you sightseeing past the shipyards, the lighthouse, or to the bullfights in July and August.

A short drive north on the road to Mertola takes you to the gull-gray castle-fortress of **Castro Marim.** This formidable structure is a legacy of the old border wars between Spain and Portugal. The ramparts and walls watch Spain across the river. Afonso III, who chased the Moors out of this region, founded the original fortress, which was brought to its knees by the 1755 earthquake. Inside the walls are the ruins of the Church of Sao Tiago, dedicated to St. James. The best way to visit the castle is to take the road through the marshes on a carriage known as a trem.

From the Algarve, we continue directly north to two provinces whose culture, architecture, and customs make them unique.

Chapter XII

ALENTEJO AND RIBATEJO

1. Évora
2. Beja
3. Vila Viçosa
4. Elvas
5. Marvao
6. Castelo de Vive
7. Estremoz
8. Vila Franca de Xira
9. Santarém
10. Tomar

THE ADJOINING PROVINCES of Alentejo and Ribatejo are the heartland of Portugal. But while Ribatejo is a land of bull-breeding pastures, that of Alentejo is characterized as a plain of fire and ice.

Ribatejo is the country of the river, where the Tagus—coming from Spain—overflows its banks in winter. It is famed for blue grass, Arabian horses, and black bulls. The most striking feature, however, is a human one: the campinos, in their stocking caps, the sturdy horsemen of the region. Theirs is the job of harnessing the Arabian pride of their horses and searching out the intangible quality of bravery in the bulls.

Whether visiting the château of the Templars, rising in the middle of the Tagus at Almourol, or attending an exciting festa brava, when the hooves of horses and rumble of bulls reverberate in the streets of Vila Franca de Xira, you'll marvel at the passion of the people of Ribatejo. Their fadistas have long been noted for intensity.

The cork-producing plains of Alentejo (literally, beyond the Tagus) compose the largest province in Portugal—so large, in fact, that the government has divided it into Alto Alentejo in the north (capital: Évora), and Baixo Alentejo in the south (capital: Beja). Even today it's difficult to reach. Take the Ponte 25 de Abril across the Tagus via Setúbal, or go all the way north to Vila Franca de Xira, then head east.

In Alentejo the locals have insulated themselves in whitewashed houses with tiny windows that keep in heat in the cold winters, coolness during the scorching summers. The least populated of Portuguese provinces, Alentejo possesses seemingly endless fields of wheat, and is the world's largest producer of cork (the trees can be stripped only once in nine years).

In winter the men are a dramatic sight in their characteristic capes, which are long brown coats with two short tiered capes—often adorned with a red-fox collar. The women are even more of a spectacle, especially when seen working in the rice paddies or wheatfields. Their skirts and patterned undergarments are short so they can wade barefooted into the paddies. Over a knitted cowl, with a "peek through" for their eyes, is a brimmed felt hat usually studded with flowers.

1. Évora

The capital of Alto Alentejo is an historical curio. Considering its size and location, it is something of a phenomenon—a mélange of styles, its builders freely adapting whatever they desired from mudéjar to Manueline, from Roman to rococo. Évora lives up to its reputation as The Museum City. As it lies only 96 miles from Lisbon, it is most often visited on a day trip from the capital.

Nearly every street in Évora is filled with 16th and 17th-century houses, many with tiled patios. Cobblestones, labyrinthine streets, arcades, squares with bubbling fountains, whitewashed houses, a profuse display of Moorish-inspired arches characterize the town—all of which used to be enclosed behind medieval walls.

Évora today is a sleepy provincial capital—perhaps self-consciously aware of its monuments. One local historian actually recommended to an American couple that they must see at least 59 monuments! Rest assured you can capture the essence of Évora by seeing only a fraction of that number.

Many conquerors have passed through Évora, and several have left architectural remains. To the Romans at the time of Julius Caesar, Évora was known as Liberalitas Julia. Perhaps its heyday was in the 16th century, during the reign of Joao III, when it became the Montmartre of Portugal, and then avant-garde artists congregated under the aegis of royalty. Included among them were Gil Vicente, sometimes known—not too accurately—as the Shakespeare of Portugal.

The major monument in Évora is the **Temple of Diana,** in the central plaza, directly in front of the government-owned pousada. Dating from either the 1st or 2nd centuries A.D., it is a light, graceful structure, with 14 Corinthian granite columns topped by marble capitals. Of course, no one can prove that it was actually dedicated by Diana (the goddess of the moon and of hunting), but with her fine physique, she's a better choice than most. Incidentally, it withstood the earthquake of 1755, and there is evidence that it was once used as a slaughterhouse. Don't fail to walk through the garden for a view of the Roman aqueduct and the surrounding countryside. A short stroll leads to the:

Sé (Cathedral): Bulky and heavy, the mother church of Évora was built in the Roman-Gothic style between 1186 and 1204, though notably restored and redesigned over the centuries. The stone facade is flanked by two square towers, both topped by cones, one surrounded by satellite spires. The interior consists of a nave and two aisles. The main altar, from the 18th century, is the finest in town, made of marble in tones of pink, black, and white.

At the sculptured work, "The Lady of Mothers," young girls pray for fertility. A French couple, whose marriage had produced no children, prayed here, and the wife found herself pregnant by the time she returned to Paris! The next year the couple returned to Évora, bringing their new child.

The museum, charging an admission of 5$ (20¢), is open from 10 a.m. to 12:30 p.m. and 2 to 5 p.m., except Mondays. It houses treasures from the church, the most notable of which is a 13th-century Virgin made of ivory (it opens to reveal what at first appears to be her innards, but is really a collection of scenes from her life). A reliquary is studded with 1,426 precious stones, including sapphires, rubies, diamonds, and emeralds—the most precious item, a piece of wood said to have come from the True Cross.

In the 14th-century cloister, the medallions of the Apostles include the Star of David, certainly incongruous in a Catholic church. A cross in the ceiling—called The Key of the Cloister—marks the last stone to be set into place.

Facing the Temple of Diana is the **Church of St. John the Evangelist.** Next door to the government-owned pousada, this private Gothic-mudéjar church is connected to the palace built by the Dukes of Cadaval. However, it is open to the public—in fact, is one of the gems of Évora, though seemingly little visited. It contains a collection of azulejos (glazed earthenware tiles) dating from the 18th century. A guide will show you a macabre sight: an old cistern filled with neatly stacked bones removed from old tombs. In the sacristy of the chapel are some paintings, including a ghastly rendition of Africans slaughtering a Christian missionary. A curiosity is a painting of a pope that not only has moving eyes, but moving feet. In addition, you can see part of the wall that once completely encircled Évora.

The **Royal Church of St. Francis** is visited by those wanting to see its ghoulish **Chapel of Bones.** The chancel walls and central pillars are lined with human skulls and other parts of skeletons. Costing an admission of only one escudo, the stone chapel dates from the 16th century. Alternate legends have it that the bones came either from soldiers who died in a big battle, or from plague victims. Over the door is the sign: "Our bones who stay here are waiting for yours!" The church itself was built in the Gothic style with Manueline overtones between 1460 and 1510.

The **Church of Our Lady of Grace** is viewed chiefly for its baroque facade, with huge classical nudes dangling their legs over the pillars. Above each group of lazing stone giants is a sphere with a flame atop. These pieces of sculpture are often compared to works by Michelangelo. The church itself was built in Évora's heyday in the reign of Joao III. The central window shaft is flanked by columns and large stone rosettes, the lower level supported by ponderous neoclassic columns.

Finally, you may want to visit the **Ancient University.** In 1559, as a natural outcropping of the cultural flowering of Évora, a university was constructed and placed under the tutelage of the Jesuits. It flourished until the Jesuit-hating Marquês de Pombal closed it in the 18th century. The baroque structure itself is double tiered and built around a large quadrangle. The arches are supported by marble pillars, the interior ceilings constructed with Brazilwood. The inner courtyard is lined with blue and white tiles. Other azulejos representations throughout depict women, wild animals, angels, cherubs, and costumed men contrasting with the austere elegance of the classrooms and the elongated refectory. The compound is no longer used as a university, although pupils (the equivalent of high-school students in America) attend class here.

THE UPPER BRACKET: Estalagem Monte das Flores, four kilometers outside Évora on the road to Alçacoves (tel. 254-90), is out of the ordinary. The owner, Don Joao de Noronha, was one of Portugal's leading bull-breeders. He has converted what formerly were adjoining stables and servants' quarters into a magnificently decorated hotel, with a rustic lounge, a roaring fire, easy chairs, and country artifacts. The dining room is pleasant and spacious, featuring another "walk-in" fireplace. Outside, a large dining terrace, surrounded by hedges, overlooks the open countryside—a summer delight. The bedrooms contain private baths and are decorated with hand-painted bedsteads and closets. Across from the estalagem is the owner's own three-story villa.

The hotel's good for those who like the sporting life. There's a large swimming pool, plus plenty of lawn, a tennis court, horseback riding, and a private lake three kilometers away. If you've ever wanted to live on an hidalgo's private estate, here's your chance to do so. A room for one costs 200$ ($7.80); for two, 300$ ($11.70). Full board (two days for two people) comes to 750$ ($29.25). If you're just having lunch or dinner, it's à la carte.

THE BUDGET RANGE: Pousada Dos Lóios, Évora (tel. 240-51), is one of the finest government-owned tourist inns in Portugal. It was built as a monastery in the 15th century, undergoing further adaptation and enlargement during the 18th century, and culminating in the mid-20th century with the installation of heating and private baths in every bedroom. Its position in the museumlike center of Évora is prime—between the Cathedral and the ghostlike Roman Temple of Diana.

Even if you're not bedding down for the night, like a pilgrim of old, you should at least stop for a regional meal of Alto Alentejo. There are 27 double rooms and one suite, now unrecognizably luxurious when compared to the monks' quarters of old. They're traditionally furnished in a provincial style, with a blending of antique reproductions. For a room, one person pays 235$ ($9.17); two persons, 330$ ($12.87). A cardinal-like suite for splurgers rents for 530$ ($20.68) for two persons, taxes and service included in all these tariffs. Breakfast is an additional 30$ ($1.17). During the peak summer season, wayfarers are sometimes housed in the simpler, top-floor "chauffeur rooms," which are smaller.

There's a salon in white and gold (a one-time private chapel), with an ornate Pompeian-style decor and frescoes. Now it's formal, with antique furnishings, hand-woven draperies, crystal chandeliers and sconces, and painted medallion portraits. A portion of the old monks' kitchen has been converted into a small bar for drinks and snacks. In addition, there's a vaulted stone pillared tea veranda where you can order breakfast or four o'clock tea, relaxing in rattan chairs and enjoying a view of a palace built by a count.

In winter meals are served in the main monks' dining hall, with its heavy chandeliers. But in fair weather most guests dine in and around the cloister, at tables set under the Manueline fan-vaulted ceiling and an ornate Moorish doorway leading to the Chapter House. You pay 130$ ($5.07) for a complete luncheon or dinner. For this, you get a basket of freshly baked bread and home-churned butter, a bowl of hot soup, followed by a fish dish, such as sole prepared in a herb-flavored tomato sauce and accompanied by mashed potatoes. For your main course, try the acorn-sweetened pork cooked with clams in the manner of Alentejo. For dessert, a trolley of assorted pastries is wheeled by.

Hotel Planície, Rua Miguel Bombarda (tel. 240-26), is Évora's leading modern hotel, built in a contemporary fashion and furnished with Nordic-style pieces. However, it nods briefly to the past (for example, in its boîte for drinks and dancing it has built an imitation Gothic ceiling; and out back a little boy porter will show you the remains of a Roman cistern). Though the street entry reception room is pocket sized, the lounges and bar on the second floor are spacious and comfortable. In the late afternoon, guests seek out the roof terrace, with its view of the Cathedral.

The lounges are laden with leather and wood chairs and lots of marble from Borba. Luncheons and dinners, generous in portions, are served in the low-key restaurant, with its black parquet floor; a complete four-course meal goes for 120$ ($4.68). The bedrooms are consistent with the hotel's up-to-date idiom, and contain fully tiled baths. For two persons, the rate range is from 220$ ($8.58) to 270$ ($10.53), depending on view, size, and plumbing—the cheaper rooms containing showers instead of tubs. The best single rents for 185$ ($7.22). Full pension for one person is 455$ ($11.75); for two, 810$ ($31.59).

O Eborense, 1 Largo da Misericordia (tel. 220-31), is a budget pension with a touch of grandeur in the form of a stone staircase leading up to an entrance lined with plants and decorated with tiles. As you come up to the first-floor terrace, you're greeted by a caged parrot and your host Senhor Barreto, who speaks English. He offers 25 rooms in this building, and an additional 17 in the annex where accommodations range from only 60$ ($2.34) in a single to 102$ ($3.98) in a double. The more expensive rooms, in the main building, cost 140$ ($5.46) for a single and 220$ ($8.58) for a double. All rooms are clean, a bit old-fashioned, and quite pleasant. You can sit on the terrace nursing a drink and peering through the cloisterlike, mullioned veranda. An adjoining rooftop garden-cafe attracts sun-worshippers. Breakfast costs 15$ (59¢).

WHERE TO DINE: Cozinha de St. Humberto, 39 Rua da Moeda (tel. 242-51), is the most atmospheric restaurant in Évora. Hidden away in a narrow side street leading down from the Praça do Giraldo, it is rustically decorated with old pots, blunderbusses, standing lamps, a grandfather's clock, and kettles hanging from the ceiling. Carnations stand on each table, and you sit in rush chairs or on divan-settees. The à la carte specialties include a seafood cocktail for 45$ ($1.76); vegetable soup, 15$ (59¢); mussels Santo Humberto, 50$ ($1.95); sole, 75$ ($2.93); duck, 60$ ($2.34); and regional cheese, 12$ (47¢) to 18$ (70¢).

2. Beja

The capital of Baixo Alentejo—founded by Julius Caesar and once known as Pax Julia—rises like a pyramid above the surrounding fields of swaying wheat. Only 116 miles from Lisbon, the women of Beja still cook on braziers on their front doorsteps, and timid donkeys draw blue carts through the narrow streets. Clothes hang on lines strung between the castle ramparts and olive trees, and children scuffle out a soccer game under the shadow of the fortress wall.

The fame of Beja, however, rests on what many authorities believe to be a literary hoax. In the mid-17th century, in the Convent of Conceiçao, a young nun named Soror Mariana Alcoforado is said to have fallen in love with a French military officer, identified as Chevalier de Chamily. He was believed to have seduced her, then to have left Beja never to return again.

The girl's outpouring of grief and anguish found literary release in the *Five Love Letters of a Portuguese Nun.* Published in Paris in 1669, they created a sensation and have remained an epistolary classic of self-revelation and remorse ever since. However, in 1926, F. C. Green, author of *Who Was the Author of the 'Lettres Portugaises'?* claimed their true writer was the Comte de Guilleragues.

The mid-15th-century convent has been turned into a **Regional Museum** (Museu Rainha D. Leonor), at the Largo da Conceiçao. It houses a varied assortment of art works, artifacts, and historical curios, including Roman axes, sarcophagi, Roman amphorae, statuary of Florentine marble, Chinese porcelains dating from 1541, paintings of Saints Jerome, Augustine, and Bartholomew assigned to Ribera, delicate silverwork, vestments, and dummies dressed in regional Alentejo costumes, 17th-century Spanish and 15th-, 16th-, 17th-, and 18th-century Portuguese paintings.

One of its most unusual exhibits is a grille through which the nun and the Frenchman were supposed to have exchanged intimacies. Also displayed are copies of early editions of the literary classic, even an engraving of the Count, revealing him to be chubby cheeked.

A modern Portuguese study, by the way, has submitted evidence that the *Lettres Portugaises* were actually written by Mariana Alcoforado, a nun in the convent.

The walls, especially those of the cloister, are profusely decorated with antique tiles, some blue and white, others emerald green. There are sacred relics as well, along with elaborate candelabra, and a gilded baroque altar with marble inlay work in pink, black, gold, and gray. The museum is open from 9:30 a.m. to 1 p.m. and from 1:30 to 5 p.m. daily, except Sunday. The regular admission is 5$ (20¢), except Saturday when it's free.

Crowning the town is the **Castelo de Beja,** which King Dinis built in the early 14th century on the ruins of a Roman fortress. Although some of its turreted walls have been restored, the defensive towers are gone, save for a long marble keep. Traditionally the final stronghold in the castle's fortifications, the old keep appears to be battling the weather and gold fungi. The walls are grown over with ivy, the last encroachment upon the structure's former glory. From the keep, you can enjoy a view of the provincial capital and the outlying fields. The castle opens onto the Largo Dr. Lima Faleiro.

THE BUDGET RANGE: Santa Bárbara, 56 Rua de Mértola (tel. 220-28), is a little gem in a town that has a lack of suitable accommodations. The residencia is a bandbox modern building still shiny clean and immaculately kept. It's all small scaled, with only a whisper of a reception lobby and elevator. The sitting room, however, is warm and personalized, with furniture arranged on the various hand-loomed or goatskin rugs. The decorations consist of an antique English desk, gilt mirrors, and cherubs, plus tiled dado around the walls.

The 26 compact rooms are adequate, with soft carpeting, good beds, tiled baths with showers, and central heating in the winter. The cost of staying here is low, 150$ ($5.85) to 220$ ($8.58) for one person; 260$ ($10.14) to 330$ ($12.87) for two. No meals are served except a continental breakfast for 26$ ($1.01).

Residenciais Coelho, 15 Praça de Republica (tel. 240-31), is simple and unpretentious, with small, unassuming rooms, somewhat cramped, but clean and modern. Some rooms have balconies overlooking the square with its large potted flowers. Singles cost 120$ ($4.68); doubles 180$ ($7.02).

WHERE TO DINE: Beja is rather lacking in first or even second-class restaurants. However, at the **Luis da Rocha,** Rua Capitao Joao F. de Sousa, on the same street as the Tourist Office, you can sit downstairs in the cafe where the whole town seems to congregate for coffee and pastries, or go upstairs where you'll find two spacious neon-lit dining rooms, featuring a tourist menu for 85$ ($3.32).

SERPA:
Languishing in the Middle Ages, Serpa is a walled town with defensive towers. All this medieval stone once had a purpose. Serpa lies only 20 miles west of Vila Verde de Ficalho (the Spanish frontier). Today the town has become a stopping-off point (for lunch or just a rest) with travelers on the way to or from Spain.

Silvery olive trees surround the approaches to the town. The whiteness of the settlement is in contrast to the red-brown of the plains. To the east at a distance of 18½ miles lies Beja; but many motorists prefer to spend the night at Serpa rather than the provincial capital because of the following hilltop pousada:

Where to Stay
Pousada de Sao Gens, Alto de Sao Gens (tel. 52-327). In keeping with the Portuguese love of vistas, this budget range government-owned tourist inn is set at the crown of the hill of Sao Gens. On clear nights guests can see all the way to Spain. Though a long way from the Algarve, the architecture is Moorish inspired, almost a pueblo-styled villa with stark white walls easily seen as you ascend the winding road past olive trees.

The pousada is family run and has a homelike atmosphere. All but a third of the 18 bedrooms have private baths, tiled in aqua and white. The furnishings are modern, making use of bold colors. A room without bath rents for 140$ ($5.46) for one person; 220$ ($8.58) for two.

Dining in winter is in a salon, with a coved ceiling, although in the warmer months it overflows onto the wide veranda. A Portuguese cuisine is offered, with many dishes of the region featured. A complete meal, including soup from a tureen, a fish course with potatoes, a meat dish with vegetables, and dessert goes for 140$ ($5.46). There are two servings for dinner. Before dinner you can have a drink in the gold and white bar, or in one of the stark white living rooms.

3. Vila Viçosa

This borough was the near-private dominion of the Dukes of Braganza, the last royal rulers of Portugal. Thirty-four miles northeast of Évora, Vila Viçosa has been a ducal seat since 1442. But what cast it into worldwide prominence was when one of its members journeyed to Lisbon in 1640 to be declared the head of a new royal dynasty. Ruling as Joao IV, he freed Portugal from 60 years of Spanish domination.

Ironically, one of the last of the Braganza kings, Carlos I, spent his last night dining under his favored antler chandeliers before making the journey to Lisbon. His staff—lined up at the Terreiro do Paço—waved him and his older son good-bye. But when they arrived at another Terreiro do Paço (this one in Lisbon), the reception was less friendly. Both died by an assassin's bullets.

The **Paço Ducal de Vila Viçosa** remains as a memorial to the Braganzas. You'll see pictures of the last king, Manuel II, who fled with his mother, Amélia, into exile in 1910. The uniforms of Carlos I are here as well. Perhaps the most remarkable personal exhibit is a gallery of Carlos' (otherwise known as the painter king) paintings and watercolors. As one critic put it, he was a better artist than a king!

The inside of the palace and its furnishings are a collage of faded mementos, foreign art influences, and nostalgic specters of a once-royal life. As with a fine tapestry, separating the diverse treasures is difficult. The trappings include a frescoed "Salon of Hercules"; tapestries based on Rubens' cartoons; 16th-century Persian carpets; 17th-century armor; a Pompeian styled oratory; a Medusa chamber; Louis XVI furnishings; a 17th-century Holy Cross with 6,500 precious stones (rubies, diamonds, pearls, and emeralds); handcarved armoires; a chapel faced with pink marble; a sword and shield collection (even spears from Angola); and cloisters dating from the 16th century. The kitchen is filled with copper pots and utensils used by the royal family (a spit for roasting the big game Carlos I was fond of bagging), and a Coach Museum, containing about a dozen carriages, some from the 17th century, and a sedan chair. After your visit, you can stroll through the "Garden of the Ladies." The palace is open daily, charging an admission of 10$ (39¢).

Today, the "white town" of Vila Viçosa rests remarkably unchanged in the midst of the olive-green carpeted marble hills which are spotted with fragrant orange trees. The town is guarded by a walled castle from the 14th century, with a quartet of tall towers and crenelated walls. It is a natural extension of the museum in the palace. Admission to the castle is 5$ (20¢). There are 22 churches in Vila Viçosa—many almost casually containing treasures—but only the most dedicated of tourists seek them out.

WHERE TO DINE: The **Restaurante Framar**, 35 Praça da República (tel. 95), is where the local people gather for an inexpensive meal or coffee. In the heart of town facing a square of potted flowering plants, it's modern, with an all-glass facade. Past the coffee and brandy-drinking Alentejo "cowboys" up front is a miniature dining area, with just four tables set on a platform.

A set luncheon or dinner is offered for 85$ ($3.32), including a bowl of soup from a tureen (perhaps a rich stock with turnips, greens, and red beans). For a second course, a sweet, lightly fried white fish is offered, accompanied by rice with sweet red peppers and a mixed salad. The main course is likely to be a platter of thinly sliced fried veal with lemon wedges and puffed potatoes. For dessert a big basket of fresh fruit is placed on the table.

There are many good à la carte selections as well, including regional dishes such as the typical soup of Alentejo for 15$ (59¢). The house specialty is febras de porco (a leg of pork simmered in wine and flavored with garlic), costing 42$ ($1.64) for one person. You pay 12$ (47¢) to 15$ (59¢) for a small carafe of wine, 8$ (31) to 12$ (59¢) for dessert, probably pudim flan.

BORBA:
The town that marble built, Borba lies only a short drive from Vila Viçosa. On the way there, you'll pass quarries filled with black, white, and multi-colored deposits. In the village itself, donkeys pulling carts loaded with chips and slabs attest to the fact that marble is king. Along the village streets many cottages have door trimmings and facings of marble, and the women get down on their hands and knees to scrub their doorways, a source of special pride to them.

On the Rua S. Bartolomeu sits an interesting church, also dedicated to S. Bartolomeu. It contains a groined ceiling; walls lined with azulejos in blue, white, and gold; and an altar in black and white marble. The richly decorated ceiling is painted with four major medallions, one depicting decapitation. As

Portuguese churches go, this one isn't remarkable. What is remarkable, however, are eight nearby antique shops (amazing for such a small town) which are filled with interesting buys. Borba is also a big wine center, and you may want to sample the local brew at a cafe (or perhaps at the pousada at Elvas).

On the outskirts is a remarkable sight—the **Museum of Christ** (on the main road to Estremoz). The entrance is inauspicious, on a farm by the side of the road. In front is an antique shop filled with a hodgepodge of oddments, including many fine pieces from Alentejo. In the rear, the museum itself is the most intimate and personal one in Portugal. It's owned by the Lôbo family.

Started more than four decades ago, the collection now includes 3,000 crucifixes. One would suspect that this figure will change, as the Museum of Christ is an organic and growing thing. The father of the family started collecting primitive crucifixes from the country people, bartering his excess farm produce, picking up more figures in his travels to North Africa, Angola, and Spain.

The present collection spans about 13 centuries, 42 countries, and countless artistic traditions. For one of the rarest crucifixes, dating from the 9th century, a museum in Philadelphia offered $15,000, but was spurned. Some of his figures were hollowed out to hide money in the 16th century. One of the finest is from 18th-century Florence, showing a skull and crossbones at the bottom. In the other rooms of the museum are regional artifacts and furnishings. The museum may be viewed from 9 a.m. to 9 p.m. in summer (till 6 p.m. in winter).

4. Elvas

This city of the plums, known for its crenelated fortifications, is less than 10 miles from Badajoz, Spain. The walled town is characterized by narrow cobblestoned streets (pedestrians have to duck into doorways to allow automobiles to inch by), and is surely an anachronism, so tenaciously does it hold on to its monuments and history.

Lining the steep hilly streets are tightly packed gold- and oyster-colored cottages topped by tiled roofs. Many of the doors leading to the houses are only five feet high. In the tiny windows are numerous canary cages and flowering geraniums. From the little plaza wells dotting the town, both men and women draw water in large copper and pottery jugs. The water is transported to Elvas by the four-tiered **Amoreira Aqueduct,** built in the 16th century.

In the Praça D. Sancho II (honoring the king who reconstructed the town) stands the **Sé (Cathedral),** forbidding and fortresslike. Under a conically shaped dome, it is decorated with gargoyles, turrets, and a florid Manueline portal. The Cathedral opens onto a black and white-diamonded square. A short walk up the hill to the right of the Cathedral leads to the Largo D. Santa Clara, a small plaza on which was erected an odd Manueline pillory, with four wrought-iron dragon heads.

In accommodations there's a good pousada, but you may have to stay at the second-class hotel inside the town, as the tourist inn is often fully booked.

THE BUDGET RANGE: Pousada de Santa Luzia (tel. 194), is not only a link in the government inn circuit, but it's also an antique emporium, where nearly everything is for sale. Hopefully, the former occupant of your room didn't purchase that handcarved bed! The bone-white stucco villa, facing the fortifications, sits on a hill, commanding a view of the town and countryside, especially from its terraces and dining room. The entire ground floor is devoted to a living room, an L-shaped dining salon, and a bar—all opening through thick arches onto a Moorish-style courtyard with fountain, lily pond, and orange trees.

Although there are some bedrooms on the upper floor, it's more interesting to be housed in the nearby annex, a villa with a two-story entrance hall and an ornate staircase. Here, the bedrooms are furnished with antiques and decorative accessories. (Tip: ask to be let into the dungeon crypt by a seven-inch iron key, the door clanking open to reveal an antique dealer's paradise—carved wooden cherubs, tapestry-covered jewel chests, Chippendale chairs, gilt candelabras.)

Depending on the plumbing, doubles go from 120$ ($4.68) to 220$ ($8.58). A table d'hôte luncheon or dinner costs 130$ ($5.07), and for a pousada the menu is extensive. Noteworthy are the fish dishes, including grilled red mullet and natural oysters.

5. Marvao

This ancient walled town, lying close to Castelo de Vide, is well preserved and is visited chiefly for its views. Near the Spanish frontier, the fortified medieval town clusters around a castle at the foot of a peak of the Serra de Sao Mamede. The castle, which is inside the town walls, dates from the end of the 13th century.

The population is very small. If you arrive in the afternoon, you may think you're in a ghost town. Most of the inhabitants are working in the fields outside the walls.

THE BUDGET RANGE: The **Pousada de Santa Maria** (tel. Marvao 10-11) contains only nine double rooms (two without bath). Singles rent for 85$ ($3.32) without bath, increasing to 100$ ($3.90) with bath. Doubles with bath go for an inexpensive 100$ ($3.90) to 145$ ($5.66). For full pension, one person pays 360$ ($14.04), that tab rising to 505$ ($19.70) for two persons. Breakfast costs 30$ ($1.17), and you need pay only 100$ ($3.90) for one main meal, if you're just stopping by.

6. Castelo de Vive

At an altitude of 1,800 feet, this spa town lies at the foot of a castle. Nature has endowed Castelo de Vive with therapeutical waters. Inside its walls stand old whitewashed houses, some on squares little changed since the 15th and 16th centuries. A view of chestnuts, pine woods, and oak trees gives the town a resort aura.

Cromlechs in the area testify to the ancient origin of the town. It was conquered by the Romans in 44 A.D. and destroyed by Vandals in 411. The Arabs who later occupied it rebuilt the castle in 1299. At this fortress the contract for the marriage of King Dinis to Dona Isabella of Aragon (later Saint Elizabeth of Portugal) was signed.

The Judiaria or Jewish Quarter is a sector of narrow alleyways and small homes, housing the richest collection of ogival doors in Portugal. This quarter also abounds with cats. A medieval synagogue is currently being restored.

It is said that the people who settled the Azores originated from this part of Portugal, as the populace speaks with a similar dialect.

7. Estremoz

From the ramparts of its **Castle**—dating from the 13th-century reign of King Dinis—the plains of Alentejo are spread before you. Although one 75-year-old British lady is reported to have walked it, it's best to drive your car to the top of the Upper Town, bringing it to a stop on the Largo de D. Dinis. The stones of the Castle—the cradle of the town's past—were decaying so badly that the city fathers pressed for its restoration in 1970.

The large imposing keep, attached to a palace, dominates the central plaza. Dinis' saintly wife, Isabella, died in the Castle. Isabella was unofficially proclaimed a saint by her loyal followers, even in life. However, one of her detractors wrote, "Poor Dinis!"

Also opening onto the marble and stone-paved largo are two modest chapels and a church. As in medieval days, soldiers still walk the ramparts, guarding the fortress.

Rising from the Alentejo plain like a pyramid of salt set to dry in the sun, fortified Estremoz is in the center of the marble-quarry region of Alentejo, 108 miles east of Lisbon. Cottages and mansions alike utilize the abundant marble in forming windows and apertures or in fashioning balustrades and banisters.

With enough promenading Portuguese soldiers to form a garrison, the open quadrangle in the center of the Lower Town is called the **Rossio de Marquês de Pombal.** The **Town Hall,** with its twin bell towers, opens onto this square, and the walls of its grand stairway are lined with antique azulejos in blue and white, depicting hunting, pastoral, and historical scenes. In front, you can buy the characteristic earthenware pottery of the region.

A LUXURY POUSADA: Pousada da Rainha Isabel (tel. 648) is one of the best of the government tourist inns. Within the old castle dominating the town, and overlooking the battlements and the Estremoz plain, it is a deluxe showcase. In perfect style, the very latest of modern comfort is provided within the framework of history. Therefore, do not be surprised that prices differ from those of the less regal pousadas.

There are 17 twin-bedded rooms, one double, two singles, and three suites (twin beds and a double), all with bath. Singles, including service charges, are 235$ ($9.17); twins and the double, 330$ ($12.87). Full pension for one person ranges from 525$ ($20.48) to 885$ ($34.52); for two, from 910$ ($35.49) to 1,430$ ($57.57). For a meal, 130$ ($5.07) is charged. Breakfast is an additional 30$ ($1.17).

WHERE TO DINE: Aguîas d'Ouro, 25 Rossio do Marquês de Pombal. The Golden Eagles faces the largest square in Estremoz, its mosaic and marble balconied facade suggesting a Doge's Palace. On the second floor are several connecting dining rooms that combine contemporary and regional design. Rough white plaster walls rest under ceramic brick ceilings; heavy sumptuous black leather modern armchairs are set around white-draped tables. The waiters are well trained, placing a dish of homemade pâté with crusted rye bread before you.

You can select an all out dinner for 140$ ($5.46). À la carte dishes are also offered, including a large bowl of the típico spinach and bean soup with crispy croutons floating on top, 22$ (86¢). A regional stew, the caldeirada de eirós, is 60$ ($2.34) for a half portion (meia dose), while a full portion is 80$ ($3.12) and enough for two. Other dishes include lombo de porco na grelha (tenderloin of pork), 75$ ($2.93) for one and 110$ ($4.29) for two.

Either en route to Évora or Estremoz, you may want to stop at:

ARRAIOLOS: This small village has been famous since the 13th century for its carpets—the early designs in imitation of those from Persia. The intricate patterns continued to develop and expand until the 18th century. After that, the craftsmen seemed to suspend their originality, and the present rugs follow the old designs religiously. The rugs are made of heavy wool (the yarns tinted by natural dyes), are handmade, and often contain elaborate needlework. Many of the most elegant are displayed at the Museum of Antique Art in Lisbon. Even if you can't stop off at Arraiolos, you may want to see a wide-ranging display for sale at the **Casa Quintao** on 30 Rua Ivens in Lisbon.

READER'S SELECTION IN PORTALEGRE: "**Hotel D. Joao III** at Portalegre is the more outstanding because there is nothing in its class for many kilometers around. The top-floor dining room with its panoramic view of the city and the amphitheater of hills in the background, was the most impressive we saw anywhere. The hotel's decor is modern, but made good use of native materials. Our rooms were large and pleasant, and each one had a balcony overlooking a lovely park. Evidently the hotel hasn't been discovered yet, as there appeared to be only a dozen guests the night we stayed there. We were overwhelmed with service, and the food was excellent. A single rents for 210$ ($8.19), a double for 285$ ($11.12)" (Roger H. Hatch, Boston, Mass.). (Editor's Note: Portalegre is just 22 kilometers from the recently opened border post at Marvao, providing motorists with the shortest route between Lisbon and Madrid. Five kilometers away lies the mountain of Sao Mamede. The town itself, a center for cork production, is filled with baroque mansions, particularly on Rua 19 de Junho. In the 16th century, it was famous for tapestries made here; the workshops can be visited today. Portalegre merits a stopover.)

8. Vila Franca de Xira

Vila Franca de Xira is the Pamplona of Portugal. Twice a year (the dates of the festivals vary), the frenzied community ordeal of the festa brava—the running of the bulls—is staged. In the countryside around Vila Franca, 20 miles north of Lisbon, are pasturelands that are breeding grounds for the black bulls. There's a modern speedway to take you there. The toll is 5$ (20¢).

At the festivals, a herd of black bulls—fresh and primed for the rings of Lisbon or Cascais—are let loose in the main street of town. With the smaller side streets heavily barricaded, the corrida is ready to begin. When the campinos (Ribatejo cowboys with their traditional stocking caps) first turn the bulls loose in the streets, they appear bewildered and confused.

The crowds hoot and holler, trying to make the massive animals break rank. When one inevitably does, mêlées and frantic dashes follow, with occasional displays—on the part of some young aspirant matador—of virtuosity with the cape. The cape, incidentally, is likely to be an old piece of sack-cloth or a quilt. The bulls are rarely intimidated by those who taunt them. Many a hopeful matador has been pulled by his arms to the safety of a spectator-filled wrought-iron balcony. Numerous injuries result, and the hospital staff is reinforced by recruits from Lisbon.

This blending of festive levity and grim reality, such as a critical injury, has made bull baiting an intriguing custom down through the ages. Although attacked and criticized by some who consider it barbaric, the pagan custom is well preserved on the streets of Vila Franca de Xira—at least on two occasions of the year. Otherwise, there isn't much reason to go there, except to have a good meal at one of the following inns:

THE BUDGET RANGE: Estalagem Do Gado Bravo, Estrada do Cabo-Camarao (tel. 231-24), lies across the toll bridge on the other side of the Tagus. It's a roadside inn, encircled by a garden, right in the heart of the bull-breeding district—hence, its name, Brave Bull. You park your car under a bougainvillea arbor and walk past lemon trees. The emphasis is on the dining rooms, which bear a strong regional stamp. On goatskin rugs, the tables are draped with brightly colored, handwoven cloths. Every diner has a view of one of the two brick and stone fireplaces. Around the walls are plastered bullfight posters, engravings, and prints.

The table d'hôte luncheon or dinner at 100$ ($3.90) is well prepared, with many Ribatejo specialties. The chef's favorite dish is linguado (sole) à brasileira. From most of the bedroom windows, there's a view of the plains; and occasionally a stray bull noses up to the nearby fence. The room furnishings are modern, but provincial, making for comfort. There are only eight bedrooms, five of which contain private baths. In a double the tariff is 250$ ($9.75), 150$ ($5.85) in a single. Breakfast is 25$ (98¢).

Estalagem de Leziria, Rua Palha Blanco (tel. 221-29), is a country inn set back from the busy highway by a tiny front garden with a bougainvillea arbor and rose bushes. It offers two old-world dining rooms, usually filled (especially during the running of the bulls) with those who appreciate regional dishes. The front room is more interesting, with tables set under a row of four wide plastered arches, an oak-beamed ceiling, and an open fireplace. The service is courteous and attentive.

True to the region, the cuisine features many Ribatejo dishes appearing on the table d'hôte dinner for 75$ ($2.93) or 100$ ($3.90). The specialties please gourmets, many of whom drive up from Lisbon to sample enguias fritas (fried eels) or ensopado de enguias (eel stew). Not only eels, but much of the fresh fish comes from the nearby Tagus, earning for the estalagem the title, The Inn of the Marshland.

166 □ DOLLAR-WISE GUIDE TO PORTUGAL

There are 15 rooms, of which six contain private baths. A double with bath is 260$ ($10.14); without bath, 150$ ($5.85). A single without bath is a bargain at 100$ ($3.90). Breakfast is 20$ (78¢).

9. Santarém

The Portuguese use the words noble or Gothic in describing this town, 49 miles north of Lisbon. The garrison here, set on a spur of land overlooking the river, has always been a key fortification. Afonso Henriques, the country's first king, drove out the Moors in 1147—and ordered the construction of the Cistercian monastery at Alcobaça to commemorate that feat.

Santarém still overlooks the low-lying lands devoted to cattle, vineyards, olive groves, even corn. It seems as if the whole of Ribatejo is spread out before one's eyes from the vantage point of the **Portas do Sol** (the Gates of the Sun), a park of tiled fountains, flowering plants and bushes, statuary, red benches, and globe lamps. At times the river is so shallow that sandy islets appear; at other moments, it overflows its banks. The gardens are reached by heading out the Avenida 5 de Outubro.

One of the main squares is **Praça de Sá da Bandeira,** lying right off the Garden of the Republic. Opening onto the largo is the **College of the Patriarchal See,** whose multi-windowed, niched and statuary-studded facade takes up an entire side of the plaza. Inside, the main altar is decorated with marble and alabaster inlays, and flanked by four serpentine columns. Alabaster statues of saints, azulejos, and a baroque trompe l'oeil ceiling add to the lushness. Across the way from the seminary (entrance at the end of the Rua Cidade da Covilhá) sits the octagonal, domed **Chapel of Our Lady of Pity,** whose neoclassic style is enhanced by trompe l'oeil paintings.

One of the town's most interesting churches, **St. Joao de Alporao,** right off the R.S. Martinho, en route to the Portas do Sol, has been converted into an **Archaeological Museum.** Built in the Romanesque-Gothic style, probably in the 12th century, it is graced with a rose window and multiple arched doorway. Inside is contained the elaborate tomb of D. Duarte de Menezes, built by his wife after he died at the hands of the Moors. So badly mutilated was the body, that the remains consisted of a lone tooth. The collection of Roman sarcophagi is more interesting.

Nearby, the Gothic **Church of Graça,** dating from 1380, has a rose window carved from a single stone. At the corner of Calçada da Graça and the Rua Vila de Belmonte, it has been completely restored and contains some carved tombs, and an architecture characterized by simple arches.

For either rooms or meals, the following establishment is recommended:

THE BUDGET RANGE: Hotel **Abidis,** 4 Rua Guilherme de Azevedo (tel. 220-17). Rated second class, Abidis is the best hotel in Santarém—a place at which to order meals or enjoy a night's sleep. Although the reception area is mini-sized, the bedrooms are personalized, with old-style furnishings given a feminine touch with matching fabrics at the windows, on the beds, and at the dressing tables. Only six of the 27 bedrooms contain private baths. The cost of a double with bath is 290$ ($11.31); 195$ ($7.61) in a single.

The dining room is decorated in the Ribatejo tavern style. Noted for its attentive service and cuisine, it offers a table d'hôte luncheon or dinner for 110$ ($4.29). A typical meal is likely to include a bowl of onion soup, followed by turbot cooked with pimiento rice, a main course of roast kid, a carafe of good wine, cheese, and fresh fruit. The waiters, in kelly green, urge you to take second helpings. The setting is winning: a blue and white tiled dado, ox-yoke chandeliers, and provincial chairs.

10. Tomar

Tomar was integrally bound to the fate of the notorious quasi-religious order of the Templars Knights. In the 12th century these militant monks of wealth and power established the beginnings of the **Convent of Christ** on a tree-studded hill overlooking the town. Originally a monastery, it evolved into a kind of grand headquarters for the Templars. These knights, who swore a vow of chastity (but didn't always keep it!), had fought ferociously at Santarém against the Moors. As a result of their growing military might, they built a massive walled castle at Tomar in 1160. The ruins, especially the walls, can be seen today.

By 1314 the Pope was urged to suppress their power, as they had made many enemies, and their great riches were coveted by others. King Dinis allowed them to regroup their forces under the new aegis of the Order of Christ, of which Henry the Navigator became the most famous of the grand masters, using much of their money to subsidize his explorations.

From its inception, the convent underwent five centuries of inspired builders, including Manuel I (the Fortunate). It also saw its destroyers, notably the overzealous troops of Napoleon in 1810 who turned it into a barracks. What remains on the top of the hill, however, is one of the most brilliant architectural accomplishments in Portugal—an amalgam of styles.

The portal of the Templars Church is like a lacy valentine in the Manueline style, depicting everything from leaves to chubby cherubs. Inside, you enter an octagonal church with eight columns, said to have been modeled after the Temple of the Holy Sepulchre at Jerusalem. The effect is like a mosque, linking Christian tradition with Moslem culture, as in Córdoba's "Mezquita." Howard La Fay called it ". . . a muted echo of Byzantium in scarlet and dull gold." The damage done by the French troops is much in evidence. On the other side, the church is in the Manueline style with rosettes. Throughout you'll see symbols of the insignia of the Templars.

The convent embraces seven cloisters in a variety of styles. The most notable one—a two-tiered structure built in 1557 by Diogo de Torralva—exhibits perfect symmetry, the almost severe academic use of the classical form that distinguishes the Palladian school. A guide will also take you on a brief tour of a dormitory where the monks of old lived in cells.

The convent possesses some of the greatest Manueline stonework to emerge from that era. An example is the grotesque west window of the Chapter House. At first, you'll think that some effusive secretion has bubbled out the window; but a closer inspection reveals a meticulous symbolic and literal depiction of Portugal's sea lore and power. Knots and ropes, mariners and the tools of their craft, silken sails wafting in stone, re-create coral seascapes—all are delicately interwoven in this chef d'oeuvre of the whole movement.

The admission-free convent is open from 9:30 a.m. to 12:30 p.m. and from 2 to 6 p.m. (closes at 5 p.m. off season). It is customary to tip the guide.

Tomar has many other sights of interest. On the way up the hilltop, you can stop off at the **Chapel of Our Lady of Conception,** crowned by small cupolas and jutting out over the town. Reached via an avenue of trees, it was built in the Renaissance style in the mid-16th century, and its interior is a forest of white Corinthian pillars.

In the heart of town, the **Church of St. John the Baptist** opens onto the Praça de República, built by Manuel I, with black and white diamond mosaics. Dating from the 15th century, the church contains a white and gold baroque altar (a chapel to the right is faced with antique tiles.)

In and around the church are the narrow cobblestoned streets of Tomar, where shops sell dried codfish, and wrought-iron balconies are hung with bird cages and flower pots.

Divided by the Nabao River, historic Tomar lies 85 miles from Lisbon, 40 from Santarém. The accommodations are excellent, for both contemporary and traditional tastes.

THE UPPER BRACKET: Hotel dos Templários (tel. 33-121) is a modern 84-room aspirant to the luxury status—incongruously placed in such a small town, which most tourists visit just for the day. It's all due to the gratitude of five local businessmen, who met success building homes, apartments, and roads, and wanted to do something memorable for their home town. Pooling their know-how, they created this five-floor structure placed on the banks of the river. Facilities include wide sun terraces, a riverside swimming pool fed by a fountain, two tennis courts, even a greenhouse.

The local people are awed by the interior with its spacious, well-styled lounges, its murals in the wood-paneled drinking lounge, and the terrace-view dining room. The bedrooms are harmoniously designed, with modern built-in features and private baths, plus air conditioning and heating. In high season (April 1 to October 31) doubles rent for as low as 315$ ($12.29) or as high as 405$ ($15.80). Singles go for 220$ ($8.58) to 285$ ($11.12). Most guests have breakfast either in their room or in a sunny salon overlooking the river. In the evenings they gather around the living room fireplace for drinks. If you're passing through, you can stop in for a table d'hôte luncheon or dinner for 115$ ($4.49).

THE BUDGET RANGE: Estalagem de Santa Iria, Parque do Monchao (tel. 324-27). It's situated on a three-acre island filled with sycamore and maple trees, right in the center of town. Just a 30-second walk across the bridge removes you from the bustle of town activity and plants you on the doorstep of a country inn. Greeted by a group of maids, you'll get comfortable and peaceful sleeping, plus substantial local fare.

The 10 bedrooms may be small, but they rate high on charm. The furnishings are brightly provincial—all hand painted with figures and flowers. Many windows overlook the river, and you'll be lulled to sleep by the slow rippling of the water. A double with private bath rents for 135$ ($5.27); 95$ ($3.71) in a single. Even cheaper are three accommodations with hot and cold running water only, with a double going for 115$ ($4.49).

Regional meals are served in the park-view dining room, costing 100$ ($3.90) for a complete luncheon or dinner. In the summer months tables are set outside. The food is good, and you'll eat too much since second helpings are encouraged. After lunch you can go rowing around the island under weeping willows and past old water wheels.

WHERE TO DINE: Bella Vista, corner Rua Marquês de Pombal and Rua Ronte do Choupo, is, as its name indicates, a restaurant with a pretty view of the town and a small canal. You can dine outside, under a bower, or in rustic dining rooms decorated with plates, flowers, plants, and racks to hang your hat on. Meals are simple but plentiful, the prices low. A bowl of homemade vegetable soup costs 8$ (31¢); fried trout or sole, 55$50 ($2.35); chicken curry with rice is 60$ ($2.34); and pork chops with potatoes cost 50$ ($1.95). Round off your meal with some of the local cheese for 15$ (59¢) and a carafe of wine, 12$ (47¢).

The Beiras of Portugal unfold in the next chapter.

Chapter XIII

COIMBRA AND THE BEIRAS

1. Leiria
2. Figueira da Foz
3. Coimbra
4. Conimbriga
5. Bussaco
6. Curia and Luso
7. Aveiro
8. Caramulo
9. Viseu
10. Serra da Estrêla
11. Castelo Branco
12. Abrantes

FORTRESS TOWNS and feudal castles . . . undulating plains . . . steep wine-producing slopes . . . the mountain blocks of Estrêla . . . pinewoods and sand dunes . . . golden beaches . . . rice paddies and a lagoon . . . poplar-lined river banks . . . Roman ruins . . . a former royal forest . . . salt marshes . . . spas with radioactive springs . . . and water wheels sending rainbow-hued spray into the air

To many observers, the three provinces of the Beiras, encompassing the university city of **Coimbra,** are the quintessence of Portugal. Beira itself is a Portuguese word meaning edge or border. The trio of provinces includes **Beira Litoral** (coastal), **Beira Baixa** (meaning low), and **Beira Alta** (high).

Embraced in the region is the **Serra da Estrêla,** Portugal's highest land mass and haven for skiers in winter, a cool retreat in summer. The Mondego River, the mainstream of the region, is navigable, and the only major artery in Portugal that has its source within the boundaries of the country.

The granite soil produced by the great range of serras blankets the rocky slopes of the Dao and Mondego River Valleys and is responsible for the wine of the region: the ruby red or lemon-colored Dao.

In all, the Beiras are a subtle land—a sort of Portugal in miniature.

Heading north from Estremadura, the first stopover is at:

1. Leiria

About 20 miles from Alcobaça, on the road to Coimbra, the town of Leiria rests on the banks of the Liz and spreads itself casually over the surrounding hills. From any point you can see the great **Castle of Leiria,** once occupied by Dinis, the poet king, and his wife, an Aragonese princess who became Saint Isabella. Tower-topped and imposing still, it has been extensively restored.

The castle lies on the summit of a volcanic outcrop, practically inaccessible to invaders. The Moors had their defense redoubt on this hill while they were taking possession of the major part of the Iberian Peninsula. The fortress was first taken for Portugal by its first king, Alfonso Henriques in the 12th century, and was twice recovered by him after the Moors had re-taken it, the last recovery being definitive.

The church of the Castle, as well as its palace, are pure Gothic. From an arched balcony, the city and its surroundings can be viewed.

To reach the Castle, you may take either a car or a bus, right to the front door. On the way to the Castle, you might also visit **St. Peter's Church,** dating from the 12th century. The fortress is open from 9 a.m. to 6 p.m. for a 3$ (12¢) admission.

Around Leiria is one of the oldest state forests in the world. In about 1300 Dinis began the systematic planting of the **Pinhal do Rei,** with trees brought from Landes, France. He hoped to curb the spread of sand dunes which ocean gusts were extending deep into the heartland. The forest—still maintained today—provided timber used to build the caravels to explore the Sea of Darkness.

Many motorists find Leiria a convenient stopping point for the night. In the past, they lamented the town's lack of accommodations. That oversight has been rectified.

THE MEDIUM-PRICED RANGE: Hotel Euro Sol (tel. 241-01) competes in position with the stone castle crowning the opposite hill. It's an 11-floor, modern, and well-styled hotel. All 52 bedrooms offer unforgettable views, and compete successfully with any first-class hotel in the north. They are smartly simple, making use of built-in headboards and wardrobe walls of wood paneling. All of them contain private baths in forest green and white tile. In a single room, the half-pension rate ranges from 315$ ($12.29) to 345$ ($13.46); in a double, from 508$ ($19.81) to 535$ ($20.87), taxes and service included. Two persons can book one of the suites for 425$ ($16.58) nightly, plus their meals.

The hotel has quickly become the social hub of Leiria, attracting businessmen to its rooftop lounge bar and dining room. Individual lunches or dinners cost 95$ on the four-course table d'hôte. Lighter meals are offered in an adjoining snack bar. The restaurant entrance lounge is decorated with a museum-caliber contemporary wall hanging, depicting the story of the building of the castle. Time your visit to enjoy a dip and sun bath in the open-air swimming pool, with its tiled terrace. There's a lower-level boîte for after-dinner diversions.

SAO PEDRO DE MUEL: If you care to relax before plunging into the Coimbra heartlands, Sao Pedro de Muel is an undiscovered place. The bracing Atlantic breezes pervade the little village, perched on a cliff over the water. Although new villas have sprung up, the old quarter retains its cobblestoned streets.

The scattered rocks offshore create controlled beach conditions—rolling breakers and rippling surf. The beaches are white and sandy, running up to the village's gray-walled ramparts. Paths border the cliffside, leading to the coastal lighthouse and a panoramic view.

The emerging resort is 14 miles west of Leiria and can be reached via a six-mile drive toward the sea from the glass-manufacturing center at Marinha

Grande. Along the way you'll pass donkeys laden with twigs, the scent of pine mingling with salt air.

Staying in Sao Pedro de Muel

Hotel Mar e Sol (Sea and Sun), tel. 911-82, is a three-story, modern hotel—starkly white, on a palisade above the beach at the residential edge of the village. This vantage point gives half of its 33 bedrooms views overlooking the ocean. It's for sun and sea addicts only, as there are no extravagant lounge facilities and only a minimum-sized dining room. The compact bedrooms—all with private baths—are simply furnished, with a mixture of modern and traditional pieces. The cost for one person, full pension, is 380$ ($14.82) in a seaview room; 325$ ($12.68) for the mountain vista. Two persons wanting full pension pay 580$ ($22.63) for the water-view rooms; 475$ ($18.53) for the mountain vista. The second-class hotel—open year round—is immaculate and comfortable. (There is a 15 percent reduction in off season—November to February.)

2. Figueira da Foz

Old villas on the sea compete with modern apartment houses. On the north side at the Beach of Brightness, Portuguese families frolic, the wealthier ones hitting the gambling casino at night. Back in the Old Town fishermen dry cod in the sun. Others make their living by reclaiming salt from the marshes, and having their wives scoop it up and carry it back to town in wicker baskets on their heads.

Situated at the mouth of the Mondego River, Figueira da Foz literally means Fig Tree at the Mouth of the River, though how it got that name remains a long-forgotten secret. North of Cascais and Estoril, Fig Tree is the best known and oldest resort along the Atlantic coastline of Iberia. Aside from its climate (city fathers claim that the sun shines 2,772 hours annually), the most outstanding feature is the town's golden sandy beach, stretching for more than two miles. Those who don't like the beach can swim in a pool sandwiched between the Grande Hotel da Figueira and the Estalagem da Piscina-Praia on the main esplanade. Should the beach crowds get you down, you can always go for a trek into the **Serra da Boa Viagem**, a range of hills whose summit is a favorite vantage point for photographers and sightseers.

Most tourists don't come to Figueira to look at museums, but there is one exceptional one—the **Casa do Paço**, known as the Grémio do Comércio, a one-minute walk from the post office and esplanade. It contains one of the world's greatest collections of Delft tiles, numbering almost 7,000 and most often depicting warriors with gaudy plumage (some blowing trumpets). The puce and blue tiles are detailed and subtly executed. The casa was the palace of Carlos I, who came here in the last century when Figueira was frequented by royalty—the equivalent of San Sebastián in Spain. The tiles may be viewed from 9 a.m. to 12:30 p.m. and from 2-5 p.m. all-year-round (no admission is charged).

Bullfights are popular in season (remember, in Portugal the bull isn't killed and the animal's horns are padded). The old-style bull ring operates from mid-July to September, with seats ranging from 90$ ($3.51) to 460$ ($17.94), depending on where you sit (the sunny or shady side) and who is performing.

The **Grand Casino Peninsular**, open from May to October, features shows, dancing, a nightclub, and, of course, gambling salons.

Just two miles north of Figueira, by-passed by new construction and sitting complacently on a ridge near the sea, is **Buarcos**, a fishing village far removed from casinos and beaches. From the central square to the stone sea walls, it is pure and unspoiled. Cod dries in wire racks in the sun, streets faintly move with activity, and native girls with loaded baskets on their heads—arms akimbo—look out with bright eyes from under dark scarfs.

Figueira lies 80 miles south of Porto, 125 miles north of Lisbon, and 25 miles west of Coimbra In accommodations it is well stocked in a number of price ranges beginning with:

THE UPPER BRACKET: Grande Hotel da Figueira, Avenida Dr. Oliveira Salazar (tel. 221-46). This seven-floor modernized establishment stands right on the beach. Just walk across the esplanade and you have a clean sandy beach at your disposal, or go next door to the open-air salt-water swimming pool where you pay 15$ (59¢). The interior of the Grande is a world of marble and glass, more like a big city than a resort hotel. Some of the rooms on the sea (and these are preferable, of course) have glass-enclosed balconies similar to the miradores for which La Coruña, Spain, is known, but most have open balconies.

One English tripper called the furnishings in the rooms "sensible," and that seems fair enough. The 110 rooms contain private baths, with tariffs on the seaview rooms set at 550$ ($21.45) to 770$ ($30.03) for half board for two persons, 305$ ($12.29) to 465$ ($18.14) for demi-pension for one. The food is good and served in a lower-floor dining room. The price is 140$ ($5.46) for a table d'hôte luncheon or dinner. The hotel stays open year round, though you may be the only guest in winter.

THE MEDIUM-PRICED RANGE: Hotel Da Praia, 59 Rua Miguel Bombarda (tel. 220-82), is a first-class tourist hotel. It sits on a raised terrace along the beach esplanade, with its overscaled, open-air swimming pool with three diving boards (one dubbed stairway to heaven). The 60 rooms and four suites contain private baths and are furnished with compact pieces, the draperies and counterpanes in Portuguese-designed fabrics. Depending on the size, placement, and plumbing, the full-board rate for two persons is from 680$ ($26.53) to 760$ ($29.64), while one person with full pension pays 380$ ($14.82) to 400$ ($15.60). Meals are served in a walnut-paneled dining room, and there's a midget-sized bar. Breakfast is 30$ ($1.17). The hotel is closed in winter.

Also opening onto the swimming pool and under the same management is the following recommendation in:

THE BUDGET RANGE: Estalagem da Piscina, 7 Rua Santa Catarina (tel. 224-20). Totally modern, the estalagem of the swimming pool is a bargain. Here every bedroom has its own private bath and a balcony overlooking the water. Bright-patterned fabrics and herringbone floors enliven what would otherwise be a streamlined decor in the bedrooms. For full board, two persons pay either 460$ ($17.94) or 490$ ($19.11), depending on the room; one person is charged from 360$ ($14.04) to 410$ ($15.99) for full pension. Serving healthy-sized and good-tasting meals, the dining room is wood paneled with indirect egg-crate lighting. A meal is 100$ ($3.90); breakfast, 30$ ($1.17). Adjoining is a bar and modern sitting room overlooking the pool. Guests are welcomed from April to October 1.

IN BUARCOS—A BUDGET INN AND RESTAURANT: Restaurante-Pensao Teimoso, Estrada do Cabo Mondego (tel. 227-85), is a regional fish restaurant right on the shore, with a wing of modern rooms reserved for overnight guests. The Teimoso (a Portuguese word meaning stubborn or mulish) is family operated. The owner António Perez Sanchez started many years ago with a simple waterfront restaurant. As business grew, he added more rooms. He attracts both tourists and locals alike who know of his bountiful meals. He's also known for his shellfish soup and regional entrees such as fresh bass baked in a tomato sauce and served with potatoes and other vegetables. In addition, he roasts kid and suckling pig. Fish soup is 9$ (35¢); fish stew (caldeirada), 50$ ($1.95). Braised sardines go for 40$ ($1.56); roast veal, 55$ ($2.15); chocolate mousse, 7$ (27¢). The decor of the dining room is barren and aseptic, but the room has a fine view of the water. Breakfast is 15$ (59¢).

There are 14 rooms, all with private bath. Tariff for a single is 156$ ($6.08); 220$ ($8.58) for a double. Some of the newer rooms, prettily decorated and equipped with private sun terraces overlooking the ocean, may go a little higher. It's hard to get in from July through September, so make reservations.

More charming and a kilometer closer to town, is the **Tamargueira,** Estrada do Cabo Mondego (tel. 225-14), where you dine in an oval-shaped room with chandeliers made of ships' steering wheels. There's a fireplace at one end of the room, and the walls are decorated with typical plates and fishermen's nets. In good weather you can sit on the spacious terrace, from which you have a view of the sea. Menu specialties are caldeirada a mista a pescador, 50$ ($1.95), or Tamargueira cutlets, 60$ ($2.34). You can finish with a mousse or custard for 14$ (55¢). There are also five rooms available, furnished in simple New England style with bath. Doubles range from 130$ ($5.07) to 195$ ($7.61).

MONTEMOR-O-VELHO: Between Figueira da Foz and Coimbra, overlooking the fertile Mondego River Valley, is the historic village of Montemor the Old. Dating from the 12th century, the ruins of the **Castle of Montemor-o-Velho,** built by Sancho I, crown the hilltop. The main road runs scenically past villas, shrines, high walls, and churches. Narrow cobbled streets will lead you to the restored walls and ramparts, from which there is a fine vista of the valley.

The Castle has witnessed many moments in Portuguese history—perhaps the most infamous being when Alfonso IV sanctioned (according to historian Leonardo Coelho) the plot to kill Inês de Castro, mistress of the king's son. The Castle is a moving medieval setting, especially when sparrows play among the air currents over its time-dated stones.

3. Coimbra

Black-caped students strumming guitars and violas and singing a serenade of their own fado hilário on narrow cobblestoned streets . . . tattered hems of fraying gowns that speak of heartbreak (some say conquest) . . . colored ribbons flying from the black student garb, signifying a young man's destined profession (but why violet for pharmacy?) . . . and a stream that "flows with the blood of the tortured Inês de Castro," who was crowned Queen of Portugal, after her death! Coimbra—"the most romantic city in Portugal"—was the inspiration for the popular song, "April in Portugal."

On the weather-washed right bank of the muddy Mondego, it is also the educational center of the country—its university the second oldest in the world, having been founded at Lisbon in 1290.

The students of Coimbra band together in republics, usually renting cramped buildings in the old quarters—some up many flights of winding stairs. An invitation to one of these student dormitories will give you an insight into Coimbra rarely experienced by the foreign visitor. Sometimes when they dart out in the morning in their black capes, they look like low-winging bats fleeing the belfry.

The republic actually isn't very democratic, run as it is on a strict seniority basis. A typical evening's bill of fare in a republic is likely to include grilled sardines, bread, and a glass of wine. If you do get an invitation, we hope the evening will be capped by the students presenting you with a fado concert. To show your gratitude, if you should happen onto an invitation, cigarettes are much appreciated.

Coimbra's charms and mysteries unfold as you walk up the Rua F. Borges passing under the Gothic **Arch of Almedina,** with its coat-of-arms. From that point, you can continue up the steep street, past antique shops, to the old quarter.

The focal point for most pilgrims, of course, is the **University of Coimbra,** entrenched in the town in 1537 on orders from Joao III. Among its alumni are Luis Vas de Camoes (the country's greatest poet, author of the national epic, The Lusiads); St. Anthony of Padua (also the patron saint of Lisbon); even the late Dr. Salazar, once a professor of economics.

If you'll ignore the cold statuary and architecture on the Largo de Dom Dinis, you can pass under the 17th-century **Porta Pérrea** into the inner core of the academy. The steps on the right will take you along a cloistered arcade, the **Via Latina,** to the **Sala dos Capelos,** the site of graduation ceremonies. You can enter into a world with a twisted rope ceiling, a portrait gallery of Portuguese kings, walls of red damask, and the inevitable azulejos. Afterwards, you can visit the **University Chapel,** decorated with an 18th-century organ, 16th-century candelabra, a painted ceiling, 17th-century tiles, and a fine Manueline portal.

Of course, the architectural gem of the entire town is the baroque **University Library** next door, with its chinoiserie motifs. It is one of the most elaborate (some say the most) decorative accomplishments in all of Portugal. Established between 1716 and 1723 and donated by Joao V, it shelters more than a million volumes, including a first edition of *"The Lusiads."* The interior is comprised of a trio of high-ceilinged salons walled by two-story tiers of lacquer-decorated bookshelves. The pale jade and sedate lemon marble inlaid floors complement the jeweled gold and emerald effect of the effusive gilt. The library tables are ebony and lustrous rosewood, imported from the former colonies in India and Brazil. Three-dimensional ceilings and the zooming telescopic effect of the room structure focus on the large portrait of Joao V, set against a backdrop of imitation curtains in wood. The side galleries, with their walls of valuable books, the supporting pillars, the intricate impedimenta—all are dazzling, even noble. You may want to save the Library for last; after viewing this masterpiece, other sights pale in comparison. Admission-free, it is open from 10 a.m. to 12:30 p.m., and from 2-5 p.m.

To wind down after leaving the Library, walk to the end of the belvedere for a panoramic view of the river—equal to scenes on the Rhine—and the rooftops of the old quarter. On the square stand a statue of Joao III and the famous curfew-signaling clock of Coimbra, known as "cabra," meaning goat.

A short walk down from the university square leads to the **Machado de Castro Museum.** Named after the greatest Portuguese sculptor of the 18th century, this museum is one of the finest in the north. Built as the Paço Episcopal in 1592, it houses a collection of ecclesiastical sculpture—especially polychrome—much of which dates from the 14th to the 16th century. The other exhibits include vestments, a relic of Saint Isabella (wife of King Dinis, the university's founder), paintings, antiques, coaches, silver chalices, old jewelry, embroideries, retables, and 16th-century ceramic representations of the Apostles and Christ. The museum is open from 10 a.m.-5 p.m., charging an admission of 5$.

Across the way is the **New Cathedral (Sé Nova),** but it isn't much admired. Dating from the 17th century, its interior is coldly neoclassic, although relief is provided by the baroque altars and a riot of angels playing horns atop the organ.

More interesting, however, is to walk down to the **Old Cathedral (Sé Velha).** At the Largo da Sé Velha, the cathedral founded in 1170 enjoys associations with Saint Anthony of Padua. Crenelated and staunch as a fortress, it is entered by passing under a Romanesque portal. Usually a student is there, willing to show you (for a tip, of course) the precincts, including the restored cloister. The pride of this monument is the gilded Flemish retable over the main altar, with a crucifix on the top. To the left of the altar is a 16th-century chapel designed by a French artist, and containing the tomb of one of the Bishops of Coimbra. The chapels house the sarcophagi of everybody from medieval kings to a lady-in-waiting to Saint Isabella, the patroness of Coimbra.

Reached by going up the Rua Visconde da Luz, the **Santa Cruz Church** is a former monastery, founded in the late 12th century when Afonso Henriques, Portugal's first king, ruled. However, its original Romanesque style gave way to Manueline restorers in 1507. The much popularized "Romeo and Juliet" story of Portugal, involving Pedro the Cruel and his mistress, Inês de Castro, reached its climax in this church. As mentioned, years after her murder at the hands of his father's assassins, Pedro—festering with vengance—had her remains exhumed and set her upon a makeshift throne at Santa Cruz. The courtiers were forced to pay homage to her royal corpse—even kiss her hand.

The lower part of the walls inside are decorated with azulejos (tiles) sweeping along the walls like cut-outs. Groined in the profuse Manueline manner, the interior houses the Gothic sarcophagi of Afonso Henriques—his feet resting on a lion—and that of his son, also a king, Sancho I. The pulpit nearby is one of the achievements of the Renaissance in Portugal—carved by Joao de Ruao in the 16th century. The choir stalls preserve, in carved configurations, the symbolism, mythology, and historical import of Portuguese exploration. With its twisted columns and 13th-century tombs, the two-tiered Gothic-Manueline cloister is impressive, with a fountain in the center.

The facade makes Santa Cruz one of the finest monuments in the land. Decorated like an architectural birthday cake, it is topped with finials and crosses, its portal top heavy with a baroque porch—a curious blending of styles. Overadorned, but fascinating.

ACROSS THE MONDEGO: On the left bank lie four of the most interesting—and least visited—attractions of Coimbra. On the silt-laden banks of the Mondego stand the gutted, flooded, and crumbling remains of **Santa Clara-a-Velha,** A Gothic convent built in the 14th century. This church once housed the body of Coimbra's patron saint, Isabella, although her remains were transferred to the New Convent higher up on the hill. Rising out of the inrushing river, the Roman arches are reflected in the canals, evoking a Venetian scene. You can walk through the upper part only, as the river has already reclaimed the floor. The former convent is reached by crossing the Santa Clara Bridge, and turning left down the cobbled street (Rua de Baixo).

Commanding a view of right bank Coimbra, the **Convent of Santa Clara-a-Nova** provides a setting for the tomb of St. Isabella. Built during the reign of Joao IV, the convent is an incongruous blending of a church and a military garrison.

The church is noted for a rich baroque interior and Renaissance cloister. In the rear, behind a grille, is the tomb of the saint (usually closed except on special occasions). When her body was removed in 1677, her remains were well preserved, even though she died in 1336. Instead of regal robes, she preferred to be buried in the simplest habit of the order of the Poor Clares. At the main altar is the silver tomb (a sacristan will light it for you), which the ecclesiastical hierarchy considered more appropriate following her canonization.

At least for youngsters, the main attraction of Coimbra is **Portugal dos Pequenitos.** Called Portugal for the Little Ones, it is reached by crossing the Ponte de Santa Clara and heading out the Rua António Augusto Gonsalves. It's a mélange of miniature houses from every province of Portugal, including Madeira and the Azores, even the distant foreign settlements of Timor and Macao. It gives one the impression of a Dr. Lemuel Gulliver strolling across a Lilliputian world. The recreations include palaces, an Indian temple, a Brazilian pavilion (with photos of gauchos), a windmill, a castle, and the 16th-century House of Diamonds from Lisbon. The children's museum is open from 9:30 a.m. to 6 p.m., charging an admission of 5$ (20¢).

Further up the road is the final attraction—the **Quinta das Lágrimas** (the Garden of Tears, tel. 232-52). In "sweet Mondego's solitary groves," in the words of Camoes, lived Inês de Castro, mistress of Pedro, and their three illegitimate children. Although the property of the Osório Cabral family since the 18th century, the gardens are visited by romantics from many countries.

176 DOLLAR-WISE GUIDE TO PORTUGAL

You can't go inside the house, but can wander through greenery to the spring fountain, known as the Fonte dos Amores.

It was at the quinta on Camoes' "black night obscure" that the Spanish beauty was set upon by assassins hired by her lover's father. Pedro returned, finding her in a pool of blood, her throat slit. He would wait until he became king to seek his revenge.

So classic and enduring a Portuguese love story is it that who would want to suggest that it wasn't true, or that the murder didn't happen at the Garden of Tears? You can visit from 8 a.m. to 8 p.m. for an admission of 2$50 (10¢).

HOTELS: Unfortunately, Coimbra is far better supplied with attractions than it is with hotels and restaurants. But there are the following two recommendations.

THE MEDIUM-PRICED RANGE: Hotel Bragança, 10 Largo das Ameias (tel. 221-71), is a bandbox modern five-floor hotel, built next door to the railway station. Primarily catering to businessmen, it does a thriving trade in the summer season. A few of its bedrooms open onto balconies overlooking the main road. All of the 83 bedrooms contain private baths; the furnishings are modern and utilitarian. The rooms vary in plumbing, size, and placement, as reflected by the tariffs. Two persons pay 260$ ($10.14). Singles are priced at 185$ ($7.22). A table d'hôte luncheon or dinner is served for 105$ ($4.10). Breakfast is 20$ (78¢).

Astoria Hotel, 21 Avenida Navarro (tel. 220-55), on the river esplanade, overlooks the New Convent of Santa Clara on the left bank. Outside, it is decorative with an ornate dome—a crusted holdover from the 19th century.

The interior disappoints. Instead of potted plants or antiques—even reproductions—you're greeted with unfortunate modern. The overall impression of public and private rooms is that of being well worn. The beds too often have "army cot" springs, although the view from one of the balconies is pleasing. Furnishings are a bit tattered and sparse—don't forget to bring your own soap. In a double, the rate is 250$ ($9.75) to 440$ ($17.16). In a single with bath, the tariff is 200$ ($7.80) to 300$ ($11.70).

Meals in the corner dining room are appetizing; average cost, 135$ ($5.27). The intimate bar in front of an open fireplace can be an attractive place for before- or after-dinner drinks. The bird-cage elevator, incidentally, can be temperamental.

READER'S PENSION RECOMMENDATIONS: "I'd like to recommend **Pensao Avis,** Avenida Fernao de Magalhaes (tel. 23-718), a 10-minute walk from the railway station. It is clean and centrally located. The cost was 75$ ($2.93) in a single room without breakfast. A hot shower extra" (Mrs. Andrea Clerico, Napa, Calif.).

WHERE TO DINE: The **Dom Pedro,** 58 Avenida Emidio Navarro (tel. 2-91-08), is an easily accessible first-class restaurant in the university town. Convenient for motorists, it has its own parking. English-speaking waiters will guide you through the menu of regional specialties, including such dishes as shrimp cocktail, 75$ ($2.93); tomato soup, 13$ (51¢); roast pork, 65$ ($2.54); veal caçador, 70$ ($2.73); and fruit tart, 20$ (78¢). To accompany your repast, why not order the regional vinho verde (the green wine)? The pleasant atmosphere is made even more so by the friendly and polite service.

Pinto d'Ouro (Golden Chicken), 68 Avenida Joao das Regras, is simpler than the Dom Pedro, but it offers a view. Alluring is a bar serving snacks or just a small coffee, a place for a rest. Preferred are the little tables in the nook adjoining the dining room. A satisfactory meal might include soup, 17$ (66¢); trout, 50$ ($1.95); breaded veal cutlet, 60$ ($2.34); and flan, 11$ (43¢). A good bottled green wine, as in the above restaurant, is the traditional accompaniment.

Café Nicola, 35 Rua Ferreira Borges (tel. 220-61), is a plain, but modern little second-floor restaurant over a delicatessen and pastry shop. It's spartan inside, even the flowers are usually wilted—but tradition is to be respected. Students gather here for strong coffee.

The window tables provide box seats for looking at the teeming street. The food is good, though plain, and the platters of fish or meat are usually large enough to be shared by two. The cuisine, as might be expected, is regional. A nourishing bowl of the soup of the day costs only 8$ (31¢). Two favorite dishes include grilled cod with potatoes for 60$ ($2.34), and cutlets of pork, also with fried potatoes, for 65$ also. The house specialty is frango churrasco (barbecued chicken) with french fries, costing 60$ ($2.34).

Democratica, 7 Travessa do Rua Nova, is a stark budget restaurant popular with students and shoe-string travelers. A few steps off the main drag (make the first left on main street after passing the Café Santa Cruz), this place couldn't be simpler, with a little dining room, tiles on the walls, and the kitchen in the back. The servings are large. A soup costs only 7$ (27¢); pescada (hake), greens, and potatoes go for 40$ ($1.56), and a rice pudding is 6$50 (25¢). Wine costs 15$ (59¢) a bottle.

Mandarim, 13 Praça Republica (tel. 268-26), near the University, serves simple local fare in a snack bar atmosphere. It's also popular with students, as are all cafes in the area. On a mezzanine is the dining room, serving soups for 7$ (27¢); trout meunière, 50$ ($1.95); salmonetes (red mullets), 50$ also; roast chicken with spicy sauce, 50$; pork chops, 50$; mousse, 15$ (59¢); and flan, 8$ (31¢).

A COFFEE HOUSE: Santa Cruz, Praça 8 de Maio is an old-fashioned coffee house-restaurant, popular not only with young students, but with Portuguese gentlemen of yesteryear. The Santa Cruz appears to have been converted from a chapel belonging to the church next door. The bar and meat refrigerator counter are probably where the altar once stood. You sit on tooled leather and brass-studded chairs, drinking or dining at dark octagonal tables with marble tops. The walls are darkly paneled, and there is stained glass.

The mood is casual, with cigarette butts on the floor, but a lively spirit dominates. Students often sing fado here. It's a stronghold of Iberian tradition, holding out against modernization. The coffee is black and unblended, and the shots of cognac overflow the glass rim. Stick to the black coffee and don't eat the pastries. You can also have a meal here, ranging from 35$ ($1.37) for sausages to 65$ ($2.54) for a Santa Cruz steak.

READER'S SELECTIONS: "North of Coimbra is the little hamlet of **Mealhada,** a one-industry town devoted to selling roast suckling pig. We had a delicious luncheon at **Pedro Dos Leitoes,** and afterward saw the ovens in a separate building where the roasting is done" (Burton Ashford Bugbee, Brookfield, Conn.). (Editor's Note: The town lies off the main road, the roast suckling pig appears on the menu in Portuguese as leitao assado.)

4. Conimbriga

One of the great Roman archaeological finds of Europe, the pre-Celtic village of Conimbriga lies less than 10 miles southwest of Coimbra. Conimbriga was first occupied by the Romans in the late first century. Since then—and up to the fifth century A.D.—the town knew a peaceful life. The town site lies near a Roman camp, but the town never served as a military outpost itself.

Roman mosaics of almost perfect quality have been unearthed in diggings in the area. The designs are triangular, octagonal, and circular—executed in blood-red, mustard, gray, sienna, and yellow. Motifs include beasts from North Africa and delicately wrought hunting scenes. Mosaics displaying mythological themes can be seen in one of the houses. Subjects include Perseus slaying the Medusa and the Minotaur of Crete in his labyrinth.

The diggings display to good advantage the complex functional apparatus of Roman ingenuity. Columns form peristyles around reflecting pools, and the remains of fountains stand in courtyards. There are ruins of temples, a forum, patrician houses, water conduits and drains. Feeding the public and private baths of the town were special heating and steam installations with elaborate piping systems. Conimbriga even had its own aqueduct.

The museum-restaurant-bar near the entrance (you can get a good meal for around $3.50 U.S.) displays a sampling of the most important finds. Some of the artifacts include coins, statuary fragments, toilet articles, scissors, beads, bracelets, swords, wine jugs, and some fine miniature bronze figures.

The museum and site are open from 9 a.m. till sunset, charging an admission of 5$. If you don't have a car, you can reach the site by taking a bus from Coimbra to Condeixa. The bus, José Maria dos Santos Transports, leaves Coimbra at 9:30 a.m. and 1:30 p.m., returning at 1:50 and 6:10 p.m. Conimbriga lies about a mile away, reached either by walking it (through an olive grove) or by hiring a taxi in the village.

5. Bussaco

The rich, tranquil beauty of the forests of Bussaco, 17½ miles from Coimbra, were initially discovered by a humble order of barefoot Carmelites, following dictates of seclusion as prescribed by their founder. In 1628, they founded a monastery at Bussaco, using materials from the surrounding hills. Around the forest they erected a wall to isolate further their lives and to keep women out.

These barefoot friars had a special love for plants and trees; and each year they cultivated the natural foliage and planted specimens sent them from distant orders. Bussaco had always been a riot of growth: ferns, pines, cork, eucalyptus, and pink and blue clusters of hydrangea. But the friars introduced such exotic additions as the monkey puzzle, a tall Chilean pine with branches so thick it confuses monkeys who climb in it.

The pride of the forest, however, remains its stately cypresses and cedars. Such was the beauty of the preserve that a papal bull, issued in 1643, threatened excommunication to anyone who destroyed a tree! Even though the monastery was abolished in 1834, the forest remains preserved. Filled with natural spring waters, the earth bubbles with many cool fountains, the best known of which is **Fonte Fria** (cold fountain).

The forest of Bussaco was the battleground where Wellington defeated the Napoleonic legions under Marshal André Masséna. The Iron Duke himself slept in a simple cloister cell right after the battle. A small, though adequate, **Museum of the Peninsular War** reconstructs much of the drama of this turning point in the Napoleonic invasion of Iberia. It's about a half mile from the hotel. The very slim museum consists of engravings plus a few pistols. Entrance is 5$ (20¢).

In the beginning of the 20th century, a great deal of the Carmelite monastery was torn down to make way for the royal hunting lodge and palace hotel of Carlos I and his wife Queen Amélia. He hardly had time to enjoy it, as he was assassinated in 1908. His son, the two-year monarch Manuel II, did use it as a hideaway for his affair with Gaby Deslys. Luigi Manini, an Italian architect, master-minded this neo-Manueline structure of parapets, buttresses, armillary spheres, galleries with flamboyant arches, towers, and turrets. After the fall of the Braganzas, wealthy tourists took their afternoon tea by the pools underneath the trellis hung with blossoming violet wisteria.

One of the best ways to savor Bussaco is to make the 1,800-foot ride to **Cruz Alta** (high cross) by car through forests, past hermitages. At the summit is a view considered by many to be the best in Portugal.

LIVING IN DELUXE SPLENDOR: Palace Hotel Do Buçaco, Mata do Buçaco (tel. Mealhada 931-01). "Goodbye forever," Queen Amelia said on her last visit to Bussaco in 1945. The government had permitted her a sentimental journey (in a limousine with ladies in waiting) to visit all the places where she had spent her reigning years before her flight to England in 1910. The palace is an architectural fantasy. The designer borrowed heavily from everyone: the Jerónimos Monastery at Belém; the Doge's Palace at Venice; the Graustark Castles of Bavaria.

Now a hotel, the palace is set in the center of a 250-acre forest. The structure is still intact and impressive, especially its grand staircase with ornate marble balustrades, 15-foot-wide bronze torchiers, and walls of frescoes, some painted by Carlos himself. There are several drawing rooms and salons—a potpourri of architectural whims. Of course, many of the furnishings were removed, replaced with a mixture of antiques, reproductions, and modern and not so modern (the latter especially dominant in the bedrooms).

In 1910, the Swiss head of the kitchen—the king's cook—persuaded the government to let him run the palace as a hotel. For half pension, two persons pay either 770$ ($30.03) to 1,030$ ($40.17), depending on the room. For one person, the half board costs 455$ ($17.75) to 640$ ($24.96). In some cases, the baths were once the adjoining rooms for a valet or maid,—now they have every convenience, sometimes including tubs on raised platforms.

The dining room is a theatrical success, the tables set with fine stemware and silver. Of note is the Gothic wooden ceiling and the view through two 20-foot-wide arched windows onto the gardens and the encircling neo-Manueline terrace. Even if you're not staying here, you should stop in for lunch or dinner, costing 200$ ($7.80) for a table d'hôte. A typical repast: first, a pastry puff stuffed high with hot creamed lobster, followed either by egg cake seasoned with herbs, or else grilled sole with spinach in butter. For a third course, perhaps filet of veal, tender and sweet, will be served with a rosette of potatoes, topped by dessert, an assortment of cheese and crackers, and the fresh fruit of the season.

6. Curía and Luso

"Luso for the liver; Curía for the kidneys" goes the saying. Two of the most popular health resorts in the country, Curía and Luso lie in heartland Portugal. Thermal spa enthusiasts flock here generally from June 1 through October, some arriving on the main-line Sud-Express (Lisbon-Paris).

The spa at **Luso** is just two miles from Bussaco. The gold-colored facade of the Grande Hotel Das Termas nestles in a valley in the midst of abundant foliage with a backdrop of rolling forests. Luso is known for the potency of its radioactive springs. In addition, the grounds feature tennis courts, indoor and outdoor swimming pools, hydrotherapeutic treatments, a radiation room, and laboratory facilities for all forms of analyses.

The secluded atmosphere and surroundings of **Curía** make a good setting for one of the most famous hotels in Portugal, the Palace. In the foothills of the Serra da Estrêla, Curía is in the wine-growing district of Bairrada, 7½ miles from Bussaco. Its waters have been compared to the famous ones of Vittel. The admission to the baths is 25$ (98¢) to 30$ ($1.17).

LUSO—A TOP SPA HOTEL: Grande Hotel Das Termas, Rua dos Banhos (tel. 93450), is a sprawling establishment offering 157 rather dated but roomy bedchambers, each with private bath. Habitués praise its thermal spa facilities. The emphasis is on good health. You can swim in a 150-foot olympic pool, lounge and sunbathe on the surrounding grassy terrace, or relax under the weeping willows and bougainvillea arbor. There are hard tennis courts, mini-golf, and, at night, a boîte for dancing.

The accommodation is comfortable in well-proportioned bedrooms, with matching furnishings. Some of the rooms open onto private terraces, with views of the tree-covered valley. The full-board rate for two persons begins as low as 690$ ($26.91) for simpler rooms, and peaks at 840$ ($32.76). The single tariff for full board ranges from 380$ ($14.82) to 525$ ($20.48), depending on the room's size and location. The meals are large (the cuisine is both regional and international) and served in a muraled dining room. Guests are welcomed from June 1 till mid-October.

CURIA—TWO TOP SEA HOTELS: Palace Hotel da Curía (tel. 521-32) is the grandest of the local watering spas. The approach is by way of an avenue of jacaranda trees and clipped hedges. Sunken gardens, green lawns, and "The Paradise" swimming pool, as well as mineral and radioactive springs, make this retreat a special mecca any time between July and October 1.

The hotel has diving boards and tennis courts, a small nightclub, and homegrown produce from its own gardens. On the grounds is a collection of rare pheasants, even a she-wolf captured in the Serra d'Estrêla. The hotel is owned by the same chain that controls the Bussaco Palace—in fact, en pension guests from Bussaco can obtain a voucher before leaving, entitling them to lunch or dinner at the Curía Palace.

The 155 bedrooms (only 87 with private baths) are old-fashioned, but spacious and comfortable. A double costs 186$ ($7.25) to 444$ ($17.32), depending on whether you have a private bath. In a single the tariff is 115$ ($4.49) to 144$ ($5.62). If you're just stopping in for a meal, the price of a table d'hôte luncheon or dinner is 135$ ($5.27), plus service. Add 270$ ($10.53) per person for full pension. The old lounges and ballroom evoke another era, with a salon for your mood: drinking, reading, dancing, bridge, whatever.

Hotel Das Termas (tel. 521-85) is imbued with the most gemütlich air of any of the spa hotels. It is approached via a curving dirt road leading through a parklike setting with lacy shade trees—quiet and secluded. Open year round, it offers facilities for health and relaxation, including a free-form swimming pool encircled with orange trees and umbrella tables. In the park a rustic wooden bridge leads over a lake to woodsy walks and the tennis courts.

The lounge is relaxed and casual, furnished with provincial pieces and handloomed rugs. The bar is actually a living room. The dining hall, with its parquet floors, brick fireplace, and overscaled painting, is really like a tavern, especially when filled with guests who aren't hesitant to chat from table to table. Even the bedrooms have a homey feeling, with lots of floral chintz, wooden beds, and walls of wardrobe space. Of the 39 rooms, 28 contain private baths. In a single the cost of a room ranges in price from 190$ ($7.41) to 500$ ($19.50), with doubles going from a low of 170$ ($6.63) to 370$ ($14.43), depending on the plumbing and placement. Full pension costs an extra 305$ ($11.90) per person.

7. Aveiro

The town on the lagoon, Aveiro is crisscrossed by myriad canals, spanned by low-arched bridges. At the mouth of the Vouga River, it is cut off from the sea by a long sand bar protecting clusters of islets. The architecture is almost Flemish—a good foil for a setting of low willow-reed flatlands, salt marshes, spray-misted dunes, and rice paddies. Oxen rigged with ornate harnesses trundle through the streets, passing racks of cod drying in the sun.

On the lagoon itself, brightly painted swan-necked boats traverse the waters. Called barcos moliceiros, these flat-bottomed vessels hold fishermen who harvest seaweed used for fertilizer. They are ever on the lookout for eels, a specialty of the region, which they catch in the shoals studded with lotus and water lilies. Outside the town are extensive salt pits, lined with pyramids, fog-white in color.

Houses built on stilts are often topped with finials and terracotta eagles. The surrounding lagoons and many secret pools dotting the landscape make a boat excursion (inquire at the Tourist Bureau) reminiscent of a trip into bayou country. Not only are the natural wonders unspoiled, but there is an uncommon wealth of artistic treasures as well.

The **Convent of Jesus,** at Praça do Milenário, is hailed as the finest example of the rococo style in Portugal. At the convent, the Infanta Santa Joana, sister of Joao II and daughter of Afonso V, took the veil in 1472. Her tomb—an inlaid rectangle of marble quarried in Italy—attracts many pilgrims. Its pale delicate pinks and roses lend it the air of a cherub-topped confection.

The convent, owned by the state and now the **Aveiro Museum,** displays a lock of the saint's hair, her belt and rosary, and a complete pictorial study of her life. A portrait of her, painted in intonaco, is exceptional. But what characterizes the convent is its carved giltwork, lustrous in the chapel, despite the dust.

In this setting is an assortment of 15th-century paintings, royal portraits of Carlos I and Manuel II (the last two Braganza kings), antique ceramics, and 16th-, 17th-, and 18th-century sculptures. There are also some well-preserved 18th- and 19th-century coaches and carriages. After viewing all this, you can walk through the cloisters with their Doric columns. The museum is open from 10 a.m. to 5 p.m., charging 5$, except on entrance-free Saturdays and Sundays. Closed Mondays.

On the same square is the 15th-century **Church of St. Domingos,** with its blue and gold altarpieces and egg-shaped windows flanking the upper part of the nave. The facade—in the Gothic-Manueline style—is decorated with four flame finials. To the right (facing) is a bell tower. There are other churches as well, especially the **Chapel of Senhor Jesus das Barrocas,** built in the shape of an octagon in 1722.

After a meal of stewed eels and a bottle of the hearty Bairrada wine, you might wish to explore some of the settlements along the lagoon, specifically **Ilhavo,** three miles south of Aveiro. Here you can stop off at the **Municipal Museum of Ilhavo,** 13 Rua Serpa Pinto, an unpretentious gallery of the sea that offers an insight into a semi-aquatic people. Inside you can see seascape paintings, boating paraphernalia, fishing equipment, ship models, and other exhibits.

From Ilhavo, drive along an avenue of olive trees to **Vista Alegre,** the village of the famous Vista Alegre porcelain works, which you enter during working hours through a gateway on a tree-shaded square. Founded in 1824, the establishment is noted for its delicate decorated china.

Back in Aveiro, the leading accommodations are the following:

THE BUDGET RANGE: Hotel Imperial, Rua Dr. Nascimento Leitão (tel. 221-41), is Aveiro's most important and most up-to-date hotel. Having cast aside its earlier pensao classification, it was rebuilt. In fact, it even attracts the youth of the community who gravitate to the lower lounge social center for drinks and TV, or to the open and airy dining room with its two walls of glass. They look forward to their Sunday dates here—the 95$ ($3.71) dinners or the drinks on the open terrace.

Many of the bedrooms and each of the lounges overlook the garden of the Aveiro Museum, the old convent described earlier. All the rooms contain private baths, as well as individually operated central heating. A double goes for from 270$ ($10.53) to 330$ ($12.87). A single rents for 190$ ($7.41) to 230$ ($8.97). The furnishings are in a satisfactory contemporary idiom, with many built-in features, and the color schemes are pleasant. A few suites are available, including a living room and a twin-bedded chamber with bath, costing 370$ ($14.43) when occupied by two persons.

The **Arcada Hotel,** 4 Rua Viana do Castelo (tel. 230-01), enjoys an enviable position in the center of Aveiro, with a view of the river traffic in the canal out front. In the summer, you can see from your bedroom window the white pyramids of drying salt on the flats. Although the hotel has been modernized, the classic facade of beige and white has remained. Many of the rooms open onto balconies, and the rooftop is decorated with ornate finials.

The hotel itself occupies the second, third, and fourth floors of the old building. Based on the plumbing you require, the tariffs range between 220$ ($8.58) and 270$ ($10.53) in a double with bath; 95$ ($3.71) and 105$ ($4.10) in a bathless double. A single with bath ranges from 155$ ($6.05) to 190$ ($7.41). Breakfast is the only meal served.

AN INN BETWEEN THE SEA AND THE LAGOON: Pousada da Ria, Bico do Muranzel, Torreira-Murtosa (tel. 461-32), is a private world on a promontory, surrounded on three sides by water. Between the sea and the lagoon, it is a modern nearly all-glass building, with rows of balconies on its second floor. To reach the government-owned pousada, you can go by boat from Aveiro (boats are not for cars, only for passengers). Or take a long drive via Murtosa and Torreira until you reach the sandy spit. Along the way, you'll pass Phoenician-style boats in the harbor, sand dunes, pine trees, and houses on high-tide stilts.

The entrance to the tourist inn has a long lily pond and planter with a stairway bridge leading to the marble-floored dining room on the upper level. The waterside terrace opens onto views of the brightly colored sails of the fishing craft or of the sunsets over the lagoon. The inn has a clubhouse atmosphere, and is popular with holiday-seeking Portuguese families who quickly book the 10 rooms. If these are taken, there are three additional, and far less comfortable rooms in the back. All three lack washing and toilet facilities which are across the hall. Singles cost 155$ ($6.05).

Accommodation with full board is recommended: 590$ ($23.01) for two persons, 340$ ($13.26) for a lone traveler. The rooms are compact, furnished with space-saving built-in pieces—a semi-modern decor with an emphasis on comfort. If you're stopping over for lunch or dinner (highly recommended), table d'hôte meals are priced at 80$ ($3.12) and 100$ ($3.90), plus service and tax. The chef's specialty is caldeirada à ria, a savory fish stew. Sunny Sundays are likely to be bedlam; otherwise, it's a peaceful haven.

A BUDGET INN IN THE VOUGA VALLEY: Pousada de Santo António, Serém (tel. 522-30), is an overscaled villa resting on a rise above the Vouga River. Near the main Lisbon-Porto highway, it is a fine location. The meadowlands and river valley are lush, filling the dining and living room windows with the colors of three-dimensional postcards. Large natural flagstones make up the front courtyard, ushering you into a renovated villa decorated like a warm provincial inn.

All 13 rooms have their own baths, and contain striped rugs and floral bedspreads. High headboards on the country-style beds and patterned stone floors give an air of simple comfort. The full-board tariff is 315$ ($12.29) in a single, 385$ ($15.02) in a double.

At dinner, whether you begin with a caldeirada or caldo verde, be sure to request (if available) the ovos moles (luscious egg sweets) typical of the area, along with fresh cheese from the mountains and the fruits of the valley. A meal is 110$ ($4.29); breakfast, 30$ ($1.17). The pousada is about 157 miles north of Lisbon.

8. Caramulo

Set against a background of mimosa and heather-laden mountains, this tiny resort is a gem. It is also a modern art center unique in Portugal. Founded by Dr. Abel de Lacerda, the bulk of the collection of the **Caramulo Museum** is made up of gifts from private donors. Many paintings, such as works by Salvador Dalí and Picasso, were donated to the museum by the artists themselves. Other famous painters represented include Dufy, Léger, Chagall, Miró, and Graham Sutherland. Of special interest is a painting of St. John the Baptist by the 16th-century Portuguese artist, Grao Vasco, and a sultry nude by Henrique Medina (1934).

There is an assortment of modern and ancient sculpture, ranging from the matronly bovine "Maternidade" by José Clara (1955), to an ethereal Lady of Fátima (1946) by Canto de Maya, to a grimacing Chinese gnome (c. 386-577 A.D.). The celebrated Tournai tapestries depict the trials of the Portuguese explorers in India. Other exhibits include enamel work, jewels and pendants, and fine 17th-, 18th-, and 19th-century Indian, Chinese, and English porcelain.

Adjoining is an **Automobile Museum,** housing at least 60 veteran and vintage cars, including a 1910 Benz; a 1909 Fiat; a 1927 Bugatti sports roadster; even a 1902 Darracq. These antique cars are restored to purring condition. A few early bicycles—one dating back to 1865—and motorcycles are also exhibited. In addition to the ground-floor car display area, workshop, and library, there is an upper gallery where more vehicles are arranged. Access to this is gained by a wide staircase at one end of the banister formed of crankshafts and camshafts from vintage engines. The admission is 10$ (39¢) to each museum. Both are open daily from 10 a.m. to 6 p.m.

These attractions are 50 miles north of Coimbra, midway between Aveiro and Viseu.

In accommodations Caramulo is provided with an inn.

THE BUDGET RANGE: Estalagem de S. Jerónimo (tel. 862-91) is placed high as an eagles's nest, near the crest of a mountain ridge. Its panoramic view is comparable to sights encountered in Switzerland and Austria. The inn is like a spread-out chalet, with a design not only aesthetically pleasing, but comfortable. You park your car and enter through a lower reception lounge, noticing a group of paintings casually hung. One is an original Dufy. You ascend to the reception, living, and dining rooms—with one salon flowing into another. In winter guests sit by the copper-hooded fireplace.

Beyond the wooden grill is a pleasant dining room, the window wall providing views of the hills. Dinner is candlelit, and guests sit on tall provincial chairs sampling the country-style cooking served by mountain girls. If you're just dropping in, a table d'hôte luncheon or dinner goes for 100$ ($3.90). There are five courses, and the helpings are generous.

The six double rooms are small, but attractive, all with private bath. Portuguese antiques and reproductions are used—ornate iron headboards, a slab of wood as a console. Wide windows open onto vista-scanning private balconies. The cost for a double with shower is 260$ ($10.14) to 295$ ($11.51). Actually, it's more sensible for two persons to take full board at 620$ ($24.18) to 645$ ($25.15).

A POUSADA ON THE COIMBRA-GUARDA HIGHWAY: The **Pousada da Santa Bárbara,** at Póvoa das Quartas-Oliveira do Hospital (tel. Oliveira do Hospital 5-22-52), is a most convenient stopover on the main Coimbra-Guarda highway. Though not luxurious, it is suitable for those seeking a mountain spot. There are only 16 double rooms, but each comes equipped with a bath and phone. One person is charged 155$ ($6.05) nightly, that tariff increasing to 220$ ($8.58) for two persons. For full pension (a pleasantly recommendable Portuguese cuisine), one person is charged 340$ ($13.26), that tab rising to 590$ ($23.01) for two clients. If you're motoring and would like to stop by for lunch or dinner, a set meal in the provincial dining room costs 80$ ($3.12) or 100$ ($3.90). Breakfast is an additional 25$ (98¢).

STAYING IN CANAS DE SENHORIM: The hotel at Urgeiriça is set amidst the forested countryside near Canas de Senhorim, and is connected by road with all the major cities of Portugal by fine highways. The hotel lies about 25 miles from the Estrêla Mountains—popular with winter sports enthusiasts—and is 186 miles north of Lisbon, 102 miles from Porto, just 50 miles northeast of Coimbra and 20 miles from the country town of Viseu.

Hotel Urgeiriça, Urgeiriça, Canas de Senhorim (tel. 672-67), is really more of a spread-out country club than a hotel. It's a place where nature lovers can live and dine in comfort and style—on 25 acres of vineyards and pine trees—without roughing it. The unique hotel is operated by Joao de Oliveira. Many discriminating guests know of this retreat, including Queen Elizabeth of England.

The bedrooms are in the grand style—and are part of the reason for staying here. All individually decorated, they are often furnished with dramatic antiques, such as carved and tufted headboards (some reaching up to the ceiling), spinet piano desks, and Queen Anne chairs. For full board in a room with private bath, two persons pay 750$ ($29.25) and 850$ ($33.15), depending on the size, quality, and placement of the room. Around the impressive building are chalets where guests such as Sir Anthony Eden have stayed. For two persons, the cost is only 800$ ($31.20) per day for one of the private suites and all meals (complete with a fireplace which the maid fills with logs every day in chilly weather).

The lounge-bar is a favorite, though there are many nooks and salons for conversation and rest. You can take your drinks in front of the wide granite fireplace, with its slow-burning chunks of pine root, or at the carved oak bar. Meals are served in the vast and impressive dining hall, lined with five palace-sized portraits of English kings. Even if it's only for a meal, you should stop over. The cost of a table d'hôte is 130$ ($5.07); the bread is made on the premises; some of the wine is made with grapes grown in the farm vineyards; and much of the fruit comes from the hotel's own orchards. Of course, the bowls of freshly picked flowers are brought in directly from the garden.

The Urgeiriça is a winner for relaxing tired nerves. The more athletic are drawn to the tennis court, the rough nine-hole golf course, and the swimming pool.

9. Viseu

The capital of Beira Alta province, Viseu is a quiet country town. But it is also a city of art treasures, palaces, and churches. Its local hero is an ancient Lusitanian rebel leader, Viriato. At the entrance of Viseu is the **Cova de Viriato,** where the rebel, a combination Spartacus and Robin Hood, made his camp and plotted the moves which turned back the Roman tide.

Some of the country's most gifted artisans ply their timeless trades in and around Viseu. Where racks creak and looms hum, the busy weaver women create the unique quilts and carpets of Vil de Moinhos. Local craftsmen of Molelos produce the region's provincial pottery, and women with nimble fingers embroider feather-fine, light bone-lace.

There is much to see and explore at random in Viseu: the cubistic network of tiled overlapping rooftops and entwining narrow alleyways; the encroaching macadam streets; the river where the women pound out the day's wash upon smooth flat stones in the clear water. However, if your time is limited, head at once to the **Ardo da Sé,** one of the most harmonious squares in Portugal, often referred to as the showplace of Viseu. There you'll find the town's three leading buildings: a cathedral, a museum, and a church.

The severe Renaissance facade of the **Viseu Cathedral** evokes a fortress. Two lofty bell towers—unadorned stone up to the balustraded summit with crowning cupolas—can be seen from almost any point in or approaching the town. The second-story windows at the facade—two rectangular and one oval—are latticed and symmetrically surrounded by niches containing religious statuary.

You can go first into the two-story Renaissance cloister on the right, adorned with classic pillars and arcades faced with azulejos. The interior of the Sé is basically Gothic, but is infused with Manueline and baroque decorations. Plain, slender Romanesque clusters of columns line the nave, supporting the vaulted Manueline ceiling with its nautically roped groining. The basic color scheme inside plays brilliant gilding against muted gold stone. However, the full emphasis is centered on the Roman arched chancel—climaxed by an elegantly carved retable above the main altar. The chancel makes ingenious use of color counterpoint, with copper, green gold, and brownish-yellow complementing the gilt work. The ceiling is continued in the sacristy.

Next door to the Cathedral is the **Museum of Grao Vasco**, named after the 16th-century painter, also known as Vasco Fernandes. The major works of this Portuguese master are displayed here, especially "La Pontecôte," with the lancetlike tongues of fire hurtling toward the saints—some devout, others apathetic.

Besides the works of this fine Portuguese primitive and his school of followers, the museum also has a moving and tender St. Raphael by the outstanding 18th-century sculptor Machado de Castro. Enameled reliquaries, Byzantine artifacts, liturgical apparel, a Manueline monstrance dating from 1533, and a chalice with vermeil pendants from 1626 are a few of the items on view.

Across the square from the Cathedral is the palatial **Misericórdia Church** from the 18th century. Its pristine facade contrasts with the Cathedral's baroque granite decorations, spirals, large windows and portal frames, balustrades, and matching towers.

In accommodations the town is well-equipped.

THE UPPER BRACKET: Grao Vasco (tel Viseu 235-11), in the heart of town and surrounded by gardens and parks, is built motel fashion, with the bedroom balconies overlooking the swimming pool. After days of driving in the hotel-lean environs, it's a pleasure to check into this top-grade, sophisticated establishment, more suited to a resort than a provincial town. Popular with both businessmen and socialites, it also attracts tourists, especially in the summer months. The decor is colorful contemporary and elegantly designed.

The bedrooms are usually large, utilizing the finest of Portuguese traditional furnishings, enhanced by flowering chintz and softly muted colors. With full board, the price for a double starts at 720$ ($28.08), goes up to 770$ ($30.03) for the better rooms, and peaks at 900$ ($35.10) in a suite. For a single, the full-board rate is from 410$ ($15.99) to 460$ ($17.94). The dining room has Mediterranean blue chairs, a baronial stone fireplace—plus an exceptional cuisine, with many international dishes. If you're just dropping in you can sample a four-course table d'hôte luncheon or dinner.

THE BUDGET RANGE: Hotel Avenida, 1 Avenida 28 de Maio (tel. 234-32), is a personalized small hotel right off the Rossio, the main plaza of town. Inside, it is the domain of the personable Mário Abrantes da Motto Veiga, who has combined his collection of antiques from Africa and China with pieces of fine old Portuguese furniture. He's created a friendly aura—bound to attract admirers of his eclectic taste. Each of the bedrooms varies in size, character, and price; and most of the 33 rooms have private shower or bath.

The nightly rate is 100$ ($3.90) to 195$ ($7.61) for one person; 150$ ($5.85) to 290$ ($11.31) for two. There's a nice room (210B) with a high coved bed and an old refectory table and chair, costing 300$ ($11.70) for two persons, including an adjoining chamber with a wooden spindle bed and a marble-topped chest, like a nun's retreat. There are a few economy doubles, with twin antique wooden beds, going for only 180$ ($7.02) nightly. Meals in the plain family-style dining room are well prepared and generous; a table d'hôte is priced at 110$ ($4.29) for a luncheon or dinner.

Estalagem Dom Duarte, 143 Rua 5 de Outubro (tel. 232-36), is a little villa at the edge of town, opening onto a tiny front garden. Here you can live in a Portuguese Hansel and Gretel atmosphere. The inn is owned and run by a white-haired woman (her reception clutter is a sight) who exudes hospitality. In reality you share her way of life, even if it's only for 24 hours. You may enjoy her personalized style: her collection of antiques, sculpture, paintings, plus good home cooking. The little drawing room is packed with old pieces, plus comfortable seats around a fireplace. The dining room has a coved wooden beamed ceiling, with painted wall plaques she rescued from an old chapel, and three carved ecclesiastical statues on wall sconces.

The hallways are lit by long decorative pole torchiers. The eight rooms, all with bath, are each one of a kind. Almost everything except the soft mattresses and the tiled baths are of another century: high wooden beds, dressers with brass handles, armchairs, and time-aged paintings. The cost for two with three meals is 410$ ($15.99) to 445$ ($17.26). One person's full pension is 215$ ($8.39) to 240$ ($9.36). The household staff is constantly turning down beds to air, waxing the parquet floors, or preparing meals. Unfortunately, no English is spoken, but the language of the smile works wonders. A meal in the pleasant restaurant is 85$ ($3.32).

10. Serra da Estrêla

From January to May, the great granite Serra da Estrêla is the winter sports center of Portugal. In summer, campers, trout fishermen, and mountain climbers dominate. Once almost completely isolated from the rest of the country, the major points of interest in the Serra da Estrêla are now linked by roads.

The land is also the home of the Cao de Sena, or "dog of the mountain." The area is a major sheep-raising district as well and is infested with wild animals, especially packs of wolves. Reader A. Wayne Magnitzky writes: "The throats of the sheep dogs are protected from the teeth of wolves by an iron collar with long sharp spikes. Imagine the wolf's surprise when he attempts to throttle the dog and ends up with a long spike through his mouth!" The dogs survive by sucking ewes' milk.

One major auto route is from Covilhà to Seia via **Torre,** the latter the tallest point in Portugal, at an altitude of 6,500 feet. From its summit, a panoramic view unfolds.

Covilhà is on the southern flank of the Serra, near the Zêzere Valley. A town of steep and narrow streets, it is known for its Monument to Our Lady of the Conception, a 25-foot statue of the Virgin Mary carved out of granite. Steps also carved out of granite lead to the statue. The sculptor was killed near this spot in a car accident, shortly after completing his work. The town is at its liveliest from June 22 to 25 when people from the neighboring hills come in for the Fair of Sao Tiago, and sell handicrafts.

Covilhà used to be known as the "dormitory" for the **Penhas da Saude** sports area, at 4,500 feet above sea level.

Now Penhas da Saude has the most attractive hotel in the district, the **Hotel Serra da Estrêla** (tel. 223-94). Handwoven fabrics, a copper-hooded fireplace (around which skiers gather in winter), modern paintings, and warm, natural colors—all these elements combine to create an outstanding first-class hotel in a remote district. A single room with breakfast rents for 261$ ($10.18), increasing to 387$ ($15.09) in a double. Even more expensive suites are available. The food is the finest in the district. A complete meal costs 125$ ($4.88). Although international dishes are offered, you may want to sample some of the regional specialties, especially the rabbit. Of course, the proper finish for any meal is the queijo da Serra, a strong cheese made from ewe's milk.

Instead of continuing to Seia, an alternate route is to go along the Rio Zêzere to **Manteigas,** a little town with several balconied 17th-century houses. It lies between mountain ranges. From there you can take an excursion to the **Poço do Inferno,** or "Hell's Mouth." This is a gorge with waterfalls. The distance from Manteigas along an unsurfaced and narrow road is about four miles.

Near Manteigas the government runs a pousada, the **Pousada de Sao Lourenço** (tel. 471-50), a stone inn at an altitude of 5,000 feet. It lies nine miles to the north of Manteigas, two miles from Penhas Douradas, and 15 miles to the south of Gouveia. Rooms are comfortably rustic. A double with bath costs 220$ ($8.58), with an additional 25$ (98¢) charged for breakfast. If you're stopping over, you can order a country-style dinner for 100$ ($3.90).

11. Castelo Branco

The capital of Beira Baixa, Castelo Branco lies near the Spanish frontier. The city is beautiful and often filled with flowers. Shoppers may want to acquire some of the multi-colored embroidery done by the women of the town. Some of the designs haven't been changed since the 17th century.

The gardens of the former Bishop's Palace are well kept and formal, with a statue-bedecked staircase, clipped box hedges, and numerous fountains. The statues are life sized, depicting the Apostles, the kings of Portugal, as well as signs of the Zodiac.

Adjacent are the ruins of a Moorish castle, rebuilt in the time of King Dinis.

The town takes about an hour to explore. Most motorists seem to stop just for a look at the gardens, then continue on to Abrantes.

12. Abrantes

After passing a dramatic view of the Tagus at Rodao, you arrive at Abrantes in central Portugal. The river must be crossed again to gain entrance to the town. Here, you see the ruins of a Roman bridge extending into the Tagus.

High on a hill, the old fortress was rebuilt during the reign of King Dinis. To reach the fortifications, you must go through a labyrinth of narrow streets. Once at its belvedere, a panoramic view of the valley unfolds.

The **Hotel do Turismo** (tel. 256) overlooks the town on one side and the castle and the mountains on the other. An olympic-sized pool, belonging to the town but available at no charge to hotel guests, is adjacent to the Turismo. Room rates depend on location and view. Including breakfast, prices range from 130$ ($5.07) to 320$ ($12.48). The half-pension range is from 265$ ($10.34) to 590$ ($23.01) for two persons. Reader A. Wayne Magnitzky writes, "This hotel serves the best bread I've eaten anywhere, certainly in Portugal." A complete meal is offered for 120$ ($4.68).

After this excursion into provincialism, a return to the atmosphere of a minor metropolis seems in order. Although Lisbon is the capital, denizens of Porto claim their hometown is the first city, the backbone of the country.

Chapter XIV

PORTO AND ITS ENVIRONS

1. The Hotels
2. Where to Dine
3. What to See and Do
4. Exploring the Coast
5. Deep in the Environs

PORTUGAL'S SECOND CITY, Porto, is the home of port wine—traditionally drunk in tulip-shaped glasses. The grapes that produce the wine come from the vineyards along the arid slopes of the Douro River Valley, many miles inland. At harvest time in autumn, the hills are alive with the trilling of flutes, the cadence of drums.

The wine is brought to lodges at **Vila Nora de Gaia,** across the river from Porto, where it is blended, aged, and processed. In the past it was transported on flat-bottomed boats called barcos rabelos. With their long trailing rudders and sails flapping in the breeze, these boats with tails skirted down the Douro like swallows. Nowadays, they have virtually given way to the unglamorous train or even the truck.

Porto not only gave its name to port wine, but to the country itself—the word deriving from the old settlement of Portus Cale, which became Portugal. The Douro—from Rio do Ouro, or river of gold—has always been the source of Porto's life blood. Though it enjoys many sunny days, at times Porto has been called a gray city of mist and rain.

It's set on a rocky gorge that the Douro cut out of a great stone mass. Of it, Ann Bridge wrote, "The whole thing looks like a singularly dangerous spider's web flung across space." Porto is most interesting in the old quarter, the **Alfândega.** Here the steep narrow streets—hardly big enough for a car to pass through—and the balconied houses evoke Lisbon's Alfama, though the quarter has its own distinctive character. The Alfândega preserves the timeless color of many of the old buildings and cobbled ruas lining the river bank.

Connecting the right bank to the port wine center of Vila Nova de Gaia and the lands south, is the **Maria Pia Bridge,** an architectural feat of Eiffel, completed in 1877. Two other bridges span the Douro, including the **Dom Luís I Bridge,** completed in 1866 by a Belgian engineer inspired by Eiffel. The other one is bright and contemporary, the **Arrábida Bridge,** totally Portuguese in concept and execution and one of the largest single-span reinforced concrete arches in Europe.

Many write off Porto as an industrial city with some spectacular bridges, but that assessment is unfair. The provincial capital and university seat sits on the cover of its own artistic treasure chest, as we will soon see.

GETTING THERE FROM LISBON: At a distance of 175 miles from Lisbon, Porto is easily reached by train. TAP, the Portuguese airline, provides quicker connections between the two cities as well. There are daily flights year round.

1. The Hotels

There has long been a lack of top-rate accommodations in this, the capital of the north. Some so-called first-class hotels can only be recommended in the direst of emergencies. However, for the 1970s, the outlook was brightened considerably by the following new topnotch establishments.

THE UPPER BRACKET: Dom Henrique, 179 Rua Guedes de Azevedo (tel. 257-55), is the biggest hotel in town. Eighteen stories high, and containing 102 rooms, this octagonal-shaped colossus towers over the whole city and provides some spectacular views from its 16th floor bar-lounge and 15th floor dining room. The decor, modern to the hilt, is somewhat impersonal and cold. The rooms are plastic and wood, all with terraces, rather narrow beds and white furniture. What the hotel lacks in style it makes up for in modern conveniences. Somewhat away from the center, the Dom Henrique charges anywhere from 330$ ($12.87) to 450$ ($17.55) for a single room, from 410$ ($15.99) to 605$ ($23.60) for a double. Meals are à la carte, and breakfast is an additional 35$ ($1.37). Clinton Gamble, Fort Lauderdale, Fla., writes: "Nowhere in Portugal will you find more kind personal attention and service."

Infante de Sagres, Praça D. Filipa de Lencastre (tel. 281-01), will coddle you in Edwardian comfort. Catering to those who prefer the glamorous old style, it gives its clients a chance to savor brass beds, crystal chandeliers, and personalized service. The reception lounge sets the pace, with its two-story-high stained glass window and baronial staircase. Done in oak, the main level bar is small enough to be intimate, large enough to be comfortable.

Breakfast is served in an Adam-style room, with ornate plaster work and shellback chairs. Dining in the main room is recommended, even if you aren't staying here. The large room is in the formal French tradition, with shimmering crystal, wood paneling, and service that is right in every detail. The food—both regional and international dishes—is among the best in the city; a complete luncheon or dinner goes for 200$ ($7.80) per person unless you order à la carte.

The bedrooms were created for large-scale living, a world of hand-loomed rugs, 19th-century furniture, and elaborate marble baths. The average double room rents for 550$ ($21.45) per person, increasing to 660$ ($25.74) in a deluxe double. In all cases single occupancy costs 30 percent less.

THE MEDIUM-PRICED RANGE: Albergaria Miradouro, 598 Rua da Alegria (tel. 278-51), is like an eagle's nest, a slim 13-floor baby skyscraper built atop a hill outside the main part of the city. One of the newest hotels on the city's skyline, the Miradouro offers vista-scanning rooms (you can watch ships laden with port making their way to the open sea). Though small-scaled, the public rooms are tasteful, even dramatic. The lower bar, with its red velvet chairs, is decorated with wall tiles from Japan and Portugal. Two plush elevators whisk you to an upper bar, with walls opening onto a view, gold glass curtains, mosaic decorations, and fire engine red carpeting. The top-floor restaurant is fine enough to be featured separately in the dining recommendations detailed below.

The bedrooms are without fault. Even the most fastidious traveler usually responds to the streamlined style. The more expensive corner rooms are preferred, of course. In these two walls have built-in wardrobes and chests (with a built-in pair of beds); the others are all glass, curtained with filmy draperies. In all the rooms, you'll find a vestibule, abundant luggage storage, a valet stand, desk, and sitting room. Bright colors are used without hesitation: golds, blues, and burnt orange. There are 30 rooms, all with private baths. One person pays from 200$ ($7.80) to 370$ ($14.43); two persons, 370$ ($14.43) to 410$ ($15.99). Breakfast only is served for 30$ ($1.17). The facilities include a subterranean garage.

Hotel Castor, 17 Rua das Doze Casas (tel. 286-91), is a personal statement—and a fine one. Maurício Macedo and his son have created a cultured, comfortable world, to be savored by those who enjoy individuality with style. The son, Doctor Francisco Macedo, is an enterprising decorator, managing one of the better antique stores in the north around the corner from his hotel. The hotel siphons off many of his best pieces, used well in the reception and lounge areas. In fact, the Castor is a glorified antique store, as every piece is for sale. In addition, a large salon has been set aside as an art gallery for contemporary painters, the artist contributing a painting for having been granted the premises.

The bedrooms have ornate antique or reproduction beds, original paintings, old mirrors, hand-screened printed fabrics covering the walls, centrally controlled heating, and individual chimes for the maid. There are 62 rooms, all with baths, designed with tiled walls. Singles range from 250$ ($9.75) to 315$ ($12.29); doubles go for anywhere from 390$ ($15.21) to 490$ ($19.11). Breakfast is included.

Meals are well prepared by a talented cook who runs the kitchen like an artist. Dining is festive: you sit in red, high-backed Queen Anne chairs, enjoying delicious dishes and personal service, for 150$ ($5.85). Pre-dinner drinks are available in the stone-walled bar, with its troubador theme. The Castor has a discotheque in modern decor, and its own garage.

Hotel S. Joao, 120 Rua do Bonjardim (tel. 216-62), is in a class by itself: the only hotel-residência of its type to be rated deluxe by the government. Such a designation shows what deep imprint human warmth can make upon a limited framework, especially when the owners have a high taste level, a certain flair, plus a concern for the welfare of their guests. Accomplishing this is the Baldaque family, who have worked miracles with the top floor of a modern building right in the heart of Porto. You ascend in an elevator and are greeted by a friendly receptionist.

The living room is inviting with its fireplace nook, deep sofa and antiques, such as a grandfather's clock. The main corridor leading to the bedrooms is like an art gallery, with old tapestries, high-backed 18th-century chairs, engravings, and large copper bowls of flowers. The bedrooms—only 14 in all, each a double—combine modern with traditional furnishings, reserving a section for a sitting area. Every room contains its own pink and white marble bath. The tariffs are based on size and outlook. One person pays 200$ ($7.80) to 285$ ($11.12); two, 285$ ($11.12) to 400$ ($15.60). Breakfast is the only meal provided, costing 35$ ($1.37).

THE BUDGET RANGE: Grande Hotel do Porto, 187 Rua Santa Catarina (tel. 281-76), is an older hotel, right in the heart of the shopping section, offering comparatively low rates. It has been given a face-lift, and now contains 100 bedrooms, each with bath and central heating.

Best of all are the brightly painted rooms—all modern, with many built-in tables. A single rents for 210$ ($8.19) to 235$ ($9.17). Depending on size and facilities, doubles are priced at 310$ ($12.09) to 345$ ($13.46). A suite costs 600$ ($23.40). Breakfast is included.

Many Portuguese families are attracted here, drawn by the low tariffs and near grandeur. Along the main corridor lounge, with its row of marble pillars and crystal chandeliers, are small lounges. At one end is a modern bar, most intimate with stained-glass windows and black leather booths. There's a fine old-world dining room with four chandeliers, a mosaic wooden floor, and ornate curtains, where an à la carte meal will cost about 130$ ($5.07). A private garage is nearby.

READERS' SELECTIONS: "**Porto-Mar,** 167 Rua Brito Capelo, in Matosinhos, is a good place to stay. Matosinhos is the sardine capital of the world and only a streetcar ride away from the railway stations in Porto. We paid 180$ ($7.02) for double with bath, which included a large room with a view of the Leixoes harbor and the ocean. Meals were copious and good, served in a huge dining room for about $6.50 (U.S.) for two, including wines. The large public market is nearby and a treat to visit, with its flowers, live chickens, fish, and other items" (Mrs. Marie Bockerdorff, Ottawa, Canada).... "I stayed at the **Pensao de Açucar,** 262 Rua do Almada, which was very reasonable. I had a small bathless single, very clean, with a wash basin and Venetian blinds at the windows, for 75$ ($2.93), including taxes and service. Larger singles were 95$ ($3.71), and most had baths for those requiring them. French is spoken by the personnel, and a simple but good continental breakfast is served for 15$ (59¢)" (J. Barrie Jones, Paulersbury, Northamptonshire, England)."

2. Where to Dine

When Prince Henry the Navigator was rounding up the cattle in the Douro Valley for his men aboard the legendary caravels, he shipped out the juicy steaks and left the tripe behind. Faced with the stuff, the denizens of Porto responded bravely and began inventing recipes for it. To this day, they carry the appellation of tripe eaters—and it has become their favorite local dish. To sample the most characteristic specialty of Porto, you can order tripas à moda do Porto (tripe stewed with spicy sausage and string beans). Of course, the city offers other viands—and quite good ones at that—at any of the following recommendations:

AN ELEGANT TAVERN RESTAURANT: Restaurante Escondidinho, 144 Rua de Passos Manuel (tel. 210-79), is an elegant regional-style tavern, popular with the leading port wine merchants and the English. The name means hidden or masked. The entrance alone is a clue, a facade in burnt orange tile framing an arch leading to the L-shaped dining room.

Inside, it's a world of time-blackened beams and timbers, a corner baronial stone fireplace, and carved wooden shelf brackets holding a collection of antique Portuguese ceramics. The chairs are just right for a cardinal, or at least a friar, with their intricate carving and brass studs. The waiters are old-world, yet proud of the prevailing informality. They feel free to speak their mind, candidly telling you the day's best dishes from the kitchen. Take their word.

The shellfish soup at 20$ (78¢) and the charcoaled sardines for 35$ ($1.37) are always reliable. The chef's special dishes include grilled jumbo shrimp, 110$ ($4.29); lobster, 200$ ($7.80); hake in Madeira sauce, 60$ ($2.34); and châteaubriand for two, 187$ ($7.29). A main course might be augmented by a tomato salad at 23$ (90¢). Desserts include a rum omelette for 60$ ($2.34) or a simple orange pudding at 20$ (78¢). Telephone for reservations; closed Sunday.

ROOFTOP DINING: Portucale Restaurante, 598 Rua da Alegria (tel. 278-61), perches on the rooftop of the Albergaria Miradouro. Seemingly on the highest point in town—outside the heart of the city—it offers wide views of the river, the boats, and rooftops. Two elevators zip you to the 13th floor, from which you ascend to the dining room via a spiral staircase, crossing a tiny lily and fish pond. Despite the infinity of the panoramic sweep, the restaurant is fairly intimate, with tables set with fine silver, china, and flowers. There's an appetizing pastry cart.

The handwoven hanging is by Camarinha, the artist who designed the à la carte menu. Specialties of the house include bacalhau (dried codfish) a marinheiro, 88$ ($3.43); cabrita à serrana (kid in wine sauce), also 88$; smoked swordfish, 78$ ($3.04); lomos do pescado, 96$ ($3.74); steak flambé, rice, and mushrooms, 98$ ($3.82); and homemade cakes, 29$ ($1.13).

A CHINESE RESTAURANT: Restaurante Chinês, 38 Avenida Vimara Peres (tel. 289-15), is Porto's leading Chinese restaurant. Housed in a modern building at the entrance to Dom Luís I Bridge, it is an incongruous combination of the new and the old. Setting the mood are traditional Chinese lanterns, three wide bamboo fans, and a dragon mural. In the spacious two-level dining room, soft music is played in the background, a good complement to the authentic dishes.

Appetizers include egg flower soup, 18$ (70¢); fried wonton, 35$ ($1.37); and fried almonds, 20$ (78¢). Main courses (which can be shared) include stewed carp in soybean sauce, 70$ ($2.73); sweet and sour meatballs, 72$ ($2.81); duckling with pineapple, 80$ ($3.12). The price of fried prawns varies according to the time of year. For dessert, there are many appetizing choices, such as fried bananas with hóney for 15$ (59¢).

SEAFOOD SPECIALTIES: Aquário Marisqueiro, 163 Rua Rodrigues Sampaio (tel. 222-31), is one of the finest seafood restaurants in Porto—actually, two, connected by a central kitchen. Its location is within sight of the City Hall, and close to either of two leading hotels: the Infante de Sagres and the Albergaria de S. Joao.

Marine fare reigns supreme at this "aquarium." Soup made from boiling the shells of mariscos is a good beginner for 14$ (55¢). Main fish orders include cod at 50$ ($1.95). An excellent fish dish is clams in the Spanish style, but the house specialty is an açorda (a type of bread panada) of shellfish. The prices of these two dishes vary according to the season. Sole costs 45$ ($1.76), and trout with ham, 48$ ($1.87). Closed Sundays.

Garrafao, Rua Antonio Nobre (tel. 93-06-93), one of the newer restaurants in town, overlooks the Praia Boa Nova. Attractively situated, with a pleasant decor, it seats about 100 and serves mainly seafood. The price of the seafood specialties varies according to the season. The Garrafao is becoming known for its large selection of good wines, also. The daily menu goes for 100$ ($3.90) and includes a four-course meal. À la carte specialties feature a shrimp omelette for 40$ ($1.56); fish soup for 20$ (78¢); trout, 65$ ($2.54); veal cutlets, 70$ ($2.73); and cassata ice cream for 12$ (47¢). The restaurant has a cozy, pleasant dining room with a nautical decor.

Neptuno, 133 Rua Rodrigues Sampaio (tel. 279-37), as its name indicates, specializes in seafood, though all other dishes are delicious as well. The decor is simple and modern, with white walls, and fruit on the counter. Non-fish specialties are the bife na frigideira, 75$ ($2.93); veal scallopine, 75$ ($2.93); chicken with ham, 50$ ($1.95); and tripe Portuguese style, 60$ ($2.34). Try the shellfish soup for 12$ (47¢), and, more expensive, the lobsters, shrimp, and clams. Desserts include a soufflé with kirsch or rum 30$ ($1.17), or a rum omelette, 35$ ($1.37).

THE BUDGET RANGE: Tres Irmaos, 101 Bomjardim, is a small, popular, economic restaurant in the heart of Porto. The owner serves up an excellent tomato soup for 14$ (55¢), shellfish rice, 90$ ($3.51); and lulas fritas (fried fish), 56$ ($2.18). Meat dishes include a medallion de carne (choice cut steak), 50$ ($1.95). Finish with a fruit salad for 18$ (70¢). The place is clean, simple, and the service is good.

DELUXE DINING IN THE ENVIRONS: The **Restaurante Boa Nova**, Leça de Palmeira, is built along the northern coast on the outskirts of the city—right on the rocks within sound and smell of the ocean surf. Leça de Palmeira lies about 1½ miles beyond the fishing village of Matosinhos. Erected in 1963—and perhaps inspired by Frank Lloyd Wright—the restaurant is lodged into a rocky cliff, its heavy wooden ceiling thrust out for a view of the sea.

You descend an open staircase to the preferred tables near the fireplace, where logs burn slowly on chilly days and evenings. You dine on modern leather and wood chairs, the mood properly set when a waiter places a plate of whole-grained homemade bread on the table to accompany your soup. Dinner might begin with cream of shellfish soup at 14$ (55¢), then move to bacalhau (codfish) à Zé do Pipo, 40$ ($1.56). Among the meat dishes, the specialty of the house is beef Boa Nova—cooked rare, smothered with mushrooms, and surrounded by spiral potatoes—costing 115$ ($4.49). A mixed salad goes for 35$ ($1.37) and a good ending is the orange soufflé, 80$ ($3.12) for two persons. Otherwise go just for drinks and sit in the cocktail lounge jutting out over the ocean.

Driving out, you shouldn't be put off by the industrial blight. Once you near the area, in the vicinity of the lighthouse, manufacturing will be behind you.

READER'S SELECTION: "I would like to suggest a restaurant in Porto. This small, dimly lit, warm place is nestled in, right on the riverfront overlooking the water and the port wine lodges on the other side. The **Taverna do Bebobos**, 24 Cais da Ribeira (tel. 313-565), is housed in one of the oldest stone buildings, which has undergone a tasteful, light-handed renovation. The à la carte menu is quite complete, with a whole spectrum of Portuguese fare—all hearty, well-flavored and served in generous amounts. A complete three-course meal goes for less than 100$ ($3.90) per person, including wine. A full bar is also available. Dinners are served on heavy crockery, and the patrons sit on high-backed leather chairs. Clearly this was one of the best places in Portugal for beautiful food" (Suzanne Dixon, Cambridge, Mass.).

3. What to See and Do

Exploring the sights of Porto requires some probing. But your discoveries will compensate for the effort. A good beginning is—

THE CATHEDRAL DISTRICT: The **Sé (Cathedral)**, at the Terreiro de Sé, has grown and changed with the city—that is, until about the 18th century. Originally founded by a medieval queen and designed in a foreboding, basically Romanesque style, it is now a patchwork-quilt monument to changing architectural tastes. Part of the twin towers, the rose window, the naves, and the vestry are all elements of the original 13th-century structure. However, the austere Gothic cloister was added at the end of the 14th century, and was later decorated with azulejos depicting events from the Song of Solomon. Opening off the cloister is the interesting Chapel of St. Vincent, built in the closing years of the 16th century.

The main chapel was erected in the 17th century; and in 1736, the baroque architect Nicolo Nasoni of Italy added the north facade and its attractive loggia. The monumental altar is flanked by twisted columns, the nave by fading frescoes. In the small baroque Chapel of the Holy Sacrament (to the left of the main altar) is an altarpiece fashioned entirely of silver—the work so elaborate that the whole piece gives the illusion of constant movement.

Outside on the Cathedral Square is a Manueline-styled pillory and a statue of Vimara Peres, the warrior of Afonso III of León, who captured ancient Portucale in 868. To the side, also on the same square, is the 18th-century **Archbishop's Palace**, sequestered for municipal offices. Noted for its granite-cased doors and windows, it also contains an exceptional stairway inside.

In back of the Cathedral is one of the most charming típico streets of Porto: the **Rua da Dom Hugo**. Along its route, you'll pass the **Chapel of Our Lady of Truths**. It's invariably closed, but you can peek through the grill work at the gilded rococo altar, with a statue of the Virgin at the center.

Down the same street, you'll reach the **Casa Museu de Guerra Junqueiro**. This famous Portuguese poet lived between 1850 and 1923. The house was built by the Italian architect Nicolo Nasoni (1691-1773). Each room is arranged to preserve the private art collection and memorabilia of Guerra Junqueiro.

The collection includes Georgian and Portuguese silver, Flemish chests, Italian, Oriental, Spanish, and Portuguese ceramics, and ecclesiastical wood and stone carvings. Joining the many examples of religious sculpture are an Italian Renaissance desk, metal plates said to have been made in Nürnberg, a 16th-century Brussels tapestry, as well as interesting Portuguese furniture.

Casa Museu de Guerra Junqueiro is open every day except Monday from 10 a.m. to 5 p.m. Admission is free.

In the same district, you can cross the busy artery, the Avenida Dom Afonso Henriques, and head down the Rua Saravia de Carvalho until you reach the Largo de 1 de Dezembro and—

The Church of Santa Clara: Although completed in 1416, the interior was transformed by the impassioned artists of the 17th century, masters of woodwork and gilding. The facade remains squat and plain, however. The number of man hours invested is staggering to contemplate. There is hardly a square inch that isn't covered with angels, saints, cherubs, patterned designs, and great knobbed bosses. All this dripping gilt is an architectural scramble of rococo and baroque—one of the most exceptional examples in Portugal. The clerestory windows permit the sunlight to flood in, making a golden crown of the upper regions.

If the keeper of the keys takes a liking to you, he'll take you on a behind-the-scenes tour of the precincts. In the Tribute Room, for example, you'll see a devil carved on the choir stalls. Through it all is a hodgepodge of a lot of bad, fading paintings, some not even hung—just propped casually in the corner. But it's intriguing to see what lies beyond all the glitter and glamor out front.

Sights Near the Cathedral

Passing along the water, you can look for a front row of buildings along the **Rua Nova da Alfândega**. Underneath these structures is an arcade that is a continuous row of Romanesque arches. Perhaps they faced the waterfront until the street was built at a high level like a dike.

Up from this major artery is one of the most colorful sectors of Porto. If time allows, it's good to wander through some of the back streets (often stepped), where the city's poorest people live. In other places, the area might be called a slum or ghetto, but in Porto, the district has such style—vegetable- and meat-stuffed arcaded markets, churches, museums, monuments, even such elegant buildings as the Stock Exchange and the British Factory—that it retains both punch and glamor.

A good point to begin your exploration is on the main **Praça do Infante Dom Henriques**, named after the Porto-born Henry the Navigator, who launched Portugal on its Age of Discovery. At this square, you can visit the big covered food market, where tripe is sold in great quantities.

Facing the square (entrance on the Rua da Bolsa) is the **Stock Exchange,** housed in the imposing 19th-century Palácio da Bolsa. It is known for its Moorish Hall, a much modified pastiche resembling a room in the Alhambra at Granada. The walls, ceiling, and balcony are a gilded mass of patterns and geometrical configurations. The pastel blue column bases glow in sunlight filtered through intricately latticed octagonal skylights and floral side windows.

The **Basilica of St. Francis,** reached by steps up from the waterfront and opening onto the Rua da San Francisco, was built in the Gothic style between 1383 and 1410. But in the 17th and 18th centuries it underwent extensive rococo dressing. The vault pillars and columns are lined with gilded woodwork: cherubs, garlands of roses, cornucopia of fruit, and frenzied animals, entwined and dripping with gold. Many of the wide-ribbed Gothic arches are made of marble resembling the Italian forest green serpentine variety. The marble almost seems to fade into an easy blending with the gray granite columns and floors.

The Romanesque rosette dominates the facade, whose square portal is flanked by double twisted columns. Above the columns, a profusely ornamented niche contains a simple white statue of the patron saint. In the rose window, 12 mullions emanate from the central circle in apostolic symbolism, ending in a swaglike stone fringe. The steps seem to spill out into the square fanlike along the base of the curved walls.

Next door you can visit the **Museum of St. Francis.** An odor of death hangs over this place—and little wonder. The sacristan estimates that 30,000 human skulls have been interred in the cellars since the 14th century. Even assuming that he may be exaggerating, this dank building was once the burial ground for rich or poor. Nowadays, it can't decide what its purpose is: museum, church, or mausoleum.

A section of it looks like an antique shop filled with ecclesiastical statuary. There are paintings, too, one of St. Francis of Assisi worshipping Christ on the Cross. Oddities include some of the first paper money printed in Portugal and a 17th-century ambulance that was really a sedan chair. The Sala de Sessoes adds a note of unexpected elegance—built in the rich baroque style, it is now a meeting hall with a Louis XIV table and Joao V chairs. Wherever you go in the room, the painted eyes of framed bishops follow you, like Big Brother watching. The museum charges only 2$ (8¢) for admission (but tip the guide), and is open from 10 a.m. to noon and from 2-5 p.m. daily, except Monday.

Also reached by steps up from the water is one of the city's leading museums, sheltered on a típico square and rarely visited. Culture seekers are usually beset with escudo-hungry children who live in the jumble of dwellings nearby.

Museum of Ethnography and History of Douro Litoral, Largo S. Joao Novo, celebrates the arts, handicrafts, and culture of the Douro River valley. It's a rustic potpourri of spinning wheels, looms, animal and fish traps nostalgically evoking the simple lifestyle of the peasant. Roman coins and other artifacts remind one that legions from far afield once marched in and settled on the banks of the river.

Earthenware jugs from Vita-da-Feira, gold filigree work, a bas relief of a provincial cottage, and a three-faced Christ are among the exhibits, along with primitive puppets, provincial bedrooms, ceramics, dolls in regional costume, ship models, decorative ox yokes, weathervanes, cannon balls, spears, antique sarcophagi, even a wine press. Any or all of the above may be viewed from 10 a.m. to noon and from 2-5 p.m. daily, except Monday, for a 5$ (20¢) admission.

THE TOP MUSEUM: The **Soares dos Reis National Museum,** Rua de Dom Manuel II, offers salon after salon of "antique" contemporary art. The museum takes its name from the sculptor, Soares dos Reis (1847-1889), a neoclassic artist in pursuit of the ideal. His most interesting work is an undraped Christ in death. One of his nudes could have found a niche in ancient Greece, and no one would have known the difference. The most important sculptor exhibited is Teixeira Lopes, who was born in Porto in 1866 (look for his bust of Amélia, the last Queen of Portugal). More remarkable, however, is his marble of "Cain the Youth."

There are numerous paintings, including a lusty 16th-century work of Susanna at her bath, as provocative as ever. Also displayed are numerous works by Jean Pillement, and other works by such Portuguese artists as Columbano (see his portrait of the poet, Guerra Junqueiro), Carlos Reis, and Sousa Pinto. You'll also find exhibits of ceramics, gold and silverwork, gilded mirrors, vestments, screens, glassware, and furniture.

The museum is open daily, except Monday, from 10 a.m. to 5 p.m., charging an admission of 5$ (20¢), except on entrance-free Thursdays and Sundays.

WHERE PORT IS KING: Across the river from Porto, in **Vila Nova de Gaia,** are the port wine lodges. Like the sherry makers at Jerez de la Frontera, Spain, the establishments are hospitable, inviting guests to tour their precincts.

The largest of these lodges, the **Real Vinícola,** is a prime example of the art of wine making. It is here that the blending, aging, and selection processes take place. Dating from 1889, the warehouses contain specially treated oaken vats where the wine is sterilized, pasteurized, blended, and aged. The wine is bolstered with brandies and vintage wines to maintain its characters.

The vast cellars—dark, cool, and moist—are the resting place for port which ranges in age from five to 70 years. However, the oldest bottle in the company's museum is dated 1765. In one tunnel section alone there are two million bottles of Portuguese sparkling wines.

If you wish to learn the intricacies of production and development of port wine—from tasting to decanting—arrive and announce yourself. You'll be guided through the cask- and vat-lined cellars and tunnels and into the laboratories. If you can resist breaking away to tap a keg, there's a free sample of port—matured for 25 years—at the end of the tour. You can purchase wicker baskets packed with fine wine at the company tavern.

OTHER SIGHTS: There are many other monuments and sights worth exploring in Porto, especially the 18th-century **Torre dos Clérigos,** the landmark tower of the city, rising to a height of nearly 250 feet (it can be scaled for a fee of 12$50). The tallest tower in Portugal, it was designed by an Italian named Nicolo Nasoni. From its summit, there's a view of the Douro River, the valley gorge, and the far reaches of the city.

PORTO AFTER DARK: The real fado is in Lisbon, but Porto does offer a club or two where you can hear these typical songs and listen to guitar music. Perhaps the best is **Arcadas Dom Vaz,** 167 Rua de Miragaia (tel. 38-07-37), right on the waterfront in a slummy part of town.

While in Porto, you shouldn't miss having coffee in one of the old-time "Brazilian" cafes. Our favorite is the **Majestic Cafe,** 120 Rua de Santa Catarina, one of those ornate places where burghers and poets congregated. It still oozes charm. The wood-and-mirror decor, jasper pillars, and sculpted cherubs over pilasters are eye-openers. Rows of leather-backed sofas line both sides of the oblong room, in front of which two rows of round-topped tables stand. In the rear is a small garden and a counter where coffee is prepared in the old way. A coffee with milk is served in a large glass placed within a bronze holder, so you won't burn your fingers. The polite waiters are dressed in maroon jackets and wear bow ties. The wood-carved decorations are reminiscent of choir stalls in a cathedral. The cafe was opened in 1922 and is still going strong. The cost of a coffee and milk is only 6$50 (25¢). A small black coffee goes for 2$50 (10¢).

BEACHING IT: The bristling fishing village of **Matosinhos** is little more than a suburb of Porto. Separated by rocky crags, its beaches are becoming more popular with visitors who enjoy the pleasures of a seaside resort mixed with the sightseeing attractions and shopping activities of a big city nearby. Part of it sadly marred by industrial blight, Matosinhos lies but six miles north of Porto.

A much more interesting beach excursion is to the fishing village of **Espinho,** only 12 miles south of Porto, and rapidly growing into a modern beach resort. The town boasts many activities: a big gray casino with gaming tables, diverse shops, swimming pools, tennis courts, an 18-hole golf course, and wooded camping sites—plus a wide sandy beach skirted by a seaside esplanade.

Although frequented by sun-seeking families from Porto in summer, it can look like a ghost town off season. If you're based in Porto and venture down for a day at the beach, you can order a good and filling regional luncheon at the **Hotel Mar Azul,** Avenida 8 (it opens onto the railroad tracks). The total cost is 85$ ($3.32) for a complete meal.

4. Exploring the Coast

An underrated stretch of coastal resorts and fishing villages lies between Porto and the southern reaches of the Minho district. The Atlantic waters, however, are likely to be on the chilly side, even in July and August. The communities along this northern highway of the sun are small—ideal spots for those desiring a sequestered beach target. In some of these places, North Americans are still viewed with curiosity—but welcomed warmly. Out first stopover is at . . .

VILA DO CONDE: Along the wharfs of the Ave River stand piles of rough hand-hewn timbers used in the building of the sardine fleet. Barefoot women repair the fish nets which hang suspended in the sun; and racks of cod dry salty and stiff. Not much has changed in Vila do Conde—that is, until recently. Now, its fortress-guarded sandy beaches, rocky reefs, and charm are being discovered.

If you arrive for lunch, you might stop off at the nicely situated dining room of the **Hotel Palácio,** Avenida Bento de Freitas (tel. 634-03). Rated first-class, the salmon-pink hotel faces a large square, and is open all year. The charge for a table d'hôte luncheon or dinner is 100$ ($3.90).

For sights, a large squat structure sits fortress-like on a hill. It is the **Santa Clara Convent,** founded in the 14th century. In the upper rooms you can see relics and paintings garnered through the centuries by the Poor Clares. Simplicity and opulence play against each other in a combination of Gothic and Romanesque styles. The plain altar offers contrast to the gilded stalls behind the communion grilles and the ornately decorated ceilings. The church also contains two 14th-century sarcophagi: one elaborately carved tomb, depicting the founder of the monastery, his feet resting on a lion; the other the coffin of the first duchess of Braganza. From the grounds, you can see an 18th-century aqueduct, utilizing 999 arches to carry spring water to the precincts.

Just 17 miles from Porto, Vila do Conde is served by a modern, convenient highway.

PORVO DE VARZIM: In the small intimate cafes of this town, beneath ornate roofs and gables, skimpily clad tourists idyllically take their afternoon glass of port wine (some have several!). Seemingly unaware of them, the pescadores (fishermen) of the bustling fishing village go on with their work. Franz Villier wrote: "Here the boat-owners are kings, and morality reigns. Drunkards and debauchees may not aspire to the honour of fishing, unless it happens that the owner is one himself."

Dotting the beach are white canvas tents known as toldo, which are suspended on two poles. Many bathers prefer to swim in the warmer waters of the olympic-sized pool. In days of yore, a fortress dominated the coastline. Nowadays, a neoclassic-style **Casino** does, drawing visitors from Porto, 19 miles away. In summer the Casino offers dancing to an orchestra and, of course, gaming tables.

If you're just passing through, seek out the **Grande Hotel,** on the Passeio Alegre, where you can order a table d'hôte meal for 75$ ($2.93).

OFIR AND FAO: Once through the pine forests of **Ofir,** you gaze down on a long white sandy spit dotted with wind-swept dunes and suffused with the sharp cries of seagulls. Imagine a pure unspoiled Cape Cod. The beach is dramatic any time of the year, but exceptional during the summer months. Ofir is considered by many as the best beach resort between Porto and Viana do Castelo. The "White Horse Rocks," according to legend, were formed when fiery steeds from the royal stock of King Solomon were wrecked upon the beach.

While the hotels of Ofir offer guests every convenience in a secluded setting, the nearest shops and more local color are found one to two miles inland on an estuary of the Cávado River at **Fao.** Framed by mountain ridges in the background and a river valley, the village is the sleepy destination of all visitors to Ofir. Interesting are the sargaceiros (literally, gatherers of sargasso), who, with their stout fustian tunics, rake the offshore breakers for the seaweed used in making fertilizer. On the quays you can lunch on sardines off the smoking braziers. At the end of the day you can soothe your overdose of sunshine with a mellow glass of port wine.

The accommodations in these two towns are the best along the coast north of Porto.

Staying in Ofir

The Hotel de Ofir, Praia de Ofir (tel. 893-83), competes in its own way with the new resort developments on the southern Algarve. One section is quite luxurious, built motel-style right along the dunes, with a row of white tents and a pure sandy beach in full view of the second-floor bedroom balconies. There are rather well-styled public rooms for the evening's activities, but the principal focus is on the wide ocean-front terrace, where guests sunbathe and order refreshments under candy-striped umbrellas.

A dining room opens onto the sea and is informal with comfortable armchairs—allowing guests to enjoy a near-constant parade of delicious meals. The nightclub, Boîte de Nuit, simulates an open patio with ceiling of heavy beams under a fake sky. Tables encircle a round dance floor, and a large stage provides an orchestra and variety shows.

It's really a resort unto itself, with a vast playground terrace, two swimming pools (one for children), two tennis courts, and a flagstone terrace bordering soft green lawns. The hotel has a discotheque and a bowling alley as well. The hotel is divided into three sections—the older central core contains bedrooms furnished in the traditional Portuguese fashion, with excellent reproductions of regionally styled furniture; the adjoining wings are totally modern.

The public rooms are large, well decorated, and have plenty of areas for quiet relaxation. The bedrooms have a well-conceived sense of style, with substantial pieces of modern furniture placed against pleasant color backgrounds. In high season (July to August 31), the full-board rate for two persons is 950$ ($37.05), dropping to 770$ ($30.03) in spring and fall. Full-board rate for one person is 560$ ($21.94) in high season, 460$ ($17.94) in spring and fall.

Staying in Fao
Hotel do Pinhal (tel. 894-73), is a modern resort hotel, but somehow it captures the regional character of Northern Portugal. The Hotel of the Pine Cones is set in the midst of pine trees beside a river. The entrance is formal, but at the rear is a lawn leading to the water. Here are two swimming pools (a smaller one for children), a tennis court, and a putting green. It's just a four-minute walk to the sea and the beaches.

The public rooms are attractive, the lounge arranged with modern armchairs clustered to enjoy the view of the gardens through the picture windows. The restaurant captures the river view with an all-glass wall. The bedrooms are impressively furnished: some are ultra-modern (walls of wood paneling, lots of built-ins); others capture the character of the region with carved fourposter beds, chintz fabrics, hand-loomed rugs, ornate wrought-iron lamps and chandeliers, and old chests or desks.

There are three price levels, according to the room you select (size, balcony, outlook). Doubles are in the 280$ ($10.92) to 350$ ($13.65) bracket; singles, 190$ ($7.41) to 245$ ($9.56). For a little more, two persons can have a suite, costing 415$ ($16.19). Add a supplement of 210$ ($8.19) per person daily for full pension. All taxes are included in the rates. Occasionally, there's dancing to music in the hotel's boîte.

5. Deep in the Environs

Before exploring the northwestern Minho, you may want to dip deeper into the Douro River valley by driving west into the mountains for a look at the Portugal rarely seen by rushed foreign visitors. If you give yourself two targets—**Amarante,** north of the river, and **Lamego,** to the south—you'll be rewarded. Hopefully, you'll be in the Upper Douro region at the end of summer for the harvesting of the grapes.

AMARANTE: Where the lazy Tâmega flows under the **Ponte de Amarante,** completed in 1790, you can see wooden balconies extending out over the river and willow trees drooping their branches over the banks. A romantic setting for the town of St. Gonçalo, the protector of old maids.

On the slopes of the Marao Hills, Amarante is worth the 41-mile trek northeast from Porto. Right at the entrance to the bridge sits the former **Convent of St. Gonçalo,** with an azulejos-faced dome. Inside, the entire altarpiece is a cherubic romp, with silvery white-haired baby angels frolicking and cavorting all over the columns and ceiling. On each side of the altar are huge pillars festooned with bouquets and wreaths of flowers. Adjacent archways display richly gilded trompe l'oeil decorations. Four supporting columns reveal bizarre figures costumed in black, gold, and scarlet. These seemingly hermaphroditic figures exhibit the face, posture, and air of women, but are in fact masculine, as their hirsute chests will testify. The right and left platforms off the main altar continue the florid rococo ornamentation.

Another oddity amidst this frantic theatrical scene is a baroque organ held by a gilded merman, the tips of his feet forming fish tails. Fellow tritons round out the supporting cast. To the right of the altar chapel is a well of wax replicas depicting particular body infirmities. Someone even placed a replica of his sick pig. In a small chapel to the left under the altar is the enemy of every young Portuguese girl: St. Gonçalo, who sees to it that elderly spinsters or widowed women find husbands, but doesn't care a bit about unattached young girls. His sculptured figure is robed, holding a staff and a book—his head resting on two bold red embroidered cushions with tasseled ends.

The saint's feast day in Amarante—on the first weekend in June of every year—produces a festa unique in Portugal. It is the custom for unmarried girls and bachelors to exchange loaves of bread shaped like phalluses. Seems like the vestige of a pagan fertility rite has survived—or else St. Gonçalo himself is having a final chuckle.

For dining or lodgings, there's a government-owned pousada in the environs:

A Budget Pousada

Pousada de Sao Gonçalo, Serra do Marao, Amarante (tel. 461-13), is on a remote mountain pass. It's almost snowbound in winter, but a sun trap in summer. A modern version of a roadside inn, it is a retreat. The approach—between Amarante and Vila Real—is forlorn, with no signs of life. The place is called Bela Vista, near the Alto de Espinho. Pinewoods grow for miles around in every direction.

Inside, it is furnished in the regional style, more like a hilltop home than an inn. Antique console tables, high wooden chests, tiled floors, country-style armchairs, an open fireplace, and statuary add to that effect. Only 18 rooms are available—14 with bath, four without—so it's wise to make reservations. The rooms are furnished with a few antiques interspersed with passable reproductions. In a room with bath, the rate is 155$ ($6.05) for one person, 220$ ($8.58) for two. Bathless rooms cost 85$ ($3.32) in a single, 120$ ($4.68) in a double.

Meals are hearty and filling, a complete table d'hôte luncheon or dinner going for 100$ ($3.90), including homemade bread and a ceramic pitcher of wine. Hopefully, you'll be served the house specialty, a baked cod casserole (generous chunks of white fish baked in a cream sauce, under a crust of cheddar cheese), with vegetables. Kid is also savory when roasted until it's brown and crispy. Desserts are the special pride of the cook: perhaps you'll receive a creamy layer cake studded with almonds and looking just like a porcupine.

LAMEGO: This old bishopric on the wooded slopes of Mount Penude is a good example of baroque harmony. Many of its public and private buildings (even the town cinema) show this unifying style, an example of community planning rarely achieved. The main square has a public garden and adjoins a leisurely, tree-lined esplanade, where the denizens of Lamego promenade in the evenings. Behind the statue of Bishop Dom Miguel is his former palace, converted into a museum displaying sculpture and French tapestries.

Across the way is the **Cathedral of Lamego (Sé),** originally built in the Romanesque style, then overlaid with Gothic and baroque ornamentation. The ceilings are frescoed, but in dire need of repair. Adjoining is a Renaissance cloister, with a chapel containing a large baroque altar. Ironically, two baroque picture frames—with their huge monsters, twisted scrolls, winged cherubs with bellies protruding, and fowl—obscure the canvases they frame. A second chapel contains pictorial tiles illustrating a touching scene of children bathing in a tub.

Crowning a forested serra, overlooking Lamego, is the well-known 18th-century mecca of **Nossa Senhora dos Remédios** (Out Lady of the Cures). Leading to it is an elegant baroque stairway—the Spanish Steps, of Lamego—broken by nine fountain-centered and profusely decorated landings. The faithful scale the steps on their knees, as they do in Rome's Scala Santa (Holy Steps).

The granite balustrade is topped with various resplendent finials and statues in Roman battle dress, vases and urns, spheres and niches, plus some saccharine pictorial tiles. The fountains are interesting—one decorated with four grotesques, each spouting water from its mouth.

VIDAGO: An international spa, Vidago lies in remote Tras-os-Montes, the far northeastern province of Portugal. Its pure sparkling waters and good climate have made it a favorite among "spa collectors."

All life centers on the **Palace Hotel** (tel. 973-56), which is set deep in a forest. On beautifully landscaped grounds, the hotel is known for its flower beds and fountains. Standing like a glistening pink birthday cake, the hotel in high season charges from 182$ ($7.10) to 385$ ($15.02) for one person, from 260$ ($10.14) to 370$ ($14.43) for two. If you request an accommodation without bath, the charge drops to 120$ ($4.68) in a single, to 200$ ($7.80) and up in a double. If you're touring, you might want to drop in for lunch, ordering a four-courser for 125$ ($4.88), including wine. Swimming, tennis, golf, horseback riding, and badminton are among the sports offered. International races are often held on a well-known race track nearby. The hotel also shelters a nightclub.

From Porto and its environs, we now head for the last stopover in continental Portugal, the Minho district.

Chapter XV

THE MINHO DISTRICT

1. Guimaraes
2. Braga
3. Barcelos
4. Esposende
5. Viana do Castelo
6. Valença
7. Pousada-Hopping in Minho

CORN GRANARIES on granite stilts... heather-covered hills... fishing villages... poplar-shaded river valleys... terraces scaling slopes... ramparts guarding against long-dead enemies... sargaceiros in fustian tunics raking for seaweed... and heavily laden vines at grape harvest.

The Minho occupies the most northwestern corner of Portugal, and is almost a land unto itself. The district begins some 25 miles north of Porto, stretching to the frontier of Galicia in northwestern Spain. In fact, the Minhotons and the Galicians share many common characteristics.

Granite plateaus undulate across the countryside, broken by the green valleys of the Minho, Ave, Cávado, and Lima Rivers. Bountiful granite quarries stand agape amidst the hills. From the great church facades in Braga and Guimaraes to the humblest of village cottages, this material has been employed for centuries. Green pasturelands contrast sharply with forests filled with cedars and chestnuts.

The small size of the district and the proximity of one town to another makes hamlet hopping easy. Even the biggest towns—**Viana do Castelo, Guimaraes,** and **Braga**—are provincial. You can see wooden carts in the streets drawn by pairs of dappled and chocolate brown oxen. These noble beasts have become subjects for the regional pottery and ceramics for which the Minho, and especially Viana do Castelo, are known.

Religious festas are excuses for bringing the hard-working people out into the streets for days of merrymaking and celebrations including folk songs, dances and, of course, displays of traditional costumes. The young girls and women often wear woolen skirts and gaily decorated aprons in floral or geometric designs. Their bodices are pinned with golden filigree and draped with heart or cross-shaped pendants hung in many layers upon chains about their necks.

Historically, the Minho was the spawning ground of Portuguese independence. It was from here that Afonso Henriques, the first king, made his plans to capture the south from the Moors. Battlemented castles along the frontier attest to the former hostilities with Spain, and fortresses still stand above the coastal villages, ruined sentinels which once protected the river accesses to the heartland.

1. Guimaraes

The cradle of Portugal, Guimaraes suffers from a benign malady which the French call embarras de richesses. At the foot of a range of serras, this first capital of Portugal has successfully preserved a medieval atmosphere which shows little sign of evaporation.

Dominating the skyline is the 10th-century **Castle of Guimaraes,** where Afonso Henriques, Portugal's first king, was born sometime between 1094 and 1111 (historians disagree). The Castle dates from 996. High-pitched crenels top the strategically placed square towers and the looming keep, said to have been the birthplace of Afonso. The view is magnificent. With the church bells ringing in the distance, and roosters crowing early in the morning, the setting seems straight out of the Middle Ages.

Almost in the shadow of the structure is the 12th-century **St. Michael of the Castle,** a squat rectangular Romanesque church where the liberator was baptized. Nearby is an heroic statue of the mustachioed Afonso—his head helmeted, his figure clad in a suit of armor, sword and shield in hand.

From the keep of the castle, you can see the four-winged **Palace of the Dukes of Braganza.** Although constructed in the 15th century, it has been heavily restored. Many critics have dismissed the rebuilt structure with contempt. However, if you're not a purist, you may find a guided tour interesting. Perched on the slope of a hill, the palace possesses a varied assortment of treasures, including a number of portraits such as of Catherine of Braganza, who married Charles II of England, the merrie monarch and lover of Nell Gwyn.

Copies of the large Pastrana tapestries depict scenes from the Portuguese wars in North Africa. The scabbards and helmets in the armor room, plus the antiques, Persian hangings, Indian urns, ceramics, and Chinese porcelains make the 5$ (20¢) admission seem small. Many of the rooms have beamed and coffered ceilings, plain gray stone block walls, and chocolate brown stone floors. The chapel opens onto the throne chairs of the duke and duchess. Nearby are the double-tiered cloisters.

By far the most dramatic interior of any church in town belongs to **Sao Francisco,** on Largo 28 Maio. Entered through a Gothic portal, the church contains Delft-blue and white azulejos decorations on its walls. At times color tones are created which seem to bathe the whole interior in moonlight. In the transept to the right of the main altar is a doll house, a re-creation of the living room of a church prelate. The detail is meticulous—from the burgundy-colored cardinal's chapeau resting upon a wall sconce, to the miniature dog and cat (slightly out of scale), to the grapes suspended from the ceiling. Found at the second altar on the right is a polychrome tree of life, representing 12 crowned kings and the Virgin, her hands clasped, her feet resting upon the heads of three cherubs. The palace next door, with its embellished tiled facade, may be visited from 10-11 a.m. and from 3-4 p.m. free. It is, at present, the site of a hospital.

If you'd like to step into the Middle Ages for an hour or two, take a stroll down the **Rua de Santa Maria,** which has remained essentially unchanged, except nowadays you're likely to hear some blaring music, in English no less. Proud town houses—once the residences of the nobility—stand beside humble dwellings. The handcarved balconies, aged by the years, are most often garnished with iron lanterns, not to mention laundry.

At the end you'll come upon a charming square in tne heart of the old town, the **Largo da Oliveira** (Olive Tree Square). Escudo-hungry children are likely to surround you at this point. You can press on, however, to an odd chapelette in front of a church. Comprised of four ogival arches, it is said to mark the spot in the 6th century where Wamba was asked to give up the simple toil of working his fields to become the King of the Goths. Thrusting his olive stick into the tilled soil, he declared he would accept only if his stick sprouted leaves. So it did, and he did—or that was the tale told.

The church itself, called the **Collegiate Church of the Olive Tree,** was originally a 10th-century temple erected by Mumadona, a Galician countess. It has changed with the seasons: Romanesque giving way to Gothic, and then to more sterile neoclassicism.

In the Romanesque cloister of the church is the **Museum of Alberto Sampaio.** Besides a large silver collection and such historical curios as the crown of Our Lady of the Olive, it displays the tunic worn by Joao I at the famous battle of Aljubarrota that decided Portugal's fate. In addition, there is a myriad assortment of vestments, paintings, ceramics, faïence from Viana do Castelo, and pottery from the Beiras. A fresco illustrates a glowering Salome, rapturous over the severed head of John the Baptist. Off the cloister you can visit a baroque chapel with two Wagnerian amazons, sans helmets, bearing torchiers.

Although Guimaraes may suffer from an embarrassment of riches in sights, in hotels it suffers from mortification. The leading hotel in town—rated third class by the government—cannot in good conscience be recommended, either for its cramped, inadequately furnished, and often dirty rooms, or for its extremely poor cuisine and faulty service. Recommendation: go to Braga nearby where you'll find far superior accommodations.

2. Braga

Nearly everywhere you look in Braga there's a church, a palace, a garden, or a fountain. The site the town occupies has always been favored. Known to the Romans as Bracara Augusta, it also resounded to the footsteps of other conquerors—the Suevi, the Visigoths, and the Moors. For centuries it has been an archiepiscopal see and a pilgrimage site (the Visigoths are said to have renounced their heresies here).

Inside the town, interest focuses on the **Sé,** the **Cathedral of Braga.** It was built in the 12th century by Count Henry of Burgundy and Dona Teresa. Following his demise, she was chased out of town because of an illicit love affair; but in death Henry and Teresa were reunited in their tombs in the Chapel of Kings.

Although built in the Middle Ages, the Sé didn't escape subsequent decorative and architectural overlays. The north triple-arched facade is austere and dominating, with a large stone-laced Roman arch flanked by two smaller Gothic ones. What appear to be the skeletons of cupolas top the facade's dual bell towers, which flank a lofty rooftop niche containing a larger-than-life statue of the Virgin and Child. Under a carved baldachin in the apse is a statue of "Our Lady of the Milk"—that is, the Virgin breast feeding the infant Jesus Christ. The statue is in the Manueline style—but somehow pious, restrained.

Once inside the structure, you'll believe you've entered one of the darkest citadels of Christendom. However, if you can see them, the interior decorations are profuse, particularly a pair of huge 18th-century organs gilded with baroque decorations. In the 1330 Capela da Glória is the sarcophagus of Archbishop

Dom Gonçalo Pereira—carved by order of the prelate himself—with an unctuous expression on his face.

For 5$ (20¢), you can visit the **Treasury of the Cathedral** and the **Museum of Sacred Art**, an upstairs repository of Braga's most precious works of art. Included are elaborately carved choir stalls from the 18th century, embroidered vestments from the 16th through the 18th centuries, a 14th-century statue of the Virgin and a Gothic chalice from the same period, plus the custódia of Dom Gaspar de Braganza. This treasure house may be visited from 8 a.m. to 12:30 p.m. and from 1:30-5:30 p.m. In the cloister is a Pietà, reflecting human grief.

Three miles southeast of Braga is the nationally renowned **Bom Jesus do Monte**. The hilltop pilgrimage site is reached via foot, funicular, or a tree-lined roadway. A double baroque granite staircase dating from the 17th century may look exhausting; but, if it's any consolation, pilgrims often climb it on their knees.

Though less elaborate than the stairway of Remédios at Lamego, the stairs at Bom Jesus (Good Jesus) are equally as impressive. On the numerous landings are gardens, grottos, small chapels, sculptures, and allegorical stone figures set in fountains.

Designed by Carlos Amarante in 1811, the hilltop **Chapel of the Miracles** contains many reminders, even anatomical re-creations, of the diseased and sick who have claimed cures. Though in foggy weather the mountain is enshrouded in mist, on most days you can walk along the mosaic sidewalks and belvederes, past white and black swans, and view the provincial capital at every turn. In accommodations you have the following:

A BUDGET HOTEL: Hotel Joao XXI, 849 Avenida Joao XXI (tel. 221-46), is a good stopover hotel in its bracket (second class). At the fringe of the town, it sits on a tree-lined avenue leading to Bom Jesus do Monte. The entry to this modern little hotel is a salute to the 19th century. The overall effect is attractively immaculate and comfortable. The social center is the living room, with well-selected furnishings featuring an open fireplace for the nippy months.

The bedrooms are halfway up—furnished well with semi-traditional pieces, the accent on efficiency. Each of the 28 rooms contains a private bath. The prices depend on the size and outlook, with doubles going for either 185$ ($7.22) to 245$ ($9.56); singles, 145$ ($5.66) to 180$ ($7.02). You can order a well-prepared table d'hôte luncheon or dinner for 100$ ($3.90).

3. Barcelos

Fourteen miles west of Braga, Barcelos is a sprawling river town, resting upon a plateau ringed by green hills. Wrought-iron street lanterns glimmer late in the evenings long after the market in the open square of **Campo da República** has closed down. Barcelos does not feature any single major attraction, only itself, taken as a whole, with its ensemble of sights and curiosities—and that is more than enough.

Market day, on Thursdays, in the fountain-centered Campo da República, almost 450 yards square, is a major event. You can purchase such local handcrafted items as rugs, dyed pillows stuffed with chicken feathers, Portuguese chandeliers, crochet work, local pottery, and, of course, the Barcelos cockerels.

These hand-painted earthenware cocks are the most characteristic souvenirs of Portugal and often seem a symbol of the country itself. The worship of the Barcelos Rooster derives from a legend concerning a Gallego sentenced to hang, despite his protestations of innocence. In a last-hour appeal to the judge (who was having dinner at the time), the condemned man made a bold statement—if his manifestation of innocence were true, the roasted rooster resting on the magistrate's plate would get up and crow. Suddenly, a gloriously scarlet-plumed cockerel rose from the plate, crowing loud and long. The man was acquitted, of course.

Opening onto the tree-studded main square are some of the finest buildings in Barcelos. The **Igreja do Terço** from the 18th century resembles a palace more than a church, with a central niche facade topped by finials and a cross. The interior tile work around the baroque altar depicts scenes of monks at labor and a moving rendition of Last Supper. Also fronting the campo, with its fountain, is the **Hospital da Misericórdia,** a long formal building of the 17th century, behind a spiked fence, taking up almost half a side of the square.

Of more interest, however, is the small octagonal **Temple of Senhor da Cruz,** with a cupola faced with azulejos. An upper balustrade punctuated by large stone finials and a latticed round window above the square portal, provide contrast to the austerity of the walls. The interior is more sumptuous, with crystal, marble, and gilt.

Overlooking the swirling Cávado River are the ruins of the **Palace of the Braganzas,** dating from 1786. The original palace site, as well as the town of Barcelos itself, were bestowed on Nuno Álvares by Joao I as a gift in gratitude for his bravery in the 1385 battle at Aljubarrota.

On the present facade is a representation of the palace, re-created in splendor. You can wander through the ruins which have been turned into an archaeological museum, left relatively unguarded and filled with sarcophagi, heralded shields, and an 18th-century tiled fountain. A museum of ceramics underneath the palace encapsulates the evolution of that handicraft (look for the blood-red ceramic oxen, with their lyre-shaped horns).

The shadow from the high palace chimney stretches across the old pillory in the courtyard below, with the structure even exceeding in height the bell tower of the adjoining **Igreja Matriz.** Fronting the river, this old Gothic church contains a baroque altar and an interior whose sides are faced with multicolored azulejos. The altar is an array of cherubs, grapes, gold leaf, and birds.

4. Esposende

Esposende is a small beach resort in an idyllic village between Viana do Castelo and Porto, 30 miles to the south. The pines and sand dunes are swept by the Atlantic breezes, and cows graze in nearby pastures. Unspoiled countryside flows around the villake like a stream—ox carts in the streets, old undistinguished chapels and simple churches, all the elements that make up a quiet village.

Men and women in fustian clothes and broad-brimmed hats work the vineyards in the foothills. The beach is large and fine, lining either side of the Cávado estuary. Small fishing vessels plod up the river carrying anglers to the bass upstream. Recent archaeological diggings have revealed the remains of a Roman city and necropolis—but that doesn't seem to have disturbed Esposende in the least.

In accommodations there are the following:

THE MEDIUM-PRICED RANGE: Hotel Nélia, is starkly modern for such a provincial town. Making much use of wood grain, the hotel offers sleekly functional bedrooms that cost 200$ ($7.80) in a single, 320$ ($12.48) in a double. The restaurant features regional cooking. Especially delicious are the pastries from the Nélia's own bake shop.

THE BUDGET RANGE: The Hotel Sauve Mar, Avenida Arantes Oliveira (tel. 894-45), is a semi-modern hotel on the river, with its own swimming pool and tennis courts. It attracts budgeteers who don't want to pay for the superior first-class accommodations at neighboring Ofir and Fao.

The lodgings are pleasant and comfortable, and of its 41 bedrooms, 33 contain private baths. Full pension for two persons costs either 620$ ($24.18) or 810$ ($31.59); whereas one person, for a room and all meals, is charged either 405$ ($15.80) or 440$ ($17.16). However, of its cuisine, the food critic Raymond Postgate wrote that its "menus are a meticulous reproduction of Anglo-Saxon nurseries of the twenties—for example, vegetable soup, followed by boiled fish with boiled potatoes and a jam cake." The Suave Mar is open year round, though you may have the place to yourself off season.

5. Viana do Castelo

Viana do Castelo sits complacently between an estuary of the Lima River and a base of rolling hills. The Princess of the Lima—as she is called—is Northern Portugal's city of folklore. The setting is enhanced by an occasional ox cart with wooden wheels clacking along the stone streets. Some of the boatmen of the city—their faces weatherbeaten—can be seen near the waterfront, offering to sell tourists a slow cruise along the river banks.

But for the best view, scale the **Monte de Santa Luzia,** reached by a 5$ (20¢) funicular ride or, if you have a car, along a twisting road. From the Hotel de Santa Luzia at the summit, a great view unfolds, including Eiffel's bridge spanning the Lima.

Viana do Castelo is especially noted for its pottery and regional handicrafts (many can be purchased in the Friday market). It is even better known for its peasant garb, best seen at the annual festa (the Friday, Saturday, and Sunday nearest to August 20) of Nossa Senhora da Agonia (Our Lady of Agony). The native women wear bright, strident colors of oranges, scarlets, and Prussian blue, with layers of golden necklaces displaying heart and cross-shaped pendants.

The center of town is the **Praça da República,** one of the handsomest squares in Portugal. At its heart is the much-photographed **Chafariz Fountain,** constructed in the 16th century, with water spewing from the mouths of its figures. The most impressive building on the square is the **Misericórdia,** a dour, squat, three-story structure, unique in the country. The lower level is an arcade comprised of five austere Roman arches, whereas the two upper levels are ponderous Renaissance balconies. All are crowned by a rooftop crucifix. The four supporting pillars of each level are primitive caryatid-like figures between which are interspersed bright red geraniums in flower boxes. Adjoining the Charity Hospital is a church fronting the Rua da Bandeira. Inside is a combination of pictorial tiles made in 1714, ornate baroque altars, a painted ceiling, and wood carvings.

The other building dominating the praça is the old **Town Hall,** constructed over an arcade made up of three wide and low Gothic arches (the Tourist Bureau occupies the headquarters upstairs). The crenel-topped facade displays a royal coat-of-arms and wrought-iron balcony windows above each arch. Originally the Paços do Concelho, it was constructed during the reign of Manuel I and completed under Joao III. From the small sidewalk tables and chairs, you can observe the square's activities and sample pastries such as torta de Viana.

The **Igreja Matriz,** down the Rua Cabral at Largo do Instituto Histórico do Minho, was begun by Joao I in 1285 and completed in 1433. Dominated by a large Gothic arched portal, the facade is flanked by two battlemented towers. The interior archway is carved with granite figures, acanthus leaves, and simplistic statuary with moonshaped faces. The inside is cold but with an excellent trompe l'oeil ceiling.

Viana do Castelo, only 44 miles north of Porto, is possible either as an overnight stopover or as the goal of a one-day trip. The beaches are large and sandy—guarded by an age-old fortress standing at the river's mouth.

Only 12 miles up the river is **Ponte de Lima**, which is exactly what one hopes a Portuguese village will be like. The drive along the north side of the river takes you through grape arbors, pastoral villages, and forests of cedar, pine, and chestnut. Red-cheeked peasants stand silhouetted against moss-green stone walls or cease their toil in the cabbage fields to watch you pass.

At Ponte de Lima, an old bridge spans the river, on the banks of which women wring out their clothes. At certain times of the year, though, this river is likely to be dry. At other times anglers try to snare trout from its waters. The numerous towers and churches reveal a secular architecture in faded elegance.

In accommodations the city is well supplied.

THE UPPER BRACKET: The **Hotel Afonso III**, 494 Avenida Afonso III (tel. 241-23), is a first-class hotel which opened in 1971. Offering eight floors of comfort, it contains 88 accommodations in all—each with its own bath. More than half are graced with a private balcony as well. The attractively furnished rooms rent for anywhere from 240$ ($9.36) to 265$ ($10.34) for one person, increasing to from 380$ ($14.82) to 440$ ($17.16) for two. Suites are more, of course. For full pension, the rate ranges from 510$ ($19.89) to 550$ ($21.45) for one, from 800$ ($31.20) to 885$ ($34.52) for two. The contemporary decor consists mainly of black and white marble. The overall tone is both simple and sophisticated. A restaurant on the seventh floor provides a panoramic view over the Lima River. Other facilities include a convention hall, a boîte, and swimming pools. Bar facilities are available. A 15 percent reduction is granted from November through February.

THE BUDGET RANGE: **Hotel Rali**, Avenida Dom Afonso III (tel. 221-76). Set back from the waterfront, this four-story modern hotel is a pleasant choice. It faces the mountains, but also opens onto a busy thoroughfare. The bedrooms—42 in all, each with a private bath—are splashed with good strong colors, often greens and blues, with floral prints at the wall-wide windows. The furnishings seem like demonstration rooms in Copenhagen. The tariff in a single is either 150$ ($5.85) or 175$ ($6.83), depending on the plumbing (shower or tub). For two persons, the cheapest double is 220$ ($8.58), increasing to 260$ ($10.14).

The lounges open one onto the other, the favored one with a raised fireplace, red lacquered armchairs, and marble coffee tables. The dining room has paneled walls, a rear clerestory window with green plants, and dramatic drop lights of cutout white metal. Depending on the weather, guests choose between a heated indoor pool or an outside one. At a boîte in the compound, records are played for dancing.

6. Valença

The walled battlements of Valença, 33 miles northeast of Viana do Castelo, stand today as a reminder of ancient hostilities between Portugal and Spain. In fact, when Afonso III ruled Portugal, the forces of Castile and León besieged and destroyed much of Valença.

Today, a narrow covered gateway across a moat takes you into the center of this walled village of cobbled streets, ancient stone houses, pots of geraniums, wrought-iron balconies, and old street lanterns. Incorporated into the 13th-century fortress, a government-owned pousada opens onto a belvedere, from which you can enjoy one of the finest views in the Minho. The old cannons are still mounted—no longer seriously—looking down on the **International Bridge** across the Minho to Spain.

On the other side of the river is the Spanish town of **Tuy**, once a blood enemy, and now a sister-town to Valença. Tuy is noted for its narrow, steep streets, and walls erected on top of ancient Roman fortifications. The battlemented turrets and towers of the Cathedral-Fortress have stood guard on the frontier since 1170.

VALENÇA & THE POUSADAS

While in Valença, you may get hooked on the local specialty, lampreys. Order them fresh from the river, served in a spicy pepper sauce.

In accommodations, there is the following in:

THE BUDGET RANGE: Pousada de Sao Teotónio (tel. 222-52). The Portuguese government tried to outshine its rival counterpart across the border, a Spanish parador. Although lodged among some of Portugal's most unspoiled antiquity, the pousada is contemporary in concept. It's built villa-fashion on several levels, with an entrance portico connecting the main building with an annex. Most of the lounges and bedrooms not only have a view of the river and Tuy, but also open onto a courtyard with a lawn and reflecting pool.

The public rooms are spacious, flowing one into another, containing wooden ceilings, tiled floors, and various retreat nooks. Favored is the lounge with a wide stone fireplace, a 15-foot plank coffee table, and hand-loomed rugs. Many of the bedrooms have balconies, and 14 of the 16 rooms contain private baths. Single rooms range in price from 135$ ($5.27) to 155$ ($6.05); doubles, 220$ ($8.58). If you stop only for a meal (and many do), the cost is 100$ ($3.90) for a five-course table d'hôte luncheon or dinner. The helpings are bountiful and the dishes good, if you like regional cooking. The wooden-ceilinged dining room takes full advantage of the view of the river and Spain.

7. Pousada-Hopping in Minho

Many visitors consider pousada-hopping the most rewarding way of exploring Portugal. Every government-owned inn lies in a characteristic region, as well as a special scenic spot. (The first pousada—a place to rest—was founded in the 12th century, offering pilgrims a roof, a bed, and a candle. That kindly motto today includes all the amenities of modern comfort.) Pousadas in this northern region of Portugal include the following:

Pousada de Sao Bento (tel. 571-90), on the Braga-Gerês highway, six miles from Vieira do Minho at Caniçada do Minho (about 27 miles from Braga). In lovely countryside stands this small pousada of only 10 double rooms, each with bath. For full pension, one guest pays from 340$ ($13.26) to 380$ ($14.82). If you're stopping by just to sample a regional meal, the charge is 100$ ($3.90). A magnet with guests is the swimming pool.

Pousada da Sao Bartolomeu, Bragança, Trás-os-Montes (tel. Bragança 379). This government-owned inn lies just outside the town, about a half-an-hour drive from the Spanish frontier of Quintanilha. Ten double rooms containing private baths are most attractively furnished. The room rate for two persons is 220$ ($8.58) with bath, 120$ ($4.68) without bath. The charge for a main meal is 100$ ($3.90), if you're just passing through.

Pousada da Santa Catarina (tel. Miranda 55), at Miranda do Douro (Trás-os-Montes). About 78 miles from Bragança, this inn overlooks the great dam at Upper Douro. Enjoying a scenic spot, the pousada rents out 12 pleasantly furnished double rooms—each with private bath—all year round. A party of two is charged 220$ ($8.58). For full pension, the tariff is 345$ ($13.46) for two. A complete luncheon or dinner costs 100$ ($3.90).

Pousada Barao de Forrester (tel. Alijó 622-15) at Alijó, Trás-os-Montes, on the Murça-Pinhao road, about 41 miles from Vila Real. In a delightful small town, this pousada is set in the midst of vineyard country, famed for its port wine. Open all year, it rents out 12 rooms, six of which contain private baths. (This was one of the first pousadas built when the idea took root some decades ago.) One person in a room without bath is charged 95$ ($3.71), that figure increasing to 115$ ($4.49) with bath. In a bathless double, the rate is 140$ ($5.46), rising to 165$ ($6.44) with bath. One person pays anywhere from 260$ ($10.14) to 310$ ($12.09) for full pension; two persons, 380$ ($14.82) to 425$ ($16.58). A main meal goes for 110$ ($4.29).

Pousada de Sao Lourenço, Manteigas, Serra da Estrela (tel. 471-50), is about 12 miles from Manteigas, standing at a height of 4,900 feet on a mountainside, with a panoramic view. Only 12 double rooms with bath are available. Singles rent for 155$ ($6.05); doubles, 220$ ($8.58). For full pension, the charge for one person is 185$ ($7.22), increasing to 370$ ($14.43) for two, plus the price of the room. One main meal costs 100$ ($3.90) if you're just stopping by.

With continental Portugal behind us, we head out into the Atlantic.

Chapter XVI

MADEIRA AND THE AZORES

1. Settling into Funchal
2. Excursions in Madeira
3. Discovering the Azores
4. Ponta Delgada
5. Exploring Sao Miguel
6. Terceira
7. Faial

THE ISLAND OF MADEIRA, 530 miles southwest of Portugal, is the mountain peak of a volcanic mass. Its craggy spires and seacoast precipices of umber-dark basalt end with a sheer drop into the blue water. The surrounding sea is so deep that large blubber-rich sperm whales abound near the shore, providing an added source of income for island fishermen.

The summit of the undersea mountain is found at Madeira's center where the **Pico Ruivo,** often snow capped, rises to an altitude of 6,105 feet above sea level. From that point project the rocky ribs and ravines of the island, running to the coast. If you stand upon the sea-swept balcony of **Cabo Girao,** one of the world's highest ocean cliffs (1,933 feet above the sea), you'll understand the Edenlike quality of Madeira. Camoes called it "at the end of the world."

Madeira itself is only 35 miles in length, about 13 in breadth at its widest point. It contains nearly 100 miles of coastline—but no beaches. In its volcanic soil, plants and flowers blaze like the Tahitian palette of Gauguin. From jacaranda and crawling masses of bougainvillea, to orchids and geraniums, whortleberry to prickly pear, poinsettias, cannas, frangipani, birds of paradise and wisteria, the land is a botanical garden. Custard apples, avocados, mangoes, and bananas grow profusely. Fragrances such as vanilla and wild fennel intermingle with sea breezes and pervade the ravines, sweeping down the rocky headlands.

Claimed by the British as a "sentimental dominion," Madeira has long been popular with Englishmen, notably Winston Churchill. The post-Victorians arrived dressed to the teeth, the women in wide-brimmed hats to protect themselves from the sun. Now that has changed: the British make their way here specifically to enjoy the sun, even though most of them visit during the rainy winter season. The climate of Madeira is mild—the mean temperature averaging about 61 degrees Fahrenheit in winter, about 70 degrees Fahrenheit in summer.

Legend has it that two English lovers discovered the island about half a century before its known date of exploration. Supposedly Robert Machim and Anna d'Arfet, fleeing England, were swept off their course by a tempest and deposited on the eastern coast. In 1419, Joao Gonçalves Zarco and Tristao Vaz Teixeira, captains under Henry the Navigator, discovered Madeira while exploring the African coastline, some 350 miles distant.

As it was densely covered with impenetrable virgin forests, they named it Madeira, meaning wood. Soon it was set afire to clear it for habitation. The holocaust is said to have lasted seven years, until all but a small northern section was reduced to ashes.

The hillsides are so richly cultivated today one would never know there had even been a fire. Many of the groves and vineyards—protected by buffers of sugar cane—grow on stone-walled ledges, which almost spill into the sea. The farmers plant so close to the cliff's edge that they must have at least a dash of goat's blood in them. The terraced mountain slopes are irrigated by a complex network of levadas.

About 25 miles to the northeast, **Porto Santo** is the only other inhabited island in the Madeira archipelago. Réalités called it "Another world, arid, desolate and waterless." Unlike Madeira itself, Porto Santo contains beaches, but is not yet developed for mass tourism.

However, at press time one first-class hotel, **Nuevo Mondo,** complete with sea-view balconies and a swimming pool, was scheduled for completion sometime in 1976. Inquire at the Tourist Bureau in Madeira before heading there, and always make a reservation.

The **Pirata Azul** sails from Funchal to Porto Santo daily, if the weather is good. The round-trip fare is 257$ ($10.02). Some hotels or quintas will pack a picnic lunch, which guests can enjoy on the beach. The boat leaves in the early morning, returning in the late afternoon, giving passengers at least four hours on the Porto Santo beach. For about the same price, you can fly over in the morning, catching a Funchal-bound plane in Porto Santo at 7:30 in the evening.

The first governor of the island was Bartolomeu Perestrelo (one of his daughters is said to have married Columbus). According to tradition, the great explorer himself lived on the island in a house still standing today.

Treasure hunters are drawn to a group of deserted islands in the Madeira archipelago, the **Selvagens.** Captain Kidd is reputed to have buried his gold here.

GETTING THERE FROM LISBON: The quickest and most convenient way to reach Madeira from Lisbon is on a TAP flight (the trip taking one hour and 30 minutes). A round-trip air passage, as of this writing, costs U.S. $139.08, but confirm that with your travel agent or by calling TAP. The plane stops at the Madeira Airport, then goes on to Porto Santo. However, if you're booking a TAP flight from, say, New York to Lisbon, you can have the side trip to Madeira included at no extra cost, providing you have a regular—that is, not an excursion—ticket.

To go by one of the steamship lines, you'll find the most regular service maintained by the **Empresa Insulana de Navegaçao.** A run from Lisbon to Funchal takes about 25 hours. Any travel agent in Lisbon will book you a seat; or you can go directly to the line's passenger department in Lisbon at 152 Rua Augusta (tel. 37-03-41).

1. Settling into Funchal

The capital of Madeira, Funchal, is the focal point of the entire island and the springboard of outlying villages. When Zarco landed in 1419, the sweet odor of fennel led him to name it after the aromatic herb, called funcho in Portuguese. Today, the southern coast city of hillside-shelved villas and narrow winding streets is the garden spot of the island. Its numerous estates—including the former residence of the discoverer Zarco, the Quinta das Cruzes—are among the most exotic in Europe.

THE SIGHTS: Funchal is the center of Madeira's wine industry. Grapes have grown in the region since the early 15th century when Henry the Navigator introduced vines and sugar cane to the slopes. In Funchal, the must (fresh wine) from the black and white grapes is used to make Bual, Sercial, and Malmsey. It's cultivated for its bittersweet tang (women used to scent their handkerchiefs with it). The wine-growers still transport the foot-pressed must in goatskin bottles carried over the rough terrain by borracheiros. Naturally, it undergoes extensive pasteurization in its refinement and blending.

The **Madeira Wine Association**, 10 Rua Sao Francisco (tel. 201-21), next to the British Consulate, offers samples from its diverse stock. Inside are murals depicting the wine pressing (by foot) and harvesting processes which proceed according to traditions established hundreds of years ago. You can savor the slightly burnt sweetness in a setting of old barrels, wine kegs, and time-mellowed chairs and tables made from aged wine kegs. Incidentally, Napoleon passed this way on his journey into exile on St. Helena in 1815. Bottles from a vintage year were given to him, but death came before the former emperor could sample them.

Of the churches of Funchal, the most intriguing is the rustic 15th-century **Sé (Cathedral)**, with its Moorish carved cedar ceiling, stone floors, Gothic arches, stained-glass windows, and baroque altars.

Just down the street from the Cruzes Museum is the baroque **Convent of Santa Clara**, Calçada de Santa Clara, with walled azulejos, a painted wooden ceiling, and the tomb of Zarco, the discoverer of Madeira. The church is said to have been built by the granddaughter of Zarco the year Columbus discovered America.

The **Museum da Quinta das Cruzes**, 1 Calçada do Pico (tel. 223-82), is noted for its orchids and a fine collection of art works and curios, much of which was brought here by expatriate Englishmen, who have made Funchal their adopted home since the 18th century. The museum, open daily except Mondays from 2 to 5, charges nothing to view its collection of ceramics from Macao, pieces-of-eight chests, French china, ivory retables, and Flemish statuary. Also displayed are such British pieces as crystal chandeliers, Chippendale dining room pieces, and Hepplewhite ballroom furnishings.

The aquatic life in the waters around Madeira is represented at **City Aquarium**, 31 Rua da Mouraria (tel. 297-61). Sea cucumbers, trigger fish, sharpnosed puffers, moray eels, eagle rays, scorpion fish, sea zephyrs, loggerhead turtles, and triton's horns are just some of the fauna exhibited. The Aquarium is open from 9:30 a.m. to 10 p.m. weekdays; Sundays and holiday hours are from noon till 4 p.m. Admission is 5$ (20¢).

The **Municipal Square** is a study in light and dark, its plaza paved with hundreds of black and white lava half moons. The whitewashed buildings surrounding it contain black stone trim and ochre-colored tile roofs. In all, an atmosphere of stately beauty.

MADEIRA: FUNCHAL

Finally, you can visit the **Iota** (fish auction) and many bazaars selling local handicrafts, such as wickerwork and Madeira embroidery. At the Iota, seafood is auctioned off to housewives and restaurant owners. Horse mackerel, grouper, mullet, tunny (sometimes weighing hundreds of pounds), freshwater eels, even a slab of whale steak or a barracuda, will find its way to the stalls.

In the bazaars you can purchase needlepoint tapestries, Madeira wines, laces, embroidery on Swiss organdy or Irish linen—plus all sorts of local crafts such as goatskin boots or Camacha basketry of water willows. The **City Market**, at the Praça do Comércio on Saturday, is a study in color—everything from yams to papaws.

The most exciting (and most crowded) time to visit Funchal is during the **End of the Year Festival**, December 30 to January 1. Fireworks light up the Bay of Funchal, the mountains in the background forming an amphitheater. Floodlit cruise ships anchor in the harbor to the delight of passengers who revel until dawn.

THE HOTELS: In summer when every other European resort is socking you with its highest tariffs, Madeira experiences its low season. And not because of bad weather. Rather, owing to the temperate climate, the early British visitors set a pattern of mass descent in the winter, thereby crowding the hotels and inflating the tariffs. Surely when more tourists know of summertime Madeira and its low-season rates, the island will build more of a year-round popularity. The hotels range from one of the finest deluxe citadels in Europe to an attractive quinta for budgeteers.

One of Europe's Great Resort Hotels

Reid's Hotel, 139 Estrada Monumental (tel. 230-01). Its position is smashing—along the coastal road at the edge of Funchal, on its own 11 acres of multi-terraced gardens cascading down the hillside to the rocky shores. Midway down are two swimming pools thrust out onto a cliff edge, the pair joined by a bridge and fountain. On a still lower terrace is yet another pool (reached by an elevator) built onto a ledge of rocks. You feel you're swimming in the ocean. The sentimental English who frequent the hotel in large numbers (famous guest of the past: Sir Winston Churchill) spend their days strolling along the scented walks lined with blue and pink hydrangeas, pink camellias, hedges of geraniums, gardenias, banana trees, ferns, and white yuccas.

Reid's has a tradition of quiet dignity in its public rooms and in a wing added in 1968—all tastefully and successfully combined. The main drawing rooms are refreshingly decorated in the colors of the sea (aqua and jade) with country estate-type furnishings, utilizing either tropical prints or soft solid colors. Afternoon tea or lunch is provided in either the chinoiserie lounge or on the open terrace. There's still another place for lunch—the Garden Restaurant, built on two levels with white and blue outdoor furniture set to face the sea view. The two-level main dining room is classically dignified with Wedgewood-style paneling and ceiling, plus the inevitable and very English silver trolley holding roast beef. The new Grill Room is recommended separately in the restaurant section.

The hotel is owned by the Blandy family of wine and shipping fame. On the full pension plan, a single with an inland view goes for 820$ ($31.98), increasing to 1,005$ ($39.20) in a sea-view room. Inland doubles rent for 1,500$ ($58.20), rising to 1,770$ ($69.03) with a sea view and 1,950$ ($76.05) with sea-view balcony. These rates include three meals for two persons as well as service and taxes. For those who want to live in bond clipping style, a suite is recommended, costing 2,450$ ($95.55) for two on the full-pension plan, including service and taxes. Of the 168 air-conditioned rooms with radio and T.V. in the suites, all but 14 face the ocean, but in each case the baths are private. The spacious rooms are conservative in the finest sense, with well-chosen pieces, plenty of storage space, sitting areas and desks. The baths are super-clean, with walls and floor of marble or tile. Life in a suite is especially gracious—for example, every day an ice bucket is refilled in your own liquor cabinet disguised in an 18th-century Portuguese cabinet. The hotel is fully air conditioned.

Although it's hard to be lured away from Reid's garden park, there are fishing, water skiing and sailing trips available. The tennis courts are at your disposal.

The Upper Bracket

Savoy Hotel, Avenida do Infante (tel. 220-31). Like Topsy, the hotel just grew and grew. Overlooking the water, at the edge of Funchal, it was started back at the turn of the century by the grandfather of the present Swiss-trained director, Rui Dias. Each generation of management has brought extensive enlargements in the face of escalating popularity. In 1970 vast public lounges were added, plus a "Cadillac" drive-up entrance—all under the designing supervision of the gracious Senhor Dias, who insists that "everything be Portuguese."

The public facilities are vast: a neoclassic lounge with fluted columns, a cocktail bar in Carmen red, two restaurants to fit your mood and attire (lunch at the swimming pool if you wish), a nightclub with four walls of glass, and an overflow terrace for warm and summer nights. In the largest hotel dining room in Portugal (80 meters long), guests sit in high-backed red upholstered chairs, enjoying a view of the ocean. Or they can dine more intimately in the Fleur de Lys grill room, with its à la carte menu.

Even clients staying at other hotels may want to consider a meal at the Savoy. The Fleur de Lys grill features two French chefs who offer elaborate à la carte selections. Especially festive is the buffet luncheon every Wednesday for 130$ ($5.07). The tables are laden with mouth-watering dishes, combining the skill of all the chefs—an international potpourri. The social and recreational life in the afternoon centers on the lido, a swimming pool and sun terrace thrust out over the water.

The regular bedrooms are keyed to the most contemporary of taste, with plenty of space and up-to-date furnishings. Usually one wall is paneled with tola wood from Africa, another is all glass, opening onto a balcony for sun bathing. The full-board tariffs for two persons are 1,808$ ($70.51) for double and twin-bedded sea-view rooms, but only 1,560$ ($60.84) with a mountain view. For a room and three meals, a single person pays 1,009$ ($39.35). Mountain-view suites are 1,950$ ($76.05), increasing to 2,423$ ($94.50) in sea-view suites, again including three meals for two persons.

Great ingenuity has been lavished on the suites (one dedicated to James Bond) and especially the bathrooms. No hotel in Portugal has spent so much—in money or attention—on its bathrooms, one or two of which would appeal to Mae West. One suite contains a real leopard skin on the bed and floor and an antique French telephone; another lace-under-glass headboards. These deluxe suites go for 2,808$ ($109.51) when occupied by two persons on the full-pension plan.

Madeira Palácio, Estrada Monumental (tel. 300-01), is on the seaside route to Camara de Lobos, about two miles outside Funchal. The hotel, formerly the Hilton, is perched on a cliff over the sea. From the establishment, Madeira's famous high cliff, Cabo Girao, can be seen looming in the near distance.

With 260 air-conditioned rooms, the Palácio is one of the largest hotels in Madeira. Each accommodation has a spacious balcony, private bath, direct-dial phone, and radio. From May to September the demi-pension rate in a single is 720$ ($28.08), increasing to 1,115$ ($43.51) in a twin. Demi-pension from October to April is 855$ ($33.35) in a single, jumping to 1,355$ ($52.85) in a twin, service and taxes included.

The hotel's category is resort deluxe: it's contemporary, star-shaped with three wings. Inside, the public salons and guest rooms are sleek, well appointed and colorfully coordinated. Local woods, local construction materials, and Madeiran fabrics are used. Facilities include three restaurants, with both local dishes and an international cuisine; a large heated fresh-water swimming pool with its own cafe; a garden with two tennis courts; shopping arcade; hairdresser, sauna, plus a nightclub whose repertoire ranges from international shows to folklore dances.

Madeira-Sheraton, Largo António Nobre (tel. 310-31), is a luxurious, 17-story, high-rise structure near the Casino and the only hotel with direct access to the sea. Built at a cost of some $12 million, the 300-room hotel offers three swimming pools, a restaurant for 450 persons, plus an English pub, a specialty grill, and a nightclub for 200. All the accommodations, many furnished in a provincial style, are air conditioned with private balconies and baths. In the high winter season, singles, depending on the view, range in price from 550$ ($21.45) to 825$ ($32.18); doubles, 790$ ($30.81) to 1,185$ ($46.24), taxes and service included. In summer, singles are in the 470$ ($18.33) to 705$ ($27.50) bracket; doubles, 670$ ($26.13) to 1,000$ ($39). Half pension is an additional 245$ ($9.56) per person.

The hotel was more than 85 percent financed and furnished with Portuguese products, and some 10 percent of its regular staff includes Madeirans who have come back home. The hotel lies on a promontory overlooking Funchal Bay in the fashionable Vale-Verde Garden district, next to the century-old landmark, Reid's. Its oceanfront exposure to the south offers dawn to dusk sunlight on all pool terraces and seaside guest room balconies and patios.

Take a ride on the cylindrical elevator: it's spectacular.

MADEIRA: FUNCHAL

The Medium-Priced Range

Vila Ramos, Azinhaga da Casa Brança (tel. 311-81), is in the western part of town with nearly all rooms offering views of the sea. All 96 bedrooms are with private baths, phones, air conditioning, and balconies. The color-coordinated rooms are well styled and comfortable, singles renting for 530$ ($20.68) for half pension, doubles ranging from 820$ ($31.98) to 850$ ($33.15), depending on the view. (These rates include half board.) The swimming pool's heated and there's bar service on the terrace. The cuisine is standard international fare, but there's an à la carte menu for guests wishing to sample regional specialties. On the seventh floor is a nightclub with an orchestra. From the top-floor solarium, a panoramic view unfolds.

Hotel Orquîdea, 71 Rua dos Netos (tel. 260-91). The Orchid blooms right in Funchal itself. A first-class hotel, it offers 70 small, but comfortable bedrooms, each with private bath and phone. Most of the accommodations open onto their own terraces. Inside, the atmosphere is sleek modern, with polished marble surfaces and much plastic. For a room with an English breakfast, one person in high season pays 240$ ($9.36), that fee increasing to 380$ ($14.82) for two, taxes included. The best feature of the hotel is its rooftop terrace, with a panoramic view of the town and port.

Santa Isabel, Avenida do Infante (tel. 231-11), was built in the early 60s to accommodate groups who wanted completely modern accommodations in the sun. In the center of the deluxe hotel belt, it was equipped with its own rooftop terrace and swimming pool. How luxurious it is to swim, sunbathe, and lunch around the pool—without having to change one's attire.

The atmosphere is somewhat impersonal, although the bedrooms are warmly decorated, each with a triangular sun balcony. Armless soft chairs, homespun striped draperies, and combined chests of drawers with lift-up mirror dressing tables give the rooms a comfortable edge. Freshly maintained and tiled baths are included with each room. There are three grades of accommodations, extending from the more expensive ones facing the sea to the cheaper rooms opening onto a garden and a mountain view.

In high season, the demi-pension rate in a double is 780$ ($30.43), dropping to 470$ ($18.33) in a single. A public lounge with an open fireplace adjoins a bricked sun terrace.

Nova Avenida, Rua da Favilla (tel. 200-43), is a stately, overgrown villa—placed in its own garden at the side of a gorge and opening onto a view of the harbor and mountains. Built by the English, it now belongs to the Portuguese government, and guests of the Nova Avenida are given free access to the facilities of the Sheraton. The main lounge of the New Avenue is dominated by a crystal chandelier, with pleasant furnishings.

The bedrooms are well-styled and, of course, immaculate. Some rooms face the sea; some the mountains; a few contain balconies—you pay accordingly. In high season, two persons are charged 820$ ($31.98), 850$ ($33.15), and 880$ ($34.33) for full pension. One person is billed either 495$ ($19.31) or 515$ ($20.09) for full board.

Hotel do Carmo, off the Avenida Joao de Deus at 10 Travessa do Rego (tel. 290-01), provides modern accommodations right in the center of Funchal. One of the newest hotels to sprout up in the city, it is erected in a cellular honeycomb fashion, each bedroom opening onto its private balcony. While there is no surrounding garden, guests gather during the day for dips in the L-shaped rooftop swimming pool (good view of the harbor from here).

Created by the Fernandes family, it was designed for guests who have limited purses and want to be near the bazaars in the heart of the city's life. The bedrooms are simple, with contemporary furnishings (wall-to-wall draperies, overhead bed lights, armchairs, tiled bathrooms). For a room and full board, one person pays 435$ ($16.97), two persons, 730$ ($28.48). Meals are served in the spacious dining room, decorated with a green harlequin tiled floor. A little lounge opens off an inner patio.

Girassol, 256 Estrada Monumental (tel. 310-51), is one of the newer little hotels, offering immaculate accommodations at reasonably low tariffs. It's on the outskirts of Funchal, overlooking the Tourist Club where guests are allowed free access to the sea. Every one of its accommodations has a sunny balcony, half overlooking the mountains, the rest viewing the sea. Each chamber also comes complete with private bath, including a shower, plus a radio and telephone. The room decor is bright and cheerful. On the demi-pension plan, two persons can stay here at a cost ranging from 770$ ($30.03) to 820$ ($31.98), including taxes and service. If double rooms are put to single use, the half-board rate goes from 480$ ($18.72) to 530$ ($20.68). Two swimming pools are available, one for children. Guests can also catch the sun on the 12th-floor solarium. On the street level is a bar and social lounge, even a discotheque and hairdressing salon. Two other special features include an entrance courtyard with a series of octagon reflection pools and a dining room with sea views.

The Budget Range

Miramar Hotel, Estrada Monumental (tel. 211-41), is one of the great old villas of Funchal, functioning now as a very personal hotel. While it appears to be much older, it was the grandiose creation of a wine and shipping merchant named Solomao Veiga França. Built in 1922, it was once considered the finest house in the city. It was dubbed Solomon's Temple, but sadly, he lost it during the Depression.

It is under the management of Ronald Garton, who also serves as the American Consular Agent. The style of the mansion is preserved but improved. It is built on several acres of gardens facing the harbor—hauntingly similar to a Beverly Hills estate. Its entrance is through formal gates and a central stone staircase, with balustrades covered with ivy. The front veranda is glass covered, with a climbing magenta-colored trumpet vine. Most impressive is the central two-story-high entrance hall, with a curving wooden staircase and paneled doorways. The drawing room and adjoining card salon are neoclassic, furnished in a homey fashion—more English than stylish. Log fires burn in the winter months.

Meals are served either in the coral and white dining room, which has window walls opening onto the garden and harbor view, or in summer in the garden bower under a giant camphor tree. Accommodations are offered in the main house as well as two chalets, some of which have little private gardens. The rooms are furnished with brightly painted pieces in pastel sea colors and most have wicker chairs and end tables, as well as sitting areas. Prices vary if you have the luxury of a private bath or a balcony. The full-board tariff for a single with a shared bath is 345$ ($13.46), increasing to 375$ ($14.63) with a private bath. The charge for a double with a shared bath is from 560$ ($21.84) for full pension, increasing to 715$ ($27.89) with private bath. All taxes are included.

The Best Bargains

Quinta da Penha de França, off the Rua da Penha de França (tel. 290-87), exists because of the dash and impulsiveness of Muriel Ribeiro, who startled the substantial citizens of Funchal by turning her gracious old quinta into a guest house. Married to a successful surgeon, she took quite seriously the announcement of her son that he wanted to learn the hotel business. After a short training period in London, he now works for her at the quinta.

Their family home, chock full of antiques, paintings, and silver, is in its own garden right on a ledge—almost hanging over the harbor. You couldn't be more dramatically positioned. It's a short walk to the center of the bazaars and is opposite an ancient chapel. The four-story antiga casa is bone white with dark green shutters, plus small-paned windows overlooking the ocean. Across the front terrace is a good-sized swimming pool with white wicker garden chairs arranged for lazy lounging. Set on the hillside in the midst of poinsettias, bamboo, sugar cane, and coffee plants is a wine lodge and stone washhouse now converted into guest rooms.

The furnishings of the public lounges and bedrooms are an heirloom mixture. She likes to mix people as well ("not too much of the same kind"). The rooms with bath on the top floor, with the slanted wooden ceilings, are "favored by the Swiss," she said, "because of the woodsy coziness." There are two bedrooms appreciated by the English as "they don't mind the hall bathrooms." Two rooms with wide windows are requested by sun-seeking Swedes. The rooms with the antiques, tiled baths, and soft beds she saves for those creatures of comfort, the Americans. Doubles with bath go for 410$ ($15.99), including breakfast. The bungalows and rooms with kitchenettes cost 450$ ($17.55) for two, but breakfast isn't included. All tariffs include taxes.

A scrumptious breakfast is provided, though the lady of the house is full of tips on nontouristy places to dine. A tray is set with family silver on hand-embroidered linen, with homemade jams, rolls, country butter, bananas, and freshly squeezed orange juice. "Americans don't like Portuguese coffee," she said, "so I got a can of Martinson's and asked my man to roast it as closely as possible." Muriel Ribeiro, who speaks English in a knowing way, treats everyone like a house guest. Snacks are also served, and a bar, the Privado, is at the end of the garden.

Pensao Vila Belo Mar, 193 Estrada Monumental (tel. 207-32), is a kind of private beach club with a dining room, swimming pool, and space enough for 33 guests in 18 bedrooms. Life centers on a flagstone terrace opening onto a cliff over the sea. Guests swim in the free-form pool, lounge on the terrace chairs, and drink at the adjoining bar. The cost for half pension for one person is 315$ ($12.29), increasing to 620$ ($24.18) for two persons. All accommodations contain private baths. The furnishings are individualized in the modern idiom, with a generous use of Scandinavian colors. Fresh flowers are put in your room to welcome you to Madeira. If you're dropping by just for a swim, the rate is 35$ per person. Even if you don't sleep in the precincts, you'll be welcome at the dining room for either lunch or dinner, enjoying an à la carte meal of such items as pepper steak flambé at 95$ ($3.71) or chicken Belo Mar at 80$ ($3.12).

Quinta Elisabeth, 65 Rua da Coronel Cunha (tel. 231-71). Operated as a hostelry since 1854, this charming quinta functioned as the first hotel in Madeira. It's run by Mr. and Mrs. Pestana.

The gardens of the quinta are replete with mosaic-pebbled paths, arbors, old stone stairways, and a small swimming pool with umbrellas, tables, and chaise longues. The quinta has kept its feeling of an old private country house, which is perched high on a mountain overlooking Funchal and the ocean. From the balustraded terraces, the view is spectacular.

The quinta has 18 rooms and 32 beds. Most of the guests arrive from Germany weekly in tour groups, but Senhora Pestana will take in a couple or so when her house isn't filled. All rooms contain a private bath and toilet. The half-board rate peaks at 350$ ($13.65) in a single, 550$ ($21.45) in a double. The most expensive sea-view doubles with balconies cost 580$ ($22.63) for two persons on the demi-pension plan. In summer, rates are reduced slightly.

A bus runs into the village about every 10 minutes during the day.

Vila Lido, 17 Rua do Gorgulho (tel. 211-00), stands on the edge of a rocky cliff directly above the sea. It's surrounded by its own lawns and gardens. Owned by Georg and Hilma Kraus, from Essen, Germany, the villa attracts a large patronage not only from their own country, but the Scandinavian countries as well. The couple speak English and bring a homelike hospitality to their place. The food is excellent, and the setting is comfortable and moderately attractive. Antiques are interspersed with more contemporary pieces, usually in floral chintz. Bright colors prevail. Tariffs for bed and breakfast range from 280$ ($10.92) in some doubles to 310$ ($12.09) for the best doubles which include balconies opening onto the sea. Two persons, with lunch included, pay anywhere from 480$ ($18.72) to 510$ ($19.89) daily. Arrangements for light evening meals at 100$ ($3.90) per person can be made. The Vila Lido lies a ten-minute ride by bus from the center of Funchal.

MACHICO: If you don't mind living at Machico on the east coast where the Portuguese first landed, you'll find two more excellent hotels. This part of land-scarce Madeira is being rapidly developed. Already a number of tiny vacation villas are climbing the hillside. In the complex is a yacht club, plus an elegant bridge club. Machico is about five minutes from the airport, but a good 30-minute run along a twisting road to Funchal.

Two Hotels

Atlantis, Agua de Pena, Machico (tel. 544-01), stands gleaming white in the Madeira sun, a mammoth complex of 300 tastefully furnished rooms, which in high season (December 1 to April 30) go for 770$ ($30.03) for one person, 1,240$ ($48.36) for two, on the half-pension plan. It's a complete resort world unto itself, featuring a heated indoor pool with a sunroof in the lobby. The outdoor Figure 8 pool is another highlight especially when the weather's right. Dining on international cuisine is either in the Algarve Restaurant, done in creamy orange, or in the Madeira dining room, decorated in rose and brown. There's also a boîte for dancing. The inn's own bus makes frequent trips back and forth from Funchal.

Nearby is the **Hotel Dom Pedro da Madeira,** Machico (tel. 544-50), a modern structure that boasts sea views, private baths, and phones for every room. The sparsely furnished rooms are well kept, comfortable, and tastefully appointed. On the half-pension plan, one person is charged 465$ ($18.14), that tariff rising to 790$ ($30.81) for two. Rooms with balconies and suites cost more. An extra meal, if you're just dropping by, is 150$ ($5.85). Good food is served in the Panoramic Restaurant. A bar, a heated salt-water swimming pool, sun terraces, a private beach, even a discotheque, make this an especially nice choice.

THE RESTAURANTS: Many of the major hotels require full or demi-pension in high season; but perhaps you'll be able to sneak away for a regional meal at one of the recommendations listed below. The list begins, however, with the pick of the hotel restaurants.

The Upper Bracket

Reid's Grill, Reid's Hotel, 139 Estrada Monumental (tel. 230-01), is generally conceded to be the island's finest restaurant. Both guests and the local gentry consider it the perfect place to celebrate a new amour or console oneself after the loss of an old love. True to English tradition, clients dress for dinner, the women often in silk, the men sedate in black tie.

The chef combines a French, Portuguese, and English cuisine that makes for a bill of fare peculiar to Reid's. For your palatable preliminaries, you can try everything from Portuguese soup at 40$ ($1.56) to homemade terrine (potted meat in a crock) at 50$ ($1.95). The kitchen offers about a dozen specialties, worth several visits just to sample them.

Favored are the fish stew Funchal style, sea bass with fennel, and espetada, chunks of beef fillet skewered on a branch of laurel tree. Americans especially are fond of the porterhouse steak for two. To top your repast, you can select from the sweet trolley. Any meal here will cost you an average of 260$ ($10.14), and you can be sure it will be excellent.

The Medium-Priced Range

Restaurante Caravela, 15-17 Avenida do Mar (tel. 284-64), is a modern restaurant right on the waterfront. You can dine on a glass-enclosed terrace with an open fireplace or else in the inner room where you sit in wicker chairs. Reached by elevator, the top-floor restaurant gives diners an intimate view of the cruise ships arriving and departing. You can order both lunch and dinner, as well as afternoon tea with open-faced Danish smørrebrød sandwiches. What to offer daily on the menu is decided by the Caravela's Swedish owner, Lennart Cederlund.

The cooking is personal, with a large choice of tasty dishes. Perhaps the finest regional dish is espetada, skewered meat flavored with garlic and bay leaves, costing 65$ ($2.54) and only served on special request. Unpretentious and proud of the native Portuguese dishes, the restaurant features Caravela fish for 55$ ($2.15), but also turns out international dishes, such as châteaubriand flambé, 85$ ($3.32). A favorite dessert is a fruit salad at 25$ (98¢). The restaurant is open seven days a week, with lunch served between 11 a.m. and 3 p.m.; dinner from 7-11 p.m.

Clube de Turismo da Madeira, 179 Estrada Monumental (tel. 203-59), is a fine place for lunch and a swim. At the edge of Funchal, it appears to be a private club, but membership isn't necessary. Approached through a lane of poinsettias, sugar cane, and bougainvillea, the club is close to the sea. It's like a small tiled villa, with a beachhouse built to adjoin a free-form swimming pool. Delicious meals are served in one of the intimate dining rooms or on a covered veranda where guests relax in rattan chairs. One interior salon is 19th-century formal, with crystal chandeliers and mahogany chairs. The bar, with iron lanterns, tavern chairs, and pine beams, is more rustic.

A typical meal begins with a well-prepared hearty soup, costing 15$ (59¢). Fish dishes include such items as grilled red mullet or a more expensive natural lobster. Meat courses include Portuguese beef or roast chicken. Regular main dishes are priced from 50$ ($1.95) to 90$ ($3.51). Even if you stop in just for a drink, you'll be welcomed. A dry martini or cognac goes for 25$ (98¢). To use the pool, you pay 20$ (78¢), the tab including a changing cabin. Lunch is served from 12:30 to 3:30 p.m.; dinner from 7-10 daily.

Jardim do Sol, Caniço, on the coast highway east of Funchal (tel. 931-23). This roadside inn is like a hunting lodge, with knotty pine walls, a mezzanine, rattan chairs, and two walls of glass with a view of the sea through tall pines. The owner has installed framed murals of the local fishermen, a bamboo bar, and window boxes overflowing with orange marigolds. The proprietor caters not only to the residents of Funchal, but to the cruise ships that tie up in port.

A 160$ ($6.24) table d'hôte luncheon or dinner is offered, though the wine is extra. You'll be given a first course, usually a big bowl of good-tasting soup, followed by a fish dish such as caldeirada (like a bouillabaisse), then a meat course, a dessert, and finally fresh fruit. The restaurant opens at noon for lunch and closes at midnight.

The Budget Range

A Seta, 80 Estrada do Livramento, Monte (tel. 203-06), is for regional cuisine suprême. The mountainside restaurant is a tavern-style place where you can order inexpensive and tasty meals. The proprietor seemingly patterns himself after Ernest Borgnine, shirt sleeves and all. The decor is rustic, with a burnt wood trim, walls covered with pine cones, and crude natural pine tables. An inner dining room adjoins an open kitchen, with a charcoal spit and oven—ideal for those who want to watch the action.

First of all, a plate of coarse brown homemade bread—still warm from the oven—is put at your place. Above each table is a hook to which is attached a long skewer of charcoal-broiled meat. You slip off chunks while mopping up the juices with your crusty bread. There are three specialties: beef, chicken, and grilled dry codfish. Seasoned with olive oil, herbs, garlic, and bay leaves, these concoctions are called espetadas. A bowl of rich-tasting soup costs 25$ (98¢); the breads, 6$ (23¢); a salad, 20$ (78¢); the fried potatoes, 20$ also; and a skewer of beef, 65$ ($2.54). The least expensive bottle of wine goes for 30$ ($1.17).

Restaurante dos Combatentes, 1 Rua Ivens, is a budget choice for regional food, a favorite of Funchal's colony of doctors and lawyers. At the top of a park, this simple Portuguese restaurant serves well-prepared meat courses, such as a mixed grill for 60$ ($2.34). The classic Portuguese codfish dish, bacalhau à Bras goes for 50$ ($1.95). Caramel pudding is the most popular dessert, 7$ (27¢).

Gavinas, Rua do Gorgulho, won't please everybody! It's in a category by itself, the most rustic dining spot in this entire guide. Reached by driving out the Estrada Monumental to the Lido, it is a little garage-like cement cottage set amongst the rocks on the sea. You pass along a field of sugar cane overlooking the water, then descend the cliff via a narrow cobblestoned pathway. Despite the ethnic setting (even an occasional drunk stumbling over to you), Gavinas draws a stream of well-heeled tourists.

The fish is as fresh as one can imagine—practically cleaned and cooked right in front of you. No fancy saucers, no elaborate service—just hearty sea fare, cooked the way many of the Madeirans cherish it. You'll spend about 100$ ($3.90) for a regular meal, including a salad, bread, plus wine or beer. Sometimes the owner-chef, Senhor Gavinas, makes a savory caldeirada (fish stew), but generally he grills or fries at his primitive stove.

Tea & Pastries

Casa Minas Ceraes ("The Corner Shop"), Avenida do Infante, is an old-fashioned tea and pastry shop which has been around for more than 40 years. At its central serving bar, waiters make pots of tea and coffee or else pour Madeira wine. Before sitting at one of the little tables, clients pick out a pastry, paying for it separately. The waiters bring only the beverages. Against the walls are tall built-in cupboards, with glass doors in bright blue and gold. Shoeshine boys ply their trade from table to table. A pot of tea costs 12$ (47¢) for two persons. The Corner Shop opens onto a circular fountain and the busy boulevard.

READER'S TIP: "Do see **Camacha**, where the wicker factory is. You can watch employees, many of them children, making the wicker products. They are very cheap and well made. Near the wicker place is a restaurant, **Flor da Achada**, that is quite good. The whole restaurant is covered in wicker—the ceiling, walls, decorations, and chairs. Two of us had a meal consisting of chicken, french fries, seasoned rice, a liter of house wine, and custard, for which we paid 150$ ($5.85)" (W. Michael Sharpe, Windsor, Ontario, Canada).

TOBOGGAN RIDES: Time was when the visiting Victorians (some of the men looking like Mr. Pickwick) were carried around the islands in hammocks—slung on poles and supported by two husky bearers. Nowadays, the government is discouraging this form of transport, though it still exists. As one official put it: "The Communists object to it. They consider it a form of slavery." A more popular means of transport in Funchal itself is to hire a bullock-pulled, wheel-less sledge on the Avenida do Mar, near the pier.

By far, the most famous ride is the descent by toboggan from **Monte,** about four miles from Funchal. You ascend by taxi, about a 20-minute trip. Before you begin your descent, you can visit the **Church of Nossa Senhora do Monte,** which contains the iron tomb of the last of the Hapsburgs, the Emperor Charles who died in Madeira in 1922 of pneumonia. From a belvedere nearby, you can look down on the whole of Funchal: the narrow streets, the plazas, and especially the cais, that long docking pier set in deep blue mirror-like water.

The descent from Monte can be by toboggan, a wide wicker basket with wooden runners. As it rushes down the slippery smooth cobblestones, it is directed and sometimes propelled by two expert, straw-hatted guides who yaw the ropes like nimble-footed seamen. You may need to fortify yourself with a glass or two of Madeira wine before taking the plunge. From Monte to Funchal, the ride costs 100$ ($3.90) per person. You can also take the toboggan ride from **Terreiro da Luta** to Funchal. At Terreiro da Luta, at a height of 2,875 feet, you'll enjoy another splendid view of Funchal. Here also are monuments to Zarco and Our Lady of Peace.

FOLK DANCING: The **Windsor** at Terreiro da Luta (tel. 235-88) offers a folkloric exhibition at an outside dancing ring. Dancers in native costumes perform in a circle to live musical accompaniment. The cost is 120$ ($4.68) per person, including a glass of Madeira wine. From the dining room, which seats 400 guests, there is a full view of Funchal and the port from a height of 13,000 feet.

FUNCHAL AFTER DARK: The **Casino,** Rua da Imperatriz, at the Quinta Vigia, is the star nightlife attraction of the island. It lies only five minutes from many of the main hotels in the center of town. Throughout the year it's open from 3 p.m. till 3 a.m. Admission is easy for foreign tourists. Take along your passport or any other identification card. The entrance fee for two nights is 40$ ($1.56), increasing to 60$ ($2.34) for one week.

There is a special room of slot machines and a gambling room with tables of roulette, French bank, blackjack, as well as slot machines. Three bars offer drinks.

As of this writing, the Casino is housed in the future Theater and Congress Hall of Funchal. This is a new building, part of a Casino complex under construction. It is decorated as a provisory casino, to be used only while the new one is being built.

The completed Casino is not expected to be ready until late in 1976. Plans call for a restaurant, nightclub, slot-machine room, European gambling room, American gambling room, and a salle privé.

Slated for an opening in the spring of 1976 is the five-star **Casino Park Hotel,** with 400 luxurious rooms.

Taverna Real, 4 Rua da Cabeia Valha (tel. 281-87), is considered the most historic and typical wine-cellar in Portugal. Today it is a bar-boîte where you can hear genuine fado and see folklore dances. Rebuilt in 1511, the cellar had been frequented by Columbus Gonçalves Zarco, the discoverer of Madeira. Some stones from Columbus' house can be seen in several parts of the wine-cellar. On the walls are the arms of Prince Henry the Navigator (who founded the nautical school at Sagres), Gonçalves Zarco, Vasco da Gama, Pedro A. Cabral, and others. Although fado is the principal attraction, food is served, including Portuguese sausages flamed in sugar-cane brandy. A typical spit-roasted meal costs 50$ ($1.95) a portion. The owner Professor César Figueroa César is proud of the remains of a secular underground prison for pirates and a cistern from the 15th century. His place is lively and popular, especially with young people.

The Prince Albert, Rua da Imperatriz D. Amélia, is a Victorian pub in Madeira, complete with cut plush velvet walls, tufted banquettes, and English pub memorabilia. You're greeted with a "Good evening, sir." Next to the Savoy, the pub serves oversized mugs of beer and a cross sampling of all the accents of England. Drinks are served at the curved bar or at one of the tables under Edwardian fringed lamps. Whiskies range from 27$50 ($1.07) to 50$ ($1.95); beer, from 10$ (39¢) to 30$ ($1.17).

2. Excursions in Madeira

To explore and savor Madeira, the adventurous visitor—with endless time—will go on foot across some of the trails. Hand-hewn stones and gravel side embankments lead one (though definitely not the queasy) along precipitous ledges, down into lush ravines, across flowering meadows. These dizzying paths are found everywhere from the hillsides of the wine-rich region of Estreito de Câmara de Lobos to the wicker-work center at Camacha.

A much easier way to go, of course, is on an organized tour, although you may prefer to risk the hazardous driving on hairpin curves by renting your own automobile in Funchal, competing for space on the narrow coastal road with overloaded banana trucks.

Heading west from Funchal, you'll pass banana groves almost spilling into the sea, women doing their laundry on rocks, and homes so tiny they're almost like doll houses. Less than six miles away lies the famous coastal village of

Câmara de Lobos (Room of the Wolves), the subject of several paintings by Sir Winston Churchill. A sheltered and tranquil shell-shaped cove, it is set amidst rocks and towering cliffs, with hill-climbing cottages, terraces, and date palms. In the late afternoon, naked youngsters loll and play in the cove, alongside the bobbing fishing boats in such colors as sunflower gold, kelly green, and marine blue.

The road north from the village through the vineyards leads to **Estreito de Câmara de Lobos,** the heart of the wine-growing region that produces the famous Madeira. The men who cultivate the ribbon-like terraces can be seen laboring in the fields, wearing brown stocking caps with tasseled tops. Along the way you'll spot women sitting on mossy stone steps, doing Madeira embroidery. At times clouds move in over the mountain tops obscuring the view, then pass off toward the sea or tumble down a hillside. One visitor compared the effect to "a very expensive production of Götterdämmerung."

A helpful reader, Herman Marcuse, Arlington, Va., adds this footnote: "One of the best kept secrets on Madeira is that you can make excursions on local buses at a fraction charged by the tour companies."

Scaling a hill studded with pine and eucalyptus, you'll reach **Cabo Girao,** the oceanside cliff mentioned in the introduction. Considered the second loftiest promontory in Europe, a belvedere overlooks the sea and the saffron-colored rocks below. Close by, you can see how the land is cultivated in Madeira, one terrace seemingly no larger than a small throw rug. (Incidentally, the blondes you see in and around here aren't peroxided. Rather, the straw-colored hair was inherited from early Flemish settlers sent to the island.)

Try to return to Funchal by veering off the coastal road, past Sao Martinho to the belvedere at **Pico dos Barcelos.** In one of the most idyllic spots on the island, you can see the ocean, the mountains, orange and banana groves, bougainvillea in every direction, poinsettias, and the capital itself. Whether it's roosters crowing, babies crying in faraway huts, or goats bleating, the sound carries for miles.

By heading north from Funchal, you can visit some of the most outstanding spots in the heart of the island. Going first through Santo António, you'll eventually reach **Curral da Freiras,** a petite village huddled around an old monastery at the bottom of an extinct volcanic crater. The site—whose name means Corral of the Nuns—was originally a secluded convent which protected the good sisters from the appetites of sea-weary, woman-hungry mariners and pirates.

If you go north in a different direction, one of the goals is **Santana.** Many visitors have described it as something out of Disney's "Fantasia." Picture an alpine setting, complete with waterfalls, cobblestoned streets, green meadows sprinkled with multi-colored blossoms, thatched cottages, swarms of roses, and plunging ravines. Of it, novelist Paul Bowles once wrote: "It is as if a 19th-century painter with a taste for the baroque had invented a countryside to suit his own personal fantasy. It is the sort of picture that used to adorn the grocer's calendar."

Southwest of the village is **Queimadas,** the site of a 3,000-foot-high rest house. From here, many make the three-hour trek to the apex of **Pico Ruivo** (Purple Peak), referred to earlier as the highest point on the island, 6,105 feet above sea level.

In the east, about 18 miles from Funchal (a short drive from the airport) is historical **Machico,** with its much-visited **Church of Senhor dos Milagres,** dating from the mid-15th-century. According to legend, the church was built over the tombs of the two star-crossed English lovers, Robert Machim and

Anna d'Arfet. Try to view the village from the belvedere of **Camoes Pequeno**. In the vicinity is a grotto 300 feet long, said to be the deepest in Madeira.

On the way back from Machico, you can detour inland to **Camacha**, perched in a setting of flowers and orchards. It's the island center of the wicker-work industry. You can buy here (although the stores back in Funchal are heavily supplied), or just watch chairs and other items being made by the local craftsmen.

Those who stay only in Funchal miss what the island is about. If you don't care to venture into the mountains in your own automobile, then take one of the many excursions to different sections of the island. The tours reach virtually every accessible point in Madeira from Porto Moniz to Câmara de Lobos, and many of the excursions are terminated in Monte where you can finish with a toboggan ride into Funchal. Various tours leave every day except Sunday; the major jaunt to Porto Moniz runs Tuesdays and Fridays, and costs 280$ ($10.92). A toboggan tour departs at 2:30 p.m. on Thursdays, costing 180$ ($7.02). The Santana tour is a Saturday destination, leaving at 9 a.m. and costing 380$ ($14.82), including lunch and tea. A regular Monday tour of the city of Funchal departs at 9 a.m., and finishes at 12:30 p.m. for a price of 80$ ($3.12). Madeira possesses a number of travel agencies, including Wagons-Lits Cook. If you go to any of them, you can receive detailed information about the island tours available. Not all are by motorcoach; some are by boat. You can also pick up information at the **Official Tourist Bureau**, on the jacaranda-lined Avenida Arriaga.

ISLAND DINING: While exploring Madeira, you may want to arrange luncheon stopovers at one of the following recommendations:

The government-owned **Pousada dos Vinhaticos**, near Serra de Agua (tel. 62344), is near the top of a pass on the winding road to Sao Vincente. Guests can visit just for a meal or else spend the night. The pousada is built of solid stone, a tavern-styled building with a brick terrace. On that terrace comfortable wicker armchairs are placed, allowing visitors to absorb the unmarred mountain views. The cooking is regional, a complete meal costing 100$ ($3.90). Most of the bedrooms are in Portuguese modern, though a few accommodations contain antiques. All have private baths, good views, and are kept immaculately. The full-board cost of staying here is 450$ ($17.55) per person nightly.

Áquario, Seixal, is a waterfront fish restaurant too often ignored by visitors who flock to the dining spots of Porto Moniz where they have to fight for a seat. In less confusion, clients at Áquario enjoy some of the tastiest cooking on the island. Although the kitchen turns out simple fare, the cooking often outdistances the table d'hôte menus served in the deluxe hotels. Everything is prepared fresh for a diner. The tall proprietor oversees every serving by the neophyte waitresses. To begin with, one gets a heaping basket of homemade bread and a carafe of the local wine. We'd recommend the grilled fish of the day, served with three vegetables. Fish plates cost 70$ ($2.73), and the less recommended meat dishes average 75$ ($2.93). Soups are hearty, the helpings generous, and the cost is 15$ (59¢) per bowl. The decor is nautical, the walls decorated with objects rescued from the sea. On sale are handmade straw and reed baskets. Lunch only is offered, and you can arrive any time before 3:30 p.m. and be served.

A Cabana, Beira da Quinta Sao Jorge (tel. 57291), is a colony of circular cottages with central roofs, arranged at the edge of a cliff on the northern coast of Madeira. True to the architecture of the region, the roofs are thatched. The furnishings are crude, though attractive. Each unit has a private bath and a bed recess, along with a Murphy bed. Two armchairs await one on either side of a fireplace. The cost is only 150$ ($5.85) per person in the winter months, rising to 200$ ($7.80) in summer. The coffee's free.

A much larger circular thatched hut with an open beamed ceiling provides good-tasting meals at about 120$ ($4.68) per person. Many of the specialties are cooked on a large open semi-circular charcoal fireplace. Specialties include beef grilled on a spit, roast chicken, roast cod, panada, and "bolos do caco," a typical bread.

3. Discovering the Azores

The lost paradise . . . legends of enchanted princesses . . . hydrangea-bordered highways . . . lakes at the bottom of extinct volcanic craters . . . natural springs of therapeutic waters . . . windmills clacking on top of hills . . . oxen plowing the fields like a tableau vivant suspended in time . . . mist- and cloud-shrouded islands . . . and men armed with hand harpoons in pursuit of the elusive sperm whale.

Those seeking an offbeat holiday in Europe can strike out for the Azores. It is an archipelago where the winds of the ocean meet, where the cyclones call on each other. Robin Bryans called the islands a "muted mood, a pianissimo untouched by the strident dissonance of industrial Europe."

Ever since the first explorers directed their ships' prows into the Atlantic, it is likely that their crow's nest sighted the volcanic slopes of the Azores. Whether the Vikings, the Genoese, the Phoenicians, or whomever, put into these lands remains unknown. There are those who believe that the Azores are all that remain of the lost continent of Atlantis.

The archipelago spans a distance of more than 500 miles from the southeastern tip of Santa Maria to the northwestern extremity at Corvo. The main island of **Sao Miguel** lies about 760 miles west of Portugal (2,110 miles east of New York), making the Azores the most isolated islands in the entire Atlantic.

Completely uninhabited when discovered, the Azores were named by Diogo de Silves (a captain of Henry the Navigator) after the hook-beaked açor (compared to both a hawk and an eagle), which sailed on the air currents over the coast. The date: 1427. It wasn't long before settlements sprang up.

Eventually it was learned that the entire island group was actually composed of three distinct mini-archipelagos: the eastern section of **Santa Maria** and **Sao Miguel;** the central with **Terceira** (site of an Atlantic air base of the United States—scene of bullfighting in the streets), **Graciosa** (about 11 miles in length, famous for its Sulphur Cave), cigar-shaped **Sao Jorge** (Raul Brandao's ethereal island of dust and dream); and the western or Horta District of **Pico** (really a cloud-capped mountain with a whaling factory); **Faial** (vulnerable to earthquakes and known for the eerie crater of the extinct volcano, Caldeira); **Flores** (Flowers) where vegetation runs riot in a setting of lakes, waterfalls, and valleys; and **Corvo** (the smallest and most westerly member—everybody knows everybody else—and a visit by a foreigner is an occasion).

The Azores are a study in color. The writer who once made the much-publicized characterization—the "Gray Azores"—must have been color blind. Much of the color of the archipelago comes from the flowers that grow rampantly in its volcanic soil: azaleas, camellias, heather, agapanthus, rhododendrons. Although occasionally lashed by violent storms, the enchanted islands enjoy a mild climate—the temperature averaging around 58 degrees Fahrenheit in winter, only 75 degrees Fahrenheit in summer.

Its rugged people who daily contend with the elements of nature have emerged friendly and hospitable to strangers—even though one would have expected such isolated islanders to be insular. Coming back from a walk in the Sao Miguel hills, two American visitors were stopped by a boy riding a mule. Under a straw hat—with a hoe slung over his shoulder—his face beamed as he bid "Bom noite." The word YALE was written across his sweat shirt. Learning that he spoke a bit of English, the visitors inquired about the letters. It seemed that his uncle had attended Yale. "Do you know him?" the boy asked. "He now lives in Boston."

Every man, woman, and child in the island chain seemingly has relatives living in the United States. Many settled in New Bedford, Mass. (of Moby Dick fame) during the whaling heyday of that port, taking jobs as sailors, fishermen, whalers, and caulkers. Many of the immigrants returned, however, after earning their fortunes across the sea.

GETTING THERE: At any TAP office or at your local travel agent, you can learn the times and frequency of flights to the Azores. For example, on your return to North America from Lisbon, you might stop off at Santa Maria airport, originally built by the U.S. in 1944 as an Allied air base. The government leased the base to the Allies in World War II, even though Portugal was officially neutral. If you hold a round-trip ticket from New York to Lisbon, you're allowed to stop free in the Azores, providing this desire is declared and arranged when you purchase your ticket. The free stopover may not be valid on special excursion tickets. From Santa Maria, you can take local SATA flights to either Terceira or Sao Miguel. Finally, you might prefer to make the Boston/Terceira flight, then go from there by SATA either to Sao Miguel or Santa Maria. Many possibilities are available for investigation and adventure.

All the red tape of the past, including such requirements as visas for Americans, has now been abandoned. You can also visit the Azores by boat; the **Empresa Insulana de Navegaçao** runs a regular service (consult the passenger department at 152 Rua Augusta in Lisbon).

SANTA MARIA: For many, Santa Maria is just a refueling stop—a place where passengers get out and stretch their legs. But don't judge this island by the scenery at the airport. You have to penetrate deeper to know its charm, and if you're pressed for time, we recommend that you go on to Sao Miguel, saving Santa Maria for another day. Those with more time can explore the serra-studded southernmost island in the archipelago, with its grazing ridges, scattered village houses (some thatched), and roads that are in some cases merely lanes, unpaved and lined with wildflowers.

Speeding around the island (as most visitors invariably do), you get the distinct impression that the clever farmers, like their fellow islanders in Madeira, have used the land to the maximum—and not just for produce, as flowers abound as well.

Vila do Porto, a village near the airport, is the capital, though the designation seems pretentious. It is noted for its old houses and a restored parish church of the 16th century. To the east, **Santo Espírito** contains a much-admired baroque church, the Holy Spirit. With a square bell tower to the right of its portal, it presents a severe facade that is topped by an overscaled baroque scroll with finials. The simple doors are framed by an intricately carved basalt casement. In and around Santo Espírito, you'll pass some of the characteristic Azorean white-sailed windmills, usually honey colored, clacking in the Atlantic winds.

On February 18, 1493, Christopher Columbus moored the Nina off the coast. The explorer's men attended church at **Anjos,** supposedly stripping off their pants and walking single file from the vessel to the chapel to fulfill a vow made at sea when it looked as if they would perish in a storm. The little church that stands today, Our Lady of the Angels, is a reconstruction. Anjos, about a half-hour ride from the airport, is in the northwestern sector of Santa Maria.

THE AZORES: PONTA DELGADA

Picos, near the center of the island, is the highest point (about 1,800 feet above sea level). From its summit, you can absorb what is considered the finest panoramic view of Santa Maria, with the sea as a backdrop.

A night on the island can be an experience to remember, as related by Robin Bryans: ". . . the invisible night ghouls of Santa Maria came to haunt the bay and to make the cliffs echo with their diabolical cries. The ghouls were Mediterranean shearwaters, or cagarros."

The island's accommodations are limited to the following:

A Medium-Priced Hotel

Aeroporto Hotel, Aeroporto de Santa Maria (tel. Aeroporto 117), is barely adequate as a hotel, but on this island you take what is available. In the closing months of World War II, this site was an Officers Club for the American Air Base of Santa Maria. With the opening of the airport to international jet travel, it was remade into a hotel rated second-class by the government to provide stopover accommodations, bungalow-style.

The living room has fireplaces, a high beamed ceiling, and groups of furniture set for conversation and beverages. There's a bar and a spacious dining room in the Terminal Building providing a hearty and very simple Azorean cuisine.

Geared to passengers making the transition between the Old and New Worlds, the Aeroporto Hotel contains 103 rooms, 65 without private baths. A double with bath rents for 280$ ($10.92), dropping to 230$ ($8.97) without bath.

4. Ponta Delgada

Hopefully, you'll arrive in the capital of Sao Miguel in the early evening after a 20-minute flight from Santa Maria. The zebra-striped Avenida Infante D. Henrique—encircling the waterfront—is alive with strollers taking their characteristic paseo. Traditionally, this affords a chance in Iberian towns and villages for the parents of unmarried girls to show off their prizes to the eligible young men.

Today, of course, foreign tourists and sailors in port for the night join in the promenade. Some stop along the ledge to admire the twinkling lights from the boats in the bay. In the 1860s, a breakwater—2,800 feet long—was built, making possible the wide waterfront boulevard. Before that, the harbor and the lower town were completely exposed to the sea.

The next morning you can explore the southern coastal town in more detail, walking its narrow streets, looking at its new buildings, but finding the older ones more interesting. Some of the tile-roofed cottages are walled with lime, and decorated with painted earthenware tiles and black lava adornments.

Founded in the 15th century, Ponta Delgada makes a good base for exploring Sao Miguel, or you can go to the hotel at Furnas, about an hour's drive from the capital. It's recommended that you spend your time not in the baroque churches or the town museum (Santo André in a 16th-century convent), but rather in exploring the natural wonders of the island, which far excel any artificial attraction.

However, you should get in at least one shopping expedition. You're likely to find bargains galore. For example, you may want to browse through a basket bazaar, with not only a wide selection of baskets, but also wicker and willow chairs, handbags, even some articles made from the pith of a fig tree. A personal favorite is the Casa Regional da Ilha Verde (The Regional House of the Green Island), 25 Largo da Matriz. Among its best items are the Azorean embroidery, the regional pottery made of red clay from Vila França do Campo, and souvenirs of sperm whale teeth pulled from Moby Dicks caught right off the shores of the Azores.

On the outskirts of Ponta Delgada, you can arrange to attend one of the pineapple factories—actually greenhouses—where the fruit is grown under slope-ceilinged glass which has been whitewashed. The plants are smoked several times during their growth, as this fumo method is said to make all of them flower at the same time.

In Ponta Delgada, you'll find the finest hotel in the Azores, as well as a few less expensive accommodations.

THE UPPER BRACKET: The Hotel de Sao Pedro, Largo Almirante Dunn (tel. 222-23). Here you can savor the ambience of past centuries, yet enjoy the comforts of the 20th. The building was the love child of the island's most colorful and legendary figure, Thomas Hickling, who came from Boston on a schooner in 1769. He and his descendants profited from a thriving business growing and exporting oranges to London and St. Petersburg (Leningrad). From their wealth, they built a family homestead, with the help of imported craftsmen, and shipped in loads of fine antiques from the continent to furnish it.

Their town house, with its Georgian Colonial interior, is on the sea, with a high garden wall to provide privacy from the street. Throughout its history, it has known many vicissitudes (it was used in World War I as a headquarters for the American Navy).

Nowadays, one can stay here in comparative luxury for moderate tariffs. Though there has been some modernization, such as the installation of private baths in each of the 30 chambers, the essential atmosphere has been preserved. The drawing room, the salons, the dining room are tastefully furnished with many museum-caliber antiques. The majority of the bedrooms are equipped with traditional pieces combined with the old. The suites are furnished in the grand manner—one with a huge Napoleonic sleigh bed, another with spindle twin beds. The rates are complicated, as some of the rooms contain shower baths; others complete baths; some are deluxe; and a few are listed as suites. Full pension for one person in one of the standard rooms ranges from 475$ ($18.53) to 565$ ($22.04); doubles are in the 740$ ($28.86) to 840$ ($32.76) bracket. For a deluxe room or suite, two persons pay anywhere from 835$ ($32.57) to 1,310$ ($51.09) for full pension. All taxes are included in the rates.

In a non-commercial atmosphere, guests are likely to intermingle freely; and the staff is remarkably attentive and considerate. The style is set by the director, Durante M. P. Pimentel, who has won many friends and admirers in America. The drawing room is not overpoweringly stiff, though it is formal, with two bronze and crystal chandeliers, a pair of fine 18th-century fruitwood chests, velvet chairs, and a sofa set in front of an Adam-style fireplace.

The dining room—scene of many excellent, bountiful meals, backed up by a good cellar—contains mahogany chairs at tables set in either the main room or in the oak-beamed alcove, with leaded glass windows and deep paneled Georgian arches. Fresh flowers are everywhere, as important to the character of Sao Pedro as changing the linen sheets. The drinking lounge seems right from Old Salem, Massachusetts, with its hand-hewn beams and Windsor chairs. Drinks are also served on the tiled loggia where you can sit in wicker and leather armchairs under deep arches, enjoying the view of the lawn, the water, the stone urns, and the century-old trees.

THE MEDIUM-PRICED RANGE: Hotel do Infante, Avenida Infante Dom Henrique (tel. 233-31), is recommended for those seeking a prominent position along the waterfront boulevard. Rated first class B by the government, it is a seven-story, honey-combed modern building, with most of its rooms opening onto a balcony with a view of the boat-studded harbor. The architectural and furnishing concept is contemporary, though not stylish.

On the top floor is a building-wide dining room, with three walls of glass that provide an unblocked view of the ships and the Azorean sunsets. Adequate lounges for drinking and conversation are on the street floor. The bedrooms—39 in all, each with private bath—are equipped in a modern style, pleasantly simple. A double with breakfast goes for 312$ ($12.17), dropping to 211$ ($8.23) in a single, also with breakfast. If you order a table d'hôte luncheon or dinner, the cost is 110$ ($4.29).

Tip: ask for fresh pineapple juice for breakfast. Grown in the glass houses nearby, it will become your comparison for all pineapple juices thereafter.

THE BUDGET RANGE: Residencial Casa das Palmeiras, 26 Rua Diário dos Açores (tel. 22-621), is a grand old free-standing villa in the center of Ponta Delgada. Its upper floors have been transformed into colorful and comfortable suites and rooms, with many sophisticated touches. The stairway leading to the residence has glistening woodwork and opera-red walls. Each private room has its own color scheme, with coordinated fabrics and furnishings. All have refrigerators stocked with drinks. Many of the chambers are decorated with antiques, though others are in a contemporary style. The better rooms have small lounge areas. Singles range from 240$ ($9.36) to 360$ ($14.04); doubles from 300$ ($11.70) to 450$ ($17.55), the higher tariffs for suites.

A continental breakfast costs 25$ (98¢) extra. The villa is easy to spot, as its gables and peaked tower, even its towering palm, can be seen from many blocks away.

5. Exploring Sao Miguel

The largest link in the archipelago chain (290 square miles), Sao Miguel is called with good reason The Green Island. It offers a widely varied landscape, ranging from mountains, to volcanic lava pools, to brooks filled with trout, to cultivated checkerboard fields, to tea and pineapple plantations—everything set off effectively by the age-old customs and manmade touches, such as windmills clacking in the wind, ox-drawn carts, medieval woolen bonnets on cowherds. Practically everything grows well in the gardens of Sao Miguel, especially the hydrangeas that border the roads in summer.

As interesting as Ponta Delgada is, the main reason for flying over from Santa Maria is to take one of the many excursions—either by rented car, inexpensive taxi, organized tour, or independently—along with the Azoreans themselves on one of the island's buses. Nearly all visitors head east from the capital—a distance of about 28 miles—to:

FURNAS: Following in the footsteps of rheumatic Victorians who shunned the sea cocktail at Brighton to take the baths at Furnas, you'll arrive at one of the richest spas in Europe. The thermal spa season lasts from July 1 to September 30, but a visit is interesting at any time of the year. The geysers and springs make the valley steamy in the district where sulphur fumes pour forth from craters.

The *New Yorker* described the springs as a place of "bare black rock, blasted by geysers, hot oozing clay, and sulphur-scented smoke. In a grim-looking cave, water boils furiously, now and then leaping up and spilling over in a smoking stream that runs steeply downhill between lava banks." David Dodge called the waters at the baths "cold, warm, boiling, carbonated, uncarbonated, radioactive, tasty, clear, muddy and as you like it, twenty-two kinds to choose from."

The major attraction is **Hickling Park**—founded in 1770 according to an inscribed boulder—by the American vice-counsul discussed earlier in the Sao Pedro write-up in Ponta Delgada. Where Hickling left off, the Marquis da Praia eventually took up. However, the latter's grandson at one point was about to destroy the park; but it was rescued by Mr. Vasco Bensuade in 1937. A pavilion was built that same year at Furnas Lake, and two years later a nine-hole championship golf course was opened.

It is a great botanical garden, filled with azaleas, ferns, camellias, hydrangeas, pines, japónica, jacaranda. Plants were brought from China, Japan, South America, Mexico, New Zealand, Tasmania, Asia, even the southern United States. White swans float majestically in the ponds studded with red and white lilies, and in the park is an egg-shaped swimming pool filled with muddy thermal waters. Changing cabins are nearby.

Before you go, you should take a trip to **Lake Furnas** for a "volcanic cooked" luncheon. This type of cuisine can be arranged through the Hotel Terra Nostra at Furnas. The cooking is known as à la caldéira; and everything from pullet to horse mackerel is covered with paper or some other wrapping after being well spiced with aromatic herbs, then is actually buried in the hot earth, the way the Haitians roast kid. Sometimes whole chickens and yams are dropped into the simmering pools. On Sundays especially, you can see families coming to the lakeside setting for picnics, washing down their meals with cheiro, a regional wine.

For dining or accommodations, try:

A Medium-Priced Hotel

Hotel Terra Nostra (Our Land), Rua dos Banhos, Furnas (tel. 541-04), is a living monument to Art Deco. The rear opens onto the famous Hickling botanical park, with its restorative waters. A long list of European and North American visitors are drawn here, finding its setting idyllic. One of its special treats, mentioned above, are the cookouts arranged by the hotel, the food slowly done to a turn by volcanic steam. But you can also dine less ruggedly at the hotel. If you're not a guest, but are visiting, say, from Ponta Delgada, you can order an 110$ ($4.29) table d'hôte luncheon or dinner.

The full-board rates are most economical. Depending on the plumbing, the tariff for two persons ranges from 655$ ($25.55) to 780$ ($30.43). One person can have full pension at rates ranging from 425$ ($16.58) to 535$ ($20.87). The rooms are furnished in a 30s style.

Of course, you have access to the thermal swimming pool, plus the tennis courts and a nearby nine-hole golf course. You can even join the British in a game of croquet.

To the west of Ponta Delgade—a distance of some 13 miles—lies the second major attraction of Sao Miguel—

SETE CIDADES: The Seven Cities were named after a legend—in fact, they are the subject of many myths. It is an hour-glass shaped lake—the upper one blue, the lower one emerald green. The lake, about eight or nine miles in circumference, was supposedly formed by tears shed over a broken love affair: one by a blue-eyed princess, the other by the shepherd boy she loved who was green-eyed. The appellation of Sete Cidades stems from a legend that claims that this site was actually the center of a powerful empire on the lost continent of Atlantis. You can visit an interesting park near the blue lake, called Jardim Pitoresco, and enjoy the wafting aroma of the pittosporum flower. The vegetation on the slopes makes this a lush setting.

6. Terceira

Pronounced ter-say-ra and meaning third, Terceira is the third largest of the nine Azorean islands. It's about two-thirds of the way between Boston and Lisbon, making it one of the nearest parts of Europe accessible to North Americans.

When you first land at Lages Airport, you'll think you're in the United States. Terceira is the site of an American Air Force Base, and its personnel have their own little community near the airport. The base was originally built by the RAF in World War II.

Once you pass this, you'll have left America far behind and the real island emerges. It is rural in nature, with most of the islanders engaged in agriculture and livestock breeding. Extinct volcanoes slope down to green pasturelands crisscrossed by low stone walls. Black-shawled women duck pass oxcarts to enter Manueline churches of the 16th century.

Life is casual here, and for some that means Terceira is an acquired taste. In fact, it's been so quiet around here that many natives were lured to America. It's estimated that more Terceira-born persons are in California than on the island itself. Others settled in New England. Many were originally drawn there during the whaling days of the 19th century.

Don't come expecting to view great monuments and museums—rather, to sample the local hospitality and Terceira's own bucolic charm. Fishing and boating are excellent, by the way.

THE AZORES: TERCEIRA

TAP now offers a Boston/Terceira service—a four-hour flight to Europe. Terceira is also connected by SATA, the local Azorean airline, to the international airport at Santa Maria and to that of Sao Miguel, some 35 miles away.

With about 18,000 inhabitants, **Angra** is the island's main city, about a 45-minute run from the airport. It's also the oldest settlement in the Azores, also the most fascinating colonial town in the archipelago.

Considered a masterpiece of Renaissance town planning, Angra still reflects its 16th-century layout. Many mansions stand from the 17th and 18th centuries.

The finest example of military architecture on the island is the Castle of Sao Joao Baptista, where the notorious sadist, King Afonso VI, was imprisoned. At the foot of Monte Brasil, it contains a carved doorway and an arched bridge. It's one of the largest 16th-century fortresses built in the Portuguese world. Behind the castle rises the pile of Sao Gonçalo Convent, filled with fine ornamental tiles and some interesting carving.

In the center of town, the Cathedral dates from the 16th century, and is noted for its carved ceiling of cedar. The Church of Sao Francisco, built in the 15th century, contains the tomb of Pedro, brother of Vasco da Gama, who buried his kin there on his way back from India in 1499.

Peculiar to Terceira is the custom of rope bullfighting known as tourada à corda. Young bulls are brought in from the pastures and allowed to run wild in the town. A long heavy rope has been fastened to the bull's horns, and this forms the means of controlling him. Reckless young men rush into the streets to taunt these bulls with objects. This bull running takes place from May to November.

At some point you'll want to rent a taxi and explore the island itself, 12 by 18 miles in distance. At the eastern end lies **Praia da Vitória,** containing the largest sandy beach in the entire Azores. It's the second town of Terceira. Whatever time of year you decide to take the excursion, the temperature's likely to be right: the average is between 50 and 70 degrees Fahrenheit all year. Terceira is still unspoiled and inviting—especially now that the following accommodations have opened their doors to new world visitors.

WHERE TO STAY: Estalagem da Serreta, Parque da Serreta (tel. 962-53), is a small and handsome modern inn perched on a hill site overlooking the ocean, a perfect retreat for good food or restful sleep. Nixon met Pompidou here in 1971. The architecture is semi avant-garde—the multi-leveled lounge furnished with leather chairs and the walls decorated with fabric hangings. Doubles cost 350$ ($13.65). The dining room seemingly is thrust out to the sea, providing clients with a view. Even if you don't stay here in one of the attached studio bungalows, then at least drop in to enjoy a regional meal costing 120$ ($4.68). To reach this tranquil spot takes some doing, however. It's a long haul from Angra by taxi.

Those who prefer to locate within the town precincts itself can stay at one of the following recommendations:

Albergaría Cruzeiro, Praça Eng. Arantes e Oliveira (tel. 24072), is the newest of the hotels built in the center of town, a most recommendable place to stay if you appreciate modern facilities. Each room has a private bath, and singles cost from 185$ ($7.22) to 205$ ($8). Doubles begin at 270$ ($10.53), rising to 320$ ($12.48). A continental breakfast is an additional 25$ (98¢). Although the hotel is contemporary, the furnishings are traditional. Each room has a private bath. The breakfast terrace contains white wrought-iron furniture and green plants. In addition, there's a drinking bar, plus a nearby lounge with all-white plastic furnishings.

Hotel de Angra, Praça da Restauraçao (tel. 240-414), is a substantial modern hotel in the heart of Angra, set back from a pie-shaped little plaza, studded with trees. Although not overwhelming in any area, it does have its own dignity and style, and at its prices, it's an especially good choice: singles from 210$ ($8.19) to 250$ ($9.75); doubles, 310$ ($12.09) to 360$ ($14.04). Complete pension is an extra 200$ ($7.80) per person daily.

At Cabo da Praia

Apartamentos Nove Ilhas Motel (tel. 531-35) is a holiday house for those seeking a tranquil retreat in a setting of natural beauty. A member of the staff of the hotel meets guests at Lajes Airport, and provides free transportation to the facilities of Nove Ilhas, about 3½ miles away.

In one of the "Nine Islands" apartments, clients are near the largest Azorean beach and only two miles from the historic town of Praia da Vitória. The Terceira Island Golf Course is 8½ miles away, and the city of Angra do Heroísmo is 11½ miles away.

Each apartment has two bedrooms and a full bath, with tub and shower. A combined living and dining room comes with the apartment, as does an equipped kitchenette, with cutlery, silverware, and dishes. Linens are also provided.

On the precincts are a restaurant, a small market, plus facilities for dry cleaning and laundry. Babysitting can be arranged for parents wanting to be free to tour Terceira. In high season, from May 1 to September 30, two persons pay 320$ ($12.48); three persons, 400$ ($15.60); and four persons, 460$ ($17.94). An extra bed costs 60$ ($2.34) a night.

7. Faial

Much less visited than any of the islands previously recommended, Faial has its own particular charm—a land of restful valleys, verdant fields, and hydrangea-hedged hillsides. It and Pico are the chief tourist islands of the Horta district. They are separated by a channel five miles wide.

The easiest way to get there is by air via Sao Miguel or Terceira, but Faial also can be reached by boat from Terceira. However, if you're planning to come by boat, check in advance with a travel agent or the tourist office, as service is not frequent.

Faial's chief town is the port of Horta, with its Church of Sao Francisco dating from the 16th century. Inside is a museum of religious art, with carving, glazed tiles, and painting. With a population of about 8,000 persons, Horta is built along a bay. From its harbor (which was used as a naval base in both world wars), you can enjoy views of the neighboring islands.

Excursionists go to Caldeira, a volcanic crater covered inside with vegetation and containing a lake. Caldeira is at the top of the island, and from this vantage point the best view of Pico and the neighboring islands can be enjoyed. In 1957 a new volcano, Capelinhos, rose up from the sea and erupted in 1958. There was also renewed activity in 1973.

WHERE TO STAY: In accommodations, Horta offers two good hotels. Preferred is the **Estalagem de Santa Cruz**, a self-contained retreat, built in an old stone fortress on the port. It provides ultra-contemporary accommodations in a resort atmosphere. Its 10 well-styled rooms have complete private baths, and the furnishings are a combination of traditional and tropical wicker. The view from your room of the snow-capped mountain (Mount Pico) is enthralling. Two persons in a room with bath pay from 275$ ($10.73) to 360$ ($14.04); one person is charged about 30 percent less. Luncheon or dinner ordered separately is another 100$ ($3.90). The lounge is in the Iberian country style, with a stone fireplace, a refectory table, and good lounge chairs. This oasis of charm and comfort is owned by actor Raymond Burr of Perry Mason and Ironside fame. He often visits the Azores and has done much to promote tourism on the island.

Hotel Fayal, Horta (tel. 221-81), is a four-star first-class hotel, consisting of a group of buildings like a village in a park. The situation is tranquil, as the Fayal is surrounded by gardens offering views onto the sea. The hotel is the major social center for Horta. The furnishings are in an ultra-modern style, with a high taste level, as reflected by the subtle autumnal colors of nutmeg, burnt orange, beige, and soft red. The rooms are well styled, often opening onto views of the bay and the inner harbor. Depending on size and location, doubles range from 325$ ($12.68) to 450$ ($17.55). The food, served in a large room, is good and typical of the region. A complete meal costs 120$ ($4.68).

Chapter XVII

A GRAB BAG OF CHARTS

1. Menu Translations
2. A Capsule Vocabulary
3. Currency Exchange

FRENCH IS STILL traditionally spoken by guides in provincial museums, but English is increasing in popularity, and is now taught in most schools.

Usually in Lisbon, Estoril, Cascais, Madeira, and on the major coastal resorts of the Algarve, you'll have no problem if you speak only English. However, if you venture inland—to towns of the Alentejo for example, you may find a few words in our Capsule Vocabulary helpful.

Likewise, menus tend to be bewildering, especially when a chef has named a bean and tripe dish after his favorite aunt. Nevertheless, a basic knowledge of the main dishes in the Portuguese cuisine is essential, especially if you're planning to stay at second-class hotels or local taverns where there's nobody around to translate for you.

1. Menu Translations

SOUPS (SOPAS)

caldo verde	potato and cabbage	**sopa à alentejana**	Alentejo soup
canja de galinha	chicken soup	**sopa de cebola**	onion
crême de camarao	cream of shrimp	**sopa de mariscos**	shellfish
		sopa de queijo	cheese
crême de legumes	cream of vegetable	**sopa de tomato**	tomato

EGGS (OVOS)

com presunto	with ham	**mexidos**	scrambled
cozidos	hard boiled	**omeleta**	omelette
escalfados	poached	**quentes**	soft boiled
estrelados	fried	**tortilha**	Spanish omelette

FISH (PEIXE)

ameijoas	clams	ostras	oysters
atum	tuna	peixe espada	swordfish
bacalhau	salted codfish	percebes	barnacles
cherne	turbot	pescada	hake
camaraos	shrimps	robalo	bass
eiró	eel	sardinhas	sardines
lagosta	lobster	salmonete	red mullet
linguado	sole	santola	crab
lulas	squid		

SPECIALTIES

bife na frigideira	steak with mustard sauce	porco Alentejano	pork in a sauce of tomatoes and clams
caldeirada	fishermen's stew		
cozido à portuguesa	Portuguese stew		

MEAT (CARNE)

bife	steak	língua	tongue
borrego	lamb	porco	pork
cabrito	kid	presunto	ham
carneiro	mutton	rim	kidney
coelho	rabbit	salchichas	sausages
costeletas	chops	vaca	beef
dobrada	tripe	vitela	veal
iscas	liver		

POULTRY (AVES)

borracho	pigeon	pato	duck
frango	chicken	perdiz	partridge
galinha	fowl	perú	turkey
ganso	goose		

VEGETABLES (LEGUMES)

aipo	celery	cenouras	carrots
alcachôfra	artichoke	cogumelo	mushroom
arroz	rice	couve-flor	cauliflower
azeitonas	olives	couves	cabbage
batatas	potatoes	ervilhas	peas
berinjela	eggplant	espargos	asparagus
beterrabas	beets	espinafres	spinach
cebola	onion	favas	broad beans

MENU TRANSLATIONS

feijao		bean	pepino		cucumber
nabo		turnip	tomate		tomato

SALAD (SALADA)

agrioes		watercress	salada verde		green salad
alface		lettuce	Russa		Russian
salada mista		mixed salad			

DESSERTS (SOBREMESA)

arroz doce		rice pudding	pêssego Melba		peach Melba
bolo		cake	pudim flan		egg custard
gelados diversos		mixed ice cream	pudim de pao		bread pudding
			salada de frutas		fruit salad
maça assada		baked apple	sorvetes		sherbets
pastelaria		pastry	queijo		cheese

FRUIT (FRUTAS)

abacate		avocado	melancia		watermelon
alperches		apricots	melâo		melon
ameixa		plum	morangos		strawberries
ananas		pineapple	peras		pears
cerejas		cherries	pêssegos		peaches
figos		figs	roma		pomegranate
framboesa		raspberry	tâmara		date
laranjas		oranges	toronja		grapefruit
limao		lemon	uvas		grapes
macas		apples			

BEVERAGES (BEBIDAS)

água		water	leite		milk
água mineral		mineral water	sumo de fruta		fruit juice
café		coffee	sumo de laranja		orange juice
chá		tea	sumo de tomate		tomato juice
cerveja		beer	vinho branco		white wine
com gelo		with ice	vinho tinto		red wine
laranjada		orangeade			

CONDIMENTS (CONDIMENTOS)

açúcar		sugar	azeite		olive oil
alho		garlic	caril		curry

compota	jam	pimenta	pepper
manteiga	butter	sal	salt
mostarda	mustard	vinagre	vinegar

MISCELLANEOUS

chocolate	chocolate	pâo	bread
biscoito	cracker	pâo torrado	toast
gelo	ice		

COOKING TERMS

assado no forno	baked	frito	fried
cozido	boiled	mal passado	rare
estufada	braised	bem passado	well done

2. A Capsule Vocabulary

		Pronounced
Hello	olá	oh-lah
How are you?	como está?	como esh-tah
Very well	muito bem	muy-toh bym
Thank you	muito obrigado	muy-toh obree-gah-do
Good-bye	adeus	adeush
Please	faça favor	fassa fah-vohr
Yes	sim	seem
No	nao	naion
Excuse me	desculpe-me	dash-culpa-meh
Give me	dê-me	deh-meh
Where is?	onde fica?	ondeh feecah
the station	a estaçao	a aish-tassaion
a hotel	um hotel	oom hotel
a restaurant	um restaurante	oom rash-tauranteh
the toilet	a casa de banho	ah cahzah de bahnhoo
To the right	à direita	aah deeraitah
To the left	à esquerda	aah ash-kerdah
Straight ahead	em frente	ym fraintah
I would like—	gostaria de	goosh-tareeah de
to eat	comer	coh-mere
a room	um quarto	oom quarr-toh
How much is it?	quanto custa	quahnto coosh-tah
The check, please	a conta se faz, favor	ah cohnta sa fahsh, fah-vohr
When?	quando	quandoh
Yesterday	ontem	ohntym
Today	hoje	hoyhje
Tomorrow	amanha	ahmain-hayh

VOCABULARY & CURRENCY

Breakfast	**pequeno almoço**	paikainoh aahlmohssoh
Lunch	**almoço**	aahlmohssoh
Dinner	**jantar**	jain-taah

1 **um** oom
2 **dois** doysh
3 **três** traishe
4 **quatro** quaahtroh
5 **cinco** sseencoh
6 **seis** ssaish
7 **sete** ssaiteh
8 **oito** oytoh
9 **nove** nohveh
10 **dez** daish
11 **onze** onzeh
12 **dôze** doze
13 **trêze** traihzeh
14 **catorze** cahtohrzeh
15 **quinze** keenzeh
16 **dezasseis** dehzaissaish
17 **dezassete** dehrzassaihteh
18 **dezoito** dehzoytoh
19 **dezanove** dehzanohveh
20 **vinte** veenteh
30 **trinta** treehntah
40 **quarenta** quaraintah
50 **cinquenta** sseenquaintah
60 **sessenta** ssaissaihntah
70 **setenta** ssaitaintah
80 **otenta** oyhtaintah
90 **noventa** nohvaintah
100 **cem** sym

3. Currency Exchange

Escudos	Dollars	Escudos	Dollars
1	$ .04	125	$ 4.88
2	.08	150	5.85
3	.12	200	7.80
4	.16	300	11.70
5	.20	400	15.60
10	.39	500	19.50
15	.59	600	23.40
20	.78	700	27.30
25	.98	800	31.20
30	1.17	900	35.10
35	1.37	1,000	39.00
40	1.56	1,500	58.50
45	1.76	2,000	78.00
50	1.95	3,000	117.00
75	2.93	4,000	156.00
100	3.90	5,000	195.00

Our gratitude for research aid to Peter Besas and especially to Margaret Foresman for her editorial assistance.

ARTHUR FROMMER, INC.
70 FIFTH AVE., NEW YORK, N.Y. 10011   Date_____

Gentlemen:
Please send me (postpaid) the books checked below:

$10-A-DAY GUIDES
(In-depth guides to low-cost tourist accommodations and facilities.)

- ☐ Europe on $10 a Day $4.95
- ☐ England on $10 & $15 a Day $3.95
- ☐ Greece on $10 a Day $3.95
- ☐ Hawaii on $15 a Day $3.95
- ☐ India on $5 & $10 a Day $3.95
- ☐ Ireland on $10 a Day $3.95
- ☐ Israel on $10 & $15 a Day $3.95
- ☐ Mexico and Guatemala on $5 & $10 a Day $3.95
- ☐ New Zealand on $10 a Day $3.95
- ☐ New York on $15 a Day $3.95
- ☐ Scandinavia on $15 a Day $3.95
- ☐ South America on $10 a Day $3.95
- ☐ Spain and Morocco on $10 a Day $3.95
- ☐ Turkey on $5 & $10 a Day $3.95
- ☐ Washington, D.C. on $10 & $15 a Day $3.95

DOLLAR-WISE GUIDES
(Guides to tourist accommodations and facilities from budget to deluxe, with emphasis on the medium-priced.)

- ☐ England $3.95
- ☐ France $3.95
- ☐ Germany $3.95
- ☐ Italy $3.95
- ☐ Japan and Hong Kong $3.95
- ☐ Portugal $3.95

GETAWAY GUIDES
(Pocket-size guides to tourist accommodations and facilities in all price ranges, with discount coupons worth up to $100.)

- ☐ Athens $1.50
- ☐ Boston $1.50
- ☐ Denver $1.50
- ☐ Honolulu $1.50
- ☐ Ireland/Dublin/Shannon ...$1.50
- ☐ Las Vegas $1.50
- ☐ Lisbon/Madrid/Costa del Sol $1.50
- ☐ London $1.50
- ☐ Los Angeles $1.50
- ☐ New York $1.50
- ☐ Paris $1.50
- ☐ Phoenix/Tucson $1.50
- ☐ Rome $1.50
- ☐ San Francisco $1.50
- ☐ Washington, D.C. ..$1.50

By the Council on International Educational Exchange

- ☐ Whole World Handbook $2.95
(A student guide to work, study and travel worldwide.)
- ☐ Where to Stay USA $2.95
(A guide to accommodations in all 50 states costing from 50¢ to $10 per night.)

Enclosed is my check or money order for $_____

NAME_____

ADDRESS_____

CITY_____STATE_____ZIP_____